SECURITY FOR BUSINESS AND INDUSTRY

A. James Fisher
Edinboro State College

Prentice-Hall, Inc., Englewood Cliffs, New Jersey 07632

Library of Congress Cataloging in Publication Data

Fisher, A James, (date)
Security for business and industry.

Bibliography: p.
Includes index.
1. Retail trade—Security measures. 2. Industry
—Security measures. I. Title.
HF5429.F498 658.4'7 78-23425
ISBN 0-13-798967-9

Editorial/production supervision and interior design by Ann Marie McCarthy
Cover design by Rudolph Svezia
Illustration courtesy of Cardkey Systems, Chatsworth, California
Manufacturing buyer: John Hall

Prentice-Hall Series in Criminal Justice

Printed in the United States of America

10 9 8 7 6 5 4 3 2 1

PRENTICE-HALL INTERNATIONAL, INC., *London*
PRENTICE-HALL OF AUSTRALIA PTY. LIMITED, *Sydney*
PRENTICE-HALL OF CANADA, LTD., *Toronto*
PRENTICE-HALL OF INDIA PRIVATE LIMITED, *New Delhi*
PRENTICE-HALL OF JAPAN, INC., *Tokyo*
PRENTICE-HALL OF SOUTHEAST ASIA PTE. LTD., *Singapore*
WHITEHALL BOOKS LIMITED, *Wellington, New Zealand*

Contents

PART IV

OTHER CRIMES AGAINST THE BUSINESS COMMUNITY

PART V

FIRE SCIENCE

APPENDIXES

Preface

The word *security* has such broad meaning that it is difficult to formulate a concise definition of the term. However, as a vocation, security means the utilization of hardware, techniques, and personnel to prevent and control crime and disaster. More specifically, the security function involves personnel and measures independent of public law enforcement.

Although most security practitioners pursue the same objectives, they possess diverse skills and knowledge, and function within a variety of commercial, industrial, and institutional settings. Practitioners in specialized fields tend to perceive the security function strictly in terms of the particular enterprise or facility they protect. On the introductory level, however, security should be presented in broader terms, since most companies and institutions are confronted by the same security problems.

The security vocation, encompassing subjects from locks to undercover investigations, is extremely broad and diverse; most security textbooks, failing to reflect this diversity, are not truly introductory. Security literature quite often consists of books and articles primarily concerned with security technology, since they are usually written by people with backgrounds in the manufacture, installation, or sale of security hardware. Because most of this literature is technical and specialized, it is of little value to a general security practitioner.

This introductory work consists primarily of material relating to the nature of crime, criminals, and selected criminal offenses, as well as disasters such as fire and other threats to personal health and safety. It also defines and analyzes major security concerns, identifying and evaluating the techniques, hardware, and personnel utilized to reduce or eliminate these security problems.

Following the introductory chapter, which discusses, among other things, the relationship between the security and law-enforcement functions, the text is divided into five parts, each part involving a major security concern.

Part I deals with unlawful intrusion, which includes burglary and criminal trespass, and contains six chapters discussing this major security concern. Part I is followed by a security exercise. Part II involves retail theft (shoplifting) and consists of two chapters dealing with this security matter. Part III contains two chapters dealing with internal theft, the security term describing a theft by an employee of his employer's property. Part IV comprises two chapters discussing some of the other crimes that seriously threaten the business community—bad checks, counterfeiting, kidnapping, robbery, and bombing matters. Part V, made up of one chapter dealing with fire prevention and safety, is followed by Appendixes A and B.

Case histories, illustrations, and fact situations are used throughout the text to illustrate key points and major concepts. Each chapter is followed by a series of discussion questions and a selected bibliography.

Chapter 1

Security and Related Fields

AN OVERVIEW

I. The Private Security Function

II. Career Opportunities in Security and Related Fields
   A. *Common backgrounds in the security field*
   B. *Specialization within the security field*
      1. Special security fields
      2. Security consultants
   C. *Private investigations*
      1. Private contract investigations
      2. Proprietary investigations
      3. Basic investigative skills
   D. *Careers in security-related fields*
      1. Private lie-detection examiners
      2. Armored-car services
      3. Private bodyguards

The Private Security Function

The security vocation is composed of personnel, hardware, procedures, and techniques developed to control crime and disaster. The most visible type of security personnel is the uniformed watchman or security guard standing watch at a main gate or on patrol at a bank, store, institution, warehouse, or factory. Also visible to the public are campus police, armored-car personnel, and security patrol-car officers. Private investigators, security consultants, retail floorwalkers, and intrusion-alarm response personnel are some of the other types of personnel working in the security field. In the area of security technology and hardware, security practitioners are involved with the manufacture, sale, and installation of fire and intrusion alarms, electronic surveillance hardware, locking devices, and fire detection and prevention equipment.

Those involved with security equipment are usually employed directly by the firm manufacturing or selling this hardware. Uniformed security guards, floorwalkers, consultants, auditors, investigators, and security administrators are employed either directly by the facility they protect or by security companies such as Pinkerton's, Wackenhut, or Burns International Security Services. Personnel who perform a security function solely for their employer are commonly referred to as in-house security practitioners, whereas those employed by independent security contractors are referred to as private contract security personnel.

Although security goals are generally the same as police objectives, the security approach to crime fighting is somewhat different. Typically, the police do not become involved with crime until an offense has actually been committed. As a result, police deal mostly with criminal offenders rather than potential victims of crime. In contrast, the security method of crime control centers on crime prevention. Deterrence, the nucleus of crime prevention, is achieved by implementing measures that render the commission of a criminal act less attractive to a potential wrongdoer. For example, the more work, planning, or time required to complete a specific criminal act, the greater the possibility that the criminal will become discouraged, quit, or be caught by police or security personnel. Most criminals are unimaginative, unskilled, and undisciplined, so they do not commit crimes that are the product of planning, skilled execution, or determination. They intrude upon, steal, vandalize, or attack only the most vulnerable targets, and so they are effectively deterred from committing crimes against premises protected by physical and psychological security barriers.

The use of uniformed security guards is the most common security crime-fighting measure. In 1969, there were about 200,000 more police officers in the country than private security guards.[1] But by 1976, the number of uniformed security guards in the United States exceeded the number of sworn public police officers. In Denver, Colorado, for example, there are 1,000 more private police

[1]James S. Kakalik and Sorrel Wildhorn, *The Private Police: Security and Danger* (New York: Crane, Russak and Company, 1977).

personnel than there are public police officers, but in the Cleveland, Ohio, area, there are 4,000 sworn police officers and 10,000 private guards. California has 95,000 licensed guards, more than double the number of its police. It is estimated that in New York City alone, there are 100,000 security guards, 15 times as many as there were in 1965. Nationally, the estimated number of private-police officers ranges from a minimum of 500,000 to 1 million. In 1975, Pinkerton's, the nation's largest private security company, employed 40,000 guards, and Burns employed 29,000. The security-guard service earned Pinkerton's over $200 million in 1975, three times its 1965 guard revenues.[2]

Fences, walls, locks, lighting fixtures, and safes are common barriers to criminal intrusion. In the security business, electronic surveillance, alarms, and automatic access-control systems are also commonly used for crime prevention and detection. Most security practitioners believe that the proper use of one or more of these measures will either physically prevent criminal intrusion, deter intruders, or result in their capture. Administratively, an employer's rules and regulations that effectively supervise and control employee conduct, although not physical barriers to crime from within, are designed to discourage and deter it. Periodic audits and surveys conducted by security personnel ensure that these security rules and policies are followed.

In many ways, the security function begins at a point where the police effort ends. For example, because of manpower and other shortages and limitations, police personnel cannot make foot patrols inside warehouses, factories, or retail establishments, or watch workers as they leave their place of employment in order to recover the employer's tools, equipment, merchandise, or supplies being illegally removed from the premises. Because the security function includes internal crime control, security complements or extends the overall crime-fighting capability of the police.

There are only a few security functions augmenting or paralleling police work. One is the patrolling of neighborhoods, shopping centers, trucking terminals, and industrial parks in marked patrol vehicles, in which uniformed security officers perform essentially the same service as police personnel patrolling these areas in their cruisers. The purposes of police and security motorized patrols are similar—to prevent crime and to discover or respond to the scene of a criminal act—but the roles and responsibilities of police and security patrol-car personnel differ. When a security patrolman discovers a crime or detains a person suspected of a criminal act, he will summon a police officer; the police are responsible for the crime-scene investigations, arrests, and subsequent inquiries that may follow the security officer's initial discovery. Thus the police service complements the security function by extending the crime-fighting effort beyond the reach of security to the arrest, investigative, and prosecutive stages of the criminal justice process.

---

[2]These data on the number of private and public police in various cities and number of guards employed by individual contract companies is taken from Clark Whelton, "In Guards We Trust," *New York Times Magazine*, September 19, 1976.

Nevertheless, a security patrol-car service provides the client who pays for this protection with a service he cannot obtain from the police. For example, a security foot patrol inside the client's premises may accompany the exterior perimeter patrol-car check. By extending the patrol to the interior of the facility, the security patrolman can shut and lock the owner's windows and doors and perform other security-related tasks. In this way, police and security efforts act to augment and complement each other, and when combined and coordinated, can form an effective crime-fighting measure.

In 1975, the Private Security Task Force of the National Advisory Committee on Criminal Justice Standards and Goals conducted a survey whose primary purpose was to acquire statistical data on subjects and issues vital to the security function. Prior to this, there had been no available information on the basis of which standards and goals for private security could be formulated. The survey questionnaire was distributed by the American Society for Industrial Security (ASIS) to its entire membership. Among other matters, the questionnaire solicited opinions from various businesses and organizations in the industry regarding the relationship between security and public law enforcement. The survey's findings failed to substantiate the notion that the working relationship between personnel of the two areas is inadequate or strained. (It should be noted, however, that public-police personnel did not participate in the survey.) The questionnaire and results from it are set out in full in Appendix B to this book.

Of those responding, 71 percent indicated they had frequent contact with public-police personnel. From this group, 87 percent considered their relations with the police to be good or excellent. Moreover, 66 percent of the survey respondents believed that the police have positive attitudes regarding the security function. It is interesting to note that in the same survey, 74 percent of those responding believed that private security personnel should *not* have the same legal authority as public police officers.[3]

Career Opportunities in Security and Related Fields

common backgrounds in the security field

In this discussion, the educational and employment experience of unarmed security guards and watchmen will not be considered. The diverse backgrounds reflected by this group of security personnel will be dealt with at length in Chapter 6. Also excluded is material dealing with the training and experience of personnel involved with the manufacture, installation, and sale of security hardware and equipment.

[3]The official report of the Private Security Task Force, including its recommendations on improving the quality of private security, is contained in *Private Security* (Cincinnati, O.: Anderson, 1977).

A significant number of security practitioners have backgrounds in public law enforcement. Security managers and executives at various corporate levels quite often have prior experience in city or state police administrative or investigative work, and many are former federal government or military investigators, retired after several years of public service. A large number of uniformed security officers working in banks and on college campuses are retired public-police officers.

Security personnel employed by utility companies, large retail chain operations, manufacturing firms, colleges, and hospitals, who perform functions of a loss-prevention, investigative, and/or managerial nature, are often employees who have been promoted or horizontally transferred from nonsecurity jobs within the same company. Safety directors, personnel managers, or controllers frequently expand their interests and job responsibilities to include matters related to security. It is not unusual for a corporate security director to have prior experience as an employee of a private contract security agency. Many contract security managers and executives started as either private contract security guards, security-guard supervisors, undercover operatives, or security investigators.

It appears that an increasing number of people entering the security field with college degrees in security, criminal justice, or police science are without civilian or military police backgrounds. The retail industry employs large numbers of young, college-educated security practitioners who begin their careers by controlling shoplifting and employee theft. Although several colleges and universities offer security courses and programs, only a few offer degrees in this field. By enrolling in a college offering a wide variety of security courses, a student has the opportunity to prepare himself for an eventual administrative position in a specialized field such as campus or hospital security.

The type of educational and employment background most suitable for security work constitutes an ongoing debate among security administrators and practitioners. More specifically, the question centers on whether or not experience and training in public law enforcement are more suitable than a background that does not include police work.

Because both police and security functions involve crime control, it is understandable that so many former police personnel are employed in the security field. But this does not necessarily mean that a background in police work is the only suitable prerequisite to a successful security career. Although many police and security crime-control principles and techniques are similar, the security function also includes knowledge and application of matters relevant to the control and prevention of fire and other disasters. Moreover, in crime fighting, the security function is less reactive than is public police work. Security methodology emphasizes crime prevention rather than crime solution and order maintenance, so security practitioners must acquire a basic knowledge of the business and administrative operation of the facility or enterprise being protected. For instance, a working knowledge of accounting, bookkeeping, and auditing principles may be required. Moreover, high-level security positions involve the supervision and handling of uniformed guards and other subordinate security personnel.

In summary, although prior police experience is often beneficial, it is rarely an absolute necessity. Those who have prior police experience must, in order to become complete and effective security practitioners, acquire additional knowledge and a new approach to crime control. The most important factors in success in the security field are the ability, interest, and desire of the individual practitioner.

specialization within the security field

Essentially, all commercial, manufacturing, and institutional facilities are vulnerable to the same kinds of crimes and disasters. Certain enterprises, however, by virtue of their operation, are vulnerable to particular types of crimes and criminals. For example, a service station that operates all night assumes the risk of being victimized by an armed robber; one that is closed all night is vulnerable to burglary. Banking institutions, because of the large amounts of cash on hand, are exposed to daytime robbery and, because of the large sums of money handled by bank employees, to embezzlement and similar white-collar crimes. Retail establishments, because they are exposed to credit-card, bad-check, and shoplifting offenses, initiate security programs specifically designed to minimize losses from these types of crimes. The theft of drugs by narcotics users plagues hospitals, doctors' offices, and pharmacies. Thefts of cargo in storage and in shipment concern trucking companies and other common carriers. Institutional facilities such as hospitals and retirement homes, because they are responsible for the care and housing of patients 24 hours a day, are particularly concerned with, in addition to crime control, fire prevention and related safety matters. Because of the various vulnerabilities associated with different facilities and business operations, and the need to effectively combat and control these specific problems, a degree of specialization has developed within the security field.

Special Security Fields. Specialized security careers are available in the following fields:

1. Campus security
2. Hospital security
3. School security
4. Freight and cargo security
5. Retail security
6. Museum security
7. Airport and airline security
8. Computer security
9. Railroad security

Security Consultants. Security practitioners with training, skill, and experience in a few highly specialized fields are qualified to function as security consultants. Many of these consultants are listed, along with their specialities or areas of expertise, in trade magazines and other publications pertinent to the security industry.

It is not unusual for a security consultant to be employed by, or affiliated with, a manufacturer or retailer of security hardware. Although many security consultants are also employed by companies offering specialized security services, a few operate independently of security product or protection agencies. An independent security consultant is free to recommend one of the many security products, services, or companies capable of dealing with a security problem beyond his expertise.

The following list sets out a few of the most common areas in security specialization and consultation:

1. Electronic surveillance (closed-circuit television and surveillance photography)
2. Audio surveillance countermeasures (debugging and antiwiretapping)
3. Protective lighting
4. Protective fencing
5. Protective dogs
6. Alarm systems
7. Access control
8. Security training
9. Locking, master-keying, and key control

The forensic scientist is another type of security consultant. In the public sector, forensic scientists are employed in crime laboratories operated by large municipal, state, and federal law-enforcement agencies. The accumulation, preservation, and analysis of physical evidence by forensic personnel representing many scientific fields have become an integral part of the public crime-solution function. The more familiar forensic sciences are ballistics, fingerprints, and handwriting.

In addition to taking physical evidence from the scene of a crime to the laboratory and examining, comparing, and analyzing it, the forensic scientist performs a vital law-enforcement function as an expert witness. His testimony at a trial carries weight and credibility beyond that of a regular witness.

Within the security field, forensic scientists perform functions analogous to the work of their counterparts in the public sector. The following list, although not complete, illustrates the variety of forensic sciences practiced by private consultants and expert witnesses:

Chemistry, Biology, and Physics

Ashes
Blood examinations
Bombs and explosives
Document examinations
Drug analysis
Firearm identification
Blast fractures
Mineral analysis
Number restoration
Poisons
Shoeprints and tire treads
Wood examinations
Hairs and fibers
Metal examinations
Paint comparisons
Powder patterns
Tool marks

Document Examinations

Handwriting
Hand printing
Typewriting
Printed matter

Fingerprints

Latent
Crime search
Comparisons

Ballistics

Electronics

Detection of unauthorized devices
Transmitters
Recording devices[4]

---

[4]This partial list of forensic abilities was taken from the *Directory of Technical Services and Consultants* (Washington, D.C.: American Society for Industrial Security, 1971).

private investigations

The private investigative function, universally recognized as an independent vocation, is nevertheless closely related to the security field. Like security administrators, private investigators frequently have backgrounds in federal, state, or city police work. And although proprietary and contract security practitioners may not consider themselves investigators, they occasionally find it necessary to conduct or supervise a private investigation. An investigation by a security practitioner to identify a person who has committed a crime against the facility under his control is analogous in many ways to a police investigation. These security-related investigations account for a major portion of the overall private investigative function.

The public image of the private investigative vocation is for the most part the product of television and motion picture characterizations, resulting in a somewhat limited and distorted perception. The private investigative field actually consists of a wide variety of practitioners and functions.

A significant proportion of this work involves preemployment inquiries. Most large companies and institutions rely upon fitness and character checks as a part of their regular personnel operation, to ensure hiring honest and reliable employees. Although the degree and depth of preemployment checks vary, most large companies budget a substantial amount of time and money to insure a thorough investigation. Employers that hire high-level executives from other companies often conduct complete background investigations before making a final employment decision. Large firms may use their own security departments for this purpose; smaller firms usually delegate these responsibilities to nonsecurity personnel or private investigative agencies. Preemployment and background investigations are discussed in detail in Chapter 11.

For purposes of this discussion, an investigation involving private crime solution will be referred to as a security investigation. For example, a security investigation would be any inquiry conducted by a proprietary or private contract investigator for the purpose of identifying an employee or other person who has committed a criminal act against the investigator's employer or client. Most of these private inquiries, although they involve criminal matters, are conducted without the knowledge or assistance of public law-enforcement personnel. When the internal thief, vandal, burglar, or saboteur has been identified and solidly linked to the crime by a security investigator, the victim may then decide to initiate criminal prosecution.

Generally, police investigations involve street crimes such as murder, rape, assault, vandalism, armed robbery, burglary, and automobile theft. Private criminal investigations, on the other hand, are more likely to involve those offenses commonly referred to as white-collar crime—offenses such as embezzlement and forgery, as well as credit-car, insurance, tax, and bankruptcy fraud.

The arrest and subsequent conviction of a subject of a private security investigation will be predicated upon the work of a private investigator. The security investigative function therefore complements the overall crime-fighting effort of the police by extending the detection and solution capability to people and places normally beyond the reach of most law-enforcement personnel, particularly in connection with white-collar crimes such as embezzlement.

Private inquiries into criminal cases being investigated by law-enforcement personnel also serve to augment the public crime-solution effort. For example, a private arson investigation conducted on behalf of an insurance company supplements the effort of the police to solve the case. Private bad-check and fraudulent-credit-card investigations serve private as well as law-enforcement interests. Telephone-company investigators conduct security-type investigations involving the fraudulent and illegal use of telephone services and thefts from utility pay telephones. Although arson, bad-check, credit-card, and other crimes against business are matters of police concern and attention, they are also frequently the subjects of security investigations initiated and financed by vulnerable and victimized members of the business community. By assisting the police, private investigators complement their work.

Another private investigative function is that of assisting an attorney in the preparation of a criminal defense. Because most criminal trials are won or lost on the facts, a private investigation on behalf of the defendant is usually helpful to the defense attorney. It is estimated, however, that criminal-defense investigations make up only 5 percent of the total private investigative workload. Private investigations of a noncriminal nature on behalf of an attorney and his client are quite common. Such investigations may be conducted on behalf of the plaintiff or the defendant in a civil suit. For example, tort cases involving wrongful death or personal-injury claims usually necessitate fact-finding effort on the part of the attorney, his client, or a private investigator. Investigations on behalf of the plaintiff in a civil suit are usually conducted by either in-house or private contract investigators. On the other hand, investigations on the defense side are usually handled by private investigators employed in-house by the defendant's insurance company. Tort and other civil court cases, like criminal cases, are decided on the facts.

Attorneys handling domestic matters often employ private investigators to gather facts in connection with divorce contests. Many private investigators, finding this kind of work distasteful, avoid or refuse these cases, as do a significant percentage of contract investigative agencies, as a matter of policy. Nationally, about 25 percent of private investigative agencies handle domestic work.

Another type of private investigation involves the locating of missing persons, frequently minors who have run away from home or spouses who have voluntarily disappeared. Private investigators with prior police experience in fugitive work have little difficulty adapting to this kind of investigation. The task of locating someone whose whereabouts are unknown is commonly referred to as "tracing."

Private Contract Investigations. All nonpublic investigators and security practitioners, whether proprietary or contract personnel, have been up to this point referred to as private investigators. For purposes of the discussion that follows, the term *private investigators* will include only those who provide investigative services for a fee as independent contractors, or the investigative employees of private contract investigative agencies. Security personnel who perform an investigative function solely for their employer will be referred to as proprietary (in-house) investigators. Proprietary investigators and their work will be discussed later in the chapter.

In 1969, James Kakalik and Sorrel Wildhorn conducted the first major nationwide study of the security industry. The results of their work, published by the Rand Corporation in 1971, are contained in four separately entitled volumes commonly referred to as the Rand Report. (See the Selected Bibliography following this chapter.) The report includes a survey of the private investigative function and industry. The findings and recommendations of the Rand Report are referred to throughout this text.

According to most estimates, there are about 5,000 private investigative agencies, with some 200,000 employees, in the United States. They include partnerships, corporations, and individuals doing business as private contractors. Although most states, and a few cities, provide some form of government regulation over the formation and operation of these businesses, only a handful of states have enacted laws controlling the investigative employees of private contract agencies, and few if any states regulate in-house investigative personnel. The findings of the Rand Report indicate that state laws regulating security, private investigative, and related enterprises are not uniform in substance or application.[5] As of 1975, 35 states required the licensing, on a statewide basis, of some aspect of the private security industry.[6]

Most of the states that regulate the private investigative business require the licensing of individuals, partnerships, and corporations providing private contract investigative services, and most have established by statute a variety of standards and prerequisites for the acquisition of such a license. Some states are, in this regard, more restrictive than others.[7] Ordinarily, the applicant must meet all or

---

[5]James S. Kakalik and Sorrel Wildhorn, *Current Regulation of Private Police: Regulatory Agency Experience and Views* (Santa Monica, Calif.: Rand Corporation, 1971). This volume sets out, classifies, and analyzes all the state and city laws and ordinances regulating private investigative and security personnel, services, and agencies. This and other cited excerpts from the Rand Report have been revised, updated, and published as Kakalik and Wildhorn, *The Private Police: Security and Danger* (New York: Crane, Russak and Company, 1977).

[6]*Private Security* (Cincinnati, O.: Anderson, 1977).

[7]In 1976, the attorney general of Michigan ruled that the educational requirement of the state Private Detective Licensing Act was not met by the acquisition of a two-year associate-in-arts degree from a community college. One of the four prerequisites for private investigative licensing, pursuant to the Michigan statute, is a degree in police administration from an accredited university or college. The attorney general, in interpreting this portion of the statute, distinguished between universities or colleges granting baccalaureate degrees and community colleges with two-year associate-in-arts degrees.

most of these requirements in order to obtain his license: He must satisfy a state residency requirement, be a citizen of the United States, have training and/or work experience as a police officer or investigator, have a clean arrest record, undergo a background investigation, pass an oral or written examination, obtain the appropriate amount and type of insurance, and pay an initial license fee. The renewal provisions and costs of private investigative licenses also vary from state to state.

In addition to state and city regulations, there are federal laws, such as the Fair Credit Reporting Act, that affect private investigators and their function. Initially, the Fair Credit Reporting Act was enacted primarily to regulate and control mercantile credit, insurance, employment, and investment agencies and the users of these services; but subsequent interpretations of this federal law have resulted in its application to, and control of, many facets of the private investigative function. Moreover, if any of the many proposed amendments to this act are passed, this law will have an even greater effect on most private investigators and agencies. The Fair Credit Reporting Act, as well as some of the numerous proposed federal laws specifically intended to limit and control private investigative activity, will be discussed pursuant to the treatment of preemployment and background inquiries in Chapter 11.

Proprietary Investigations. As a general rule, proprietary investigative personnel are not subject to licensing and other government regulations. Many companies, businesses, and professions, because of the nature of their operation or function, require in-house investigators. Large law firms often employ them to assist in the preparation of civil and criminal cases for trial. Insurance companies use them to investigate matters involving arson, life insurance fraud, large theft claims, product liability, workmen's-compensation fraud, and automobile accidents. Oil companies employ investigators to identify and locate the users of stolen, canceled, or fraudulent gasoline credit cards. Utility firms such as telephone companies utilize investigative personnel for a variety of purposes; for example, telephone-company investigators handle matters involving obscene and threatening telephone calls, toll-call billing frauds, pay-telephone burglaries, and the unauthorized use and possession of illegal telephone communications equipment.

Large industrial firms, institutions, and retail operations employ their own investigators to conduct inquiries of an internal nature, such as the identification of employees who have committed criminal acts against the company or other company personnel. Although a majority of these internal investigations involve theft-related offenses, investigations into arson, assault, rape, and burglary are not infrequent. Moreover, proprietary investigative personnel are often utilized to investigate such noncriminal matters as employee violations of company rules and policies.

Basic Investigative Skills. In view of the fact that the investigative function is more art than science, and that it takes many years of continued and active experience before an investigator becomes completely effective, there are a few basic skills that have to be learned and used by every practitioner.

In order to be effective, an investigator must develop the ability to elicit information from all types of people, including those who are reluctant to cooperate. Investigators should also have the personality, communicative skills, and intelligence to elicit admissions of guilt from uncooperative or reluctant interviewees. Also necessary is the ability to communicate effectively in writing. An investigative report, letter, memorandum, written interview, or signed statement should be clear, concise, and grammatically correct, so investigative personnel must be able to organize their thoughts quickly and to take complete and accurate notes. In short, investigative work requires the personality and ability to communicate effectively.

In addition, numerous facets of private investigative work require the ability to inconspicuously follow and observe persons and activities. This surveillance capability can be developed only through training and experience.

careers in security-related fields

Private Lie-Detection Examiners. A scientific lie-detection process is composed of three basic functions: the use of an instrument capable of detecting, recording, and measuring human bodily responses; the formulation and administering of examination questions; and the analysis of the bodily responses that correspond to, and are created by, the examinee's answers to these questions.

A polygraph instrument, commonly referred to as a lie detector, is an extremely effective investigative tool. It is capable of detecting, measuring, and recording three bodily responses. The polygraph operates on the scientific principle that a lie will trigger a change in the liar's heartbeat and breathing patterns, and a corresponding and measurable galvanic skin response.

A polygraph examination is usually conducted in a room designed and constructed to eliminate extraneous noise and visual stimuli that might distract the examinee and cause irrelevant bodily responses. The examiner, prior to asking his questions, attaches the instrument to the subject's body. Two leads, or galvanic skin response detectors, are taped to the examinee's fingers, and his upper arm is wrapped in a device identical to the instrument used by a doctor to measure a patient's blood pressure. This attachment senses and measures changes in the examinee's heartbeat or pulse rate and relative blood pressure. The third attachment, placed around the examinee's waist or chest, is a connection resembling a telephone cord; it detects and records changes in breathing patterns.

The polygraph instrument is somewhat analogous to a camera. That is, just as a properly adjusted camera that is in good working order will always produce a photograph if it is operated correctly, the polygraph in good working order and operated correctly will never fail to sense, measure, and record a response caused by an untruthful answer. Although a polygraph examinee may attempt to fool the instrument by intentially altering his breathing pattern, he cannot eliminate an involuntary bodily response triggered by deception. Whenever the results of a polygraph examination are erroneous or inconclusive, the cause usually lies in the question formulation and/or analysis function of the process. It should be noted that a polygraph test cannot be effectively administered to an examinee who has taken drugs or consumed alcohol shortly before the examination.

Before the test, the polygraph examiner carefully prepares questions calling for a yes-or-no answer. These questions, usually grouped in series of ten, must be formulated and selected in such a way as to facilitate an accurate analysis of the record produced by the examinee's physical responses to each question. The responses appear as pen lines on a graph produced by the polygraph instrument. By analyzing the data contained in this chart, the examiner formulates his conclusions regarding the truthfulness of the answers. For this reason, the degree of reliability associated with the polygraph lie-detection process is primarily determined by the training, experience, and ability of the examiner.

Most courts refuse to recognize and accept the opinions of polygraph examiners as expert testimony, but security and law-enforcement personnel consider this method of lie detection exceedingly reliable and useful. Although the polygraph is usually perceived as a device to uncover deception, a more positive aspect of its use is its capacity to confirm what is true.

Both police and private polygraph examiners acquire their training in polygraph training schools, 15 schools certified by the American Polygraph Association and various state education boards.

For those private examiners who work closely with contract or in-house security investigators, experience in criminal investigations, while not a necessity, is extremely helpful. It is not unusual for a private investigator, seeking to increase his vocational effectiveness, to acquire the training necessary to become a polygraph operator.

Most states have statutes that in some way regulate the use of the polygraph. Fifteen states restrict the use of polygraph results, most often in relation to employee hiring, firing, and promotion.[8] And the objection to polygraph utiliza-

---

[8]In Pennsylvania, the use of polygraph examination results are regulated by Section 7321 of Title 18, Consolidated Pennsylvania Statutes, Crimes and Offenses. Section 7321, entitled Lie detector tests:

(a) Offense defined.—A person is guilty of a misdemeanor of the second degree if he requires as a condition for employment or continuation of employment that an employee or other individual shall take a polygraph test or any form of a mechanical or electrical lie detector test.

(b) Exception.—The provisions of a subsection (a) of this section shall not apply to employees or other individuals in the field of public law enforcement or who dispense or have access to narcotics or dangerous drugs.

tion by many trade-union personnel is reflected in collective-bargaining provisions that control or restrict its use under a variety of circumstances.

The polygraph instrument is not the only device associated with a scientific lie-detection system. An instrument called the Psychological Stress Evaluator (PSE) detects and records vibrations in the examinee's voice. The PSE operates on the principle that vibrations in the human voice become more rapid when the speaker is under stress, and that therefore, the telling of a lie, because it creates psychological stress in the speaker, results in a discernible speech variation that indicates deception.

The PSE examinee's oral responses to the examiner's questions are recorded on audio tape. Then the tape is processed through the PSE instrument, which analyzes the examinee's voice and produces a written record, on a narrow strip of paper, of the speaker's voice pattern.

The PSE instrument, slightly smaller than a polygraph, is housed and carried in a container similar in appearance to an attaché case.

Formal PSE operator training consists of three- to eight-day training sessions provided by the manufacturer or seller of the instrument. PSE training is less costly, intense, and time-consuming than the more formalized polygraph-examiner training programs. As a result of the nature and quality of most PSE examiner training, the newness of the instrument itself, and the fact that only one bodily response is analyzed, this lie-detection process has not been fully accepted by all police and security practitioners.

Armored-Car Services. There are between 70 and 100 armored-car companies currently doing business in the United States. These firms own and operate about 4,000 vehicles, which on any given workday transport from $10 to $12 billion in cash, bullion, and other valuables. Typical users of armored-car services are commercial banks, Federal Reserve banks, industrial firms, and the U.S. Mint. Armored-car companies regularly serve almost every large city bank in the country. The cost of a particular armored-car shipment usually depends upon the monetary value of the cargo.

Armored-car firms are independently insured against the loss of the cash and valuables temporarily in their control. The necessity for this insurance is one of the major reasons why in-house armored-car operations, if not nonexistent, are exceedingly rare.

Brinks, Inc., the largest company of its kind, is responsible for about 50 percent of the total armored-car revenue in the United States. Three other large companies—Loomis, Inc., Wells Fargo (Baker Industries), and Purolator Security, Inc.—account for 25 percent of the total business.

Although interstate armored-car operations are regulated federally by the Interstate Commerce Commission, armored-car services are generally unregulated by state licensing and other regulatory laws. However, they are regulated as common carriers by state public utility commissions. In most states, an applicant for a PUC license who desires to engage in the armored-car business must show, among other things, that there is a need in the community for another armored-car firm, that he is fully capable of providing a reliable service, and that he has acquired adequate cargo insurance coverage.

Armored-car drivers and guards are uniformed and armed. A significant percentage of them, unlike other security employees, are members of the Teamsters and other trade unions. Because of the responsibility and trust associated with this type of security work, armored-car personnel are more carefully screened, better trained, and higher paid than most contract security guards or watchmen. Their responsibilities, as distinguished from those of other uniformed security personnel, involve the protection of the assets in their temporary care and control rather than the protection of a specific company, premises, or group of people.

Armored-car work is dangerous; for obvious reasons, the risk of work-related injury or death is higher for armored-car guards than it is for most other uniformed security-guard personnel. For example, from February 1971 through September 1972, twelve armored-car guards were killed while on duty. In April 1976, two Purolator Security, Inc., guards were ambushed as they entered a New York City theater to make a cash pickup. Both were shot and killed by gunmen who had taken the theater employees hostage while they awaited the arrival of the armored car. And one week earlier, two Wells Fargo armored-car guards had been robbed of $851,000 while working a few blocks from the site of that shooting.

Private Bodyguards.[9] In the past, it was usually only entertainers and celebrities that hired private bodyguards as protection against overzealous fans. Since the mid-1970s, however, in response to increased threats of kidnapping, extortion, and political terrorism, the business of personal protection has grown significantly. High-level corporate executives and their families have joined the ranks of the more traditional users of private bodyguard services.

During the mid-1970s, the larger security companies, such as Burns and Wackenhut, experienced annual increases in the private bodyguard business of from 10 to 15 percent. Officials of Pinkerton's said in 1974 that they were being flooded with inquiries regarding their personal protection services. In 1975, it was estimated that there were 20,000 people working as private bodyguards in the United States, and that by 1980 there would be 70,000.

Unlike other private-police personnel, bodyguards are well paid, receiving annual salaries of $15,000 to $20,000. People with previous civilian or military police experience in personal protection are the most suitable and sought-after candidates for this work.

---

[9]The statistics in this section have been taken from "Bodyguard Business Booms as Kidnapping and Crime Rate Rise," *Wall Street Journal,* November 20, 1975, pp. 1 and 20.

DISCUSSION QUESTIONS

1. Using your knowledge of the security function, how would you characterize most police–security working relationships?
2. Assuming that the working relationship between police and security agencies is sometimes less than adequate, what aspect of the security function, in your opinion, would be most likely to cause hard feelings on the part of the police?
3. What part of the security function, in your opinion, is the most effective measure against crime?
4. What type of educational background and work experience do you believe to be the most appropriate prerequisites for the following security positions?
   a. Investigative employee of a private investigative firm
   b. Private polygraph examiner
   c. Bodyguard
5. Distinguish:
   a. Security investigation from private investigation
   b. A proprietary investigator from an investigator employed by a private investigative agency
   c. A private contract investigator from an investigator employed by a private investigative agency
6. Under Pennsylvania law (see footnote 8), is an employer guilty of a crime when his termination of an employee is based upon the results of a polygraph examination?
7. Create several fact situations to illustrate instances that would require a surveillance by a private investigator.

SELECTED BIBLIOGRAPHY

BEATTIE, LINDA, "Ambiguity/Challenge/Change—What Does the Young Woman Looking at Security as a Prospective Career Find?" *Security Management,* May 1977.

Directory of Technical Services and Consultants. Washington, D.C.: American Society for Industrial Security, 1971.

CARROLL, JOHN M., *Computer Security*. Los Angeles: Security World Publishing Co., 1977.

GELBER, SEYMOUR, *The Role of Campus Security in the College Setting*. U.S. Department of Justice, Law Enforcement Assistance Administration, National Institute of Law Enforcement and Criminal Justice, 1972.

"A Guide to Security Investigations." Washington, D.C.: American Society for Industrial Security, 1973.

KAKALIK, JAMES S., and SORREL WILDHORN, Vol. 1, *Private Police in the United States: Findings and Recommendations;* Vol. 2, *The Private Police Industry: Its Nature and Extent;* Vol. 3, *Current Regulation of Private Police: Agency Experience and Views;* Vol. 4, *The Law and Private Police*. Santa Monica, Calif.: Rand Corporation, 1971. This report has been updated, revised, and published as Kakalik and Wildhorn, *The Private Police: Security and Danger*. New York: Crane, Russak and Company, 1977.

LIPSON, MILTON, *On Guard: The Business of Private Security,* Chap. 9, "Armored Car Services," New York: Quadrangle, 1975.

NELSON, FRANCIS B., JR., "Factors Affecting the Relationship Between Public Police and Private Police," *Security Management,* January 1977.

NORWOOD, FRANCIS W., "Licensing, Standards, and Certification in the Private Security Sector," *Security Management,* November 1976. A discussion of the LEAA Private Advisory Council's model legislation dealing with the training of armed and unarmed security guards and the licensing of companies providing security services.

PEEL, JOHN D., *The Story of Private Security*. Springfield, Ill.: Charles C. Thomas, 1971. Contains a discussion of the history, role, functions, and objectives of the uniformed security guard.

"The Private Security and Public Police Interface," *Security World,* August 1977. Condensed by Carol Deck from "Law Enforcement and Private Security Sources and Areas of Conflict," a report prepared by the Private Security Advisory Council, LEAA, U.S. Department of Justice.

REALI, SILVESTRO F., "Does the Polygraph Belong in Business?" *Security World,* January 1977.

Private Security. Cincinnati, O.: Anderson, 1977. A publication of the report of the Task Force on Private Security of the National Advisory Committee on Criminal Justice Standards and Goals, Arthur J. Bilek, Task Force Chairman. This was a project awarded to the LEAA, U.S. Department of Justice.

WATHEN, THOMAS W., "Careers in Security—One Professional's View," *Security Management,* July 1977.

WHELTON, CLARK, "In Guards We Trust," *New York Times Magazine,* September 19, 1976, pp. 21-41.

PART I

UNLAWFUL INTRUSION

Chapter 2

Burglary and Related Offenses

AN OVERVIEW

I. Criminal Law Regarding Burglary and Related Offenses
   A. *Basic criminal-law elements of burglary*
   B. *Selected burglary statutes*
   C. *Criminal trespass*

II. Burglary—A Major Security Concern
   A. *The burglar—a profile*
   B. *The receipt of stolen property*

Security measures against unlawful or criminal intrusion are a major part of the overall security function. Burglary and criminal trespass are the two most common intrusion offenses. For purposes of this discussion, the offenses of burglary and theft will be distinguished, on the basis that theft consists of an unlawful taking, whereas the material element of burglary is an unlawful intrusion. Although burglaries are usually motivated by theft, a burglary offense can be established without an unlawful taking. And many types of theft, including shoplifting, embezzlement, and robbery (taking by force or threat of force), are committed without an unlawful intrusion. The fact that theft is often one of the elements in burglary does not make theft and burglary synonymous offenses.

Although efforts to control burglary are primarily motivated by the desire to protect assets from theft, the security measures employed reflect the intrusion aspect of the crime rather than the theft aspect. Security measures preventing or reducing theft by shoplifters, employees, and other persons lawfully on the premises are different from and usually unrelated to the techniques and methods employed to prevent and deter burglary. Therefore, the burglary–theft distinction is relevant for security as well as for legal purposes.

Criminal Law Regarding Burglary and Related Offenses

basic criminal-law elements of burglary

The substantive-law definition of burglary differs from state to state. Most modern burglary statutes, however, reflect in various degrees the common-law concept of the offense. Since in our discussions of the various criminal offenses throughout the text, the common-law version of the crime will be considered, let us refer to the *Black's Law Dictionary* definition of common law:

> As distinguished from law created by the enactment of legislators, the common law comprises the body of those principles . . . which derive their authority solely from usages and customs of immemorial antiquity or from the judgments and decrees of the courts recognizing, affirming, and enforcing such usages and customs; and, in this sense, particularly the ancient unwritten law of England.[1]

In the past, a criminal conviction might have been based upon a violation of an unwritten common-law crime such as burglary, arson, or larceny. Many of these unwritten common-law offenses have since been incorporated into modern state and federal criminal statutes, and these statutes make up most modern criminal substantive law in the United States. However, criminal statutes include not only modified versions of common-law offenses, but also crimes without a

---

[1]Henry C. Black, *Black's Law Dictionary* (St. Paul, Minn.: West Publishing Company, 1951).

common-law heritage—for example, antitrust offenses and obscene telephone calls.

By definition, the common-law version of burglary comprises four specific parts or elements:

1. A physical breaking into and entering
2. A dwelling (residence)
3. At night
4. With the intent to commit a felony therein

Burglary, at common law, applies to a very specific and limited fact situation. For example, a daytime breaking into a barn to steal a cow would not be considered burglary under the common-law definition of the offense. At present, most state burglary statutes do not involve the dwelling element. However, in the statutes that have retained this common-law element, the nature of the premises entered is relevant in determining the degree or seriousness of the offense.

The common-law element of "breaking into" has also been eliminated from most state burglary statutes. At common law, this requirement became more symbolic than actual; the element was satisfied if the intruder merely compromised the security measures established by the occupant of the home. That is, the breaking-in element could be met by showing that the offender had opened an unlocked door or window to gain entry, or used a key to open a locked door. Entry through an *open* door, however, did not at common law establish breaking in, a distinction based upon the rationale that when a person leaves his door open, he has by his own negligence contributed to the crime.

selected burglary statutes

The New York State burglary law illustrates the modern statutory treatment of the offense:

Section 140.30 Burglary in the First Degree

A person is guilty of burglary in the first degree when he knowingly enters or remains unlawfully in a dwelling at night with intent to commit a crime therein, and when, in effecting entry or while in the dwelling or in immediate flight therefrom, he or another participant in the crime:

1. Is armed with explosives or a deadly weapon; or
2. Causes physical injury to any person who is not a participant in the crime; or
3. Uses or threatens the immediate use of a dangerous instrument; or
4. Displays what appears to be a pistol, revolver, rifle, shotgun, machine gun or other firearm; except that in any prosecution under this subdivision, it is an affirmative defense that such pistol, revolver, rifle, shotgun, machine gun or other firearm was not a loaded weapon from which a shot, readily capable of

producing death or other serious physical injury, could be discharged. Nothing contained in this subdivision shall constitute a defense to a prosecution for, or preclude a convicion of, burglary in the second degree, burglary in the third degree or any other crime.

Section 140.25 Burglary in the Second Degree

A person is guilty of burglary in the second degree when he knowingly enters or remains unlawfully in a building with intent to commit a crime therein, and when:

1. In effecting entry or while in the building or in immediate flight therefrom, he or another participant in the crime:
   (a) Is armed with explosives or a deadly weapon; or
   (b) Causes physical injury to any person who is not a participant in the crime; or
   (c) Uses or threatens the immediate use of a dangerous instrument; or
   (d) Displays what appears to be a pistol, revolver, rifle, shotgun, machine gun or other firearm; or
2. The building is a dwelling and the entering or remaining occurs at night.

Section 140.20 Burglary in the Third Degree

A person is guilty of burglary in the third degree when he knowingly enters or remains unlawfully in a building with the intent to commit a crime therein.

Thus, under New York law, burglary involves entering or remaining unlawfully in a building with the intent to commit a crime therein. If this element is present, with no aggravating circumstances, the crime is burglary in the third degree. The absence of terms such as "breaking in" or "breaking and entering" in the statute indicates that in New York, forceful entrance into the premises is not an element of the burglary offense. However, the use of force to gain entry is a relevant fact, because it clearly reflects the offender's intent to unlawfully intrude.

The New York statute does not require a commission of a felony to be the purpose of the intrusion—just the commission of a "crime," which has been interpreted by the New York courts to include any felony or misdemeanor. And in New York, the more serious offenses of burglary in the first and second degrees include, in addition to the elements necessary to establish burglary in the third degree, either an entrance into a building classified as a dwelling, or an intrusion at night, plus any one of the statutory "aggravating factors."

The interpretation of the New York statute in connection with its application to a specific fact situation requires the legal definition of such words and phrases as "night," "building," "deadly weapon," and "enters or remains unlawfully." Nevertheless, it is apparent that burglary in New York involves numerous elements applying to a variety of fact situations. For example, unlawful intrusion into a dwelling during the day, without an aggravating factor, constitutes a burglary in the third degree, whereas intrusion into a dwelling at night, with any one of the three aggravating factors, establishes burglary in the first degree.

The statute clearly reflects the concept that an invasion of one's home at night is a very serious and dangerous criminal act. In fact, during the period when common law ruled, it was a felony punishable by death.

The distinction has been made between the offenses of burglary and theft. To further illustrate the independence of these two crimes, in most states an intruder can be prosecuted for burglary as well as the crime committed pursuant to the unlawful intrusion. For example, an intruder who enters a home and rapes the occupant can be prosecuted, in most states, for both burglary and rape. Similarly, in most states, an intruder entering a business establishment to steal a typewriter is guilty of burglary and larceny.

The Model Penal Code, a complete collection of criminal substantive-law statutes drafted by the American Law Institute and adopted in whole or in part by several states, contains the following burglary provisions:

Section 221.1 Burglary

1. Burglary Defined. A person is guilty of burglary if he enters a building or occupied structure, or separately or occupied portion thereof, with purpose to commit a crime therein, unless the premises are at the time open to the public or the actor [intruder] is licensed or privileged to enter. It is an affirmative defense to prosecution for burglary that the building structure was abandoned.
2. Grading. Burglary is a felony of the second degree if it is perpetrated in the dwelling of another at night, or if, in the course of committing the offense, the actor:
   (a) purposely, knowingly or recklessly inflicts or attempts to inflict bodily injury on anyone; or
   (b) is armed with explosives or a deadly weapon. Otherwise burglary is a felony of the third degree.

   An act shall be deemed "in the course" of an offense if it occurs in an attempt to commit the offense or in the flight after the attempt or commission.
3. Multiple Conviction. A person may not be convicted both for burglary and for the offense which it was his purpose to commit after burglarious entry or for an attempt to commit that offense, unless the additional offense constitutes a felony of the first or second degree.

Under the Model Penal Code, there are two degrees of burglary. The more serious, burglary of the second degree, involves an armed intrusion into a dwelling at night, or entrance into premises for the purpose of inflicting bodily injury upon another. If an unarmed intruder enters a home at night with the intent of stealing property, the more-serious burglary offense has been committed. In contrast to burglary at common law, the Model Penal Code distinguishes between two types of burglaries; one that primarily involves a crime against property, and the other a crime against habitation, which is the more serious.

Since most burglaries affecting the security function involve thefts from industrial, commercial, and other nonresidential premises, most security practitioners deal with the offense as a crime against property and not as a crime of habitation or intrusion. As a result, many security practitioners do not perceive the legal burglary–theft distinction.

Under the Model Penal Code, unlike many other state burglary statutes, the general rule is that an intruder cannot be convicted for both burglary and the crime he committed pursuant to the unlawful intrusion. However, there is an exception to this rule. When the intruder commits a crime that is more serious than burglary of the second degree, he can be charged with both offenses. For example, a burglar who has committed rape can be convicted of both crimes under the Code.

criminal trespass

Criminal trespass, like burglary, is classified as a crime of intrusion. However, unlike burglary, it does not involve an intent on the part of the intruder to commit a "felony," "theft," or "crime" on the premises. Nevertheless, in order to establish a criminal-trespass violation, it must be shown that the intruder knowingly entered in or onto the premises without a license or privilege to do so.

In New York, criminal trespass, like burglary, is divided into three categories or degrees according to the seriousness of the offense. Criminal trespass of the third degree involves an unlawful entry onto land that is not fenced or otherwise physically protected against unlawful intrusion; criminal trespass of the second degree is trespassing within a fenced area, or an intrusion into a nonresidential building; and the first-degree violation relates to an unlawful entrance into a dwelling. Since most unlawful intrusions, especially into homes and nonresidential buildings, are motivated by an intent to commit a crime therein, many criminal-trespass convictions are the result of plea bargaining. In these situations, the intruder pleads guilty to criminal trespass, a crime involving a lesser sentence than burglary, and in return, the prosecution is not put to the test of proving the intruder's intention to commit a crime within the building.

The following are the Model Penal Code criminal-trespass provisions:

Section 221.2 Criminal Trespass

1. Buildings and Occupied Structures. A person commits an offense, if, knowing that he is not licensed or privileged to do so, he enters or surreptitiously remains in any building or occupied structure, or separately secured or occupied portion thereof. An offense under this Subsection is a misdemeanor if it is committed in a dwelling at night. Otherwise it is a petty misdemeanor.

2. Defiant Trespasser. A person commits an offense if, knowing that he is not licensed or privileged to do so, he enters or remains in any place as to which notice against trespass is given by:
   (a) actual communication to the actor [intruder]; or
   (b) posting in a manner prescribed by law or reasonably likely to come to the attention of intruders; or
   (c) fencing or other enclosure manifestly designed to exclude intruders.

   An offense under this Subsection constitutes a petty misdemeanor if the offender defies an order to leave personally communicated to him by the owner of the premises or other authorized person. Otherwise it is a violation.
3. Defenses. It is an affirmative defense to prosecution under this Section that:
   (a) a building or occupied structure involved in an offense under Subsection (1) was abandoned; or
   (b) the premises were at the time open to members of the public and the actor complied with all lawful conditions imposed on access to or remaining in the premises; or
   (c) the actor reasonably believed that the owner of the premises, or other persons empowered to license access thereto, would have licensed him to enter or remain.

The Model Penal Code's version of criminal trespass involves a distinction between unlawful entry into a "building or occupied structure" and intrusion into other types of premises such as a lot, a field, or open land. This distinction, similar to the differentiation under New York law, relates to the seriousness of the offense.

Burglary—A Major Security Concern

Every premises is vulnerable to some degree to unlawful entry. Burglars, in selecting their victims, are not restricted to a particular type of business enterprise or facility. If a building is the site of an item even remotely attractive to the thief, the potential for burglary exists. This is why burglary is the most frequently committed felony offense. The following discussion of burglars and burglary will relate primarily to situations involving forced entry into nonresidential buildings and areas for the purpose of theft or vandalism.

Unlike burglary, which threatens and victimizes the entire community, crimes such as armed robbery, forgery, shoplifting, counterfeiting, and kidnapping plague only specific kinds or groups of victims. For example, bad-check passers, counterfeiters, and armed robbers victimize banks or commercial enterprises such as stores and service stations; kidnappers and extortionists select their victims from the ranks of the wealthy or influential; and shoplifting is obviously limited to retail establishments. But *all* these people or enterprises are threatened by burglary.

The fact that burglary is usually very easy to commit accounts for its popularity among offenders. A building that can be easily entered is for this reason alone extremely vulnerable to burglary. Burglary statistics tend to verify the fact that most burglaries involve victims who have failed to establish or maintain effective physical and psychological barriers to intrusion. Burglary, like automobile theft and shoplifting, is a crime of opportunity.

The Federal Bureau of Investigation's *Uniform Crime Reports*, hereafter referred to as the *UCR*, defines burglary as ". . . housebreaking, safecracking, or any breaking or unlawful entry of a structure with the intent to commit a felony or a theft." Note that this definition includes forcible entry of a structure.

The *UCR* contains data on the number of major crimes committed during a particular time period in the United States, and compares crime-rate figures for each major offense classification. Crime rates are determined by the number of times a particular offense is committed per 100,000 inhabitants, so they provide an indication of the risk, within a particular geographical area, of one's becoming a victim of this offense. Crime rates vary from time to time and, of course, from place to place.

Pursuant to the discussion of the various criminal offenses throughout the text, relevant *UCR* and other crime statistics will be cited.

In 1975, over 3 million burglaries were committed in the United States, for a national burglary rate of 1,526 offenses per 100,000 inhabitants. This amounted to a 6 percent increase over the 1974 rate and a 41 percent increase over the rate calculated for the period 1970 to 1975. Except for 1972, the burglary rate has risen steadily every year since 1955. In 1975, the western portion of the United States suffered the highest regional burglary rate and the North Central states the lowest. Burglaries of nonresidential buildings accounted for 36 percent of all burglary offenses. Most of these intrusions (75 percent) involved forced entry into the premises.

Statistics regarding the various methods of forced entry, including the percentage of burglaries committed by each of these methods, were part of a report to the 91st Congress by the Small Business Administration in 1969:[2]

Break front windows	22%
Break front door glass	16%
Break rear or side windows	14%
Enter through basements, coal chutes or other openings	14%
Break rear door glass	10%
Forced front door locks	9%
Enter roof or skylight	2%
Other	13%

[2]Small Business Administration, *Crime against Small Business*, Report to the Select Committee on Small Business, 91st Cong., 1st sess., Report N. 91-14 (Washington, D.C.: U.S. Government Printing Office, 1969).

According to this set of statistics, 62 percent of the forced entries were made by breaking glass, and 71 percent were made through either a door or a window. These figures substantiate the widely held belief that such gaps in the structure are usually weak points in the physical security barrier.

UCR statistics show that most residential burglaries are committed during the daylight hours, and that the most substantial increase in the burglary rate over the years has been in daytime residential intrusions. The 1975 rate increased by 9 percent over 1974, and from 1970 to 1975, the increase was 60 percent. In contrast, the nighttime nonresidential rate, although it remains high, has shown only slight annual increases—16 percent for the period from 1969 to 1974. It is clear that the rise in the overall national burglary rate is due mostly to the increase in residential burglaries; and this in turn has caused greater interest in the home burglar alarm on the part of the intrusion-alarm industry.

In most cities and sections of the country, more burglaries are committed in December than in any other month. Although numerous variables may account for this, the fact that there are fewer daylight hours during December may explain it. To the security practitioner, who generally works in a nonresidential setting, burglary is essentially a nighttime offense. In 1975, 60 percent of all burglaries were nighttime intrusions.

It has been estimated by the Small Business Administration that burglary costs the business community about $958 million per year. The *UCR* shows the 1975 monetary losses from residential burglary to be $925 million, with nonresidential losses in that year amounting to $446 million. But to these figures must be added the costs associated with burglary prevention, and also the very large indirect costs to the public—those involving many police man-hours spent investigating burglaries, the processing of accused burglars through the criminal justice system, and the incarceration of convicted burglars.

Federal Bureau of Investigation crime statistics show that in 1973, one-third of all police costs in California were related to the offense of burglary. In cases involving the investigation, arrest, and conviction of burglars who had not been caught at the scene of the crime, the cost of this police effort has been estimated at $2,000 per conviction.

Members of the Western Burglar and Fire Alarm Association (WBFAA) assert that increased alarm usage would significantly reduce police and prosecutive costs created by the handling of burglars and burglary offenses. This assertion is based on the following three assumptions: that it costs the public less money, on the average, to convict a burglar who has been caught at the scene of the crime; that the use of a silent-alarm system is an effective method of catching burglars; and that those intruders caught inside an alarmed premises are more likely to be convicted of burglary than those who are not arrested at the scene of the crime.

The WBFAA has suggested the granting of tax incentives to those business enterprises bearing the expenses of a silent-alarm system, on the principle that increased silent-alarm use will indirectly save the average taxpayer money and will also serve the public interest by reducing crime through a higher burglar apprehension and conviction rate.

the burglar—a profile

The average burglar is young, amateurish, and motivated by the desire to achieve immediate material gain. And most burglaries, even though they involve forced entry, require few tools, little planning, and almost no skill or dexterity.

The nature of criminal intrusion and the profile of the burglar have changed over the past 10 to 15 years. As a result of advanced alarm, lock, safe, and electronic-surveillance technology, and the increased use of these effective anti-intrusion measures in banks, jewelry stores, museums, and other highly vulnerable establishments and institutions, most burglaries have become crimes of opportunity committed upon unprotected premises by unskilled intruders. The current profile of the burglar may be a direct result of the advent of effective anti-intrusion technology, since unskilled opportunistic offenders, in order to steal substantial amounts, now have to steal by force. For example, the decrease in the number of bank burglaries over the past 15 years, coupled with a corresponding increase in bank robberies during this period, reflects such a change in criminal methodology.

Even though the average burglar is unskilled and amateurish, he is difficult to catch. By preying on unprotected premises, he can enter the structure with ease and speed, making his detection improbable. The National Institute of Law Enforcement and Criminal Justice has estimated that the probability of a burglar's being caught at the scene of the crime ranges from 20 percent if he stays there two minutes to 70 percent if he is there eight minutes or longer.[3] A variety of lesser physical or psychological barriers to intrusion, even though they are less ambitious and effective than the measures used by such institutions as banks to physically prevent or deter burglary, act to slow the intruder down and, in so doing, increase the chance that he will be caught.

The statistics published by the FBI's *Uniform Crime Reports* regarding the number and rate of burglary arrests strongly indicate the improbability that an intruder will be identified, caught, and convicted in connection with a burglary he has committed. Moreover, the risk of a convicted burglar's going to jail for his crime is slight. According to the 1975 *UCR*, only 18 percent of the burglary cases reported to the police that year resulted in an arrest. In view of the fact that many burglaries are never even reported to the police, it becomes obvious that most burglars are seldom, if ever, processed through the criminal justice system and convicted. In 1975, only 71 percent of the adults arrested for burglary were prosecuted for this offense, and of this group, only 60 percent were found guilty.

Of burglaries solved by arrest in 1975, only 47 percent nationally involved adult offenders; people under 18 made up the remainder. The number of juvenile burglary arrests in 1975 amounted to a 43 percent increase over the period from 1970 to 1975. As reflected by the 1975 *UCR* statistics, which indicate that 85

---

[3]Harry A. Scarr, Joan L. Pinsky, and Deborah S. Wyatt, *Patterns of Burglary*, a 1973 report to the National Institute of Law Enforcement and Criminal Justice.

percent of all those arrested for burglary during this year were under 25, burglary is truly a crime committed predominantly by young people.

In 1973, the California Bureau of Criminal Statistics published a research report, entitled *The Burglar in California, a Profile*. This report, which will be referred to as the *California Profile,* was compiled from criminal offense and offender data collected during the period from April 1972 to June 1973 from seven California counties. The following discussion concerning the profile of a burglar is based upon some of the statistics and findings of that report.

Burglary offenders, in the seven California counties, are young and have been getting younger. In 1972, about 90 percent of those arrested for burglary were under 30, and almost half were 17 or under. In 1960, only 39 percent were under 18.

Both in California and nationally, burglary is predominantly a male crime. In 1974, females accounted for only 6.7 percent of burglary arrests in California and only 5 percent nationally.

According to the *California Profile*, a juvenile arrested for burglary is less likely than an adult arrestee to have a prior criminal arrest record. The study shows that 76.2 percent of those 30 or older and only 8.5 percent of the juveniles arrested had records. It is clear that most adult burglars are repeat offenders.

According to the *California Profile*, most burglars do not work alone. Over 70 percent worked with others—juveniles more often than adult burglars, who had partners about half the time.

Although professional burglars may travel extensively to commit their crimes, the findings of the *California Profile* indicate that most burglars commit their crimes close to home. Overall, 50.5 percent committed their offenses within one mile of their places of residence and 85 percent within three miles. Juveniles tend to commit burglary closer to home than adult offenders.

In summary, the composite burglar in California is a white male, under 30, who commits his crime with an associate within three miles of his place of residence.[4]

---

[4]It should be noted, in connection with this research report, that the California burglary statute is very similar to the Model Penal Code version:

> 459. (Burglary defined.) Every person who enters any house, room, apartment, tenement, shop, warehouse, store, mill, barn, stable, outhouse or other building, tent, vessel, railroad car, trailer coach as defined by the Vehicle Code, vehicle as defined by said code when the doors of such vehicle are locked, aircraft as defined by the Harbors and Navigation Code, mine or any underground portion thereof, with intent to commit grand or petit larceny or any felony is guilty of burglary.
>
> 460. (Degrees of burglary.) 1. Every burglary of an inhabited dwelling house, trailer coach as defined by the Vehicle Code, or building committed in the nighttime, and every burglary, whether in the daytime or nighttime, committed by a person with a deadly weapon, or who while in the commission of such burglary arms himself with a deadly weapon, or who while in the commission of such burglary assaults any person, is burglary of the first degree. 2. All other kinds of burglary are of the second degree.

the receipt of stolen property

Most thefts are motivated by the thief's desire for cash rather than a personal need for the item he has stolen. Because of the need to convert stolen merchandise into cash, it has to be sold to its ultimate receiver or to another person, a middleman, for resale. The middleman who regularly and knowingly buys, sells, or otherwise traffics in stolen merchandise is commonly referred to as a fence. A fence pays the thief only a fraction of the market value of the stolen property, so he is in a position to resell the merchandise at bargain prices while making a substantial profit for himself. He may, for example, sell his merchandise to a retail outlet, also classified as a receiver of stolen property, which in turn will sell it, at a slightly reduced price, to an innocent buyer. The fence is therefore the conduit through which stolen property flows from the thief to a retail outlet or the ultimate purchaser.

Each fence has several suppliers of stolen merchandise, most often shoplifters and burglars. Thieves often steal in direct response to the marketing needs of the fence or his customers. The fence may have an "order" to fill and specifically contract with a thief to steal a specific item, such as a fur coat of a particular size, color, and animal.

Although very few burglars are convicted for their offense, even fewer receivers of stolen property are successfully prosecuted. One of the major difficulties is proving that the fence "knowingly" or "intentionally" had possession of stolen property, since it must be shown that the receiver knew that the item he bought, possessed, or sold had been stolen. Closely related to this problem is the difficulty of identifying a specific piece of property as being stolen. For example, a thief who steals a ton of electrical wire from a construction site may burn off the insulation and sell the bare copper to a scrap dealer. The copper wire is without identifying marks or characteristics, so it cannot be specifically identified as the wire that was taken from the construction site. And once it has been commingled with other scrap material in the junkyard, it will be even more difficult, if not impossible, to identify. Stolen diamonds and other precious and semiprecious stones, once cut and reset, are also extremely difficult to identify. Investigators who search for these stolen items look for them in their original condition, which minimizes any chance that they will be located for possible identification by the owner.

For obvious reasons, a fence is primarily interested in merchandise that cannot be specifically identified by serial numbers, unusual marks, initials, or unique characteristics. Since the fence pays the highest price for useful, valuable, or unidentifiable items, the thief is encouraged to steal merchandise meeting these criteria. Old coins, jewelry, and small, unmarked business machines, for instance, are especially vulnerable to theft.

If law-enforcement efforts could significantly curtail the major fencing operations, most theives would be forced to sell stolen property directly to individuals or retail receivers. And because such direct sale would necessarily be unwieldy and complicated, it would be less profitable to them and would probably facilitate their detection and conviction.

In addition to their attempts to prosecute professional fences, many law-enforcement agencies have attempted to indoctrinate citizens and legitimate retail establishments against the knowing purchase and sale of stolen merchandise. A fence cannot exist without a market for his goods, and burglary and shoplifting, without a fencing operation, would become less profitable.

Ethical businessmen are subjected to a double defeat: (1) They suffer the loss of stolen goods and endure the many ensuing dislocations (production and advertising schedules may suffer, sales may be lost or delayed, insurance premiums and deductibles increase, and so on); and (2) they may have to compete with firms that achieve a substantial and illegal competitive edge by purchasing cut-rate goods from the criminal distribution system.

Police in New York City and Washington, D.C., aware of the close relationship and interdependence of burglars and fences, recently identified and arrested 200 burglars and other thieves by posing as operators of large-scale fencing operations. In the spring of 1976, police in these two cities, in two separate police "fencing" operations, recovered over $4 million worth of stolen property.

In Washington, the police and FBI operated out of a warehouse in the northeast section of the city. Over a period of five months, thieves came to the warehouse to sell, among other things, stolen cars, television sets, stereos, credit cards, government checks, refrigerators, and hospital equipment. The value of the recovered merchandise was estimated at $2.4 million. The U.S. attorney in Washington who handled the case expressed concern regarding the apparent lack of security in the commercial and government office buildings that were victimized by the thieves.

In New York, the police, operating out of a Brooklyn storefront, posed as buyers of stolen property. As a result of this six-month operation, 79 pickpockets, burglars, and shoplifters were arrested, and $2 million worth of property was recovered.

Some states have attempted to attack the fence and his operation through criminal statutes easing the prosecutor's burden of proving the "knowing" element necessary to establish a successful case of receiving stolen property. The following provision of *Purdon's Pennsylvania Statutes* (Title 18, "Crimes and Offenses") illustrates a legislative effort to facilitate successful prosecution of a receiver:

Section 3925 Receiving Stolen Property

> (a) Offense defined. A person is guilty of theft if he intentionally receives, retains, or disposes of moveable property of another knowing that it has been stolen, or *believing that it has probably been stolen* [italics added], unless the property is received, retained, or disposed with intent to restore it to the owner.

Note that the Pennsylvania statute requires only that the receiver of stolen property *believe* that the merchandise was *probably* stolen. For example, if it can be shown that a receiver purchased 25 pairs of new tennis shoes from a 15-year-old at a price of $1 a pair, it can reasonably be established that the buyer, under Pennsylvania law, believed that these shoes were probably stolen.

A fence acting as a middleman may never physically receive or come into actual contact with the stolen property he traffics in. Nevertheless, fences are "receivers" under most statutory definitions of the offense. Chamelin and Evans state:

> The word *receiving* does not necessarily mean the receiver must have manual and actual control over the property. He need not hold the property in his hands any length of time. All that is necessary is that the accused exercise dominion and discretionary control over the property. How does a person gain dominion over property without actually touching it? He can direct the property to be delivered to a certain place over which he has control. If this is done, he has received. For example, Sam tells Joe to put the stolen radios in Sam's garage. Sam never sees or touches the radios before his arrest for receiving stolen property. He has received.[5]

The incidence of burglary, as well as other theft-related offenses, will continue to be high as long as the thief can easily convert his loot into cash.

DISCUSSION QUESTIONS

1. Company A and Company B are located across the street from each other. The incidence of burglary in the vicinity of these two firms has been exceedingly high. As a result, Company A has installed a fence completely surrounding the building. The premises are also protected by a newly installed exterior lighting system. Company A has hired a uniformed security guard who patrols the perimeter every night. Company B, on the other hand, is not protected by a fence, security lighting, or a guard. Neither company has an alarm system and both facilities are unoccupied at night.
   a. Will its new security measures significantly reduce Company A's chances of being burglarized?
   b. Will Company A's security effort result in a lower burglary rate in that neighborhood?
   c. Will the new security measures taken by Company A increase Company B's chances of being burglarized?
   d. In your estimation, what is the effect of the security function on the overall burglary rate in the United States?

---

[5]Neil C. Chamelin and Kenneth R. Evans, *Criminal Law for Policemen* (Englewood Cliffs, N.J.: Prentice-Hall, 1976), p. 140.

2. A day-shift employee of Company A returned to the company premises at midnight and stole tools belonging to his employer. Because daytime employees are forbidden, by company policy, to enter the plant at night, the employee took care to enter the building without being observed by the security guard and the other employees. He gained entry by using a key that had been issued to him by his employer.
   a. Why hasn't this employee committed burglary pursuant to the common-law definition of the offense?
   b. According to the Model Penal Code, has this employee committed burglary? If so, what degree of burglary has he committed?
   c. What degree of burglary has the employee committed according to the provision of the New York State burglary law?
   d. In prosecuting this employee for burglary under the Model Penal Code or in New York State, what element of the offense will be the most difficult to prove?
3. In your opinion, why are so few burglary cases solved?
4. Why would homicide solution rates be higher or lower than those for burglaries?
5. If every business and residential structure were protected by a physical barrier or barriers making criminal intrusion difficult, what effect would this have on most burglars and the overall crime rate?
6. Is the daytime burglary rate for dwellings higher than it is for nonresidential buildings? Justify your answer. Also, regarding the daytime burglary of nonresidential facilities, what day of the week do you think would involve the greatest vulnerability to intrusion?

SELECTED BIBLIOGRAPHY

''Burglary—A White Paper,'' *Security World,* Vol. 11, No. 10 (November 1974), 11 and 29.

CHAMBER OF COMMERCE OF THE UNITED STATES, *A Handbook on White Collar Crime.* Washington, D.C., 1974.

CHAMELIN, NEIL C., and KENNETH R. EVANS, *Criminal Law for Policemen.* Englewood Cliffs, N.J.: Prentice-Hall, 1976. This work contains a complete substantive-law discussion of both common-law and statutory burglary, as well as the offense of receiving stolen property.

DENZER, RICHARD G., and PETER MCQUILLAN, *Practice Commentary,* pp. 331–35. St. Paul, Minn.: West Publishing, 1967. A complete discussion of the modern offense of burglary and its common-law origin.

DEPARTMENT OF JUSTICE/DEPARTMENT OF TRANSPORTATION, *Cargo Theft and Organized Crime—A Deskbook for Management and Law Enforcement.* Washington, D.C.: U.S. Government Printing Office, 1972. This pamphlet contains excellent discussions regarding fences and other receivers of stolen property, operational patterns of fences, and organized crime's fencing network.

FEDERAL BUREAU OF INVESTIGATION, *Crime in the United States: Uniform Crime Reports*. Washington, D.C.: U.S. Government Printing Office, 1975.

KERPER, HAZEL B., *Introduction to the Criminal Justice System*, Chap. IV, "Elements of the Major Offenses Against Property." St. Paul, Minn.: West Publishing, 1972.

KLOCKARS, CARL B., *The Professional Fence*. New York: Free Press, 1974. An in-depth sociological study of the fence, his aspirations, motivations, and achievements.

PENN, HUGH S., and QUINTON HEGNER, *The Burglar in California, a Profile*, Research Report No. 15. Sacramento, Calif.: California Department of Justice/Division of Law Enforcement/Bureau of Criminal Statistics.

ROSELIUS, TED, and BENTON DOUGLAS, *Marketing Theory and the Fencing of Stolen Goods*. Report prepared for the National Institute of Law Enforcement and Criminal Justice (NILECJ), LEAA, U.S. Department of Justice, August 1971.

SCARR, HARRY A., JOAN L. PINSKY, and DEBORAH S. WYATT, *Patterns of Burglary*, 2nd ed. Report prepared for the National Institute of Law Enforcement and Criminal Justice (NILECJ), LEAA, U.S. Department of Justice, June 1973. An exhaustive study of burglary offenders, burglary victims, and methods of entry. Numerous tables and figures.

SMALL BUSINESS ADMINISTRATION, *Crime against Small Business*. Report to Select Committee on Small Business, 91st Cong. 1st sess., Report 91-14. Washington, D.C.: U.S. Government Printing Office, 1969.

Chapter 3

Common Methods and Techniques of Unlawful Intrusion

AN OVERVIEW

I. Surreptitious Entry
   A. *Unlocked doors and windows*
   B. *Unauthorized use of keys*
   C. *Picking the lock*
   D. *Other methods of surreptitious entry*

II. Forcible Entry
   A. *Forced entry through windows*
   B. *Forced entry through doorways*
   C. *Forcing the lock mechanism*
   D. *Forced entry through the wall and roof*
   E. *Forced entry into the safe*
      1. Attacking the combination lock
      2. Other methods
      3. Profile of the safe burglar

For purposes of the discussion in this chapter, an unlawful or criminal intruder is any person who enters a premises, safe, or other area with the knowledge that he is not privileged to do so, for the purpose of committing any criminal act, including theft, vandalism, or industrial espionage. Not considered in this chapter is the situation of the employee who comes unauthorized to his employer's premises to steal company property. This kind of criminal behavior is discussed in Part III.

In this chapter, unlawful intrusion will be discussed pursuant to two basic methods of entry: (1) entry without force, and (2) entry gained by physical force against the structure. The first method will be referred to as surreptitious entry and the second as forcible entry.

Surreptitious Entry

Surreptitious entry may be made, among other ways, by the unauthorized use of a key, by entrance through an unlocked or open door or window, or by entering a building through crawl spaces, vents, sewers, or other man-made gaps or holes in the structural security of the premises.

unlocked doors and windows

Most intruders attempt to enter a building or area through the constructed openings in the barrier or building itself, such as gates, doors, and windows. Security experts agree that an opening 96 square inches or larger and less than 18 feet above the ground is susceptible to human entry and therefore constitutes a weak point in the physical barrier or structure. Since most intruders inspect exterior doors and windows before relying on force to enter their target, they usually discover and take advantage of unlocked or open doors and windows. Failure to secure all exterior doors and windows prior to leaving a building unattended for the night or over the weekend significantly increases the risk of burglary and often precludes recovery under an insurance policy covering a burglary loss. Using the common-law rationale as discussed in Chapter 1, when a person leaves his front door open, he has contributed by his own negligence to his loss.

One of the security functions provided by private patrol-car or guard services is the locking of exterior doors and windows left open or unlocked by careless employees. Operators of these agencies agree that the incidence of unlocked or open doors, windows, and gates is surprisingly high.

unauthorized use of keys

A theft accomplished by an intruder's unauthorized possession and use of a key results in a burglary-related loss without evidence of the unlawful intrusion. It is not unusual for a victim of a surreptitious entry to encounter difficulty in collecting insurance because there was no "proof" that a burglary took place. Moreover, the victim may be unsure as to whether his loss was the result of unlawful intrusion or employee pilferage.

A key can find its way into the hands of a burglar in many ways. A former employee may have forgotten to return the key his employer issued him, or may have had a duplicate made in case he lost it, and returned only the original. He himself may be the unlawful intruder, or he may lose the key and someone else may find it. A key that is marked to identify it with a particular lock may thus, if it is lost or stolen, become a potential burglar tool, and if the employer is not alerted to the fact that one of his locks has been compromised, he is not in a position to plug this gap in his security.

Loss of company keys by current employees has become a frequent and costly occurrence. In addition to the cost of replacing lost keys, including the administrative costs, the company must sustain the high cost of replacing all the compromised locks or accept the risk of an even greater loss through criminal intrusion.

In an effort to solve the security problems associated with keys, some employers have issued keys to fewer employees, made key duplication more difficult, and imposed fines on employees who have lost their keys. Studies have shown that this last technique has deterred careless key handling by employees, with the result that fewer keys are lost.

A master key, giving the holder access to many or all of the locked doors in a facility, creates an even greater security concern. A master key in the wrong hands will allow an intruder total accessibility to a building, the worst kind of vulnerability to criminal intrusion. When a master key is lost, several locks usually have to be replaced; such a loss is therefore a costly mistake.

The establishment and implementation of a key-control system is one of the subjects discussed in Chapter 4.

picking the lock

Lock picking is opening a lock without a key, and without physically destroying or abusing the lock mechanism. There is probably no such thing as a totally pick-proof lock, but very few intruders possess the skill, tools, time, and good fortune to manipulate the internal parts of a high-security lock in such a way to produce a keylike effect on the mechanism.

Poor-quality, unsophisticated lock mechanisms are easier to pick than top-quality, high-security devices. Warded, wafer, and some lever locks are minimum- and medium-security devices requiring less skill and time to pick than most pin-tumbler-type lock mechanisms. Chapter 5 deals with the principles of operation and security application of the various types of locking devices.

Exterior doors are usually secured by pin-tumbler-type locks. Pin-tumbler mechanisms, either installed into the doorknob or set into the door itself, in order to be picked, require the use of specially designed lock-picking tools, plus skill and time; this makes them pick-resistant and therefore not as vulnerable to this method of unlawful intrusion. A warded padlock, on the other hand, can be picked by an unskilled intruder without the use of commercially manufactured lock-picking tools.

Highly skilled and determined burglars have removed lock mechanisms from the target premises for the purpose of producing a key. They install a substitute lock so that the loss is not noticed, and when they remove it and reinstall the original, they have easy access, by key, to the facility. A similar method of entry involves making an impression of a key inappropriately or temporarily possessed, allowing the duplication of the key by the intruder at a more convenient time and place.

other methods of surreptitious entry

There are several other ways an intruder can enter a building without physically breaking into the structure. Intruders have been known to enter buildings by crawling through ventilation shafts, utility tunnels, sewer drains, and small service openings designed for the after-hours receipt of packages and materials. These openings are located underneath, on the sides of, or on the roofs of many buildings, and a determined intruder can use building blueprints to plan a successful entry through these constructed gaps. Every so often, an intruder becomes stuck in an air vent or similar place and is discovered hours later by employees coming to work. There are also police cases involving the apprehension of would-be intruders who got lost in the matrix of underground tunnels beneath large, complex facilities. In a building protected by a sophisticated alarm system and high-security lock mechanisms, this type of surreptitious intrusion may be the most feasible method of entry.

Burglars also enter retail establishments and other premises open to the public and hide inside until after closing hours. Once he is alone in the building, the intruder has ample time to steal without a significant risk of being detected.

Intruders may enter automatically controlled building entrances by joining groups of employees and other authorized people who are going in. This "tailgating" technique is commonly used to enter exterior doors that can be opened only by someone with a card key that is inserted into a card reader. In large office buildings or industrial facilities utilizing this type of access-control system, it is extremely difficult to control "tailgating." Moreover, whenever an authorized holder loses his card key, the door may be compromised. In the more sophisticated card-key access-control systems, however, the card reader can be adjusted to reject lost, stolen, or canceled cards.

To control this type of surreptitious intrusion, many facilities use security guards or other personnel to check identification cards, passes, or badges issued to employees and others authorized to enter the premises. But many intruders still gain entry into these facilities by using stolen, forged, or canceled identification. The vulnerability to this type of entry depends upon, among other things, the size of the facility and the number of employees authorized to enter.

Forcible Entry

Even the most substantial structural barriers are vulnerable to physical penetration by a skilled and determined intruder using the proper tools and equipment. The most that can be achieved is to make unlawful entry difficult and slow, since there is a better chance of detection if an intruder must spend a significant amount of time in gaining entry.

forced entry through windows

Windows, like doors and other openings in the building, because they offer little resistance to force, are frequently the point of forced entry. As we saw in the statistics cited in Chapter 2, it is estimated that 36 percent of all forced entries are achieved by breaking window glass, and 26 percent by breaking glass doors and windows on doors. Although most window locks can be forced open, most intruders break or cut the glass to allow manipulation of the lock, often taping the window first to eliminate the noise of falling glass. Or a burglar may remove the entire pane of glass from a window frame by removing the molding or window putty that holds the glass in place.

In most cases, the glass in a retail-store display window can be broken easily. For example, after breaking the glass in a jewelry-store display window, the thief can reach through the broken window and steal a handful of watches. This type of burglary, commonly referred to as the "smash and grab," is effective even against stores that have window-glass alarms, since the burglar, after activating the alarm, immediately flees the area with his loot.

forced entry through doorways

Hollow-core wooden doors, often constructed of a thin skin of soft decorative wood, offer little resistance to force, thus constituting weak links in the security of the buildings they supposedly protect. Moreover, auxiliary locks are useless on these doors, because there is no place to solidly attach the lock mechanism. Even a solid-core wooden door 1¾ inches thick, or a metal door of sufficient thickness, provides inadequate protection if it is hinged on the outside. A door hinged in this fashion can easily be removed from the doorframe by an unskilled intruder. Doors attached to weak and unsupported doorframes are also ineffectual, because the doorjamb can be pried from the door and the locking bolt. A spread of ¼ inch between the frame and the door will allow the insertion of a crowbar or similar prying tool. Once the locking bolt is pried out of its place in the strike, the door is "unlocked." A metal doorframe, if properly installed, is superior to a wooden doorjamb.

Doors containing large glass windows or constructed entirely of glass should not contain locking devices capable of being operated without a key from the inside. If a door can be unlocked in this way, the burglar will merely break the glass and unlock the door himself.

forcing the lock mechanism

Because most exterior doors are equipped with locks of the pin-tumbler type, the discussion of locking devices will be limited to pin-tumbler mechanisms (as opposed to warded and lever types), which are housed in cylinders mortised into the door itself.

Forced entry into a building through a doorway may be accomplished by pulling the cylinder out of the door with a tong, wrench, or chisel. This usually leaves a 1⅜ inch hole in the door that exposes the locking bolt, allowing its manipulation by the burglar. An intruder using the correct tool and technique on a cylinder not designed or equipped to withstand this type of force can enter a premises quickly. To combat this type of attack, high-security lock cylinders are manufactured with collars or protective rings that prevent the intruder from gripping the cylinder firmly with the lock-pulling tool.

Many low-quality lock cylinders can be dislodged from the door by merely striking them several times with a hammer. High-security locks, however, are manufactured and installed so as to withstand this type of attack.

Most lock cylinders are secured by a set screw that prevents them from turning or rotating in the door. On some lock devices, this screw is set into the face of the cylinder, thereby allowing its removal by an intruder. And once the set screw is withdrawn, the mechanism can be disassembled to expose the locking bar and allow its manipulation. In most cylinders, the set screw enters the cylinder from the side and is covered by a protective plate that is fastened to the edge of the door.

Another technique used to forcibly defeat a lock is by the use of a high-speed drill. Once the keyway has been drilled out, the pin tumblers will not be in a position to impede the insertion of a screwdriver or similar tool to move the locking bolt. (See Figure 3-1.)

In many instances, forced entry is achieved by successfully attacking the locking bolt itself. The locking bolt is the metal bar that protrudes from the lock into the corresponding hole (strike) in the doorframe when the door is locked. Locking bars are either "deadbolt" or of the spring-loaded type. The spring section on the latter type of bolt automatically sends the bolt into the strike whenever the door is closed. This kind of locking action generally provides little resistance to forced intrusion. For example, one of the most frequently used methods of forced entry is by the insertion of a knife blade, screwdriver, or credit card between the door and the doorframe to push the spring-loaded bolt out of its locked position in the strike. Regardless of the sophistication and effectiveness of the internal locking mechanism, a lock set manufactured with a spring-loaded bolt is vulnerable to this type of defeat, commonly referred to as "knifing." Spring-action-lock hardware should never be used on exterior doors or on interior doors protecting high-security areas.

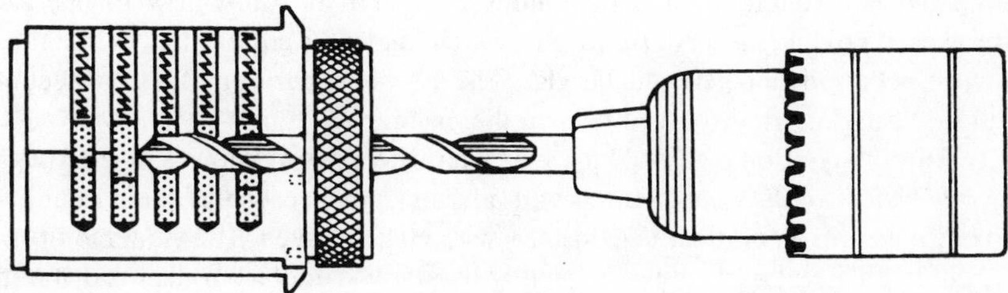

FIGURE 3-1. A pin-tumbler lock cylinder being drilled out

From Marc Weber Tobias, Locks, Safes, and Security: A Handbook for Law Enforcement Personnel, *1st ed., 1971. Courtesy of Charles C Thomas, Publisher, Springfield, Illinois.*

A locking device manufactured with a deadbolt action provides greater protection against intrusion than spring-loaded mechanisms do. The locking bolt in this type of mechanism is projected into the strike by the turning of the key or a turn knob, and withdrawn or unlocked in the same manner. In order to physically compromise a deadbolt, the intruder must resort to hacksawing through the bolt itself. Although this method of attack is often successful, it is time-consuming, so it increases the burglar's chances of being caught. A deadbolt that is too short, however, can be defeated by prying or jimmying the door away from the doorjamb.

Doors are frequently equipped with locking mechanisms that are housed in the doorknob. Even though many of these locks are of the pin-tumbler type, they are usually less burglar-resistant than cylinder-type mechanisms, because an intruder can use several techniques to remove or destroy the doorknob. Once the doorknob has been removed, the intruder can unlock the door by manipulating the locking bar.

forced entry through the wall and roof

Although walls and roofs provided an obvious barrier to forced intrusion, many buildings that are poorly constructed offer little resistance to a determined intruder. A burglar can batter a large hole through most concrete-block walls in a matter of seconds. The only tool necessary is a sledgehammer of sufficient size.

Banks have been entered by intruders who have gained access to an adjacent building and broken through a common wall. This type of entry circumvents the bank's high-security locks as well as the alarms protecting its doors and windows.

Walls of more substantial construction have been penetrated by the use of an instrument known as a "burning bar." The burning bar, or thermal lance as it is sometimes called, consists of a pipe filled with twelve lengths of metal bars. When oxygen is forced through this pipe over the metal rods and ignited, extreme heat is produced that is capable of burning through every kind of material, including concrete and steel. A burning bar is relatively easy to construct, or it can be purchased commercially, and it requires little skill or know-how to operate. However, it produces a very bright light, which, under the circumstances, operates as a distinct disadvantage to the burglar. The use of the burning bar in connection with safe burglary is discussed later in the chapter.

Entry may also be gained by an intruder who saws or chops a hole through the roof. Most roofs are not fitted with alarms and, because of their location, provide cover for an intruder to gain entry without being seen. The vulnerability of the roof to unlawful intrusion is frequently overlooked until a burglary is committed by this method.

forced entry into the safe

Unfortunately, many burglars have been able to open safes without the use of force. Written records of the combination, including unauthorized notes made by users of the safe, if not carefully handled and securely maintained, can be used by an intruder. The indiscreet operation of a safe's lock within the view of an unauthorized person may enable a burglar to acquire the combination. Moreover, safe owners or users often fail to periodically change the combination to the lock, so that too many people, including former employees, end up knowing the combination. And every once in a while, a burglar with more luck than skill will break into a premises to find that the safe has been left wide open.

Safe burglaries, however, usually involve forced entry. Safes, like locking devices, are of numerous sizes, shapes, and types, and provide varying degrees of protection against burglary. Most safes are constructed of pressed steel or other metal alloys, welded rather than riveted together. The more burglary-resistant safes are manufactured with combination rather than key-operated locking mechanisms. Some are equipped with time locks, which limit the opening of the safe to brief, predetermined times such as short periods at the beginning and end of the business day. The use of time locks has operated to deter daytime intrusion into safes and vaults by armed robbers.

Safes are graded or classified by the Underwriters Laboratories (UL) according to their resistance to fire and intrusion. It should be noted that safes with a high fire resistance are usually less resistant to burglary. The better safes are manufactured and designed to successfully withstand drilling, burning, and explosion. Almost all good-quality safes, because of their construction and design, are nearly burglar-proof. The process of forcibly entering most safes, even those classified as the least burglary-resistant, frustrates most burglars, because tools, time, and skill are needed to accomplish the job successfully.

Combination locks, unlike key-operated mechanisms, cannot be picked, because the internal working parts of the mechanism are not exposed and therefore cannot be manipulated. Also, it is impossible for a burglar to discover the combination of a lock through luck or trial and error. Most three-tumbler combination locks allow, for example, 1 million different combinations. Older and low-quality combination locks, however, can be defeated by a skilled burglar using his senses of touch and hearing.

A combination lock consists of the dial (the outer disk bearing the numbers), the spindle (a rod connecting the dial to the tumblers), and the locking bolt. Most contain from three to six tumblers, which are nothing more than disks that rotate on the spindle when the outer dial is turned. Each tumbler disk contains a notch, and when all the notches are aligned, an arm (fence) slips down into the gap formed by the alignment and the locking bolt can be retracted. A few skilled burglars, as they turn the outer dial, can feel and hear the fence hit on each tumbler notch, and thus can align the tumblers and unlock the mechanism. Modern combination locks, however, for several reasons related to their design and construction, cannot be compromised in this fashion.

Attacking the Combination Lock. A few older safes with low-quality locks can be entered by physically attacking the locking mechanism itself. One method is to knock off the outer dial, then hammer or punch the spindle back through the tumblers. Once the spindle and tumblers are out of position, the locking bar can be moved and the safe unlocked. Most modern combination locks are designed and manufactured to withstand this type of abuse.

A knowledgeable intruder may defeat a combination lock by drilling a hole on the safe door so as to allow direct contact with the tumblers, to move and align them. The success and feasibility of this technique depends upon the burglar's skill as well as the thickness and construction of the safe.

Another method is to use a cutting torch to burn out the dial, thereby exposing the internal parts of the mechanism. Instruments capable of cutting through metal have been developed and widely used in connection with the various construction and industrial trades. Since thousands of people, such as welders, have training or experience in the industrial use of cutting equipment, there are thousands of potential intruders with the skill to enter a great many safes.

Other Methods. In addition to attacking the lock itself, a cutting torch can be used on a safe in other ways. It should be noted, however, that careless and unskilled burglars have burned up the cash in a safe while using a cutting torch to burn through its surface.

Although cutting equipment is readily available and operates quietly, it must be inconspicuously delivered to the scene of the burglary. Moreover, after it is used, it is usually left at the scene, where it is valuable evidence contributing to the solution of the crime. These two aspects of cutting-torch use create a definite disadvantage to the burglar.

The burglar who steals his cutting equipment from a welding supply company for use on a safe located elsewhere adds to his chances of being caught by committing the extra burglary. On the other hand, a burglar who uses his own cutting equipment takes the chance of being associated with this evidence through his ownership and previous possession of the gear.

There are many ways in which a burglar can be connected to the burglary tools left at the scene of the crime. One burglar, for instance, left his sparker at the burglary scene. The piece of broken string attached to it had previously secured the device to a belt loop on the intruder's pants. When the string attached to the sparker was scientifically matched with the string tied onto a pair of pants in the burglar's possession, the case was solved.

A few safes are susceptible to being "peeled" or "ripped." Peeling a safe involves prying out the edge of the door for access to the locking mechanism. Once the lock mechanism is exposed, the locking bar can be manipulated and the safe door opened.

Another method of physically attacking a safe is to enter it through its floor. The undersides of many safes are poorly constructed and thus easily destroyed by an intruder using a hammer, hatchet, or saw. The difficulty in this method of entry is moving the safe into a position that allows access to the underside.

Almost all safes are vulnerable to explosives. Although this method of safecracking is rarely used today, the most common explosives used for attacking a safe are nitroglycerine, dynamite, black powder, and plastic. If the charge is too large, the contents of the safe—as well as the burglar—may be destroyed by the blast. The noise obviously associated with this technique is a distinct disadvantage to the burglar.

Finally, another method of safe burglary involves the complete removal of the safe from its site. Burglars using dollies, handtrucks, and similar devices have taken large safes from the premises. Once a safe has been relocated in this way, the burglar may utilize all the time and tools necessary to gain entry. Most burglars, given this opportunity, will be successful.

When investigating a safe burglary, investigators are particularly interested in the burglar's method of operation (MO). By noting the MO and associating the technique with a known burglar and his methods, an investigator can develop a suspect. Moreover, the MO may also tie the crime to several other, similarly committed offenses.

Profile of the Safe Burglar. In 1971, 204 California safe-burglary cases were selected for analysis from the files of the Safe Burglary MO Unit of the California Bureau of Criminal Identification and Investigation. Each of these cases, burglaries committed in the calendar year 1968, was what the researchers refer to as "professional quality." The findings of this study are contained in a report from which selected tables and the summary of findings are reprinted below.

TABLE 3-1

Safe Burglar's Reported Occupation

Occupation	*Persons*	*Percent*
Total	204	
Unknown/not stated	37	
Total known	167	100.0
Laborer—skilled	75	44.9
Laborer—unskilled	67	40.1
White-collar	21	12.6
Other	4	2.4

TABLE 3-2

Criminal History of Safe Burglars

Type of Crime	*Persons*	*Percent with History*	*Number of Charges*	*Average Number Charges*
Total	204	100.0		
Total with prior record	175	85.8		
Property crimes	168	82.4	—	—
Burglary	143	70.1	527	4
Grand auto theft & other major property thefts	117	57.4	315	3
Receiving stolen property	44	21.6	53	1
Petty theft	71	34.8	133	2
Crimes of personal violence	91	44.6	—	—
Robbery	56	27.5	99	2
Homicide, assaults	62	30.4	106	2
Consensual crimes	76	37.3	—	—
Drugs	47	23.0	134	3
Alcohol-related (drunks, etc.)	37	18.2	87	2
Other (gambling, etc.)	6	2.9	8	1
Other miscellaneous crimes				
Possession of burglary tools	20	9.8	23	1
All other—includes traffic, ordinances, unspecified	152	74.5	754	5

TABLE 3-3

Premises Attacked

Premises	*Persons*	*Percent*
Total	204	
Unknown/not applicable	13	
Total known	191	100.0
Commercial	160	83.8
Retail sales, services	130	68.1
Industrial, building trades	18	9.4
Medical practices	5	2.6
Private offices	7	3.7
Noncommercial	31	16.2
Homes	6	3.1
Schools	9	4.7
Churches	3	1.6
Public offices	13	6.8

TABLE 3-4

Methods of Attack on Safes

Method	*Number*	*Percent*
Total	204	
Unknown/not stated	38	
Total known	166	100.0
Works combination (left open)	1	0.6
Punch spindle	7	4.2
Haulaway	62	37.3
Drills	10	6.0
Rip, pry, peel	50	30.2
Pounds or chops	4	2.4
Cuts	4	2.4
Burns	28	16.9

Source: Tables 3-1, 3-2, 3-3, and 3-4 are from John Dumbauld and Homer Porter, Safe Burglars, Part II, A Study of Selected Offenders *(Sacramento: California Department of Justice, Division of Law Enforcement, 1971).*

An analysis of the safe burglars selected for study resulted in the following findings:

1. Male whites appeared to be the most active safe burglars, constituting 75 percent of the cases studied.
2. Safe burglars had a median age of 26.8 years.

3. In terms of interstate mobility, 88 percent were California residents, most having lived in the state at least a year.
4. Sixteen percent of the safe burglars were on bail at the time they committed their offense, and another 25 percent were on probation or parole.
5. Safe burglars were a criminally experienced group; 90 percent had prior criminal records.
6. Property-related offenses, and especially burglary, were a specialty of safe burglars; 82 percent had a prior record involving such crimes.
7. Only 23 percent had any official record of drug involvement, and only 4 percent were registered as narcotics addicts with the Department of Justice.
8. Safe burglars were prime probation and parole risks, as revealed by their prior records, which indicated that 72 percent had had probation revoked and 50 percent had had parole revoked.
9. Although safe burglars tended to work with partners, the study showed that only 12 percent were gang-affiliated.
10. The safe burglars identified in the study preferred to enter by breaking glass or prying doors.
11. The largest group, 37 percent, removed safes from the premises to another area to open them; 30 percent were classified as rip-pry-peel men; and another 16 percent used cutting torches.
12. Forty-five percent of those convicted were convicted of the offense for which they were originally charged; 55 percent were convicted of different or lesser offenses.
13. Of those prosecuted, 24 percent committed offenses while on bail or freed on their own recognizance.

DISCUSSION QUESTIONS

1. The fire-exit door at Company A is equipped with standard panic hardware. For reasons of safety, this door, by design, cannot be locked from the inside. Although it can be opened from the inside by pressing against the panic bar, it cannot be opened without a key from the outside. The door is not alarmed.
   a. Based upon what you know about this door, do you consider it to be susceptible to forced entry?
   b. What method or technique of forced entry would you expect to be tried on this door?
   c. Assuming that the door is constructed of standard glass, can you describe another method of forced entry through it?

d. How could an employee of Company A, assuming that he has not been issued a key to the door, facilitate the surreptitious entry of an intruder through it?

2. In view of the difficulty and risk involved, why would an intruder attempt to burglarize a safe or vault?
3. Why is it advisable to change the combination of a safe shortly after its purchase?
4. Why are most burglaries committed by two or more people?
5. In what ways does the profile of a safe burglar differ from the profile of an ordinary intruder?
6. In the light of the findings in the California study regarding safe burglars and their MO's, what advice would you give a person considering the purchase of a safe?

SELECTED BIBLIOGRAPHY

DUMBAULD, JOHN, and HOMER PORTER, *Safe Burglars; Part II, A Study of Selected Offenders*. Sacramento: California Department of Justice, 1971.

HEALY, RICHARD J., *Design for Security*, Chap. 3, "Physical Barriers—The Three Lines of Defense." New York: Wiley, 1968. A thorough discussion, including photographs and illustrations, of the various methods of forced entry into a building.

TOBIAS, MARC W., *Locks, Safes, and Security: A Handbook for Law Enforcement Personnel*. Springfield, Ill.: Charles C Thomas, 1971.

TOEPFER, EDWIN F., "The Doors That Locks Must Go On," *Security World*, Vol. 11, No. 11 (November 1974).

WALSH, TIMOTHY J., and RICHARD J. HEALY, *Protection of Assets Manual*, Vol. 1, Chap. 3. Santa Monica, Calif.: The Merritt Company, 1974. A discussion of structural barriers, including roofs, walls, ceilings, and floors.

WEBB, DONALD G., *Investigation of Safe and Money Chest Burglary*. Springfield, Ill.: Charles C Thomas, 1975.

Chapter 4

Security to Control and Deter Criminal Intrusion

AN OVERVIEW

I. Security Planning
   A. *Criticalness of the facility*
   B. *Vulnerability of the facility*
   C. *Other factors relevant to security planning*
   D. *Building design and security*

II. Protective Lighting
   A. *Protective-lighting terminology*
   B. *Planning an outside protective-lighting system*
   C. *The four basic types of protective-lighting systems*
      1. Continuous lighting system
      2. Movable lighting system
      3. Standby lighting system
      4. Emergency lighting system
   D. *Three sources of artificial light*
      1. Incandescent lamp
      2. Gaseous-discharge lamp
      3. Quartz lamp
   E. *Four basic types of protective-lighting fixtures*
      1. Floodlights
      2. Street light
      3. Fresnel units
      4. Searchlights

F. *Protective-lighting patterns*
   1. Perimeter lighting
   2. Lighting other areas

G. *Relation of public outdoor lighting to crime rates*

III. Protective Fencing
   A. *General principles and objectives*
   B. *Fenced or caged areas within the perimeter*
   C. *The number and construction of gates*
   D. *Types and specifications of protective fencing*
      1. Chain link fence
      2. Barbed-wire fencing
      3. Concertina fencing

IV. Maintenance Personnel

V. Protective Dogs
   A. *Sentry dogs*
   B. *Guard dogs*
   C. *Costs of protective-dog use*

VI. Window Security
   A. *Security glazing*
      1. Burglar-resistant glass
      2. Burglar-resistant polycarbonate transparent security material
      3. Burglar-resistant acrylic material
   B. *Security coverings for windows*
      1. Security screens
      2. Window gratings
   C. *Window-glass alarm devices*
      1. Window foil
      2. Vibration glass alarms
      3. Glass-breakage alarms

VII. Visitor-Access Control
   A. *Methods of visitor-access control*
      1. Registering the visitor
      2. Escorting the visitor
      3. Identifying the visitor

The possibility of an unlawful entry even into a well-protected structure or area can never be totally eliminated. A determined intruder with sufficient time, skill, equipment, and luck can physically compromise any structural barrier, and security goals and objectives are likely to be more realistically perceived by a security practitioner who has accepted this premise.

In addressing the problem of criminal intrusion, the primary security objective is not the apprehension or identification of the person who committed the burglary, but rather reduction of the risk that intrusion into the facility will be attempted or achieved. For example, the apprehension of a burglar who effortlessly gained entry into a structure reflects in reality a security weakness. If the apprehension was the result of a lucky break, the premises are not secure. Therefore, the basic security objective has not been met.

In combatting criminal intrusion, the specific security goal should be the proper application and use of personnel, procedures, techniques, and hardware to deny easy access to the protected area. Once this goal has been achieved, the possibility of unlawful intrusion will be slight. Burglary is a crime of opportunity; therefore, once the opportunity for easy access has been removed, most intruders are deterred. In short, it is the function of security to place stumbling blocks in the path of an intruder.

In this chapter, we shall identify and consider many of the personnel, procedures, techniques, and hardware available to the security practitioner as tools in the prevention and control of unlawful intrusion.

Security Planning

To be effective, a security system or program should be the product of a carefully thought-out plan, based upon the consideration and evaluation of numerous factors. The ultimate determinations made by the security practitioner are the amount of security necessary to accomplish his basic objective, and the cost and practicality of his program. Some of the factors relevant to security planning and decision making are identified and discussed below.

criticalness of the facility

Criticalness is the degree of importance placed upon the facility being considered for protection. Several factors must be taken into account in determining this. Although the security administrator may be consulted, the final determination is made by others. For example, a factory that provides many jobs in the community and produces a useful product is critical to the well-being of many.

The controlling factors in determining criticalness, however, do not necessarily include such considerations. With most business enterprises, the primary determinant is the importance of the enterprise to the owner. If, for example, a factory has been losing money at an increasing rate and there is little hope of financial recovery, the safety and security of the physical plant may not be important to the owner. Moreover, if this factory is heavily insured against loss from fire and burglary, he may not be predisposed to spend more money than is absolutely necessary to maintain the appropriate insurance coverage. This plant, although it may be critical to the public, is not valued by the owner and therefore will not receive much security attention.

Most commercial, institutional, and industrial enterprises, however, are critical to their owners, managers, and employees. But there are various kinds and degrees of criticalness associated with each, differences that are usually reflected in the varying amounts of security required to protect each facility.

Industrial machines and equipment used directly in the manufacture of a product, if they cannot be replaced or repaired within a reasonable time, are critical to the entire manufacturing operation. A plant shutdown resulting from damaged or stolen manufacturing equipment or material may cause irreparable harm to the owner and loss of work to the employees. A computer containing irreplaceable data vital to the day-to-day operation of a business is also considered critical, so it requires intense security protection from theft, vandalism, and fire. In most instances, supplies of raw materials, trade secrets, and sales data are critical to the continued operation and success of a business or institutional enterprise.

Although most employees can be replaced, so they are not critical to the operation of a business or institution, they should be protected from crime as well as from fire and other safety hazards. Historically, at least in an industrial context, employee safety has received less attention and priority than has property protection. (It was only in 1971 that the federal government passed the Occupational Safety and Health Act.) However, institutions entrusted with the care and housing of patients, students, or tenants usually consider their ''clients'' critical to their operation, and they provide for their protection.

vulnerability of the facility

A facility's vulnerability is its susceptibility to crime and disaster. A security planner, in determining security needs for the purpose of establishing and implementing an effective and practical security system, should take into account the degree of vulnerability associated with the premises or area to be protected. To determine this, many factors should be taken into consideration, some of which are discussed below.

In evaluating the vulnerability of a facility, the effectiveness of existing security measures should be considered. For example, if a warehouse is not alarmed against intrusion or patrolled by a security guard during nonoperational hours, its vulnerability to burglary may be high even though there are quality locks on the doors. Although locking devices are a necessary and effective security measure, they will not, by themselves, adequately protect this warehouse against intrusion.

Another factor is the attractiveness of the material being stored. Fences and other receivers of stolen property are primarily interested in small, valuable, or useful items that are difficult to identify. Therefore, if a warehouse contains small appliances, jewelry, fur coats, cigarettes, or liquor, its vulnerability to burglary will be high. On the other hand, if it holds large transformers, its vulnerability to burglary will not be as high, but the transformers may be vulnerable to fire, or to vandalism by a competitor or a disgruntled former employee. If these transformers are critical to a business enterprise, a security effort reflecting this criticalness and vulnerability should be planned and implemented.

Another factor relevant to vulnerability is the geographic location of the premises. A warehouse, for example, may be vulnerable because of its location in a remote area where police patrols are infrequent or nonexistent. Remoteness also encourages the commission of burglary and arson, because of the privacy afforded the criminal. Facilities situated in neighborhoods suffering from a high crime rate are also more vulnerable to burglary, arson, and other crimes against property.

The final determinant of vulnerability has to do with the nature of the structure itself, including its physical layout. Older buildings in disrepair or in a state of deterioration are extremely difficult to protect against intrusion. Buildings constructed with many doors and windows on the street level also tend to be susceptible to unlawful entry. Complex and sprawling structures with many nooks and crannies provide an intruder with the opportunity to physically compromise the structure without being seen. Moreover, buildings with unprotected and poorly constructed doors and windows are difficult and expensive to alarm. Fencing a large and complex industrial layout is costly and requires the installation of several gates. Providing adequate outside lighting is also complicated and costly whenever large and poorly laid-out facilities are concerned.

Older buildings constructed of wood are highly susceptible to fire. And highrise structures, although they are not necessarily more vulnerable to fire, are susceptible to total destruction in the event of fire, and people who live and work in them are more susceptible to death or serious bodily injury, because they cannot be reached by most modern fire-fighting equipment.

other factors relevant to security planning

A security planner soon realizes that most people are oblivious to security, so they do not share his interest or concern over matters important to the security program. Most employees expect to be personally protected from crime and disaster, and they understand the employer's need to protect his assets from these hazards, but they are annoyed whenever a physical security barrier or procedure restricts their freedom of movement. The deactivation of an alarm, the use of a key, or the possession and exhibition of an identification card may serve a security purpose, but it will also restrict and impede the flow of authorized people entering or leaving a building or protected area. Although the security planner should anticipate and not be too concerned about employee complaints arising from these petty annoyances, he should take into consideration the effect his security program will have on the overall operation of the facility. Because operational and security requirements often conflict, he must be aware of the necessity to strike a balance between them.

For example, most companies will not authorize the search of an employee's lunch pail at the end of his work shift. Hundreds of employees may leave the plant together through one exit, and an inspection of this nature, although it might result in the recovery of company property and effectively deter internal theft, would result in employee inconvenience and delay. Although the security planner may not agree with this policy, he must adapt his program to the operational needs of the enterprise and, in so doing, perhaps compromise the intensity and corresponding effectiveness of his security system.

Another factor to be considered in security planning is the cost of establishing and implementing the security program. In reality, this cost factor is probably the most important and controlling consideration. In order to justify the expense of his security program, the planner must show the owner that his system can save an amount equal to its cost. Of course, such a justification is somewhat subjective, since it is impossible to determine empirically whether a particular security measure has actually deterred burglary, theft, or vandalism. And it is inadvisable for a security practitioner, in order to enlarge his budget, to personally guarantee that a particular measure will result in the capture or identification of a burglar or internal thief.

Factors such as criticalness and vulnerability are also relevant in justifying the cost of a security system. If, however, a business enterprise is in financial difficulty, one of the first expenses to be eliminated or reduced is usually a security-related cost. Security planners, realizing that a drastic cut in the security budget amounts to a gamble that could result in irreparable damage to the business, often become frustrated over management's apparent failure to perceive the importance of the security function.

building design and security

Few architects and construction planners take physical security into consideration when planning and designing new structures. And building codes, while leaning heavily to fire safety requirements, seldom impose physical-security standards upon builders.[1]

Since most architects and builders are uninterested and unschooled in physical security, they seldom develop construction techniques to reduce criminal opportunity, and so crime prevention through physical design has been neglected.

---

[1]Oakland, California, was one of the first municipalities to develop a Model Burglary Prevention Ordinance. Los Angeles's building code contains numerous physical security requirements. The following municipalities and county governments have included minimum security standards in their building codes: Indianapolis, Ind.; Trenton, N.J.; Arlington Heights Village, Ill.; Arlington County, Va.; Prince George County, Md.; and Live Oak, Texas.

Moreover, built-in physical security may compete with safety and aesthetic considerations. Nevertheless, physical-security consultants should have a hand in the planning and design of new buildings. For example, it is easier and less expensive to install locking devices during construction than afterward, and it is extremely expensive and time-consuming to change window and door locations after a building has been completed.

Poor physical-security design features of a building not only fail to prevent crime, but actually operate to facilitate its commission in or about the structure. For example, elevators, enclosed stairways, pedestrian underpasses, and underground parking garages provide seclusion and screening from public view and, as a result, often become the scenes of crimes against persons and property. But buildings can be architecturally designed to eliminate criminal concealment: Stairways can be enclosed in glass and be well illuminated; visibility can be improved by selecting, locating, and trimming trees and shrubbery; closed-circuit television systems can open up areas previously out of view. Elevators in particular, commonly the scenes of crimes against the person, can be monitored with electronic surveillance devices.

The National Advisory Commission on Criminal Justice Standards and Goals, in its 1973 report, *Community Crime Prevention,* made the following recommendation regarding building design and crime reduction:

> The Commission recommends that agencies and professions involved in building design actively consult with and seek the advice of law enforcement agencies on physical design to reduce the opportunity for the commission of crime. These agencies and firms should make security a primary consideration in the design and construction of new buildings and the reconstruction or renovation of older structures. Interaction with law enforcement agencies and *security experts* should be sought during preliminary planning and actual construction to determine the effects of architectural features and spatial arrangements on building security and security costs. Careful consideration should be given to the design and placement of doors, windows, elevators and stairs, lighting, building height and size, arrangement of units, and exterior site design, since these factors can have an effect on crime. [Emphasis added.]

The commission also made the following recommendation:

> The Commission recommends that States and units of local government include security requirements within existing building codes. The formulation of these requirements should be primarily the task of building, fire, and public safety departments, but there also should be consultation with community criminal justice planners, transportation and sanitation departments, architectural firms, and proprietors. Government and private construction and renovation loan sources should make adequate security and compliance with security requirements of the building code a condition for obtaining funds.

The remainder of this chapter will deal with structural, mechanical, electrical, and human barriers to criminal intrusion.

Protective Lighting

Familiarity with basic protective-lighting terminology is a prerequisite to a full understanding of the principles and application of protective lighting, so the following glossary has been included to augment the discussion of this subject.

protective-lighting terminology

Area lighting–The installation and arrangement of lighting fixtures for the purpose of illuminating a specific area. The light fixtures (luminaries) may be installed in groups or individually at heights that provide the most effective illumination per unit.

Brightness–The luminous intensity of a surface, one of the basic elements of human sight. A lack of brightness reduces sight capability; excessive brightness, or glare, causes eye fatigue.

Candlepower–A unit of intensity of a source of light, the level of intensity emitted from one candle. The candlepower of a light source remains constant regardless of the distance between the light source and the observer.

Continuous lighting system–A lighting system composed of stationary lighting fixtures or luminaries providing controlled glare projection or area patterns of light on a continuous or regular basis.

Controlled pattern lighting–Perimeter lighting involving the illumination of a limited or well-defined strip to the exclusion of adjacent places not to be exposed to the brightness. This type of lighting pattern is necessary when highways, airports, or railroads adjoin the illuminated perimeter. Such a pattern along a fence line may silhouette the patrolling guard and so become a security weakness. (See Figure 4-2.)

Emergency lighting–A backup lighting system that is ideally capable of replacing the regular continuous system in the event that all or part of the normal lighting source is damaged, destroyed, or otherwise out of order. Emergency lighting systems operating on alternate power sources will also anticipate and provide light during periods of power failure, interruption, or shortage.

Floodlight–A lighting unit designed to produce an intense beam of light that can be projected over a distance and/or focused on a specific spot. Floodlights are capable of forming narrow, medium, or wide beams.

Fluorescent lamp–An electric discharge lamp in which the radiant energy from the electrical discharge is transferred by phosphors into wavelengths producing an intense light.

Footcandle–One footcandle is the unit of illumination on a surface located one foot from the source of a one-candlepower light. It is also the amount of illumination produced when one lumen falls on one square foot of area.

Fresnel unit–A lighting unit (luminary) that produces a fan-shaped beam of light. These units are utilized in glare-projection lighting systems where care must be taken to avoid illuminating an adjoining area. This type of fixture, using an incandescent light bulb, produces on the illuminated surface a pattern of light that looks like a long horizontal strip.

Gaseous-discharge lamps–Lamps producing light as the result of an electric current passing through a tube of conducting and luminous gas. Mercury and sodium vapor lamps are of the gaseous-discharge type, as distinguished from incandescent lamps, which are the most common kinds of light source. (See the definitions of mercury and sodium vapor lamps.) Although they offer many advantages over incandescent bulbs, gaseous-discharge lamps are slow to start in cold temperatures and take even longer to relight when they are hot.

Glare-projection lighting–A perimeter lighting arrangement whereby the beam is projected out and away from the lighting fixture to the perimeter and beyond. Because this technique makes it difficult for an intruder to see into the protected area, it operates as an effective deterrent to criminal intrusion. This type of lighting pattern also protects the guard patrolling the perimeter by enabling him to spot intruders without being observed. A group of floodlights angled outward provides considerable protection pursuant to this principle. (See Figure 4-1.)

Horizontal illumination–The illumination of a horizontal surface at ground level.

Incandescent lamp–A common glass light bulb in which light is created by the resistance of a filament to an electric current. Distinguished from gaseous-discharge lamps.

Lamp–The general term for an artificial source of light.

Lumen–A quantity or unit of light required to light an area of one square foot to one candlepower. A level of light intensity.

Luminary–A complete lighting unit, consisting of a light source and its appurtenances, such as the globe, reflector, and housing.

Mercury vapor lamp–A gaseous-discharge lamp that produces a blue-green light by passing an electric current through a tube of conducting and luminous gas. A mercury vapor lamp uses the same wattage as an incandescent lamp but is more efficient. These lamps are frequently used in areas, both exterior and interior, where people are working.

Movable lighting system–A system that, as distinguished from a continuous lighting system, is composed of luminaries, such as searchlights, that are either permanently or temporarily mounted to allow movement in all directions. Movable lighting systems frequently complement a continuous lighting system composed of rigid or fixed luminaries. Usually, movable lighting fixtures are turned on only during specific periods or in response to a particular need or problem.

Reflector–The part of the lighting fixture that redirects the light by reflection.

Sodium vapor lamp–A gaseous-discharge lamp producing a golden-yellow light. Sodium vapor lamps are more efficient than incandescent and mercury vapor lamps. They are often used in fixtures that illuminate parking lots, large outdoor storage areas, highways, and bridges.

Standby lighting system–A lighting layout composed of stationary and rigid luminaries that supplement the same kind of continuous lighting fixtures. A standby system is

Stationary luminary–A light fixture that is a part of a continuous lighting system.

not capable of duplicating or replacing the regular continuous system and should not be confused with an emergency lighting system. A standby system operates as an auxiliary and is commonly activated, manually or automatically, under special circumstances, such as when an alarm has been activated, during periods of disruption, or when an intruder is detected on the premises.

Street lights–Luminaries with incandescent or gaseous-discharge lamps, usually rated by the size of the lamps and the characteristics of the light produced. Street lights distribute their light in either a symmetrical or asymmetrical fashion.

Vertical illumination–The illumination of a vertical surface, such as the side of a building.

planning an outside protective-lighting system

The security practitioner planning a protective-lighting system should keep in mind that his primary objective is to prevent criminal intrusion. Protective lighting, although it does not by itself create a physical barrier against intrusion, operates as a psychological deterrent. In addition, it allows the effective utilization of other security measures and devices. A well-lit and isolated fence line, for example, provides a better perimeter protection than a fence line situated in a remote and darkened area. A well-lit perimeter also aids a patrolling security guard by increasing his ability to detect intruders.

In determining what type of lighting system to install, the security planner must consider not only the vulnerability and criticalness of the facility as well as other relevant factors, but also matters specifically pertinent to the establishment of a protective-lighting system.

Protective lighting involves artificial illumination that provides a source and level of light allowing the same degree of protection at night as that provided during daylight hours. After all, most facilities are unoccupied at night and thus even more vulnerable to intrusion than in the daytime.

As a general rule, protective lighting requires less intensity than working light. However, each facility has its own protective-lighting needs, depending upon the physical layout of the premises, the surrounding terrain, and its operational characteristics. The perimeter and the points of access, for example, require more intense light than a parking lot or an outdoor storage area. A brighter light is usually necessary also at pedestrian and vehicular entrances, where security guards check employee and visitor identities and examine identification cards, material passes, and shipping documents.

Other protective-lighting considerations are the availability of municipal and other luminaries near the facility; the location and size of the parking area; the location, size, and nature of outside storage areas; the hours of business operation; and such aspects as the fact that dark and dirty surfaces require more light to illuminate than clean and light-colored surfaces. As a rule of thumb, the intensity of outdoor protective lighting should at least allow the reading of a newspaper's subheadings.

the four basic types of protective-lighting systems

Continuous Lighting System. This system is the most common type of lighting arrangement. It is made up of stationary luminaries providing basic area and perimeter illumination. This system should provide the facility with its basic illumination needs pursuant to a regular lighting schedule.

Movable Lighting System. A movable system consists of luminaries that can be moved from place to place or mounted on a pedestal allowing free movement in all directions. Most movable systems include searchlights, which are operated in response to occasional situations requiring more illumination, such as a beam focused on a particular area or on a movable target. A movable system is usually an auxiliary lighting source operating within a continuous lighting system.

Standby Lighting System. A standby lighting system consists of stationary lighting fixtures that provide an additional source of light whenever the need arises. These are stationary luminaries and, unlike the fixtures in a continuous system, are not used on a continued and regular basis.

Emergency Lighting System. An effective emergency system should include the number and type of luminaries necessary to duplicate the lighting capability of a continuous lighting system in the event this system fails to operate. An emergency lighting system, along with an alternate source of power, should be considered a backup rather than an auxiliary source of illumination.

three sources of artificial light

Incandescent Lamp. The incandescent lamp, producing light by the resistance of a filament to an electric current, is the most common source of artificial light. Because it provides immediate illumination when turned on, it is used more frequently in protective-lighting systems than are gaseous-discharge lamps. Incandescent lamps are of many sizes and wattages and produce a variety of light beams. They are used in street lights, Fresnel units, and floodlight-type luminaries.

Gaseous-Discharge Lamp. Not so common a source of artificial light is the gaseous-discharge lamp, which produces illumination when an electrical current passes through a tube of conducting and luminous gas. Mercury and sodium vapor lamps are of this type. Although they have a longer lamp life and produce more efficient light than incandescent lamps, they are slow to relight when hot. Some require 15 minutes to reach their full brightness when relit after having been turned off. A cold gaseous-discharge lamp usually takes from two to five minutes to achieve full illumination when it is turned on. Sodium vapor lamps, because they produce a yellow light, are especially effective in penetrating fog and mist.

Quartz Lamp. The third major source of artificial light is the quartz lamp. This is usually of high wattage (up to 2,000 watts) and produces an intense glare-type light. Quartz lamps are used in perimeter luminaries or to light outdoor areas where people are doing detailed work or being closely observed.

four basic types of protective-lighting fixtures

The source of artificial light, the lamp, is only one part of the complete luminary or lighting fixture. Therefore, luminaries are classified and discussed not only according to the type of their lamps or light sources, but according to their other features also. Some of the basic types of protective-lighting fixtures are discussed below.

Floodlights. Floodlights are lighting units that produce illumination in the form of a beam. Although different types of floodlights produce beams of various widths, all emit a concentrated light to focus on and illuminate a specific area. Because floodlights produce considerable glare, they are used to light and protect a fence line or other type of perimeter barrier. Lamps utilized as floodlights can be of any wattage; however, when used as a part of a protective-lighting system, they are usually of from 300 to 1,000 watts.

Street Lights. Street-lighting luminaries, containing either incandescent or gaseous-discharge lamps, are used to illuminate streets, parking lots, parks, building grounds, and outside storage areas. The light produced by this type of fixture is usually of low intensity and diffused, rather than a beam or narrow cone of light. Street lights produce little glare, so they are not used to produce perimeter glare-projection lighting patterns. Illuminating large surface areas, they produce either symmetrical or asymmetrical lighting patterns: Symmetrical fixtures distribute their light evenly; asymmetrical units direct the light in an imbalanced manner.

Street lights are commonly housed on the ends of overhanging arms mounted at the top of poles usually 25 to 30 feet high. "Center-of-the-road" type street-light units are constructed with overhanging arms about 15 feet long, whereas "side-of-the-road" fixtures have arms extending outward about two feet. Street-light poles along thoroughfares are usually spaced from 50 to 225 feet apart.

Fresnel Units. Fresnel lighting units are used to light and protect a perimeter. They produce a fan-shaped beam of light about 180 degrees in the horizontal and

15 to 30 degrees in the vertical. Incandescent 300-watt lamps are commonly used in these units. Unlike the round and highly focused beam produced by floodlights and searchlights, the Fresnel pattern is flat and wide, making these fixtures especially applicable along a perimeter that adjoins another building or area.

Searchlights. Searchlights are luminaries containing 250- to 3,000-watt incandescent lamps from 12 to 24 inches in diameter, which produce a highly focused beam of light. Because a searchlight can be aimed in all directions, it is capable of illuminating a moving object or being directed to a particular spot. Searchlights are most commonly used to complement an existing continuous protective-lighting system.

protective lighting patterns

Perimeter Lighting. Ordinarily, the nature of the perimeter, including its geographic location and the type of structural barrier involved, determines—and in many cases limits—the kind of luminary and lighting pattern that can or should be used. For example, if a fenced perimeter is situated in an isolated area, floodlights can be used to produce a glare-projection lighting pattern without disturbing or endangering the users of nearby or adjacent facilities. A glare-projection pattern, created by arranging luminaries in a row along the edge of a roof, on top of a fence, or on poles situated a few feet inside the protected area, produces a barrier of light along the perimeter. The floodlights should be directed down and away from the area within the perimeter, so that a patrolling security guard is not silhouetted or blinded by the light, but would-be intruders are blinded and illuminated by it. (See Figure 4-1.)

Although the glare-projection method is the most effective and therefore desirable for protective purposes, it is not always feasible. Perimeters located in

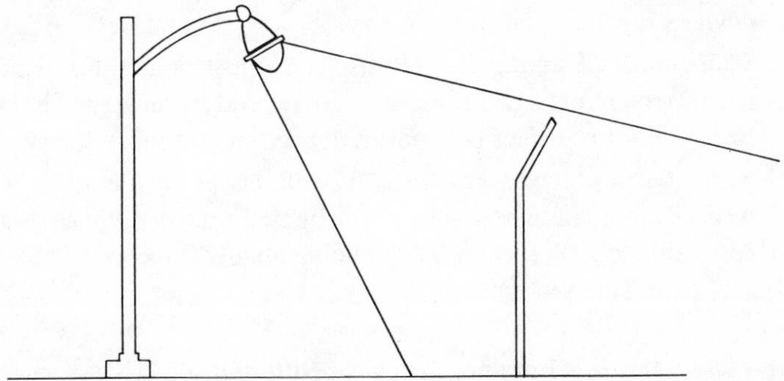

FIGURE 4-1. Perimeter lighting pattern, glare-projection method

Reproduced from FM 19-30, 3 November 1965, by permission of the Department of the Army.

nonisolated areas that are close to highways, railroads, buildings, and other perimeters cannot be illuminated in this way. To protect this kind of boundary, a controlled lighting pattern must be used, in which only a narrow strip outside the perimeter fence, wall, or other barrier is illuminated. (See Figure 4-2.) As the perimeter becomes more isolated, the illuminated strip can be widened, and vice versa.

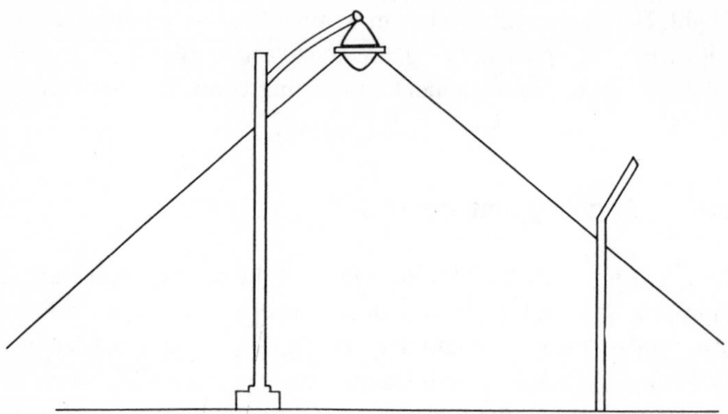

FIGURE 4-2. Perimeter lighting near adjoining property, controlled lighting method
Reproduced from FM 19-30, 3 November 1965, by permission of the Department of the Army.

The following are guidelines to the type of luminary and lighting pattern most applicable for perimeters of varying isolation:

1. *Isolated fence.* As stated earlier, glare projection is applicable where the perimeter is isolated. In these situations, the lighted zone should be an area from 25 feet within the perimeter to 200 feet beyond the fence line. Floodlights and Fresnel luminaries are the most appropriate lighting devices for this type of boundary.
2. *Semi-isolated boundaries.* Because glare must be minimized along these perimeters, street lights tilted outward to produce an area of light from 10 feet within to 70 feet beyond the fence line are most appropriate.
3. *Nonisolated fenced perimeters.* Floodlights or Fresnel units should not be used along these perimeters. The lighted zone in these areas should be approximately 60 feet wide, extending about 40 feet outside the boundary. (See Table 4-1.)

Lighting Other Areas. Entrances should be illuminated with street-light-type luminaries that produce little glare. Where appropriate, the light intensity at an entrance should be high enough to allow a security guard to read employee and visitor identification cards, passes, or badges. Vehicular access points should be

TABLE 4-1
Lighting-Area Coverage

Type of Area	*Type of Lighting*	*Width of Lighted Strip (in feet)* — *Inside Fence*	*Outside Fence*
Isolated perimeter	Glare	25	200
Isolated perimeter	Controlled	10	70
Semi-isolated perimeter	Controlled	10	70
Nonisolated perimeter	Controlled	20–30	30–40
Building face perimeter	Controlled	50 (total width from building face)	
Vehicle entrance	Controlled	50	50
Pedestrian entrance	Controlled	25	25
Railroad entrances	Controlled	50	50
Vital structures	Controlled	50 (total width from structure)	

Reproduced from FM 19-30, 3 November 1965, by permission of the Department of the Army.

illuminated well enough to allow the rapid identification and observation of all vehicles and passengers. Moreover, luminaries at these points should provide vertical illumination on both sides of the entrance. If a guardhouse is located at an entrance, the level of light inside the structure should be of a lower intensity than the surrounding outdoor illumination; otherwise, the guard would not be able to observe entrance activity from within the guardhouse. The lighted area at a pedestrian entrance should include the entire entrance walkway or road and extend at least 25 feet beyond the perimeter gate. Vehicle entrances should be illuminated in the same fashion, with the light pattern extending 50 feet on each side of the entrance. All entrance lighting systems should include backup luminaries in case a fixture fails to operate. In planning an emergency lighting system, entrance areas should be given priority.

Unlike points of egress and ingress, areas within the perimeter that surround buildings require low-level illumination. Street-light luminaries or floodlights mounted on poles are commonly used for these areas. Storage areas, however, ordinarily require a higher level of illumination. Lighting a storage area involves the consideration of many factors, including the size and shape of the area, the nature and vulnerability of the material to be protected, and the placement of poles in such a way as not to interfere with material-handling operations.

The illumination of a parking lot must be uniform and at a level that discourages vandalism, theft from vehicles, and personal attack on the users of the parking area. Street-light luminaries are frequently used to illuminate parking lots.

Other areas that may require protective lighting are vital structures or buildings located within the perimeter. Street lights can provide vertical illumination from nearby poles, or floodlight beams may be directed at the structures. In many cases, the luminaries are attached to the building being illuminated.

relation of public outdoor lighting to crime rates

Most physical-security specialists agree that an adequate lighting system will act to deter crime and, in most cases, significantly reduce the crime rate within the illuminated area. In support of this proposition, the following examples of improved lighting and lower crime rates are cited in a 1973 report by the National Advisory Commission on Criminal Justice Standards and Goals, entitled *Community Crime Prevention:*

> A program of improved street lighting was first begun in St. Louis, Missouri, in 1964. The first area completed was the downtown business district, which consists of large department stores, brokerage firms, investment companies, hotels, and comparable business establishments.
>
> In a comparison of criminal acts in 1963, the last full year before improvements, and in 1965, the first full year after improvements, it was found that crimes against persons in the improved lighting area decreased by 40.8 percent. Auto theft incidents decreased by 28.6 percent, and *business burglaries decreased by 12.8 percent.* [Italics added.]
>
> The Park Department of New York City relighted some of its playgrounds in the hope of reducing vandalism. Within a year, vandalism in Staten Island's play areas has been virtually eliminated; in Brooklyn, it was down 86 percent; in the Bronx and Queens, down 50 percent.
>
> In Detroit, Michigan, a former police commissioner reported that after a lighting program was implemented, street crimes were reduced by as much as 55 percent in the improved areas.
>
> In Washington, D.C., statistics for one area show a marked decline in crime since sodium vapor lights were installed on April 1, 1970. Within three months, robberies in the area declined by 25 percent from the preceding three months. The citywide decline was 8.3 percent. In the same period, *burglaries in the area dropped 62.7 percent;* the citywide drop was less than 6 percent. [Italics added.]

Protective Fencing

There are two basic types of physical barriers: natural and man-made. Natural barriers capable of providing perimeter protection include rivers, mountains, marshes, deserts, and terrain that is difficult to negotiate. Man-made or structural barriers include walls, floors, roofs, and fences.

general principles and objectives

A fence is a structural barrier that defines and limits physical access to an area. It constitutes a psychological as well as physical deterrent to casual trespass and criminal intrusion. Although every fence, regardless of its size or construction, can be penetrated or scaled by a human being, the barrier makes entry more difficult, and thus tends to deter intrusion. Fences also aid in the observation and detection of intruders, since, in scaling or cutting the fence, they may activate an alarm or be seen by a security guard. Another function of fences is to direct and restrict the flow of people and vehicles through designated points; security personnel can watch these points personally or electronically in order to identify and stop those not authorized to enter the premises.

The proper use of a fence can significantly expand the scope and effectiveness of a security-guard force without a corresponding increase in manpower. Moreover, security patrols along a fenced boundary constitute more effective protection than patrols around an unfenced perimeter.

fenced or caged areas within the perimeter

Fences are commonly used to protect highly critical or vulnerable areas or material situated within the outer perimeter or building. For example, small and valuable merchandise stored in a warehouse or in a stockroom in a retail establishment is usually maintained in cribs or cages constructed of fencing material. Truck terminals often use cages to secure otherwise vulnerable cargo on the dock or in a storage area awaiting shipment. A related technique is to place a weighted net over the cargo; the net functions as a barrier, deterring unlawful intrusion into the material.

When fencing material is utilized to protect areas within the perimeter, the fence should be at least ten feet high, extend to the ceiling, or be covered with a wire-mesh roof. Cages and cribs provide security depth, a second line of defense against criminal intrusion.

the number and construction of gates

The number of gates in a fenced perimeter should be kept to a minimum. The number is usually determined by the physical and operational characteristics of the facility being protected. If possible, operational procedures should be altered to allow a reduction of the number of gates. The more gates there are, the more difficult and costly it is to effectively control pedestrian and vehicular traffic. Moreover, gates, like doors and windows, constitute weak points in the structural barrier.

The most common way to secure a gate is with a chain and a padlock. In addition, the gate should be equipped with a top guard (strands of barbed wire along the top of the fence that face outward and upward at an angle of 45 degrees) equal to that on the adjoining fence. The bottom of the gate should be within two inches of hard ground or pavement. Finally, the area surrounding a gate should be well lit to facilitate the observation of people or vehicles moving through the passageway.

types and specifications of protective fencing

The three basic types of fencing commonly used to protect a restricted area are identified and discussed below.

Chain Link Fence. Chain link fences are extremely effective and should be used to secure areas requiring continued and permanent protection. An outside-perimeter chain link fence should be as straight as possible and at least eight feet high. It is advisable to erect it 50 feet or more from the building, structure, or object it is protecting. Physical-security specialists agree that a fence should be constructed of wire of number 11 gauge or heavier. For trucking facilities, the Department of Transportation recommends the use of number 9 gauge wire or heavier for fencing.

The top of the fence should be equipped with a top guard consisting of supporting arms at least two feet in length, bearing four strands of taut barbed wire, no more than six inches apart, facing outward and upward at an angle of 45 degrees. The mesh openings in the fence should not be larger than four square inches. In addition, the fence should be constructed with a barbed and twisted wire selvage at both the top and the bottom. A well-constructed fence will come within two inches of hard ground or pavement or, if constructed on soft ground, will extend a few inches below the surface. When the fence traverses openings or troughs in the terrain larger than 96 square inches, additional grillwork or fencing should be utilized to block entry from underneath the barrier.

Barbed-Wire Fencing. Barbed-wire fences are less effective than chain link fences and should not be used to secure critical or vulnerable areas requiring permanent protection. Standard barbed wire is constructed of a pair of number 12 gauge wires, twisted and barbed every four inches. Barbed-wire fences should be at least eight feet high, with vertical support posts spaced six feet apart. The space between the parallel strands of barbed wire should not exceed six inches, and at the bottom of the fence, the strands should be two inches apart.

Concertina Fencing. Concertina fencing consists of coils of barbed wire clipped together at intervals to form cylinders weighing approximately 55 pounds. A section of concertina fencing is 50 feet long and about three feet in width. One coil piled on another creates a fence six feet high. This type of fence, because it can be quickly laid and easily retrieved, is ideal for the temporary protection of an area. Also, it is the most difficult to cut, and when two coils support a third to form a pyramidlike structure, it is the most difficult of all fencing to penetrate.

Concertina fencing can effectively plug a hole in the damaged chain link or barbed-wire fence, so it can be used as emergency or auxiliary fencing.

Maintenance Personnel

Maintenance personnel, whether in-house or employed by a janitorial agency, are frequently scheduled to work on premises at night or during weekends when the facility is not in operation. It is not uncommon for a security consultant to suggest using janitorial personnel during such periods as an alternative to security-guard coverage. Smaller enterprises without a substantial security budget may find this suggestion particularly attractive and schedule their maintenance personnel accordingly. As a general proposition, because occupied premises are less likely to be victimized by burglary than unoccupied buildings, the use of janitorial personnel at night or during the weekend does constitute a degree of protection against criminal intrusion; that is, it is better than no coverage. But janitorial employees are not an adequate alternative to uniformed security guards, and a security consultant should take care not to mislead his client into thinking otherwise. In many ways, false security is more dangerous than no security.

A few janitorial agencies have openly advertised the added security benefits derived from their regular service, and a few have presented their employees as security personnel who will not only protect the premises but keep it clean. In the states that require special licensing, insurance, and security-guard training as a prerequisite to the offering of security services on a contract basis, this practice is probably illegal.

In addition to being untrained in security and usually supervised by others also untrained, janitorial personnel are primarily concerned with their cleaning responsibilities and therefore are not alert to security hazards and signs of criminal intrusion. In addition, they do not make supervised and scheduled security patrols; they themselves may be serious security problems; and agencies providing janitorial services are not insured against false arrest, libel, slander, and malicious prosecution.

Protective Dogs

A protective-security dog will provide either a physical or psychological barrier to criminal intrusion. A small dog that merely barks at the sound of an intruder—commonly referred to as an alarm dog—is a psychological deterrent; a larger dog, trained to attack a human, constitutes a physical barrier. Of course, an alarm dog's effectiveness is minimized if it is obvious that his barking cannot be heard by anyone other than the intruder. And all dogs are vulnerable to being anesthetized, poisoned, bludgeoned, or shot by a determined burglar.

The following discussion of security dogs is limited to two types of trained attack animals, sentry and guard dogs. Although untrained dogs may growl and even bite an intruder, these animals, unlike trained sentry and guard dogs, will threaten rather than attack and seriously injure a burglar, and when confronted by an aggressive person, they usually give ground.

German shepherd and Doberman pinschers, because of their size and temperament, are the most suitable attack dogs. Most experts in the field agree that the male German shepherd is the better breed of protective dog. However, like any other breed, German shepherds have a wide range of temperament; therefore, only intelligent, strong, and courageous ones should be selected for attack-dog training. Because only a few German shepherds have these required traits, it is advisable to have the dog tested first by an experienced trainer to determine its potential as an attack dog. A German shepherd that has been obtained from an animal shelter probably has not been bred to perform as a police or security dog, and it will not possess the necessary physical strength and emotional conditioning to perform effectively in this capacity. Dogs that have the potential for security work are usually ready for attack training when they are a year old.

sentry dogs

A sentry dog, usually kept on a short leash, makes rounds with a security guard, so that it makes up one half of a security patrol team. The guard's patrol effectiveness against criminal intrusion is significantly increased, especially at night, when he is accompanied by a trained dog with a keen sense of hearing and smell.

A trained sentry dog can easily detect and, on command, attack an intruder. It will also attack without command if an intruder resists detention or physically threatens or harms the dog's handler. A German shepherd has the strength in his jaws to break a man's arm.

In addition to augmenting the security guard's patrol effectiveness, the sentry dog keeps his handler alert, provides companionship, and contributes to his confidence. Sentry or patrol dogs are most effective at night and in remote and quiet settings. Industrial noise, for example, will significantly intefere with a dog's sense of hearing, and a strong odor of petroleum will detract from its sense of smell.

Sentry dogs are often used to accompany security patrolmen on motorized patrols. Station wagons are the most suitable vehicles for this type of patrol operation, but sedans can be modified to accommodate a protective dog by the removal of the rear seat and the installation of a platform. The vehicular patrolman should take care not to leave his dog in a parked car, especially when it is hot, without making arrangements for sufficient ventilation.

Notwithstanding their effectiveness as measures against criminal intrusion, the use of sentry dogs has a few disadvantages. Many security guards do not enjoy, or are not capable of, handling attack animals. Moreover, once they have been individually trained, the security guard and his dog must spend a lengthy break-in period being trained to work as a team. Although a few sentry dogs can work with any untrained security guard, most will not. Every attack dog should be considered potentially dangerous to any person who comes in contact with it, including a trained handler. The disadvantage associated with in-house protective-dog use is the need for kennel facilities and personnel to clean, feed, and care for the animal. And a significant segment of the general public considers the use of an attack dog barbaric and a threat to public safety. In view of these facts, a protective-dog user should consider the public relations effect this security measure may have upon his business.

guard dogs

A guard dog, unlike a sentry dog, patrols alone inside fenced areas and buildings. It will attack, without command, any intruder who penetrates the area under its control—and that includes police and firemen.

Ordinarily, guard dogs are placed inside the protected area or building after the occupants and employees have left the premises for the night or weekend. The dog patrols the premises until it is picked up by its handler and removed from the area. Common users of guard dogs include new- and used-car dealers, retail establishments, scrap yards, and warehouses. Packs of dogs are commonly used inside multistory department stores and warehouses.

The user of a guard dog, to minimize the possibility of a civil suit, should provide sufficient notice in the form of warning signs and posters in the vicinity of the premises patrolled by his dog, and should take care to ensure that the dog does not escape the confines of the protected area. Arrangements should be made to have a dog handler on call in case an intruder penetrates the barrier and is confronted by the dog, or in case the dog escapes the confines of the area it is to protect. Because of the potential danger involved, the appropriate police agencies should be advised of the identity of the area or building under the dog's protection and the times it is on patrol. If possible, the area or building should be monitored so that a handler can be summoned in the event of an intrusion. A closed-circuit television system, intrusion alarms, or a patrolling security guard can be used to perform this function.

costs of protective-dog use

The cost of using a protective dog, as compared to most other security services and measures, is minimal. The initial cost, however, is somewhat high for the user who wishes to own and maintain his own animal. For example, a pedigreed and trained German shepherd sentry dog, capable of obeying from six to ten commands, may cost up to $2,000. In addition, the owner will need kennel facilities and the services of a trained security guard. Most protective dogs eat approximately 50 cents worth of food per day. Other costs of owning and maintaining a dog are medical and retraining expenses.

A person who owns a dog with security potential must sustain the initial cost of having the animal tested and trained by professional protective-dog-agency personnel. The cost of this training will depend upon the nature of the dog's function and the amount of training necessary to prepare it for its work. Sentry dogs, because they have to be taught to obey commands such as "sit," "stay," "come," "heel," "down," and "no," and attack commands like "watch him," and "get him," are more costly to train than guard dogs, which, because of their more limited function, do not obey commands. For example, to train a German shepherd to become a sentry dog costs from $800 to $1,000, depending upon whether it is fed and cared for by the training agency or the owner, and whether or not the dog has been trained to accept food only from this handler. The normal training period takes from four to six weeks. The initial cost of training a guard dog is $400 to $600, depending upon whether there are kennel fees during the training period. A quality dog, purchased from a breeder, will cost from $500 to $1,000.

Because of these initial costs, many protective-guard-dog users find it more appropriate to lease a trained protective dog from an agency. Dog agencies normally charge about $300 to $450 a month for the use of a trained sentry dog, and $100 to $175 for a guard dog, according to whether the dog is maintained by the user. The higher monthly fees are applicable where the supplier transports the dog to and from the user's property before and after the patrol or guard shift.

Window Security

It is common knowledge that windows are a major weak point in the physical security of most buildings. Windows that can be opened and closed should be equipped with quality lock hardware. But because most window surfaces are constructed of glass, a particularly weak building material, window openings are vulnerable to forced entry even when they are securely locked.

The fact that over 50 percent of all criminal intrusions are achieved by the breaking of window glass makes window security a vital topic. A detailed discussion concerning this method of forced entry is found in Chapter 3.

security glazing

The term *security glazing* refers to the fitting of a window frame with a transparent barrier that has been manufactured to withstand a degree of force far greater than that sustainable by a regular sheet of window glass. Functionally, there are two types of security glazing: One is of bulletproof material, and the other of weaker barriers that are nevertheless strong enough to be burglar-resistant. Although our discussion of security glazing will primarily involve burglar-resistant material, the Underwriters Laboratories' glazing standards and classifications pertaining to both will be examined.

Underwriters Laboratories places transparent bulletproof material into three classes, according to its ability to resist various powers of weapons and bullet calibers. Bulletproof glazing material that can resist medium-power small arms, up to a .38-caliber handgun, is defined as Class I. Class II glazing material is capable of resisting high-power small arms up to and including the .357 magnum, and Class III glazing resists superpower small arms up to and including a .44-caliber magnum handgun. Most glazing applications are satisfied by Class I material.

Before a glazing material can be classified as burglar-resistant by Underwriters Laboratories, it must resist penetration under the following conditions:

1. Five 40-foot-pound impacts at room temperature, at 120° F., and at 14° F.
2. Five 50-foot-pound impacts at 95° F. and at 55° F.
3. One 200-foot-pound impact at 75° F.

Burglar-Resistant Glass. Burglar-resistant glass, a laminate, consists of five or more layers of glass bonded together with polyvinyl butyl plastic and sealed under heat and pressure. This glass, often referred to as laminated safety glass, at a 5/16-inch thickness meets both Underwriters Laboratories' bullet- and burglar-resistance standards.

The advantages of safety glass as a transparent security barrier over the modern plastic glazing materials discussed below are its durability and better weathering characteristics. In addition, glass is the only noncombustible glazing material.

The disadvantages of safety glass, when compared to the polycarbonate and acrylic glazing materials, are numerous. Specifically, safety glass is weaker, heavier, more difficult to install, and more costly than the plastic barriers. The only exception is that safety glass is stronger than acrylic glazing.

Burglar-Resistant Polycarbonate Transparent Security Material. Security barriers constructed of polycarbonate glazing are manufactured by the Rohm and Haas Company under the trade name Tuffak, and by General Electric under the trade name Lexan. Burglar-resistant polycarbonate sheets are monolithic (non-laminated) and from ⅛ to ½ inch thick. Bulletproof polycarbonate material, however, is laminated and from 1 to 1¼ inches thick.

Both burglar- and bullet-resistant polycarbonate glazing meets Underwriters Laboratories standards. The burglar-resistant material is optically clear, thin, and easy to work with and install. In the light of all the relevant factors, most physical-security experts agree that a polycarbonate is superior as a burglar-resistant barrier to safety glass and acrylic glazing materials.

Burglar-Resistant Acrylic Material. Burglar-resistant acrylic glazing is manufactured by the Rohm and Haas Company under the trade name Plexiglas. As a burglar-resistant material, it does not meet Underwriters Laboratories standards. However, it is several times stronger than regular glass, so it has many window security applications. Burglar-resistant acrylics are ¼ to ½ inch thick, and unlike polycarbonate material, the thicker the acrylic, the stronger the barrier. Moreover, the larger the window opening, the thicker the acrylic. Burglar-resistant Plexiglas is lighter in weight and less expensive than safety glass, Lexan, and Tuffak.

In addition to its relative weakness as a burglar-resistant material, another disadvantage of acrylic use is its lack of durability when compared to safety glass and polycarbonate material. Acrylic glazing material is easily scratched, so it should be cleaned only with soap and warm water. It is also more combustible than polycarbonate and glass.

But there are several advantages of using acrylic glazing material as a bulletproof barrier. For example, a UL-approved 1¼-inch-thick sheet of acrylic glazing, transmitting 92 percent of the light, is more optically clear than bulletproof glass and polycarbonate materials. Safety glass, transmitting only 55 percent of the light, bears a heavy green color around its edges. Polycarbonates, transmitting 66 percent of the light, have a dirty gray color, which also tends to distort. Because of their color and the illusion of thickness they create, the latter materials when installed create a massive fortresslike appearance. And because bullet-resistant acrylics are the only transparent bulletproof barrier that is not of laminated construction, they are the only glazing materials that can be cut and drilled on the job by standard power tools.

Burglar-resistant glazing has application whenever a window has a security vulnerability by virtue of its accessibility, or because particularly attractive items are stored within the structure. It is therefore useful in homes, stores, and financial institutions. Its use is vital in the construction of, for example, display windows for jewelry stores, camera shops, and gun stores, where a barrier exceeding the physical strength of glass is mandatory. Also, bulletproof glazing material can be installed on standard cars and trucks for greater personal and cargo safety. New, lightweight UL-approved armored cars, heavy-duty stock vans plated with Class III polycarbonate material, are taking their place alongside the Brinks-type armored vehicles.

security coverings for windows

The second major method of protecting a window opening is by the use of window guards or coverings, most commonly heavy-duty security screens and window gratings. Large display windows in jewelry stores and similar establishments located in high-crime areas are often protected by steel gates that are closed and locked every day at the close of business, but our discussion primarily concerns security screens and window gratings.

Security Screens. Most heavy-duty security screens are constructed of steel or stainless-steel wire cloth (mesh) welded to aluminum frames. The screens are either permanently screw-mounted to the structure surrounding the window opening or hinged to a frame and equipped with locking hardware. In installation, most manufacturers of security screens suggest leaving a space of two to three inches between the screen and the window glass.

Effective window protection can be achieved through the use of alarmed security screens. Although these are not manufactured with heavy-duty wire cloth, entry through the screen and window is made difficult by the alarm feature. A window-screen alarm system is usually composed of electrical wires woven into the mesh at four-inch intervals to form an electrical circuit. Whenever one of these wires is cut or broken, the electrical circuit is interrupted, activating the alarm. Screens alarmed in this way can be unplugged from the electrical circuit when they are to be removed for window-cleaning purposes. The manufacturers of alarmed security screens claim a very low false-alarm rate for these devices.

As an alternative to heavy-duty wire-cloth screens, window-protection devices are manufactured from expanding solid metal sheets welded to metal frames, with openings about the size of the holes in a standard chain link fence.

Window Gratings. Window grating is composed of a framework of parallel or latticed bars permanently set in the window opening. This method of guarding a window is extremely effective, but because it is not usually aesthetically pleasing, it is often used on, for example, warehouse and basement windows. It can, however, be made ornamental, and it can also be adapted to the requirements of fire safety.

window-glass alarm devices

The third and final method of securing a window against unlawful intrusion is alarming the glass itself. In addition to the use of alarmed glass, a multilayered glass sheet with the alarm wiring actually incorporated into it (similar in principle to alarmed screens), there are three basic types of glass alarm systems. These are identified and discussed below.

Window Foil. One of the most common methods of alarming window glass is taping the inside surface of the window with a lead foil that is silver in color, ⅜ to 1 inch in width, and paper thin. Window foil is purchased in 1- to 3-pound rolls, containing from 100 to 270 feet of foil. (See Figure 4-3.)

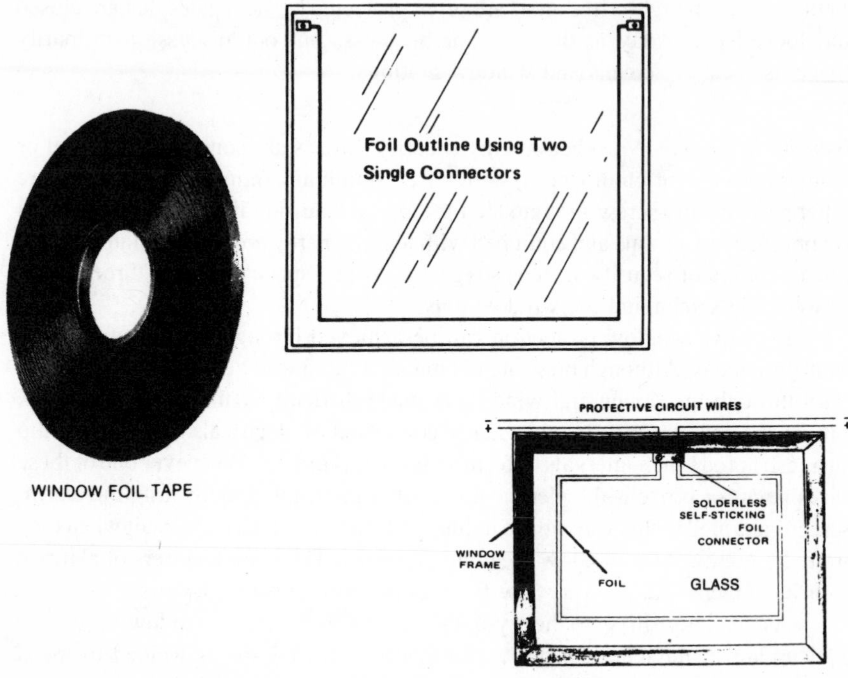

FIGURE 4-3. A roll of window foil and two methods of window-foil installation

Window foil is often used to protect store fronts, picture windows, skylights, and nonresidential glass doors. It is either self-adhesive or bonded to the glass by a special glue or foil adhesive varnish. An electrical current passes through the foil and, in the nonalarm state, the foil forms a closed electrical circuit. A break in the glass, and therefore the foil, interrupts the electrical circuit and triggers the alarm.

The major advantage of window foiling is the system's operational reliability. Also, it is inexpensive and requires minimum maintenance. Disadvantages include the relative ease by which this type of alarm system can be neutralized by a slightly knowledgeable burglar; the glass can be broken or cut in such a way as to leave the foil intact, and the electrical circuit can be bridged to keep it closed and in a nonalarm state. Also, the fact that the tape is visible may detract aesthetically from a display window or similar surface.

Although a hairline break in the tape will cause the alarm to go off, window foil is seldom affected by high vibration or surrounding sound levels. Foil that has been in place for a long time, however, may become torn or ripped through normal wear and tear. Moreover, severe changes in temperature and humidity may cause the tape to expand and contract, causing small fissures in the foil.

Vibration Glass Alarms. An alarm system specifically designed to protect window glass, marketed under the trade name InertiGuard Corp., was introduced to the U.S. security market in 1975. InertiaGuard is distribued by the Morse Products Manufacturing Company. Basically, this alarm system has two components: a sensor activated by vibration or shock, and an analyzer that distinguishes between an actual intrusion and everyday environmental disturbances such as wind, vehicle traffic, and window shoppers. The sensor itself consists of a gold-plated ball seated on three contacts and contained in a sealed enclosure about the size of a small perfume bottle. (See Figure 4-4.) The sensor is normally attached to the window frame, even on multipane windows.

In its nonalarm state, the shock sensor forms a closed switch. When a shock impacts the window, the sensor ball bounces off the three pedestal prongs, breaking the circuit and causing a signal to be sent to the analyzer. The weight of the sensor ball and the position of the prongs mechanically provide the ability to discriminate between intrustion-type vibrations and low-frequency false-alarm disturbances. In the case of loose-fitting windows, the sensor ball can be magnetically restrained. An InertiaGuard system can be installed on windows that are in easy reach of passersby, if the sensor is restrained and the analyzer is adjusted to ignore all but a major attack on the window.

The analyzer component of an InertiaGuard system "reads" sensor output to determine if an alarm condition exists. An alarm condition is initiated whenever a certain time-frequency pattern (the amount of bounce experienced by the sensor ball in a set period of time) is registered. According to the manufacturer, once the system has been properly adjusted, the false-alarm rate is low.

InertiaGuard vibration-alarm systems can be used not only to protect window glass but to alarm walls, fences, and, in some cases, valuable paintings.

The Lassen Electronics Corporation manufactures a vibration-type window-alarm system composed of a solid-state shock sensor. A Lassen sensor

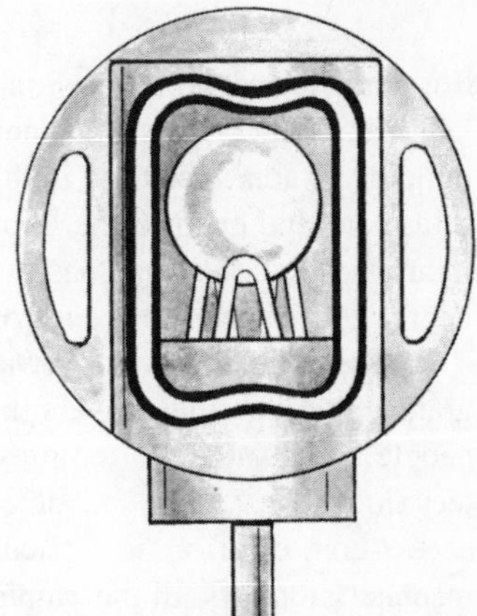

FIGURE 4-4. Illustration of the InertiaGuard window-glass-alarm shock sensor

Courtesy InertiaGuard Corporation

costs substantially more than an InertiaGuard device and, according to the manufacturer, protects 80 square feet of window surface. Unlike foil, it works on laminated glass, and it is considered to have a very low false-alarm rate.

Glass-Breakage Alarms. Many companies produce alarm devices that are generally referred to as glass-breakage detection systems. These use sensors that respond to glass breakage rather than to a shock or vibration. Most of these systems are capable of detecting glass breakage up to six feet from the sensing device. A single glass-breakage sensor, commonly called a "bug," will protect from 30 to 100 square feet of window surface. It is attached directly to the glass and is about the size of a small cigarette lighter.

A glass-breakage alarm system may be "supervised"—that is, designed to transmit a trouble signal whenever it is for any reason inoperable. Other alarm systems may or may not be supervised. An alarm system is unsupervised if it emits an electrical signal only when it is in working order and activated.

There are two types of glass-breakage alarm sensors. The first type detects breakage through the operation of a tuning fork, which is tuned to the frequency pattern produced when glass is broken. This type of sensor operates without electrical power (on a dry circuit) and is relatively inexpensive. When activated, it breaks an electrical circuit, causing an alarm.

The second kind of glass-breakage sensor requires power and responds only to the intermolecular noise generated within glass upon its breakage. This type involves analyzer hardware. The sensor itself consists of a solid-state microphone and an electronic amplifier, and it protects larger areas than do tuning-fork detectors. Both types of glass-breakage sensors can be tested, through the use of special equipment, without the actual breaking of glass.

Visitor-Access Control

For purposes of the discussion that follows, visitor-access control is the surveillance and supervision of nonemployee traffic to, from, and within a restricted building or area. Visitors, in this context, include vendors, suppliers, customers, salesmen, and even former employees. Premises such as large office buildings, industrial facilities, and institutions usually require and utilize some form and degree of visitor-access control.

Remember that visitor-access control and employee identification programs, although they have similar security objectives, apply to different sets of people. (The subject of employee identification is dealt with in Chapter 10 as a technique to prevent and deter internal theft.) However, an effective visitor-access-control effort is difficult, if not impossible, without the ability to immediately identify all the employees within a particular facility. Company identification cards or badges, worn or carried by the employee, or cards or passes used by employees to open doors on the employer's property (see Chapter 5), provide this ability.

By restricting and supervising nonemployee activity within facilities partially open to the public, the security practitioner will significantly lessen the opportunity for criminal intrusion.

methods of visitor-access control

Registering the Visitor. Whether those posted at points of entry into the facility in order to log visitor traffic both in and out are security guards or personnel working primarily as receptionists, the objective is the same—to identify the visitor and to make a permanent record of his visit. Visitor logs are often referred to and examined by criminal investigaors; if the data collected are complete and relevant, this information may contribute to the solution of a criminal case. There have been many instances where a register of this nature has produced evidence instrumental in a criminal conviction.

A record of a nonemployee visit should include at least the following data:

1. The full name of the visitor
2. The time of the visit
3. The purpose of the visit
4. The person or department visited
5. The visitor's temporary pass or badge number

When the visitor leaves the premises, an entry should be made of the time of the departure, and the visitor pass or badge should be collected.

Escorting the Visitor. In addition to making a record of a visitor's presence on the premises, many security programs include physically escorting the visitor to his point of destination within the facility. For example, when a salesman enters, the guard or receptionist, after making an entry in the visitor's log, personally escorts him to his destination or telephones the department or person being visited to obtain an escort.

Identifying the Visitor. In most cases, visitor-access-control programs call for identification badges or passes to be temporarily issued to visitors while they are on the premises. These passes and badges are found in a variety of forms, but regardless of the type used, a personal identification device should be displayed prominently on the person of the visitor. Oftentimes, a personalized pass or badge bearing, say, his photograph and signature, can be produced and issued to each regular visitor to the facility. When he arrives, he is issued his badge, and he returns it to the guard upon his departure. Irregular and new visitors to the premises are usually given standard passes or badges, which are numbered and signed by the bearer.

Visitor passes and badges should include at least the following information:

1. The holder's full name
2. The holder's signature
3. The area or person being visited
4. Information as to whether or not the visitor is to be escorted
5. A pass or badge number
6. The date and time of the visit
7. Information regarding time limitations imposed upon the visit

In order for a visitor-access-control program to remain effective, the passes and badges must be properly issued and always collected, and every pass or badge, whether issued or not, should be accounted for.

The daytime theft of office equipment and other items by nonemployees from large office complexes and smaller offices in buildings open to the public has developed into a major criminal offense. This crime, committed during business hours by intruders, "legitimate" visitors, and employees, is classified by the Federal Bureau of Investigation's *Uniform Crime Reports* under the general category of "Larceny-Theft," and into a more specific category called "Theft from Buildings." Larceny-Theft is defined by the *UCR* as "the unlawful taking or stealing of property or articles without the use of force, violence or fraud," and it includes, among other offenses, shoplifting and theft from motor vehicles.

Trends concerning the loss of assets caused by dishonest visitors to office facilities are reflected in the *UCR*'s statistics on Theft from Buildings. The rate of these crimes increased 34 percent from 1970 to 1975; the sharpest annual increase was between 1974 and 1975, amounting to a 9 percent jump. In 1975, this type of theft made up 17 percent of all Larceny-Theft offenses, and the average value of items reported stolen from buildings that year was $258. It is interesting to note that in 1975, only 20 percent of all reported Larceny-Theft offenses were solved.

Even the partial prevention and control of "visitor theft" from an office facility is difficult to achieve. A visitor-access-control system will not by itself automatically produce adequate results. If the program is poorly administered and loosely supervised, dishonest visitors will take advantage of this weakness by using the system itself to enhance their take and avoid detection. Here is a true story, with the names changed, illustrating one of the ways a thief can take advantage of a poorly implemented access-control system:

For many years, ABC Company's typewriters have been cleaned and repaired by the Ajax Business Machines Company. Whenever a typewriter requires work, a repairman from Ajax is sent to the ABC office to pick it up. Although every visitor pass is supposed to be collected from the holder by the ABC security guard, it is not unusual for the Ajax repairman to leave the facility still in possession of his pass. And because the Ajax Company suffers from high personnel turnover, many repairmen have been given such passes.

Robert Smith, a former Ajax repairman who has since been fired, managed to retain one of his visitor passes. Following his termination, Smith returns to the ABC Company and slips past the security guard during a period of heavy employee traffic into and out of the facility. Once inside, Smith enters the ABC office area wearing his old visitor pass, takes possession of a new electric typewriter, and leaves the office carrying the machine. Although several ABC employees are in the area, Smith's activities do not arouse suspicion. Moreover, because Smith bypassed the security guard coming in, no entry has been made on the visitor log to record his visit. Not only has the ABC company lost an expensive business machine; because the loss appears to have been caused by an employee thief, the theft is not reported to the police and remains unsolved.

DISCUSSION QUESTIONS

1. Can a security planner honestly make any assurances regarding the success of his physical-security program? If so, what kind of guarantee would be the most appropriate?
2. Explain why "total security" is never achieved.
3. Why must the security administrator coordinate his security program with the operational branch of the enterprise?
4. How might the presence of a perimeter fence help establish a criminal-trespass offense?
5. Does a protective-lighting system constitute a physical or a psychological barrier to criminal intrusion?
6. Physical security is premised upon the idea of a relation between physical environment and crime. Provide an example that illustrates and explains this relationship.
7. A drop in the crime rate within a particular geographical area may involve factors unrelated to physical security. Identify some of the nonsecurity variables that may affect the crime rate within a given place and time span.
8. Draft a building-code provision setting out a few basic physical-security requirements.
9. In designing a new building with physical security in mind, will a security planner run into problems when he attempts to balance safety and security interests? In this regard, are aesthetic and crime-prevention considerations mutually exclusive?
10. Ignoring cost and aesthetic considerations, what basic method of window

security would you, as a security consultant, recommend? Detail the rationale behind your recommendation.

11. In addition to determination and prevention of criminal intrusion, what other security benefits are derived from the utilization of security glazing?
12. How would you define to a nonsecurity person the problem visitor-access control attempts to remedy?

SELECTED BIBLIOGRAPHY

security planning

JEFFREY, C. RAY, *Crime Prevention through Environmental Design*. Beverly Hills, Calif.: Sage Publishers, 1971.

MURPHY, RALPH, "Design for Physical Security," *Security Management*, May 1976.

NATIONAL ADVISORY COMMISSION ON CRIMINAL JUSTICE STANDARDS AND GOALS, *Community Crime Prevention*, Chap. 9, "Programs for Reduction of Criminal Opportunity." Washington, D.C.: LEAA, 1973.

NEWMAN, OSCAR, *Defensible Space*. New York: Macmillan, 1972.

———, *A Design Guide for Improving Residential Security*. Report prepared for the Office of Policy Development and Research, Division of Building Technology, U.S. Department of Housing and Urban Development, 1973.

———, *Design Guidelines for Creating Defensible Space*. Report prepared for the National Institute of Law Enforcement and Criminal Justice, LEAA, U.S. Department of Justice, 1975.

protective fencing

Guidelines for the Physical Security of Cargo. Chap. IV, "Barriers." Washington, D.C.: Department of Transportation, 1972.

HEALY, RICHARD J., *Design for Security*, Chap. 3, "Physical Barriers—The Three Lines of Defense." New York: Wiley, 1968.

Physical Security, Field Manual FM 19-30. Washington, D.C.: Department of the Army, 1965.

protective lighting

Guidelines for the Physical Security of Cargo, Chap. V. "Lighting." Washington, D.C.: Department of Transportation, 1972.

HEALY, RICHARD J., *Design for Security*, Chap. 6, "Security Lighting." New York: Wiley, 1968.

LES Lighting Handbook. New York: Illuminating Engineering Society, 1969.

Physical Security, Field Manual FM 19-30. Washington, D.C.: Department of the Army, 1965.

Protective Lighting, Technical Bulletin TB PMG-34. Washington, D.C.: Department of the Army, 1966.

TYSKA, L.A., "Security Lighting for the Cargo Terminal." *Security Management,* July 1976.

WRIGHT, ROGER, "The Impact of Street Lighting on Street Crime." Washington, D.C.: National Institute of Law Enforcement and Criminal Justice, LEAA, 1974.

protective dogs

BLAKLEY, ANDREW M., "Guard Dogs as a Security Aid: A Case Study," *Security Management,* May 1977.

MANDELBAUM, ALBERT J., *Fundamentals of Protective Systems.* Springfield, Ill.: Charles C Thomas, 1973.

WALSH, TIMOTHY J., and RICHARD J. HEALY, *Protection of Assets Manual,* Vol. 2, Chap. 28, "The Use of Dogs for Assets Protection." Santa Monicao, Calif.: Merritt, 1974.

general

SAGALYN, ARNOLD, *Residential Security.* A report prepared for the National Institute of Law Enforcement and Criminal Justice, LEAA, U.S. Department of Justice, 1973.

WHITE, THOMAS W., and others. *Police Burglary Prevention Programs.* Washington, D.C.: U.S. Government Printing Office, 1975. This prescriptive package, supported by a grant awarded to the Urban Institute by the National Institute of Law Enforcement and Criminal Justice, LEAA, U.S. Department of Justice, outlines seven burglary-prevention programs. These programs involve crime-pattern and vulnerability analysis, community education, property marking, fencing operations, patrol efforts, and intrusion alarms. This work also contains an appendix that includes, among other things, Oakland, California's, Model Burglary Code and the physical-security requirements of Los Angeles's building code.

Chapter 5

Locking Devices

AN OVERVIEW

I. Lock Terminology

II. Key-Operated Locking Devices
   A. *Components of a key-operated lock*
      1. Bolt and latch
      2. Keyway and surrounding tumbler or key-obstacle mechanism
      3. The key
   B. *Types of mechanical locking bolts and latches*
   C. *Types of mechanical key locks*
      1. Warded mechanisms
      2. Lever mechanisms
      3. Pin-tumbler mechanisms
      4. Wafer-tumbler mechanisms
   D. *Typical key-lock hardware for doors*
      1. Cylinder-lock hardware
      2. Key-in-knob lock hardware
      3. Padlocks
      4. Panic door locks

III. Master-Keyed Locks and Master-Key Systems

IV. Interchangeable-Core Locks

V. Key Control

VI. Combination Locks
   A. *Dial-type combination locks*
   B. *Pushbutton combination locks*

VII. Electrically Controlled and Coded Locking Devices
   A. *Card-operated locks*
      1. The card key
      2. The card reader
      3. The minicomputer
      4. The electronic locking device
      5. Uses of the card-key system

This chapter contains a detailed discussion of the various mechanisms, systems, and components that have been manufactured and designed to perform a locking function. The principle of operation, security application, and effectiveness against criminal intrusion of each device is considered. Since most doors, gates, windows, drawers, strongboxes, vending machines, vehicles, lockers, safes, and vaults are secured in one way or another by some kind of locking mechanism, every security practitioner should be familiar with this subject matter.

Almost all the locking devices currently on the market can be placed in one of the following categories: key-operated locks, combination locks, card-activated locking devices, and electrically operated locks.

A lock is one of the basic components of a physical-security system. Like any other security measure or barrier, all locking devices, regardless of their quality, can be opened or physically defeated by a determined and skilled intruder. But a lock's primary purpose is to eliminate the opportunity for *easy* access into the protected area. A knowledgeable security practitioner does not expect too much from a locking device, so he relies upon a carefully selected combination of security measures that, used together, make up a formidable barrier against criminal intrusion.

Hardware expenditures make up from ½ to 1½ percent of the total construction cost of a building, and locks usually constitute 25 to 40 percent of the hardware costs. But it has been estimated that over 75 percent of the locks initially installed by building contractors are of poor quality. Most of these devices can be surreptitiously defeated or forced open by a relatively unskilled intruder in less than one minute. On the other hand, quality lock hardware can ordinarily withstand physical abuse from an intruder using standard burglary tools for from three minutes to half an hour, depending upon the type of lock mechanism being attacked.

Lock Terminology

Let us first learn some of the basic terms used in discussing locks.[1]

Barrel key–A type of key, mainly used in warded locks, having a long barrel or post, hollow at one end, that fits over a corresponding-size pin in the lock. (Commonly referred to as a skeleton key.)

Bit–The projection from the tip of the key, which is cut to allow the key to turn past obstacles or wards in the lock.

Bitting–The portion of the key blade that is cut or notched to correspond to, and allow the manipulation of, the tumblers in the keyway.

Blank key–A key that has not been cut. There are no bittings on a blank key.

Bolt–A metal bar that, when actuated, is projected either horizontally or vertically into a solid mass to prevent any door, window, or other object from moving or opening.

Bow of key–The part of the key that does not enter the lock, and allows the key to be held for operation by the user.

Cam–A rotating piece attached to the end of the cylinder plug to operate the locking mechanism.

Case knifing–A technique used to retract the bolt of the lock other than by the use of a key.

Change key–A key that will operate only one lock in a series, as distinguised from a master key, which will operate many or all locks in a series.

Combination lock–A lock in which no key is used to actuate the lock mechanism. Instead, a dial, marked by letters or numbers, is rotated in a certain sequence to actuate it.

Connecting bar–A flat metal bar attached to the plug of a cylinder lock to operate the bolt mechanism.

Core–The round central part of a lock, containing the keyway and rotated by the key to operate the lock mechanism.

Cylinder–The housing containing the tumbler mechanism and keyway.

Cylinder lock–Usually a pin-tumbler lock having its mechanism contained in a cylinder, as opposed to the types of housings used in warded and lever-type locks.

Cylinder ring–A collar or washer applied over the head of a cylinder.

Deadbolt–A lock bolt having no spring action. The bolt is usually rectangular or square in shape, is actuated by a key, and becomes locked against end pressure when projected.

Disc tumbler–A flat metal tumbler used in medium-security wafer-type locks to hold the core of the lock in one position until the correct key is inserted.

Double-bitted key–A key that is cut on two surfaces, usually opposite each other. These surfaces come into contact with the internal mechanisms of the lock.

Driver pins–The upper set of pins in a pin-tumbler lock, which project downward into the plug or core.

---

[1]This glossary of lock terminology is largely reprinted, by permission, from Marc Weber Tobias, *Locks, Safes, and Security: A Handbook for Law Enforcement Personnel* (Springfield, Ill.: Charles C Thomas, 1971). Courtesy of Charles C Thomas, Publisher, Springfield, Illinois.

Fence–A projecting piece that passes through the gating of the tumblers when they are properly aligned. Usually used in reference to lever locks.

Gate–The opening in lever tumblers through which the fence passes to permit the bolt to be actuated. Also found in combination locks.

Grandmaster key–A key that operates locks in several series, all of which have their own group master key.

Jamb–The inside vertical face of a door or window frame.

Keyway–The opening in a lock plug (core) into which the key is inserted.

Lever-tumbler lock–A lock mechanism operated with flat metal tumblers having a pivot motion. The tumblers are actuated by the bitting of the key.

Master key–A key designed to operate two or more locks having different change keys.

Mortise–The opening made to receive a lock or other hardware.

Mortise lock–A lock designed to be cut into the edge of the door or other frame.

Picking–A technique used to actuate the mechanism of a lock without the use of a key and without damage to the lock.

Pin tumbers–Small metal pins making up the internal mechanism of a pin-tumbler lock.

Pin-tumbler lock–A lock employing metal pins to retain a rotating core or plug in one position until the correct key is inserted into the lock.

Plug–The round central part of the lock, containing the keyway and rotated by the key to operate the lock mechanism. Also called the core.

Rim lock–A lock that is applied to the surface of a door.

Shackle–The link by which a padlock is secured to the hasp or other opening to effect a closed joint.

Shear line–The level to which all pins (in a pin-tumbler lock) must be raised in order for the plug to rotate.

Shim–A very thin, flat piece of metal or other material, several inches in length, used to open pin-tumbler locks.

Shoulder of key–that part of the key that stops the key from moving forward in the keyway.

Strike–A metal plate, mortised into, around, or on the doorjamb, to accept and restrain the bolt. The strike may be simply an opening in the doorjamb.

Wafer lock–A lock mechanism employing a flat metal wafer tumbler.

Warded lock–A minimum-security lock containing internal obstacles or wards, intended to block the entrance or rotation of all but the correct key.

Key-Operated Locking Devices

components of a key-operated lock

All mechanical key-operated locking devices are made up of three basic parts: (1) a locking bolt or latch, (2) a keyway passing through obstacles or tumblers, and (3) a key, which, when inserted into the keyway, bypasses the obstacles and, when turned, projects or withdraws the bolt or latch from the strike.

Bolt and Latch. It should be noted that the only type of key-operated lock that does not employ the use of a bolt or latch is a padlock. Padlocks are discussed later in the chapter.

The term *bolt,* as distinguished from *latch,* refers to a non-spring-loaded metal bar that is operated manually. Because they are not spring-loaded, bolts (commonly called deadbolts) offer the greater protection against forced entry. Deadbolts are usually ½ inch to 1¼ inches in length. Latches, on the other hand, being spring-loaded, are less resistant to surreptitious and forced entry. They are end-beveled to facilitate their spring-loaded, automatic entry into the strike when the door is closed. Latches usually extend beyond the edge of the door ½ inch. Bolts and latches are constructed of a variety of metals, some being more hacksaw-resistant than others. Most bolts and latches are slid horizontally into the strike or pivoted down into the locking position. (See Figure 5-1.) Some bolts, however, are secured vertically into a strike. (See Figure 5-2.)

Of course, any bolt secured in a strike that is housed in a poorly constructed or weak doorframe will be ineffective against forced entry. The installation of a metal strike plate onto the doorjamb surrounding the strike receptacle will increase the overall strength and effectiveness of the locking device. A more detailed discussion regarding the various kinds of locking bolts and latches follows shortly.

Keyway and Surrounding Tumbler or Key-Obstacle Mechanism. All key-operated locks, including padlocks, are operated by the insertion of the correct key into a corresponding passageway (keyway). The key's particular shape and dimension, by bypassing or arranging the obstacles or tumblers housed inside the mechanism, allow the key and keyway to be rotated. The rotation of the core (the part of the lock cylinder immediately surrounding the keyway) results, directly or indirectly, in the movement of the locking bar. This part of all key-operated locking devices, regardless of the type or principle of operation of the component itself (warded, lever, wafer, or pin-tumbler), will be housed in, for example, a padlock, a cylinder, or a doorknob. The five types of locks, classified according to the nature of the internal locking mechanism, are discussed in detail later in the chapter.

It should be noted that both mortise (cut into the door) and rim (surface-mounted) key-lock hardware are ineffective when installed on weak and poorly constructed doors.

The Key. The key is the third basic component of all key-locking mechanisms. The type, shape, and operation of a given key depend upon the nature of the tumbler apparatus it unlocks. It has been estimated that 90 percent of all key-operated lock systems are compromised within 30 days following their installation, because of poor key control. Matters relating to keys, key control, and master-keying will also be discussed in detail later in the chapter.

Because there are several different kinds of internal tumbler assemblies,

FIGURE 5-1. Horizontal locking bolts

Courtesy of Adams Rite Manufacturing Co.

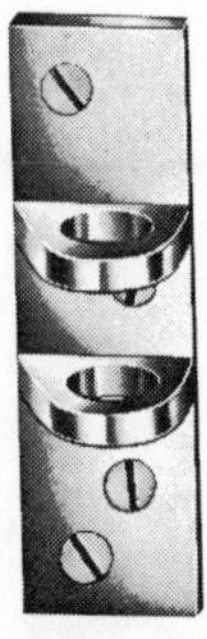

FIGURE 5-2. Vertical locking bar and corresponding strike assembly

From Marc Weber Tobias, Locks, Safes, and Security: A Handbook for Law Enforcement Personnel, *1st ed., 1971. Courtesy of Charles C Thomas, Publisher, Springfield, Illinois.*

locking bars, lock housings, methods of installation, and keys, a specific lock mechanism merely reflects one of many possible combinations of these components. For this reason, it is difficult to discuss and study the broad subject of locking devices without first learning basic lock terminology. It is also helpful to organize and classify lock mechanisms according to the nature of these basic components. For example, a locking-bar assembly may be deadbolt, spring-loaded, horizontal, or vertical; a keyway may enter the doorknob or a cylinder; cylinders are either single or double; lock hardware can be mortised or surface-mounted; the internal tumbler arrangement can be of the warded, lever, wafer, or pin-tumbler type; and finally, a lock can be either keyed to a single key or a part of a master-key system.

types of mechanical locking bolts and latches

The bolt or latch is the part of the lock that secures the door, gate, window, drawer, or other movable object to a surrounding and stationary structure. Therefore, all bolts and latches, regardless of the type of internal assembly of the locking device, perform the same function.

Bolts and latches are either attached to the surface of the door or mortised into the structure itself along with the other components of the locking mechanism. Surface-mounted bolt assemblies, commonly referred to as rim locks, are usually attached to the interior side of the door. With rim locks, the locking action is produced when the bolt or latch projects across the door into the strike, which is mounted on the doorframe. Rim-locking bars are manipulated by key or by turn knob. A surface-locking device that is operated by a turn knob should not be installed on a glass door or on a door with a window, because an intruder can break

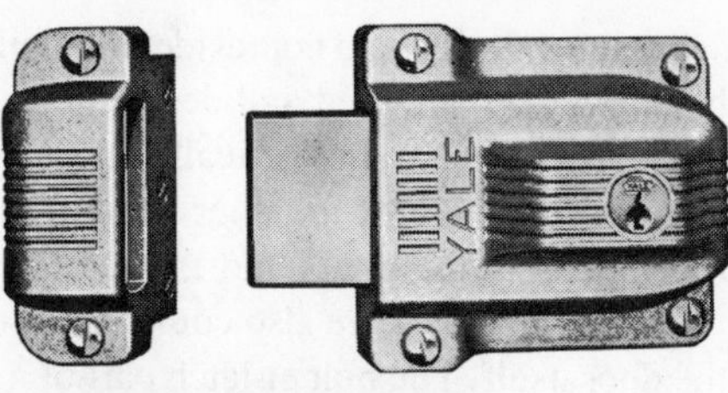

FIGURE 5-3. Key-operated rim lock

From Marc Weber Tobias, Locks, Safes, and Security: A Handbook for Law Enforcement Personnel, *1st ed., 1971. Courtesy of Charles C Thomas, Publisher, Springfield, Illinois.*

FIGURE 5-4. Rim lock operated by a turn knob

From Marc Weber Tobias, Locks, Safes, and Security: A Handbook for Law Enforcement Personnel, *1st ed., 1971. Courtesy of Charles C Thomas, Publisher, Springfield, Illinois.*

the glass, reach through the door, and unlock the mechanism. On such a door, or on one otherwise weak and vulnerable, a key-operated rim lock should be utilized. (See Figures 5-3 and 5-4.) An interior rim lock can be manipulated by key from the outside through the installation of a rim cylinder on the outside surface of the door. (See Figure 5-5.) Surface locks that are used as night latches can be locked and unlocked only from the inside.

Surface locks should be held in place by one-way screws that can be turned only clockwise. Rim locks with vertical deadbolt assemblies, because they hold the door to the door frame, are jimmy-resistant. (See Figure 5-2.)

Surface-mounted locking bolts that are "thrown" without the turn of a key or knob are commonly referred to as throw bolts. These relatively simple devices are mounted on the interior surface of the door. Because the bolt cannot be manipulated from the outside, throw-bolt mechanisms are used as auxiliary locks to secure occupied dwellings overnight, and to secure, from the inside, out-

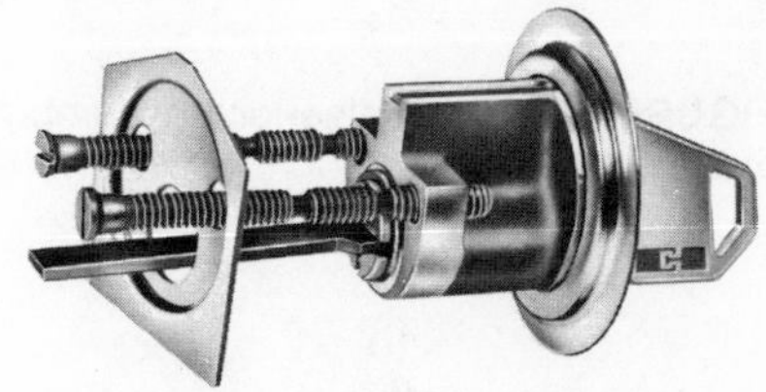

FIGURE 5-5. Cylinder for a rim lock

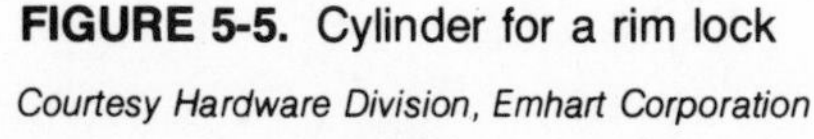

Courtesy Hardware Division, Emhart Corporation

swinging exit doors to nonresidential buildings when they are unoccupied. Throw bolts are manufactured and desigend to slide horizontally across the door into a strike, be pushed down vertically into a receptacle in the floor, or be pushed up into a strike at the top of the door frame. Throw-bolt hardware is secure only when mounted on solid doors and frames.

Locking bars are also components of mortise-lock hardware installed inside the door itself. The bolt or latch part of a mortise-lock assembly projects or pivots into the strike from an opening that has been cut into the edge of the door. One of the two kinds of mortise locking-bar assemblies consists of a thin rectangular case containing the bolt or latch and installed in a hole cut into the edge of the door. The cylinder part of a mortise lock screws directly onto this bolt encasement. (See Figure 5-6.)

FIGURE 5-6. A mortise deadlocking bolt with cylinder

Courtesy Medeco Security Locks, Inc.

The other type of mortise locking-bar assembly is called a tubular lock. This type is the easiest to install and consists of a tubular-shaped bolt or latch housing rather than a rectangualr casing. The cylinder part of the lock is not attached directly to the locking-bar encasement, so it involves a more indirect bolt-manipulation process. (See Figure 5-7.)

FIGURE 5-7. A mortise-lock assembly of the tubular type

Courtesy Schlage Lock Co.

In order to discuss the subject of locking bars more fully, let us define and distinguish the general term *bolt* and the two basic types of latches.

As we said earlier, a bolt is not spring-loaded; therefore it has to be manually moved into its locking position within the strike, and a lock with a bolt-type mechanism does not automatically secure a door when it is shut. Moreover, when a bolt in its locked position protrudes from an open door, the door cannot be closed until a key or knob is turned to withdraw the bolt. Bolts of this nature (deadbolts) are usually rectangular in shape, not end-beveled. (See Figure 5-6.) They provide a higher degree of security than do latch-type locking bars.

There are two kinds of latches, which, for purposes of our discussion, will be termed spring-loaded latchbolts and spring-loaded deadlatches. A spring-loaded latchbolt, in its normal position, protrudes ½ inch beyond the edge of the door. Whenever a door containing a latchbolt is closed, the latch is forced back into the door by the doorjamb until it aligns with the strike opening, at which time it springs automatically into the strike receptacle. Spring-loaded latchbolts are end-beveled to allow the depression of the latch against the doorframe when the door is shut and to facilitate its entrance into the strike. Regardless of the type of locking device involved, spring-loaded latches are withdrawn from a strike upon the turn of a key, turn knob, or doorknob, or upon pressure applied to a thumbpiece on a door handle.

A locking device manufactured with a spring-loaded latchbolt provides minimum security, because the latch can be withdrawn from the strike whenever force is applied directly to the latch itself (end pressure). A common method of defeating locks equipped with a spring-loaded latchbolt is called "knifing"—the insertion of a credit card, screwdriver, ice pick, or metal shim between the door and the doorframe for the purpose of pushing the latch out of the strike and back into the door. Special hardware can be installed to protect a spring latch from being "knifed" out of the strike. A metal plate mounted on the outside of the door and extending from the edge of the door to a few inches beyond the doorjamb will act as a latch guard by preventing the insertion of a tool between the door and its frame. (See Figure 5-8.) Most exterior doors, because of their construction and design, provide this kind of spring-latchbolt protection.

A deadlatch is also a spring-loaded and end-beveled locking bar that automatically enters the strike whenever the door is closed. It differs, however, from a regular spring-loaded latchbolt in that it will withstand end pressure. Once projected into the strike, a deadlatch locking bar is locked into position like a deadbolt and cannot be forced back into the door by a knife or similar tool. It is secured by the operation of an extra latch piece that, when depressed against the edge of the doorjamb, locks the deadlatch into place. (See Figures 5-9 and 5-10.)

In addition to being "knifed," locking bars and the doors they secure are also vulnerable to being jimmied. A door is jimmied by being forced away from its frame, causing the bolt to be free from the strike. Double doors and doors with

FIGURE 5-8. Latch guard

Courtesy Latch-Gard Division of Air-Flo Co., Inc.

short locking bolts are particularly vulnerable to this type of forced entry. One solution is to use locking bars that pivot rather than slide from the door into the strike. (See Figure 5-1.) Pivot-action locking bolts can be longer than projection-type bolts because they do not require as much space within the door to house. For this reason, they are especially adaptable for use in double doors constructed of glass where there is no place on the door to accommodate a long and recessed horizontal projection-type bolt. A vertical locking bar (Figure 5-2) also cannot be

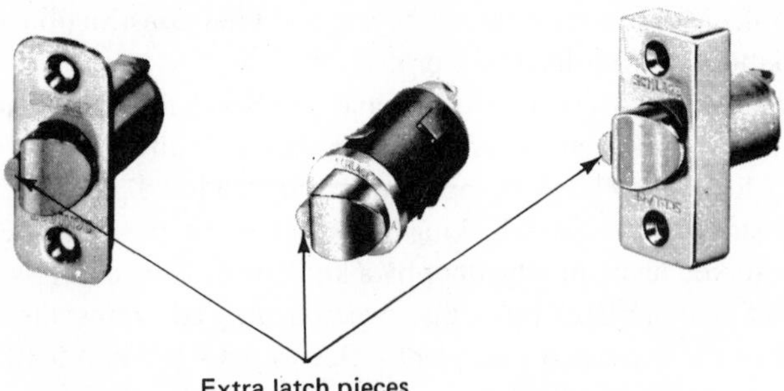

FIGURE 5-9. Deadlatch locking-bar assemblies with extra latch piece

Courtesy Schlage Lock Co.

FIGURE 5-10. Mortise-lock assembly with an antishim deadlatch locking bolt

Courtesy Folger Adam Co.

jimmied away from the door jamb, because it interlocks within the strike. There are horizontal-type locking bars on the market that achieve a similar antijimmying result by means of two spring-loaded pins that project out of the locking bolt when it enters the strike. Other horizontal locking bolts and latches designed to resist jimmying are end-notched so as to hook onto a portion of the strike.

types of mechanical key locks

The discussion in this section pertains to the mechanical and internal part of a key-operated lock, which by design cannot be actuated, rotated, or manipulated without the use of a corresponding key.

Warded Mechanisms. Today, a warded lock has limited use and security application, because it provides minimum security against forced or surreptitious intrusion. Locks of the warded type, however, were standard on almost all doors up until the 1940s, and many older homes still have interior doors equipped with these locks. Warded door locks are operated by keys commonly referred to as skeleton keys, or passkeys. Skeleton keys are designed to bypass obstacles (wards) built inside the lock encasement. Upon the insertion and rotation of the correct key, the spring holding the locking bolt in place is released and the bolt is manipulated. Because of the simplicity of its design and operation, as well as the accessibility provided by the keyway, warded locks can be manipulated easily without the use of the correct key. For example, a stiff wire bent into an L shape can be inserted into the keyway to release the spring and move the bolt. The security application of this type of lock is also limited by the fact that it cannot be master-keyed. Moreover, the key combinations to a warded lock cannot be changed, so once a warded lock has been compromised by the loss or unauthorized use of the key, the mechanism has to be removed from the door or remain vulnerable.

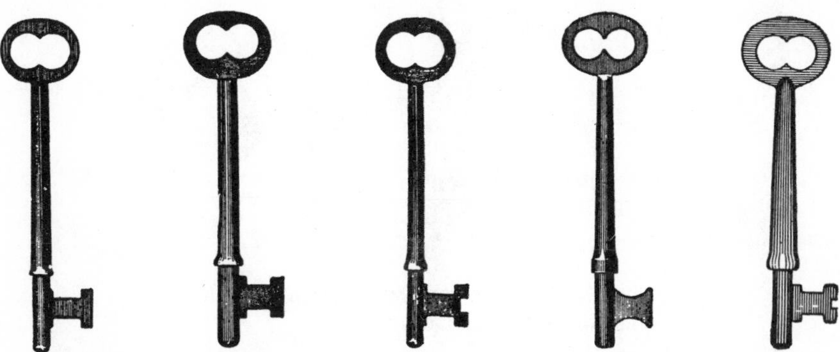

FIGURE 5-11. Warded skeleton or passkeys. These will fit a majority of warded residence and hotel-type locks.

From Marc Weber Tobias, Locks, Safes, and Security: A Handbook for Law Enforcement Personnel, *1st ed., 1971. Courtesy of Charles C Thomas, Publisher, Springfield, Illinois.*

Low-quality padlocks often contain warded mechanisms. Because handcuff locks are of the warded type, they should be treated as weak and temporary restraining devices. Inexpensive file boxes are usually manufactured with warded-type locks as well.

Lever Mechanisms. A lever locking mechanism is composed of one or more flat metal tumblers attached together at one end to create a pivotal action. At the other end of each tumbler is a notch (gate) that, when aligned properly with the pin (fence), allows the bolt to retract or unlock. When the pin is not properly positioned inside the tumbler gate, the bolt cannot be withdrawn, so it remains protracted or locked. The tumblers are held in a locking position against the pin by the pressure of a flat spring. When the correct key is used to raise each tumbler to a level causing the gates to align with the pin, the bolt can be withdrawn.

To facilitate your understanding of the principle of operation of a lever lock, see Figure 5-12.

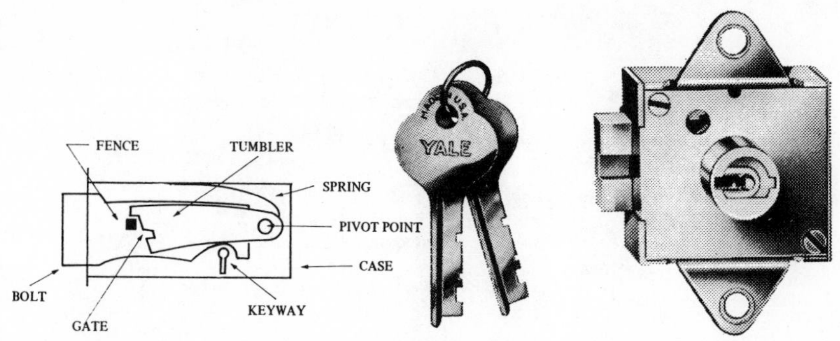

FIGURE 5-12. Identification of the parts of a lever-tumbler lock

From Marc Weber Tobias, Locks, Safes, and Security: A Handbook for Law Enforcement Personnel, *1st ed., 1971. Courtesy of Charles C Thomas, Publisher, Springfield, Illinois.*

The more sophisticated lever locks have gates (notches) cut at different places on each tumbler; making it necessary, in order to align all the gates, for the key to raise each tumbler to a different height. Lever locks are ordinarily manufactured with one to four tumblers; the degree of security they offer can be determined by the number of tumblers in the mechanism. The more tumblers, the more pick-resistant the lock.

Although lever locks are more difficult to pick than warded-type devices, they are easier to defeat than most pin-tumbler mechanisms. However, most lock experts agree that while the average pin-tumbler lock provides more security than the average lever lock, the *best* lever lock offers more security than the best pin-tumbler lock. These high-security lever locks are commonly used to secure bank safe-deposit boxes. The less-secure devices are frequently installed on school lockers, cabinets, desks, and coin telephones.

Pin-Tumbler Mechanisms. The pin-tumbler mechanism was an American invention, created by Linus Yale, Jr., in 1844. Yale continued to refine his device until 1861, at which time it was offered to the public.

This type of inner lock mechanism is characterized by tumblers in the form of pins, which rest vertically inside individual chambers housed in the cylinder shell. (See Figure 5-13.) The shell, or outer portion of the cylinder, surrounds a passageway (keyway) penetrating the cylinder core or plug. The core rotates when the correct key is inserted into the keyway and turned. (See Figure 5-14, *a* and *b*.) In its normal position, without the insertion of a key, a plug cannot rotate because of the presence of the tumbler pins extending from the cylinder shell down into the core and locking it to the cylinder shell.

A pin tumbler has two parts, the upper or driver pin and the lower pin. (These locks are usually made with from four to six pins.) Each driver pin extends into the core and is held in this position by a small spring. The lower pins, resting inside the

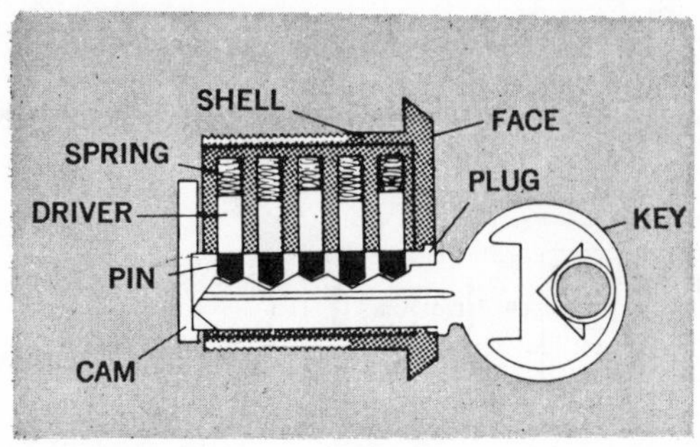

FIGURE 5-13. Pin-tumbler-lock part identification

From Marc Weber Tobias, Locks, Safes, and Security: A Handbook for Law Enforcement Personnel, *1st ed., 1971. Courtesy of Charles C Thomas, Publisher, Springfield, Illinois.*

core, come into contact with the key, which, on its insertion into the keyway, raises the lower pins against the drivers and the tension provided by the spring. In order for the core to rotate and cause the locking bolt or latch to move, each lower pin must be raised by a key to the top of the core. When all the drivers have been pushed back into the shell by the raised lower pins, a shear line is created, allowing the rotation of the core. (See Figure 5-15.) Since each pin is of a different length, each bitting on the key blade must be correspondingly cut to raise each lower pin to the correct height. If, for example, a bitting is cut too high (or shallow), the lower

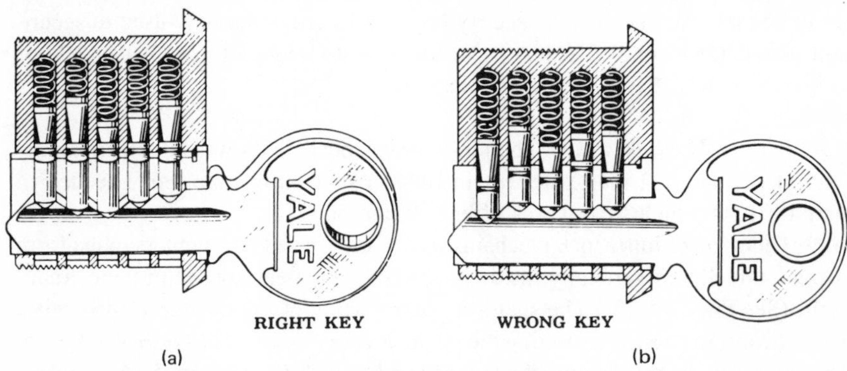

FIGURE 5-14. Illustrations showing correct and improperly cut keys in a pin-tumbler-lock cylinder. With the improperly cut key, the pins and drivers are in irregular positions, forming obstructions preventing rotation of the core. Correct key usage lines up the pins and drivers at their intersections so that the plug may be turned to operate the lock.

From Marc Weber Tobias, Locks, Safes, and Security: A Handbook for Law Enforcement Personnel, *1st ed., 1971. Courtesy of Charles C Thomas, Publisher, Springfield, Illinois.*

pin will be raised above the shear line, thus impeding the rotation of the core. (Figure 5-14*b*.) If the key bitting is cut too low (or deep), the lower pin will not be raised to the shear line, and the driver or upper pin will remain in the core, thus impeding the rotation of the plug.

Since the initial development of the pin-tumbler lock, many lock-manufacturing companies have modified and refined the mechanism to minimize the possibility of lock picking, unauthorized key duplication, wrong-key usage, and key impressioning. The more sophisticated pin-tumbler lock mechanisms also resist defeat by high-speed drilling and other types of physical force applied directly to the cylinder core or keyway. Because they are difficult to defeat and are capable of being master-keyed, pin-tumbler or similar types of locking mechanisms are found in most modern or quality door-lock hardware and most high-security padlocks.

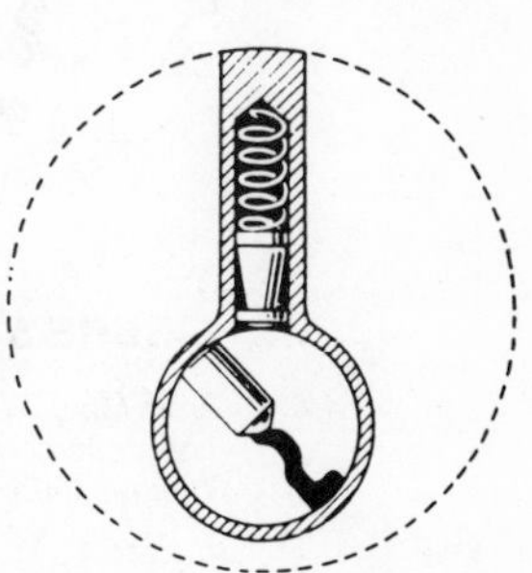

FIGURE 5-15. End view of a pin-tumbler lock, showing the tumbler positions in the open position

From Marc Weber Tobias, Locks, Safes, and Security: A Handbook for Law Enforcement Personnel, *1st ed., 1971. Courtesy of Charles C Thomas, Publisher, Springfield, Illinois.*

Wafer-Tumbler Mechanisms. Wafer locks, commonly referred to as disc-tumbler locks, operate on the same principle as pin-tumbler mechanisms except that spring-loaded flat metal discs, rather than pins, are used to bind the core to the cylinder shell. The proper key, when inserted into the keyway, enters through an opening in each disc tumbler, causing the tumblers to align and withdraw their protruding parts from the cylinder shell. Once a shear line has been created, the plug can be rotated inside the cylinder to move the locking bar.

Most automobiles are secured by wafer-locks, as are vending machines, cabinets, desks, and many padlocks. It should be noted that wafer locks, unlike pin-tumbler and most lever locks, are vulnerable to defeat by the use of the improper key, and most vehicles, cabinets, and vending machines equipped with wafer locks can be jimmied. These locks are designed and manufactured primarily for the automotive industry, and they are often inexpensively mass-produced out of brass and other less-durable metals.

typical key-lock hardware for doors

The discussion in this section, except for the material dealing with padlocks and panic door locks, will pertain to mortise-type hardware.

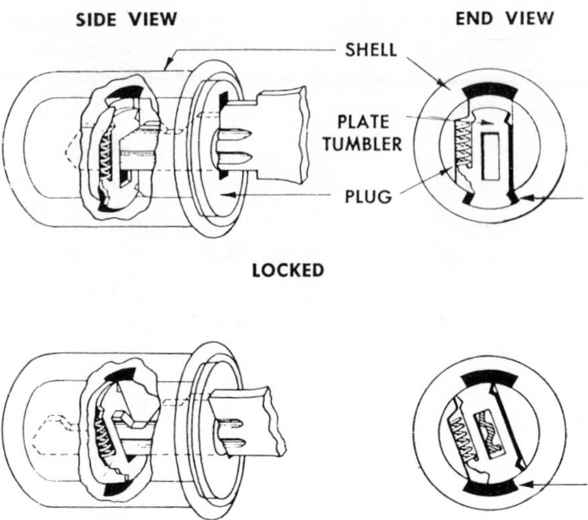

FIGURE 5-16. Illustration of water mechanism

From Marc Weber Tobias, Locks, Safes, and Security: A Handbook for Law Enforcement Personnel, *1st ed., 1971. Courtesy of Charles C Thomas, Publisher, Springfield, Illinois.*

Cylinder-Lock Hardware. Cylinder-lock assemblies (without door-operation hardware) are commonly added to exterior doors containing previously installed door-opening hardware. Because cylinder locks are usually of the deadbolt type, they are often installed on doors equipped with the less-secure, latch-type locking bars, to augment existing door security. It should also be noted that most cylinder locks, mortise or rimmed, contain pin-tumbler mechanisms.

Double-cylinder locks are operated by key on both sides of the door, whereas single-cylinder hardware is key-operated from the exterior and by turn knob from the inside. As suggested earlier in connection with rim locks, double-key cylinders should be used on glass, windowed, and poorly constructed doors.

A cylinder lock is vulnerable to being pulled out of the door by a large vise grip or by a specially constructed lock-pulling tool. The installation of a tapered cylinder ring (collar) to preclude a solid grip on the cylinder by such a tool will protect the lock from this type of physical attack. (See Figure 5-17.) Most high-security cylinders, however, by design, cannot be gripped by a vise or lock-picking tool. Exterior cylinder-lock assemblies on fire exit doors can be protected from lock-pulling devices by door handles that surround the cylinder.

A cylinder can also be protected against physical attack by a hinged shield clamped over the face of the cylinder like a hasp and secured by a padlock. This device, in addition to protecting against lock pulling, will prevent the use of a

FIGURE 5-17. Beveled steel cylinder-guard attachment

Courtesy Adams Rite Manufacturing Co.

high-speed drill to bore out the keyway and, because it involves covering the keyway, also prevents lock picking.

Some of the other standard cylinder-lock hardware includes devices equipped with handles and thumbpieces or doorknobs. A variety of mortise-lock sets are manufactured with handgrips and thumbpieces. (See Figure 5-18.) Lock and door-operation hardware containing standard doorknob assemblies are referred to as cylindrical mortise sets. (See Figure 5-19.)

Key-in-Knob Lock Hardware. The key-in-knob mechanism is probably the most common type of door-lock hardware. (See Figure 5-20.) It is usually manufactured with either a pin-tumbler or a wafer (disc-tumbler) locking mechanism. As the name implies, the keyway in this type of assembly, as distinguished from cylinder hardware, penetrates the doorknob.

Standard key-in-knob hardware, manufactured for residential and most commercial use, contains a single keyway inside the exterior doorknob. The inside knob contains a button that, when depressed, locks the door against outside entry, and the key is used only on the outside. Single-keyway devices, because they can be unlocked from the inside without a key, are ineffective protection when installed on glass, windowed, or otherwise weak doors. Double key-in-knob

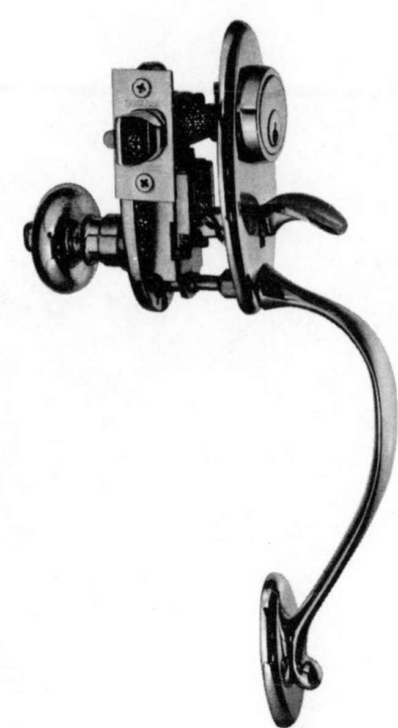

FIGURE 5-18. A mortise-lock kit with a handle and thumbpiece

Courtesy Schlage Lock Co.

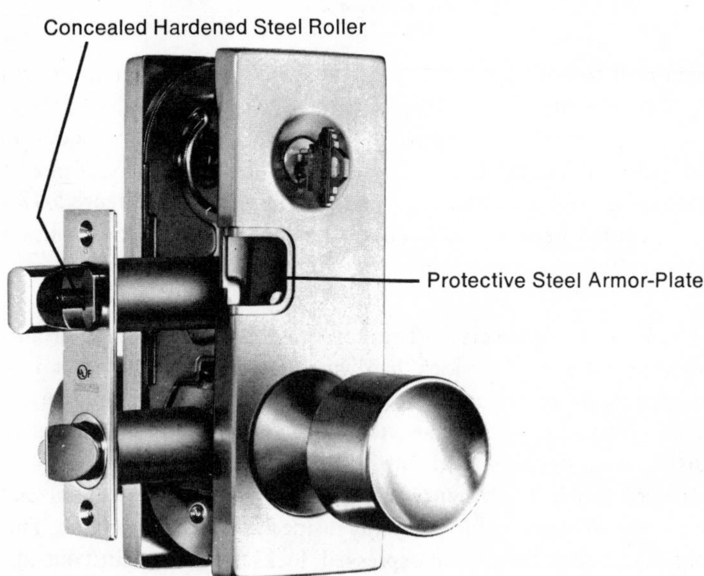

FIGURE 5-19. A knob or cylindrical lock kit

Courtesy Schlage Lock Co.

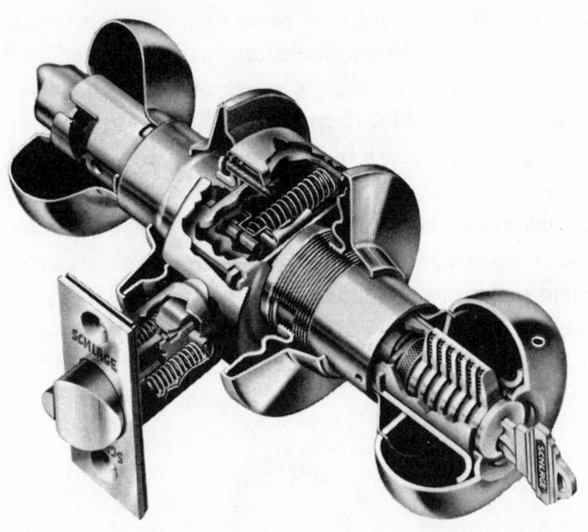

FIGURE 5-20. A key-in-knob lock
Courtesy Schlage Lock Co.

locks, manufactured with keyways running into both doorknobs, provide greater security. They can be operated only by key from both inside and out, and when shut, doors containing them will be automatically locked against entry from both sides. For this reason, double key-in-knob sets are often used to secure doors to highly critical or vulnerable buildings and rooms.

However, because most key-in-knob locks are made to automatically lock when the door is shut, this type of lock set is usually manufactured with a spring-loaded locking bar, and so it is vulnerable to being knifed open. Higher-security-type key-in-knob devices are manufactured with deadlatch-type locking bolts, and these should be used on exterior doors. (See Figures 5-8 and 5-9.) It should be noted, however, that as a general rule, a double-cylinder locking device with a deadbolt locking bar provides greater protection against forced intrusion than do most key-in-knob lock sets. Key-in-knob mechanisms are easily defeated when force is applied directly to the doorknob itself. Vise grips, hammers, and other tools have been used to wrench, knock, or tear off the entire knob assembly, exposing the locking bar and allowing its manipulation by the burglar.

Padlocks. The discussion in this section is limited to key-operated padlocks. Combination padlocks are dealt with later in the chapter, under the heading, "Combination Locks."

A key-operated padlock has three basic parts: the key, the casing (housing the keyway and the internal locking mechanism), and the shackle. The internal locking mechanism in an older or lower-security padlock is usually of the warded type. (See Figure 5-21.) Warded padlocks are easily defeated by the insertion of a stiff wire into the keyway to spread the piece of flat spring steel, which in turn releases the hold on the shackle. (See Figure 5.22.) Padlocks specifically manufactured and designed to secure bicycles usually contain warded-type locking mechanisms.

Higher-security padlocks are manufactured with lever, wafer, or pin-tumbler lock mechanisms. Many of those with pin tumblers are capable of being master-keyed, and pin-tumbler padlocks are also made with removable and interchangeable cores. In these, the core housing the keyway and the tumbler assembly can be removed from the casing by a control key, and a different plug can be

FIGURE 5-21. A modern warded-type padlock with key

Courtesy Master Lock Company

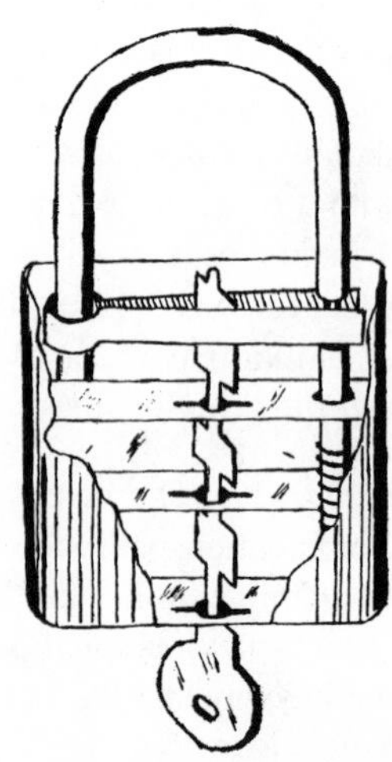

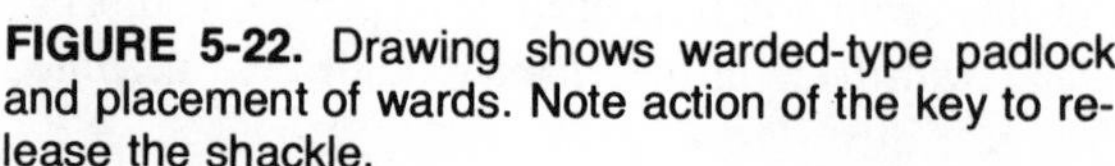

FIGURE 5-22. Drawing shows warded-type padlock and placement of wards. Note action of the key to release the shackle.

From Marc Weber Tobias, Locks, Safes, and Security: A Handbook for Law Enforcement Personnel, *1st ed., 1971. Courtesy of Charles C Thomas, Publisher, Springfield, Illinois.*

installed in its place, eliminating the necessity of discarding the entire locking device.

A shackle, analogous to a locking bar, is the locking or holding part of the padlock. Shackles are held in place in numerous ways; one of the common methods is by the use of a spring-loaded "locking dog," which is inserted into a notch cut into the shackle. (See Figure 5-23.) When the locking dog is pulled out of the notch by the rotation of the key, the shackle is cleared and can be removed from the casing. Shackles locked in this fashion can be released by applying force directly to the locking dog through the use of a shim, ice pick, or similar tool, forcing it out of the notch in the shackle.

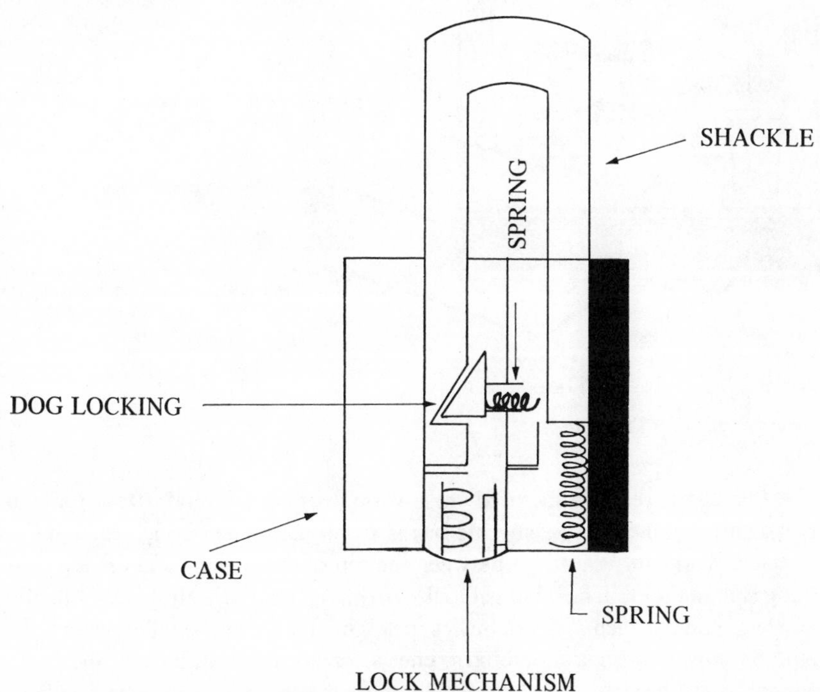

FIGURE 5-23. Drawing shows shackle locking

From Marc Weber Tobias, Locks, Safes, and Security: A Handbook for Law Enforcement Personnel, *1st ed., 1971. Courtesy of Charles C Thomas, Publisher, Springfield, Illinois.*

High-security padlocks are locked in a "heel-and-toe" fashion. In these, the shackle is held in place by locking dogs inserted into two notches on the shackle. (See Figure 5-24.) Padlocks with toe-and-heel locking are more resistant to manipulation by shimming, and they can withstand greater force applied directly to the shackle by a crowbar or similar prying tool. For example, medium- and high-security padlocks of standard size are capable of withstanding from 4,000 to 10,000 pounds of pull. A few regular-sized maximum-security padlocks, according to the manufacturers, are capable of withstanding over 20,000 pounds of pull.

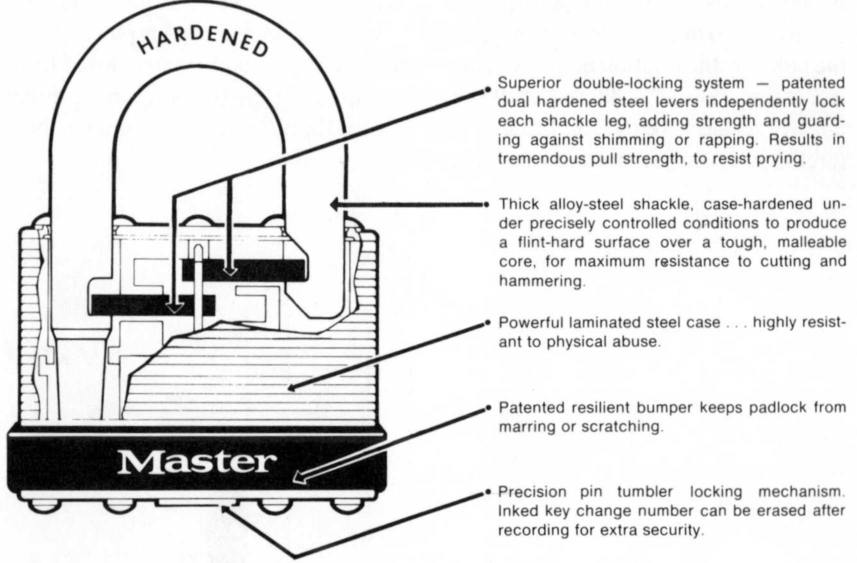

FIGURE 5-24. Toe-and-heel locking

Courtesy Master Lock Company

Shackles are manufactured in a variety of shapes and sizes. On most high-security padlocks, the shackle bar is from just under ½ inch to ¾ inch in diameter. Normally, the space between the top of the shackle and the top of the casing is about four inches, but padlocks are manufactured with shackle openings from less than one inch to seven inches in height. Those with smaller openings are commonly used to secure toolboxes, chests, or drawers. Because of the lack of space between the shackle and the casing, these resist attack by crowbars and other prying tools.

Most shackles are constructed of brass, bronze, or steel. But since all shackles are vulnerable to being hacksawed, many of those in high-security padlocks are of steel hardened with one to three plates of copper, nickel, chromium, or zinc, and several have cases that form a shroud to protect the shackle from being cut.

Like other lock mechanisms, padlocks are effective only when the surfaces upon which they are installed are solid. Because they are ordinarily used in conjunction with a hasp-type device, it is important that the hasp be installed securely and properly onto the door and the doorframe. For example, a hasp secured to metal should be welded rather than mounted with screws; and on a wooden door, the locking-bar portion of the hasp should be bolted completely through the door onto a metal plate on the other side. A padlock on a gate normally secures a chain looped through the fence and gatepost, and a weak fence, gate, or chain will minimize the effectiveness of the entire locking operation.

Whenever an object secured by a padlock is unlocked, the padlock itself should be secured in a locked position onto the hasp or other locking hardware, or else it could be stolen. Also, an enterprising intruder could remove an unsecured padlock, substitute his own, and enter the protected area later by using the key to the substitute padlock. The security guard, when entering an exterior door that is secured by a padlock, should lock the device onto the hasp, or take possession of it, until he completes his interior round. Otherwise, he risks being locked inside the building by an intruder.

A security practitioner should make certain that the serial number that is usually printed on the padlock casing is obliterated. This key-identifying number can be used by a would-be intruder to acquire a key to the padlock.

Panic Door Locks. By law, panic-lock hardware must be installed on all doors designated as fire exits. When the building is occupied, these fire exit doors must be unlocked from the inside. Most are operated from the inside by horizontal levers or metal arms, commonly referred to as crash or panic bars. (See Figure 5-25.) All fire exit doors are necessarily out-swinging and equipped with spring-loaded latchbolts locking the door against outside entry.

Single and double fire exit doors are classified as either "active" or "inactive." An active fire exit door is one that is also used as a passageway and is therefore usually equipped with outside door-operation and locking hardware. An inactive panic door, although it may be equipped with a door handle, will not contain a key-operated locking mechanism. In most instances, its exterior door handle is used to open the door from the outside during periods of building occupancy, when the locking bar is being held in its retracted position. But both active and inactive exit doors can be equipped with a "dogging device," a key-operated mechanism that is used to hold a spring-loaded latchbolt in its retracted or unlocked position even when the door is closed.

Active fire exit doors are ordinarily equipped with exterior key-operated cylinder-lock mechanisms, and many also with door-operation handles, with or without thumbpieces. Whenever an active fire exit door is used during business hours by employees who do not have a key to it, a dogging device may be used to secure the latchbolt in an unlocked position. It is also common practice to equip a fire door with a vertical bar housing a latchbolt secured in a strike at the top and bottom of the door. (See Figure 5-25.) These vertical latchbolts are retracted whenever the panic bar is depressed to open the door.

Although the use of panic-lock hardware is justified solely by the need for

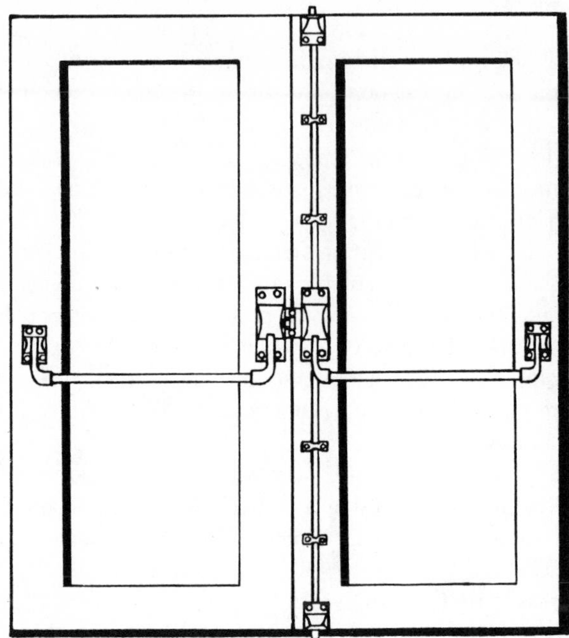

FIGURE 5-25. Double exit door with panic-lock hardware

From Marc Weber Tobias, Locks, Safes, and Security: A Handbook for Law Enforcement Personnel, *1st ed., 1971. Courtesy of Charles C Thomas, Publisher, Springfield, Illinois.*

fire safety, it does add significantly to the building's vulnerability to criminal intrusion because all fire exit doors are out-swinging and therefore hinged on the outside. To prevent an intruder from pulling the pins out of the hinge and removing the door from its frame, a pin can be installed to protrude from the inside edge of the door into the doorjamb. When the door is closed, the pin will operate in the same fashion as a locking bar and, even with the hinge pins out, will prevent the removal of the door. There are also high-security hinges on the market that have been manufactured and designed to prevent the removal of the hinge pin.

As a general rule, all doors with spring-loaded latch-type locking bars are susceptible to unlawful entry by knifing. But in panic doors, these latches cannot be manipulated from the outside by ice pick or similar tool, because panic hardware is mounted on the inside surface of an out-swinging door, so the latch is usually protected behind a protruding strike assembly that physically blocks outside access to it.

An active exit door should be equipped with an astragal (automatic door closing device) to ensure that it is not left ajar by careless employees. Moreover, it is not unusual for an employee to intentionally leave an exit door ajar to accommodate entry after business hours; and an intruder can gain after-hours entry through an exit door when the locking bar has been taped or held back into its retracted position.

Double exit doors are particulary vulnerable to unlawful entry by the insertion of an adapted coat hanger into the crack between the two doors. This type of entry can be prevented by the installation of an astragal bar running vertically along the door edge to close the gap between the doors. Moreover, the installation of the proper threshold hardware will prevent the insertion of a wire underneath the door to actuate the crash bar.

The need for fire safety makes the control of internal theft exceedingly difficult. Because fire exit doors cannot be locked from the inside, employees can use them to sneak out of the building with stolen property. The most effective solution is installtion of alarmed locks or exit alarm devices connected to and activated by the existing panic-door operation and locking hardware. Exit-door alarms are discussed in detail in Chapter 7.

Master-Keyed Locks and Master-Key Systems

Ordinarily, a key-operated lock, regardless of its type or kind of mechanism, is made to accept only one key, which has been specifically cut and designed to fit it. This standard type of key, commonly referred to as a change key, will operate a lock manufactured to accept keys of this one particular shape. On the other hand, a key-operated lock that has been altered to allow manipulation by two or more differently shaped keys is said to have been master-keyed.

Although lever and wafer-lock mechanisms are capable of being master-keyed, master-keying should be limited to high-quality, pin-tumbler locking devices. Pin-tumbler mechanisms are master-keyed whenever segments or discs are added to the existing tumblers. With a disc added to a particular driver- and lower-pin assembly, the pin can be split at another place to form a second shear line. With the installation of more of these discs, a variety of keys will align the tumblers to form one of several possible shear lines. (See Figure 5-26.)

As a general rule, a lock that has been master-keyed to accept two to four different keys is easier to pick than a single-keyed lock. A related problem, called cross-keying, is the operation of a master-keyed mechanism, because of the increased number of tumbler splits, by a key not intended to work in the lock. This cross-key problem has been solved in a variety of ways by several of the lock-manufacturing companies.

To illustrate the nature and application of master-keying and a master-key system, let us refer to a hypothetical institution, "City College." Figure 5-27 is the floor plan of two City College dormitories, North Hall and South Hall. Each building has three wings, and each wing consists of three dormitory rooms.

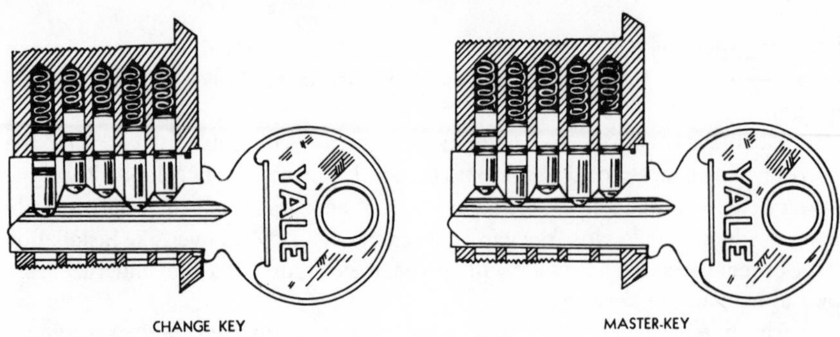

FIGURE 5-26. Diagram showing the regular and master-key pin configurations

From Marc Weber Tobias, Locks, Safes, and Security: A Handbook for Law Enforcement Personnel, *1st ed., 1971. Courtesy of Charles C Thomas, Publisher, Springfield, Illinois.*

Key-operated locks have been installed on all 18 dormitory-room doors. For purposes of our discussion, the exterior doors to each wing are without locking devices.

From a security point of view, it would be in the college's best interest to install single-keyed locks on the room doors. However, this would create some inconvenience, since anyone authorized to have access to every room would need to have 18 individual change keys. (In the case of facilities with hundreds or even thousands of locks, such inconvenience would of course, be greatly magnified.)

The security advantage of individually keyed locks, as compared to master-keyed devices, relates to matters of key control. For example, if City College installs a single-key system, the loss of a key to room 16 will not cause the other 17 rooms to be compromised. In this instance, only the lock to room 16 will have to be removed or rekeyed. In most lost-key situations, unless the room is particularly vulnerable or critical, a duplicate change key is issued to replace the lost one.

One method of avoiding the inconvenience of single-keyed locks is to install locks containing identical internal mechanisms, all keyed to the same change key. Then, one change key will open all 18 dormitory doors. However, it would create a security problem by allowing too many unauthorized people access to every room in both buildings.

It should be noted that when all the locks in a facility are keyed alike, they have not been master-keyed and do not make up a master-key system. Locks that have been master-keyed are capable of being operated by a change key, a master key, a grandmaster key, and/or a great-grandmaster key, depending upon the number of tiers or levels in the master-key system. Therefore, all the locks making up a master-key system can be operated by several sets of differently cut keys. A well-planned and well-administered master-key system eliminates the inconvenience of a single-keyed operation while making possible key control, a feature unavailable in systems composed of identically keyed locks. Thus the master-key concept balances two otherwise conflicting interests, security and convenience.

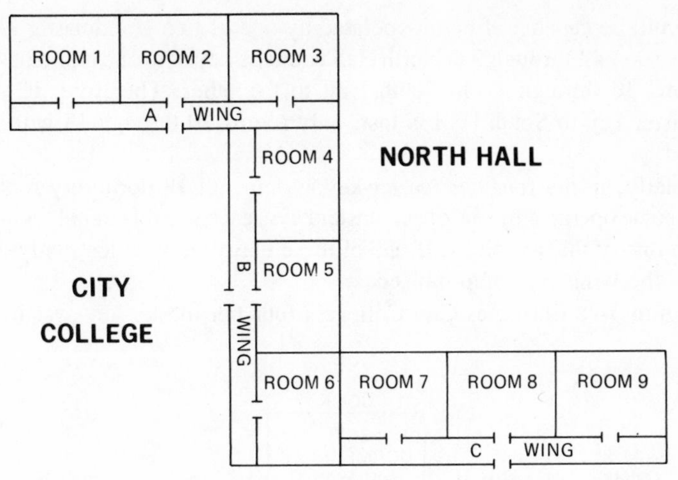

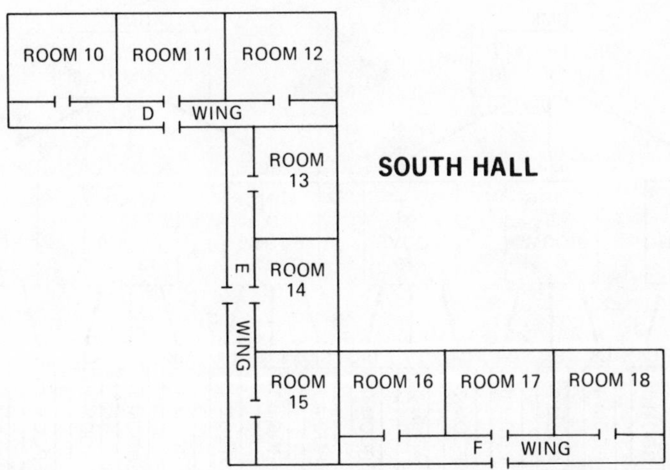

FIGURE 5-27. Diagram of North and South Halls, City College

Using City College as an example, a four-tier master-key system will be established. In this system, a great-grandmaster key can operate all the 18 locks in both dormitories. In the event that a great-grandmaster key is lost, all 18 will have been compromised and will have to be replaced. Because of the cost of such a loss, the issuance of great-grandmaster keys should be limited to as few people as possible. Also, as the number of those with great-grandmaster keys increases, the less private and secure each dormitory room becomes.

In addition to accepting a change key and a great-grandmaster key, all 18 locks would be capable of being operated by one of two grandmaster keys. For example, rooms 1 through 9 in North Hall could be keyed to one grandmaster key, and rooms 10 through 18 in South Hall to the other. Therefore, if, say, the grandmaster key to South Hall is lost, only rooms 10 through 18 will be compromised.

Finally, in the four-tier master-key system, all 18 dormitory room locks would also be operated by one of six master keys, each capable of unlocking all the rooms in one of the six wings. If one of these master keys is lost, only the three rooms in the wing are compromised.

Figure 5-28 illustrates City College's four-tier master-key system.

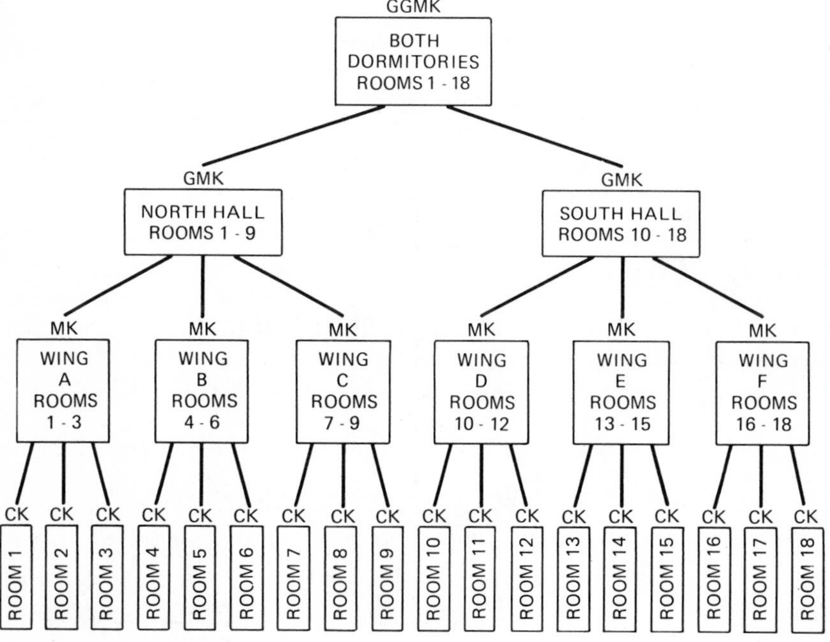

FIGURE 5-28. Chart showing four-tier master-key system for City College

When deciding whether or not to master-key, a security planner should consider several factors. The obvious advantage of master-keying is convenience; but there are other advantages. For example, in the event of fire, a broken water pipe, a bomb threat, or similar emergency, the existence of a single master key that will open every door in the building is a major safety feature because of the time and cost it would save. In an emergency situation, with no time to sort through a large number of change keys, a fireman, policeman, or security practitioner will break down a door, and if the emergency turns out to be a false alarm, the resulting cost and inconvenience will be great.

In addition to added convenience and safety, a master-keyed system will contribute significantly to the overall efficiency of a facility's operation. For example, an employee authorized to enter many secured portions of a large factory spends a considerable amount of time merely selecting the correct key from a bulging key ring. The security planner must decide if the cost of these unproductive man-hours can be justified by the security of a single-keyed system.

There are two basic disadvantages to master-keying. The first, decreased protection against criminal intrusion, has been discussed. The second is the cost of locks, keys, and related hardware. Master-keyed locks are more expensive than single-keyed, and changing from an existing change-key system to a master-key plan is also costly. Finally, master-keyed locks are about 30 percent more costly to rekey than single-keyed mechanisms are.

Once the decision to master-key has been made, the security practitioner should design a system that corresponds to the specific operational and security needs of his facility. The basic considerations are normally the nature and function of the organizational hierarchy and the physical layout of the facility.

Master-key systems are primarily characterized by the number of tiers or levels established, the grouping of locks operated by a particular master or submaster key, the overall number and types of master keys issued, and the classification and identity of those who will be issued submaster or master keys. City College's master-key system is not fully developed, because there are no provisions regarding the identity of those employees authorized to possess master and submaster keys. As far as it goes, the plan is primarily designed according to the physical layout of the structure—a grandmaster key for each dormitory building and a submaster key for each of the six separate dormitory wings. If City College's master-key system is going to be designed strictly pursuant to physical-plant considerations, all maintenance personnel and every security guard with dormitory-patrol responsibilities, because they require access to each room, would be issued great-grandmaster keys. On the other hand, the president of the college, because his duties do not normally take him into each dormitory room or wing, would not be issued even a master key. So we see that in determining key distribution, the physical layout of the facility may not be the only factor to be considered.

At City College, the organizational hierarchy of the institution should also enter into the decision. For example, great-grandmaster keys should not be issued to maintenance employees; but it might be wise to issue to the head of maintenance the six master keys to each dormitory wing, assuming that his character and reliability so dictate. A regular janitor should only be temporarily issued the change keys he needs to perform his most immediate tasks. Most janitorial personnel, low on the administrative totem pole, receive minimum wages and have a high turnover rate.

The decision of whether to issue master or submaster keys to security guards depends on many factors, including need and whether the guards are in-house or contract personnel. At City College, it would be advisable to temporarily issue all six master keys to the guard on duty. The campus security director, by virtue of his position, should be responsible for the overall master-key program and should therefore be in possession of at least all the original change, submaster, and master keys.

Beyond maintenance and security personnel, the issuance of master and submaster keys to high-level administrators, managers, or supervisors should be based upon need. Although it is not always advisable, it can be generally stated that the higher an employee is in the organizational hierarchy, the more likely it is that he will have possession of a master key.

Master key issuance, duplication, and record keeping are dealt with later in the chapter, under the heading "Key Control."

Our final reference to City College's master-key system involves the six exterior doors to North and South Halls. (See Figure 5-27.) If the decision is made, for example, to lock these perimeter doors at night, it would be inadvisable to integrate these locks into the master-key plan. For purposes of convenience, however, all six exterior door locks could be keyed to a single change key, and these change keys issued to all those requiring access to both dormitories.

"City College" has been used here as merely a device to aid in your understanding of a master-key system. A four-tier plan was established because such a system would probably be appropriate for two dormitories and 18 locks. Nevertheless, you should realize that the number of tiers and other considerations in the establishment of a master-key system must be relevant to the individual facility.

Interchangeable-Core Locks

The subject of interchangeable-core locks was dealt with briefly in the section on padlocks. Several lock manufacturers produce a mechanism with this feature. The most obvious advantage of interchangeable cores, particulary in facilities with a master-key system, is the ability to immediately change the key combination to a compromised lock. Ordinarily, the change of a key combination involves the service of a locksmith. With interchangeable-core locks, however, this change can be made by a layman using a special control key. Once the existing core has been removed by the use of the control key and another plug has been inserted in its place, a different key has to be issued to anyone authorized to operate the lock. A person with the old key still in his possession, such as a former employee, will no longer have access to the protected area.

Furthermore, if a master key capable of operating 50 interchangeable-core locks is lost, stolen, or not returned by a terminated employee, a substantial portion of the facility becomes vulnerable to criminal intrusion. Under these circumstances, the replacement of 50 interchangeable cores involves less time, cost, and inconvenience than would the changing of regular key-lock combinations. And the rapidity of the replacement eliminates the vulnerability that would be present if the time were taken to alter 50 conventional or fixed-cylinder locks.

Key Control

A lock, regardless of its quality or capability, is a worthless security measure if unauthorized people have keys to it. It is an unfortunate fact that most locks are compromised shortly after their installation by a lack of key control. In addition to the security risk, a lack of key control can cause a tremendous waste of money.

Effective key control is made particularly difficult by the common practice of permanently issuing keys to employees who do not absolutely require them. Having a key may confer convenience and status, but unnecessary key issuance continues to result in substantial security-related losses. In a facility equipped with hundreds of locks operable by large numbers of employees, effective key control is extremely difficult, if not impossible, to maintain.

Key control is defined as the ability to account for every key and every lock. Therefore, the primary purpose of key control is to establish a system whereby the security practitioner is alerted whenever a lock has been compromised by a lost, stolen, or duplicated key, and every employee authorized to possess a key is held accountable for his use of it. As an example, the investigation of a surreptitious entry into and theft from a locked room usually begins with the identification of those who possess keys to it.

The administration of a key-control system in a large corporation is usually handled by the security director or a member of his department. In facilities utilizing private contract security services, this function is usually performed by the head of maintenance. Quite often, in smaller industrial or commercial establishments, the manager in charge of operations has key-control responsibilities. But regardless of the size, operation, and type of business or institution, a key-control officer should be selected and held solely responsible for the administration of all keys and locks.

The first step in establishing a key-control program is the acquisition of a lockable cabinet in which all the unissued original and duplicate keys are to be securely maintained. Every key should be numerically tagged and hung on a hook correspondingly numbered. A key, particularly a master or submaster key, should never be marked or tagged with information identifying the lock it fits. Each key should instead be assigned a code number. This number, engraved on the bow of the key, will identify a corresponding lock and a hook in the key cabinet where all extra keys to this particular lock will be maintained. Ideally, the cabinet should be secured by a high-security combination padlock.

The second major element of a key-control program is the establishment of a record-keeping system that includes information regarding the identity of every key and corresponding lock, the number of existing keys, a list of those who possess each key, and the identity of every key permanently or temporarily issued. A sophisticated record-keeping system will consist of three sets of key information, filed according to the coded key number, the identity of the lock operated by the key, and the identity of the person to whom the key has been issued.

The first step is to write each key number on an index card, to be filed numerically. The card should show the corresponding lock and the number of available duplicate keys to it. A second group of index cards, containing data regarding each lock, should be filed alphabetically according to the door, gate, or other object it secures. This information should be cross-referenced to each key-code number.

The third set of records should be an alphabetical list of all those who have been issued keys. In addition to the name of the employee and the code number of his key, this set of records should indicate exactly when the key was issued, whether it was permanently or temporarily given out, the identity of the corresponding lock, whether it is a master key, and any information regarding the return of the key.

As a general rule, the fewer keys issued, the more effective the key control, especially in connection with master and submaster keys. Ideally, a master key should never be permanently issued to any employee. If it is at all possible, security personnel should be the ones to open and lock protected areas daily, or on demand. If it becomes necessary for a guard to temporarily provide an employee with a key for the purpose of unlocking several doors at the beginning of the workday, the guard should make a record of the time the key was lent and returned, as well as the identity of the person to whom it was issued. When not in use, all keys should be locked in the key cabinet under the security guard's control.

Whenever a key is permanently issued to an employee, a lock becomes vulnerable to being compromised through the theft, loss, unauthorized dissemination, or duplication of the key. In an effort to reduce the number of unauthorized key duplications, all keys should be stamped "Do Not Duplicate." Moreover, letters should be sent to all reputable locksmiths identifying, by code number, those keys that are not to be duplicated without the appropriate approval.

As mentioned in Chapter 3, keys are often duplicated by employees who fear they might lose the one originally issued, in order to avoid the embarrassment and possible disciplinary action caused by their negligence. But if an employee does lose his key and does not inform anyone, he eliminates the chance for the compromised lock to be rekeyed or removed. Unauthorized key duplications are often made also by terminated employees who then turn in their original keys but retain the ability to enter the employer's property.

Procedures should be established to ensure that all keys are routinely collected from every terminating employee. If such a key is not returned, the key-control officer should be advised. The administrator of a key-control program should continually update his records to reflect the identity and current number of lost or duplicated keys. He should also indoctrinate key-holding employees not to lend their keys to anyone without prior approval, and not to handle them carelessly and thereby expose them to theft.

A security practitioner should conduct periodic audits consisting of a physical check of each key holder to determine if the employee is in actual possession of his assigned key, and also if the key in the employee's possession is an unauthorized duplicate. Audits of this nature frequently disclose unreported incidents of lost or stolen keys and expose employees who are not giving their keys adequate security. The specific findings of a periodic key-control audit should be the basis of corrective action to remedy any weaknesses found in the overall key-control program.

In addition to the rekeying or replacing of locks known to have been compromised, all the locks in a facility should be periodically rekeyed as a matter of procedure. Facilities equipped with interchangeable-core locks can achieve the same result by simply switching lock plugs.

A final note regarding key control concerns the use of "construction keys." During the latter phases of new-building construction, the exterior doors to the building are sometimes equipped with locks to protect the material, tools, and machinery left inside overnight, and construction workers are often given keys to these locks. Because of the possibility that some of these "construction keys" will not be returned, or will be duplicated by construction personnel, all these locks should be rekeyed upon the completion of the building.

Combination Locks

dial-type combination locks

Combination locking devices, because they provide a greater degree of security than most key-operated mechanisms, are used to secure safe and vault doors and high-security filing cabinets and lockers. Maximum-security padlocks are also manufactured with keyless, combination-type locking devices. As a general rule, combination locks are more expensive than key-operated ones.

Beside the numbered dial on the outer face of the lock, combination locks comprise a set of circular and rotating disk tumblers (wheel pack) and a metal rod (spindle) that connects the tumblers to the dial. Most combination locks are manufactured with two to six tumblers, each with a slot or notch cut into its edge. When all these notches are aligned by the proper turning of the dial, an arm (fence) drops into a slot created by the alignment and the locking bar can be retracted from the strike.

The operator of a combination lock is instructed by the set of numbers making up the combination on how to align each disk tumbler. After spinning the dial a few times, the user starts by turning the dial, either to the right or to the left, to the first predetermined digit. As the dial is turned, all the tumblers are rotated in the same direction until the dial indicator is lined up with the correct number, causing the first tumbler to align. Then, turned in the opposite direction, the dial causes all but the first aligned tumbler to rotate. When the dial stops at the next number, the second tumbler aligns. The process is continued until all the tumblers are in place; the fence will not drop until every tumbler has been aligned. Combination mechanisms are relocked when the operator spins the dial, causing all the tumblers to rotate out of position.

As we saw in Chapter 3, it is virtually impossible to open a combination lock by randomly trying many combinations, since a three-tumbler combination lock may have any one of 1 million different combinations. As a general rule, combination locks with six disks provide more security than comparable locks with fewer tumblers. And because a combination lock does not have a keyway, its internal parts are not exposed to surreptitious manipulation or picking.

Some of the older combination locks can be defeated by skilled burglars who can hear and feel the fence align with the notch in the tumbler. But modern, quality combination locks are designed to eliminate this vulnerability. For example, in most modern combination locks, the fence does not come into contact with the wheel pack until all the disks are aligned, so the intruder cannot feel or hear the fence bump the notch in each disk.

Most modern combination locks are made to withstand force applied directly to the mechanism itself. However, some of the older ones can be defeated by knocking off the dial and punching or driving the spindle back through the wheel pack. Against a quality combination lock, this type of physical attack will merely render the mechanism temporarily inoperable.

The fact that combination locks do not require keys constitutes economic as well as security advantages. For example, whenever a lock is compromised by the termination of an employee who knows the combination, the combination can be changed without the services of a locksmith. Moreover, there are no keys to initially purchase, duplicate, or discard, or to be lost, stolen, or inappropriately duplicated. For these reasons, the integrity of a combination lock, in comparison to a key-operated mechanism, can be more effectively maintained.

Combination locks are, however, capable of being compromised; therefore, they should be subject to the following security procedures and controls: Because the manufacturer, installer, and/or retailer of the lock may have a written record of its combination, it is advisable to change the combination shortly after its purchase. The combination should also be changed at least once every year, as a matter of procedure. It should be changed whenever an employee who knows the combination or has worked in close proximity to the lock resigns, or is terminated, laid off, or transferred to another department or company. The combination should also be changed whenever, for any reason, there is the slightest suspicion that the lock has been compromised.

If he can possibly help it, the user of a lock should never make a written record of the combination. If he absolutely must, the information should be afforded top security. Combination locks manufactured with numbers positioned on the face of the dial should not be operated in the presence of unauthorized people. To alleviate this vulnerability, combination locks are manufactured with dials specifically designed to conceal the numbers from casual view.

Most combination padlocks cannot have their combinations changed after they have been manufactured. As a result, these padlocks can be said to be continually compromised to the extent that the manufacturer, a locksmith, or the retailer has a record of the combination. However, when a combination padlock has been significantly compromised, it should be removed and permanently replaced.

pushbutton combination locks

Dial-type combination locks, although they provide maximum security for safes, vaults, and file cabinets, are not usually utilized to secure doors and other passageways. The security advantages of a mechanical and keyless locking device can be applied to doors through the use of a pushbutton mechanism. This type of door-lock hardware consists of five numbered buttons, allowing the user thousands of possible lock combinations. (See Figure 5-29.)

The operation of this type of combination lock requires the user to depress one or more of the pushbuttons, together or in sequence. For example, the correct combination might be three numbers in a particular sequence, or the simultaneous depression of two buttons. Because of the convenience, economy, and security of a mechanical keyless device, these locks are particularly suitable for use on individual dormitory-room doors, hotel and motel rooms, and entrances to semiprivate rest rooms within large office buildings.

Pushbutton combination locks are manufactured with either deadbolt or spring-latch locking capabilities and are relatively easy and inexpensive to install. Although they are obviously incapable of being master-keyed, a similar effect can be achieved by the placement of a keyway near the combination dial. Upon the insertion of the correct "master" key, the combination tumblers are bypassed, allowing the key holder to open all locks in the system without knowledge of the individual combinations. This feature, of course, while it offers master-keying convenience, significantly reduces the security of the lock. The loss of the bypass key, for example, would compromise every lock in the system. It would seem that if the use of a combination lock is justified, the addition of a bypass-key feature is somewhat incompatible. Moreover, the presence of a key-lock mechanism on a combination lock eliminates the lock's pick-resistance.

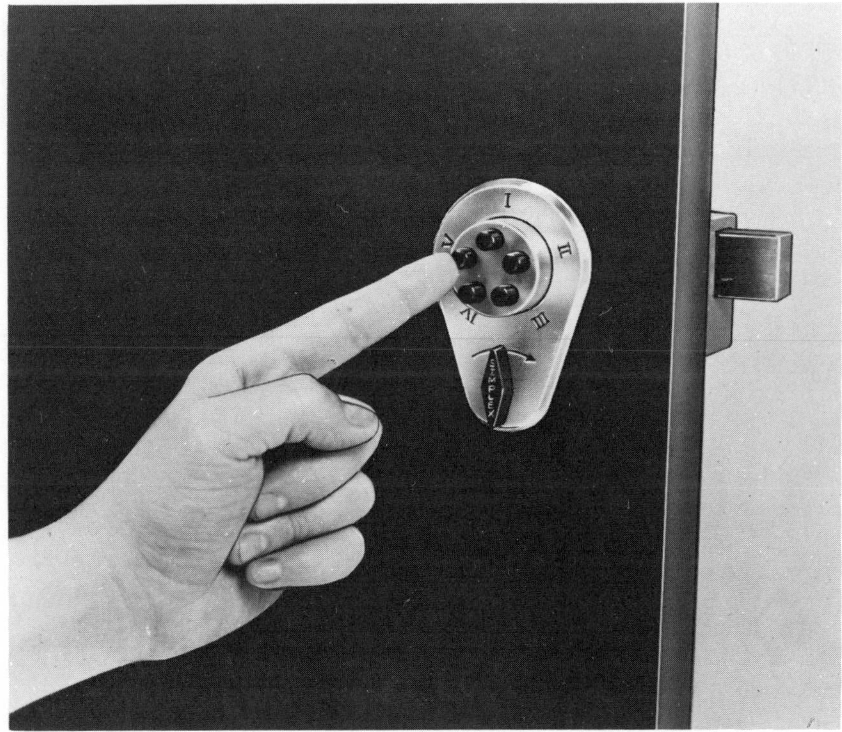

FIGURE 5-29. Mechanical pushbutton combination lock

Courtesy Simplex Security Systems, Inc.

Pushbutton combination locks, like dial-type devices, are vulnerable to being surreptitiously entered by intruders who have observed the mechanism being operated. The susceptibility to this type of entry can be somewhat reduced by the installation of a shield that acts to remove the pushbuttons from casual view. And the combination to a compromised pushbutton combination lock may be quickly changed by an authorized layman.

Electrically Controlled and Coded Locking Devices

card-operated locks

Card-operated locking devices are commonly used to control access to rooms, buildings, parking lots, and elevators. Every computerized or electronic card-key-operated locking system consists of four basic components, identified and discussed below.

The Card Key. The key that operates this type of locking device is usually a plastic, wallet-sized, invisibly encoded card resembling a gasoline credit card. The insertion of the card into the reader operates the lock. Those authorized to enter a restricted area are issued these cards, which contain a serial number or other identifying data that make every card, or a particular group of cards, unique. These cards are virtually impossible to duplicate, thus eliminating a basic key-controlled problem.

A card key can also be used as an employee identification badge or pass and may, if it is so used, be color-coded and contain the holder's photograph.

The Card Reader. The reader is usually a boxlike device housing the slot into which the card key is inserted to activate the lock. The reader, in a computerized system, transmits data that have been electronically encoded onto the card into a minicomputer memory bank. A reader that is a part of a less-sophisticated, electrical mechanical hard-wire-type system merely scans the card itself for acceptance or rejection. A card reader must be installed near each door or passageway where entrance is being controlled by this type of locking system.

A hard-wire system, as distinguished from a fully automatic, computerized card-key system, is inflexible, in that the reader is electronically wired to accept a fixed number of individually encoded cards to the exclusion of all others. It cannot be programmed, without being rewired, to accept additional cards or to reject a card that has been lost or stolen. A card used in this type of system, embossed or encoded magnetically, does not contain or correspond to data placed into a computer memory bank. The reader either compares the data on the card for acceptance or rejection or presents a logical puzzle to be solved by the card.

The rest of the discussion of card-key access control will be limited to the more sophisticated and fully automatic computerized card-key-type systems.

The Minicomputer. A minicomputer is a digital machine that operates in the same fashion as a larger computer, but is smaller and less expensive. Most minicomputers, weighing from 50 to 100 pounds and costing from $5,000 to

$10,000, do not require more than normal voltage. A minicomputer can be programmed to limit a cardholder's access to a specific door or a group of passageways during a particular time period. When the cardholder is no longer authorized to enter—for example, when a card-holding employee is terminated—the computer can be programmed to reflect this change by rejecting his card. If a card key is lost or stolen, a different card can be issued to replace it. In such a case, the lost or stolen card will be removed from the computer's memory bank.

Minicomputers are manufactured to produce a written printout tape that is a permanent record of every entry or attempted entry, by point of entrance, date, time, and person involved, including whether access was granted or denied. These computers are also capable of activating an alarm whenever a person attempts to gain entry with an improper card.

The Electronic Locking Device. The fourth component of a fully automatic card-key access-control system is the locking device itself. This is the mechanism that, when activated by the computer, opens or secures the door, gate, or turnstile.

Uses of the Card-Key System. A card-key operation, as distinguished from a conventional key-operated locking system, is particularly applicable in those situations where entry into a building must be denied to the general public while permitting convenient access to employees and other authorized people during business hours. For key-control reasons alone, it would be inappropriate to issue exterior door keys to hundreds of employees working in the building. Moreover, using a key to unlock a door is usually less convenient than simply inserting a card into a reader slot; and during periods of heavy employee traffic, requiring each employee to use a key would significantly impede the flow.

A card-key access-control system is of particular value in facilities where the employee turnover rate is high. Because the system can be quickly and economically updated to reject cards that are no longer valid, the locks will not be continually vulnerable to surreptitious entry by large numbers of former employees.

Card-key systems are also used to control and restrict vehicular traffic in private parking areas. (See Figure 5-30.) The use of a card reader to activate a parking-lot gate without the holder's leaving his car is a convenient method of keeping unauthorized vehicles out of a parking area.

Regardless of the type of access-control system used, fundamental security weaknesses are present whenever large numbers of people have access to a building or other restricted area. For example, any unauthorized person can enter a building if he is in possession of a card key that has been improperly given to him by an authorized cardholder. Another security hazard is "tailgating"—gaining unlawful entrance into a building by joining a group of employees or other authorized people who are entering together. A building's vulnerability to this type

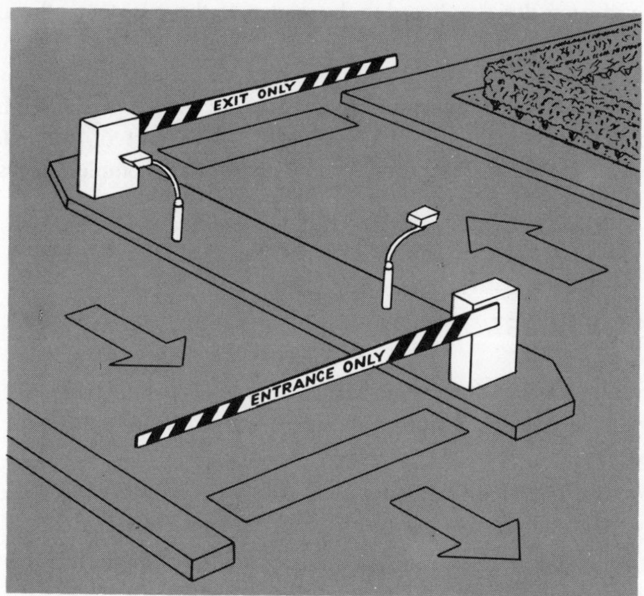

FIGURE 5-30. Vehicle access control using a coded-card-key system

Courtesy Rusco Electronic Systems

of entry can be significantly minimized by the installation of a set of outer and inner doors, with the reader positioned in a "booth" between them. Ideally, one set of double doors should be used for entering and a separate set for exiting. Under this system, the outer entrance door is unlocked until the authorized person inserts his card into the reader to unlock the inner door. Then the outer door is automatically locked behind him until he enters the building. When he is inside, the outer door unlocks and the inner door is resecured. This type of door configuration in a card-key operation will reduce tailgating by restricting entry through the passageway to one person at a time.

Another method of preventing tailgating is by the use of turnstiles that are operated by a card key. A turnstile may be set to be inoperable for a period of, say, ten seconds immediately following the authorized use of a card key.

A common security weakness associated with card-key access control is the authorized holder's passing his card back to an unauthorized person who can use it to enter the building later. This "passback" technique also defeats the antitailgating effect of card-key-operated turnstiles. However, the card-key system can eliminate unlawful entry by this technique; it can be set in such a way that each card key, once it is used to gain entry, will not operate any of the entrance doors in the system until it has been used by the holder to exit the premises.

The security of a card-key access-control system can be tightened by the installation of a ten-digit keyboard in the reader. In these systems, the authorized cardholder must recall an individaully assigned combinaion number and punch it out on the keyboard. This combination, along with the data encoded on the card key, is transmitted to a computer and verified before entry is permitted. Electronically operated keyboard-type locking devices, as a part of computerized or hard-wire systems, are also operated without card keys as complete access-control systems.

DISCUSSION QUESTIONS

1. Look at the keys in your possession. Can you determine from this examination whether each key operates a warded, wafer, or pin-tumbler locking mechanism?
2. By examining the lock hardware illustrated in Figure 5-20, can you determine the type of internal locking mechanism built into this device?
3. Identify the major disadvantage of using double-cylinder lock hardware on residential doors.
4. What is the primary advantage associated with using a combination rather than a key-operated lock?
5. In addition to gates, doors, and various chests, boxes, and other containers, what other things can be secured by a padlock?
6. What are some of the services provided by a qualified locksmith?
7. Why would the installation of a locking device that cannot be surreptitiously operated (as opposed to one that can) increase the possibility of recovering a burglary loss under an appropriate insurance policy?
8. What is the meaning of the term *key combination*?
9. As security administrator and planner, how would you economically solve or make provision for the problem created by the following hypothetical fact situation:

    > Lester, a long-standing employee of ABC Company, has been caught stealing company property. When informed of his termination, Lester says that he has lost his great-grandmaster key. He also threatens to return to the company premises to "get even" with his former employer. It is late Friday afternoon, and the locks on the premises cannot be changed until Monday morning. The existing lock mechanisms do not contain interchangeable cores. Although the plant is not in operation during the weekend, a few employees must have access to the facility during this period.

10. Can it be determined if a key operates a master-keyed lock by merely examining the key blade and bittings?

11. Pursuant to City College's four-tier master-key system, designate and identify, by job title, those employees you believe should be authorized to have a master key, and assign the appropriate key, by level, to each of them.
12. With regard to the six exterior doors to each wing of North and South Halls, why would it be inappropriate to install master-keyed locks integrated into City College's master-key system? How would you key these six doors?
13. What part of the record-keeping function of a key-control program do you consider to be the most important? Justify your selection.
14. The following is an excerpt from the Oakland, California, Model Burglary Security Code: ". . . If a padlock is used, it shall be of hardened steel shackle, with minimum five pin tumbler operation with nonremovable key when in an unlocked position." Specifically, what is the security advantage of a padlock with a nonremovable-key feature?

SELECTED BIBLIOGRAPHY

ALTH, MAX, *All About Locks and Locksmithing*. New York: Hawthorn Books, 1972.

"The Decision to Masterkey," Parts I and II, *Security World*, July/August 1974 and October 1974.

HEALY, RICHARD J., *Design for Security*, Chap. 9, "Lock." New York: Wiley, 1968.

SLOANE, EUGENE A., *The Complete Book of Locks, Keys, Burglar and Smoke Alarms, and Other Security Devices*. New York: Morrow, 1977.

TOBIAS, MARC WEBER, *Locks, Safes, and Security: A Handbook for Law Enforcement Personnel, 1st ed*. Springfield, Ill.: Charles C Thomas, 1971.

TOEPFER, EDWIN F., "Locks, Safes, Alarms," *Security Distributing & Marketing*, Vol. 5, No. 9 (September 1975).

WALSH, TIMOTHY J. and RICHARD J. HEALY, *Protection of Assets Manual*, Vol. 1, Chap. 4, "Locking." Santa Monica, Calif.: Merritt, 1974.

Chapter 6

Security Guards

AN OVERVIEW

I. Security-Guard Patrols
   A. *Foot patrols*
      1. Watchclocks
      2. Automatic guard-monitoring systems
      3. Designing patrol routes and schedules
      4. Perimeter patrols
      5. Interior patrols
   B. *Vehicular patrols*

II. A Profile of the Security Guard
   A. *Security-guard unionization*
   B. *Security-guard training*

III. Proprietary or Contract Security Guards?
   A. *Proprietary guards*
   B. *Contract guards*

The treatment of security guards in this chapter primarily concerns their use as an anti-intrusion measure. Uniformed security guards are discussed elsewhere in the text in connection with their roles in combatting shoplifting, preventing armed robbery, and controlling employee and visitor access, and in Part V in connection with fire control, prevention, and safety. In the more general discussion in this chapter, in-house guards are compared with contract personnel, and security-guard training and the common sources of security-guard personnel are dealt with.

The use of a security guard or uniformed watchman, like any other security measure, does not by itself provide adequate protection against criminal intrusion. The extent of a guard's effectiveness depends to a large degree on the nature and extent of other security measures being taken on the premises. In the same way, protective fencing and outdoor lighting, as individual security systems, cannot provide adequate protection. Used together, however, these two measures are complementary and form a first-line defense against criminal intrusion.

A security barrier consisting of a security guard, outdoor lighting, and a fence can be further augmented and strengthened by intrusion alarms. The installation of an alarm system may reduce the number of guards needed to protect the premises; however, security guards are often used to activate, deactivate, and monitor alarms, and they may respond to activated sensors, thus minimizing unnecessary police reaction to false alarms. Also, a local alarm may be useless without the response of a security guard to the bell, siren, or light.

Security guards also control and prevent unlawful intrusion by being stationed at doors and gates to oversee pedestrian traffic and deny entry to unauthorized personnel. The utilization of closed-circuit television cameras and monitors, along with remote-control locking devices, makes possible the observation and control of many doors and gates by one security guard.

In comparison to other security expenditures, security-guard usage is costly. It is a continuing security expenditure, as opposed to, for example, the installation of a $25,000 perimeter fence. After its purchase, the fence is relatively cost-free except for occasional maintenance and repair. However, guards provide security services that go beyond the control and prevention of criminal intrusion, so the cost of their service does not have to be justified entirely in terms of the money saved through burglary prevention.

The cost of uniformed-guard use pursuant to a specific security program depends mostly upon the number of hours a guard is on duty on the premises. For example, having one guard on duty 24 hours a day, seven days a week, constitutes 168 hours of guard coverage per week; therefore, the continuing weekly cost of security coverage will include, among other things, the guard's hourly wage times 168. In addition to wages and related payroll costs—workmen's compensation, and personal injury and liability insurance, for example—there will be uniform and security equipment expenses. During a period of one year, at normal turnover rates for security guards, the coverage described above will involve uniforming and equipping nine to twelve full- and part-time security guards, and although uniform and equipment expenses can be considered an initial cost, the costs of their replacement and maintenance are of a continuing nature. In addition, security-guard usage involves numerous administrative expenditures such as guard recruitment, training, and supervision.

The cost of having one security guard on duty 24 hours a day for a period of one year is estimated at between $26,000 and $30,000.

Security-Guard Patrols

foot patrols

As combatants against criminal intrusion, security guards are most commonly used in manufacturing facilities, warehouses, trucking terminals, and large institutions. The number of guards and periods of guard usage needed to protect a particular facility depend upon the physical size and layout of the facility, its operational characteristics, its vulnerability, its criticalness, and the nature of the guard's duties and responsibilities.

For example, a foot patrol within a large factory complex may require two hours to complete, so a guard on duty for eight hours, assuming he has no other duties, can make four rounds. But because he would have no time to rest between rounds, this patrol schedule is unreasonable; the effectiveness of a guard who attempted to follow it would be limited, owing to his fatigue. In this case, in order to establish more reasonable and effective guard usage, either the patrol route must be shortened or the rounds made less frequently during the eight-hour shift. If these alternatives are unacceptable, a second guard must be added to provide the degree of protection desired. Two guards would also be needed in a facility that requires both regular and complete security patrols and continuing surveillance at a door or gate.

Not all users of security guards have them on the premises 24 hours a day, seven days a week, because of the cost. A security-guard user, in determining what times and days of the week a guard will be employed, usually takes into consideration work schedules and other operational characteristics of the factory, warehouse, or institution. Since most facilities are more vulnerable to intrusion at night and on weekends when the premises are unattended, it is during these periods that security-guard shifts are most often scheduled. A factory, for example, operating two eight-hour production shifts each weekday, may utilize third-shift guard coverage (11 P.M. to 7 A.M., or midnight to 8 A.M.) Monday through Friday, with a security guard on duty 24 hours on Saturday and Sunday. Such a schedule calls for 88 hours of weekly guard coverage. Small institutions frequently employ a guard eight hours per night, seven days a week. This schedule, 56 hours of weekly coverage, most often includes third-shift duty. Many plants and warehouses use 48-hour guard coverage during the weekend; larger enterprises maintain guards on the premises from 3 P.M. to 7 A.M. each weekday, and from 7 A.M. Saturday to 7 A.M. Monday. The latter schedule, of 128 guard-hours per week, is quite common.

In addition to working regularly established guard shifts, security guards are frequently utilized during periods of scheduled plant shutdowns, during strikes, and on holidays.

Since an alert security guard, patrolling the premises on foot, constitutes an effective measure against criminal intrusion, most security-guard jobs involve a predetermined number of patrols or rounds during an eight-hour tour of duty. It is not unusual, for example, for a guard to make a 30-minute patrol every hour. Between his rounds, he is usually stationed at a place such as a desk in the office area of the facility, at a post near the building entrance, in a guardhouse adjacent to a perimeter gate, or in a central guard office that houses alarm panels, closed-circuit television monitors, and a two-way communications system. Regardless of the nature and location of his security post, a guard should have access to an outside telephone line.

Watchclocks. Most security patrols consist of a preplanned route to be followed by the guard. To be effective against intrusion, the route should require the guard's periodic presence at those places that have been deemed particularly critical and/or vulnerable by the security administrator or supervisor. The watchman's clock, or watchclock, carried by the guard as he makes his rounds, is an instrument designed to control and supervise guards and their patrols. It is operated by keys that are housed in key stations or metal boxes installed within and about the premises in areas requiring the guard's attention.

A watchclock is a seven-day timepiece encased in plastic or stainless steel, with a strap attached to a leather carrying case. (See Figure 6-1.) The watchclock corresponds to and moves a paper tape or dial (disk) that is divided into clearly marked time segments. The security guard inserts the key (usually secured on a chain attached to the key station) into the watchclock and, in so doing, makes an impression, in the form of a number, on the tape or disk. (See Figure 6-2.)

An examination of the disk or tape will determine if the guard visited each key station according to his schedule of rounds. Whenever a guard fails to visit a key station, the omission shows up on the tape or disk (see Figures 6-3 and 6-4), and the reason for it is noted on his daily report. Most guards are required to maintain these daily reports; in addition to recording the security patrols, they make up a written record of other data and occurrences pertinent to each tour of duty. For example, if a guard's rounds are interrupted by an emergency, the information about it that is found in his daily report will correspond to the gap on the watchclock tape, thereby providing a reasonable explanation for the partial round.

A watchclock, in addition to its supervisory function, produces proof that

FIGURE 6-1. Detex Guardsman Watchclock

Courtesy of Detex Corporation

the scheduled rounds were actually made. Since regularly scheduled patrols often qualify the guard user for lower fire and burglary insurance rates, these watchclock records are maintained for periodic inspection by insurance personnel.

In laying out a patrol route, the security practitioner should not install too many key stations on the premises. If there are too many for the guard to visit, he will be forced to hurry from station to station, and he will not be as alert to intruders, signs of forced entry, and security hazards such as doors and windows

FIGURE 6-2. Security guard inserting the key into the watchclock

Courtesy of Detex Corporation

FIGURE 6-3. Interior of watchclock with tape

Courtesy Detex Corporation

FIGURE 6-4. Interior of watchclock with disk

Courtesy Detex Corporation

left open or unlocked. When locating the key stations, the security planner should consider, in addition to fire and related safety matters, placing the keys in areas where the guard's presence will deter criminal intrusion.

Automatic Guard-Monitoring Systems. Another method of supervising security patrols is by the use of an automatic guard-monitoring system. Because of the cost of this method, watchclock use is considerably more prevalent.

The key stations in a sophisticated guard-monitoring system are visited in a predetermined order according to an established and rigid time schedule. Whenever the guard fails to visit a key station within the appropriate time period, the deviation is immediately transmitted by telephone line to a central monitoring station, which consists of a receiver that prints out a record of the time and the identity of the key station missed. The operation of such a system necessitates the use of personnel to continually monitor the receiver and react whenever a guard deviates from his programmed patrol route.

The use of an automatic guard-monitoring system entails certain advantages and a few disadvantages. Recommending it is the fact that whenever the guard fails to visit a key station within the appropriate time span, notification of his omission is instantaneous, thereby allowing the immediate implementation of corrective measures. In comparison, when a guard supervised by a watchclock misses a key station or neglects to make all his scheduled rounds, these omissions remain undisclosed until the watchclock tape or disk is examined by a guard supervisor, possibly several days or even weeks later. In other words, a watchclock system provides only a historical record of a guard's patrol; an automatic monitoring system not only produces a permanent record of each patrol but does so on a continuous and current basis. This system also allows the guard to immediately alert central-station personnel in the event he becomes ill, has an accident, or encounters a dangerous or hazardous situation.

Among the disadvantages of the automatic system are the higher costs associated with the purchase and maintenance of sophisticated hardware, and the added payroll costs brought on by the use of central-station personnel. In addition, an automatic monitoring system is by its nature inflexible, so it will not adapt to most existing security-guard and patrol programs. Almost all guards, because of their overall security responsibilities and duties, find it necessary to frequently alter or temporarily interrupt their regular patrols; in most instances, these interruptions take precedence over the guard's immediate patrol duties. Some of these nonpatrol security functions are the logging in of visitors, issuing of guest passes or keys, surveillance of vendor activity, unlocking of doors, and telephone answering. Also, the automatic system requires the guard to visit each key station in numerical sequence, and the inflexibility of such a routine creates a pattern that can help a potential intruder successfully predict the guard's whereabouts at any given time.

Designing Patrol Routes and Schedules. In establishing a patrol schedule, the security administrator should not require the completion of too many rounds within an eight-hour tour of duty, and the patrol route should not be over too large an area for one guard to cover thoroughly within a reasonable time. As a general rule, the guard should not have to make more than one 45-minute round every hour; a one-hour round every 90 minutes is not uncommon.

The security guard, with or without a watchclock, should periodically alter his route to avoid establishing a pattern that could be helpful to a would-be intruder. The fact that a patrol route consisting of key-station visits is completed in a variety of ways will not necessarily detract from its effectiveness as a fire-prevention measure.

Guards are sometimes assigned duties and responsibilites that do not relate to the security function—for example, to turn industrial machines on and off, perform janitorial work, carry messages, shovel snow, deliver mail, run errands, and operate telephone switchboards. But guards with too many nonsecurity responsibilities do not have time to make frequent and thorough patrols, and their use is not an effective anti-intrusion measure.

The decision of whether to utilize armed or unarmed security guards should be based on several factors, such as the facility's vulnerability to intrusion and armed robbery, the ability and training of the guard personnel, relevant state regulatory statutes, and cost. As a general rule, armed guards are not needed or used in industrial settings where fire and burglary prevention is their primary function. Nevertheless, unarmed industrial guards or watchmen should know their arrest powers and limitations, and they should receive instruction in their employer's policies regarding arrest, use of force, and police notification. Recent studies have shown that most industrial guards perceive their powers of arrest incorrectly. Since they are utilized to combat criminal intrusion, it is imperative that they understand the criminal procedural laws relevant to arrest, search and seizure, and the use of force. A discussion regarding the extent and nature of most in-house and contract-agency training programs follows later in this chapter, and material on the training of guards and floorwalkers in a retail setting is found in Chapter 9.

Perimeter Patrols. A perimeter patrol around a building or property line constitutes the first line of defense against criminal intrusion. If the premises are protected by a fence, the patrolling guard should continually check on its physical condition and be alert to signs of forced entry, paying close attention to gates and other openings in the fence to make certain that they are locked. When patrolling around the outside of a building, the guard should look for open and unlocked windows and doors. If a door or window is found unlocked or open, this security weakness should be corrected and, if appropriate, investigated. The guard should also note and report luminaries that are not functioning and be alert to the presence of suspicious vehicles and people in the vicinity of the premises he is protecting. Suspected prowlers, loiterers, and other trespassers should be confronted and identified.

When the security guard discovers evidence of a recent forced entry through a fence or into a building, he should immediately notify the police and then return to the scene of the crime to await their arrival. He should not himself search for the intruder or gather evidence of the crime. If the compromised barrier or structure is equipped with a silent alarm, the guard should telephone the police to verify the intrusion and to give directions to the premises. Incidents of this nature, as well as other security-related occurrences, are usually reported separately by the guard to his supervisor.

As a part of his perimeter-patrol function, the security guard should be trained to recognize and correct situations that invite and facilitate criminal intrusion. For example, ladders and stacked material left near a fence or building should be removed; unattended vehicles parked inappropriately close to a fence or building should be investigated. Security hazards that cannot be corrected by the guard should be noted on his daily report, which will find its way to the interested parties.

Interior Patrols. When making his first interior round, the guard should make certain that there are no unauthorized people in the building and make note of those employees who are working late on the premises. Employees, salesmen, visitors, and delivery personnel have been known to surreptitiously remain inside a facility until after business hours, so the guard must have information regarding the identity of anyone authorized to be present in the building while he is on duty. Maintenance and janitorial personnel frequently work in a factory, warehouse, or large retail establishment during nonproduction or nonbusiness hours, and the guard on patrol should attempt to keep track of the whereabouts of such after-hour workers and take note whenever he finds one of them in an inappropriate section of the building.

On his first interior round, the security guard should also examine all fire exit doors to make certain they have been securely closed. If exit alarms have been installed on these doors, the guard may activate them, as well as other local intrusion alarms, at this time.

Security patrols are most effective when they are conducted by guards who are observant, conscientious, and methodical. A security patrol is a passive and somewhat boring task that seldom produces tangible or measurable results that give job satisfaction. Moreover, because the effectiveness of a guard and his patrol cannot be empirically gauged, quality control is difficult to achieve and maintain. The fact that a break-in has never occurred during a particular guard shift may reflect the efforts of an efficient, knowledgeable, and alert security guard, or it may be unrelated to the guard and his performance on the job.

A security administrator should superivse his guard force closely and see that they are indoctrinated and trained in the nature, objectives, and techniques of the security-patrol function.

vehicular patrols

A private motorized security patrol can be obtained from an agency specializing in this service, or from a firm that provides a full range of security services. Subscribers to private vehicular patrols are usually visited regularly by a security patrolman on a predetermined schedule. These periodic visits include a perimeter check of exterior doors and windows, and, if appropriate, fence lines and other boundaries. In addition, the vehicular patrolman may also enter the facility and make an interior foot patrol. The frequency and duration of each patrol depends upon the security requirements of the facility and the amount of money the user is willing to invest in the service. Since most of these security checks are made after normal business hours, private patrol activity is the heaviest during nighttime and weekend periods.

The objectives of the vehicular patrol are generally similar to those of a regular security guard who is continually on the premises. The difference is in the degree rather than the kind of protection offered. The vehicular patrolman, after he makes an interior or perimeter round on the subscriber's premises, leaves the facility; a regular security guard remains on the property between his patrols. Like a regular security guard, the vehicular patrolman confronts suspicious persons, corrects security hazards, and reports signs of criminal intrusion to the subscriber and the police.

Subscribers to motorized patrol services usually pay on a per-visit basis. The cost of a single patrol-car check depends upon the amount of time spent on the premises and the nature of the work performed by the patrolman while he is there. Most patrol-car subscribers are visited from three times per week (usually on weekends) to four or five times every night. Since most patrol cars are equipped with police radio receivers, the security patrolman monitoring police calls can also go to a subscriber's premises in the event of fire or burglary. And private patrol-car firms also offer escort services, which usually involve transporting personnel to night depositories at banks.

Motorized patrol services are utilized by subscribers who employ security guards as well as by those that do not. The primary advantage of patrol-car use over regular guard coverage is in cost. Having several patrol-car visits to the premises every night comes to only a fraction of the cost of a security guard who is continuously on duty there.

Of course, because a security patrol-car service does not provide continued security coverage of the subscriber's premises, motorized patrols are less effective against criminal intrusion than is regular guard use. However, three or four nightly motorized perimeter checks, accompanied on each occasion by a brief interior foot patrol, may provide sufficient protection for those facilities that are not particularly critical or vulnerable to burglary. In any event, if vehicular patrolmen secure doors, windows, and gates that have been left open or unlocked by careless employees this will usually be enough to justify the cost of the service.

Most patrol-car agencies provide their clients with a written log showing the time of each visit, a description of security weaknesses observed and corrected, and an account of other security-related happenings or situations.

The private patrol-car function is one of the few security services that supplement or augment existing police efforts. However, a private patrol-car service that involves more than a perimeter check of the premises is complementary, in that it extends protection against burglary beyond that which is offered by regular police patrols.

Common users of private motorized security-patrol services are trucking terminals, scrap yards, residential neighborhoods, municipal parks, zoos, factories, industrial parks, convenience food stores, and cemeteries.

A Profile of the Security Guard

In discussing the security guard and the nature of the conditions under which he works, the distinction between in-house and contract personnel often becomes relevant, so it will be made here whenever appropriate. It is estimated that 70 percent of the country's private police are in-house, and the remainder contract personnel. There has recently been a trend, however, toward the use of contract over in-house guards.

In 1969, James Kakalik and Sorrel Wildhorn conducted the first major nationwide study of the security industry. The results of their work, published by the Rand Corporation in 1971, are contained in four separately entitled volumes (this and the other cited excerpts from the Rand Report have been revised, updated, and published as *The Private Police: Security and Danger* by Kakalik and Wildhorn. (See bibliography to Chapter 1.). The volume pertaining to private security guards is entitled, *The Private Police Industry: Its Nature and Extent.* The following excerpt is found on page 67:

> The typical private guard is an aging white male who is poorly educated and poorly paid. Depending upon where in the country he works and on his type of employer (contract guard firm, in-house firm, government), he has the following characteristics: His average age is between 40 and 55; he has had little education beyond the ninth grade; he has had a few years of experience in private security; he earns a marginal wage of between $1.60 and $2.25 per hour and often works 48–56 hours per week to make ends meet. If employed part-time, he works only 16–24 hours per week. Often he receives few fringe benefits; at best, fringe benefits may amount to ten percent of wages. Guards have diverse backgrounds: Many are

> unskilled; some have retired from a low-level civil service or military career; younger part-timers are often students, teachers, and military personnel on active duty. Annual turnover rates range from less than ten percent in some in-house employment to 200 percent and more in some contract firms. Few guards are unionized.

Although it is somewhat dated, this Rand Report profile of the security guard, especially with regard to unarmed and contract security-guard personnel, is accurate.[1] Most contract security guards are paid hourly wages that are as low as state and federal laws allow. Few receive what employees in other industries and trades consider standard fringe benefits. A few of the larger contract security firms provide free life insurance after six months or one year of employment. A guard working for one of these firms may also receive a week's paid vacation after one year's work and a two-week vacation after three or more years. Very few contract security guards receive free medical insurance and sick-pay benefits, but most contractors furnish free uniforms and equipment and pay workmen's compensation insurance premiums to cover their guards in case they are injured on the job. In-house security-guard personnel, however, often receive the same benefits the company provides for its nonsecurity employees. Also, in-house guard personnel, as a general rule, receive higher hourly wages than contract guards.

security-guard unionization

The following material from Volume II (page 75) of the Rand Report:

> The precise extent of unionization of private security personnel is unknown. One large protective services firm reported that ten percent of its guards were unionized; another reported twenty-five percent of its guards were unionized. One of these firms estimated that ninety percent of all *unionized* ("theirs") guards were employed *in-house,* rather than by contract agencies.
>
> The United Plant Guard Workers of America (UPGWA), the largest private guard union, has twenty thousand members, or about eight percent of all private sector guards. The union estimates that its membership accounts for between two-thirds and three-quarters of all the unionized guards in the country. If true, there ought to be between 27,000 and 30,000 unionized guards in the United States. Ten percent (or 2,000) of UPGWA guards work for General Motors; that force represents almost half of the total 4,200 guards employed by GM.
>
> It is no accident that most unionized guards work in-house rather than for contract guard firms. Since contract firms obtain contracts through a competitive bidding process, they resist unionization vigorously in order to keep costs, and hence

---

[1]A more recent study of the security industry, including a complete profile of proprietary and contract guards, is the Private Security Task Force Report on private security. This report was published in 1977 by the Anderson Publishing Company and is entitled *Private Security.* See the ASIS questionnaire and security results in Appendix B. The results of this survey were the basis of many of the findings in the report. Note the data reflecting the different wage and training levels of the various types of security personnel.

> wages, low. Even if a union obtains a foothold in an agency, or in a local office of a large contract guard firm, it is difficult to increase or even maintain membership. If a contract agency is unionized and the union pushes for higher wages and fringe benefits, the client can simply change to a non-unionized agency. Or, as it is alleged to have happened in at least one case, the large contract security firm can deunionize a local office, using the following technique. A newly unionized local branch bids high for both new business and repeat business when the contract expires. As bids are lost, business declines and guards are fired. When the business of the local office has declined to almost zero, the firm is deunionized in that area. Then the firm begins to bid competitively for new business, using non-union personnel.

The American Society for Industrial Security (ASIS) survey of industrial and retailer users of security personnel and of contract security suppliers showed that 79 percent of their security forces were non-unionized. It is interesting to note that 26 percent of the security personnel involved in the survey were contractural, 60 percent were in-house, and 24 percent were mixed. (See Appendix B.)

Section 9(b)(3) of the National Labor Relations Act prohibits the National Labor Relations Board from certifying any labor union that represents both security guards and other types of employees. According to the act, a security guard is any individual employed to enforce against other employees and other persons rules to protect the property of the employer or to protect the safety of persons on the employer's premises. This prohibition has kept the more powerful national and international unions from representing security guards. It is a widely held belief among security executives that if security guards and the personnel against whom they enforce company regulations become members of the same union, the guards will become union members first and management representatives second. Under these circumstances, the implementation of an effective security program would be difficult, if not impossible.

security-guard training

The authors of the Rand Report conclude that, as a general rule, most security guards are poorly trained. Specifically, they found that most contract security firms provide no formal classroom security training for their personnel, and that firms that do provide this type of training offer only a few classes, mostly consisting of training films and/or lectures from a company executive or security manager. The training of in-house security guards, they found, although somewhat better than that received by contract personnel, was also inadequate. The more recent ASIS survey indicates that guards are still inadequately trained.

Most security guards receive their training on the job, from a supervisor or a more experienced guard, usually by accompanying the experienced guard on his rounds. For examaple, the most basic form of security-guard training involves an industrial contract security guard's learning the locations of the watchclock key stations, how to operate the facility's telephone system, and his duties and responsibilities between his security patrols. Security agencies, through guard supervisors, periodically inspect their personnel to determine whether the guards are performing adequately.

Most private contract security firms provide their guards with manuals or security handbooks, typically including subject matter such as general duties, company rules and regulations, legal aspects of plant protection, fire protection and prevention, first aid, report writing, traffic matters, bomb-threat procedures, and the use and care of firearms. The value of these security manuals as training aids is questionable, since it is doubtful that most security guards read or refer to them for guidance.

Most executives in the private contract security industry agree that security training for guards is minimal. One of many reasons for this situation is the fact that private security firms must keep their rates low in order to compete successfully against other agencies as well as proprietary-guard utilization. Since training is costly, this facet of the private-security effort is often sacrificed. Moreover, few states have laws requiring minimum security-guard training. A few states have, however, established legislation requiring security and law-enforcement training for armed security-guard personnel. Pennsylvania has recently enacted what is referred to as the Lethal Weapons Act, which requires private security guards carrying lethal weapons in the course of their employment to become certified. In order to be certified, a security guard must be fingerprinted by the State Police, undergo a physical examination, and have a professional psychologist administer a reading-achievement and personality test. After completion of these requirements, formal application is sent to the state for final approval. Once the applicant has been approved, he attends a course that includes firearms qualification on a firing range, 40 hours of classroom work in a variety of law-enforcement techniques and lectures on relevant procedural and substantive criminal laws.

Although armed guards make up only 10 percent of the nation's private police force, they, more than any other group of private-security personnel, should receive some minimum security training. It should be noted that despite the absence of legislation in this area, a few private contract security firms have initiated substantial security-training programs. *Security Distributing & Marketing* magazine carried an article profiling a Phoenix, Arizona, guard agency's efforts to provide trained security-guard personnel through their own training program.[2] This firm, Continental Security Guards, Inc., not only operates its own security-training academy; it owns a mobile training van in which an instructor travels to various guard sites where a relief backup guard takes over the trainee's duties while he enters the van to view training films and receive personal instructions on relevant security subjects. If the trainee is an armed guard, he can use the van's pistol-range facility, which operates with reusable plastic bullets.

---

[2] "Innovation: Key to CSG's Growth and Success," *Security Distributing & Marketing*, March 1976.

Notwithstanding the example above, most private contract agencies, by virtue of the kind of people attracted to the guard business, the high turnover rates, and the nature of the work itself, are unable to significantly upgrade their services through active training programs. To maintain even a narrow profit margin and at the same time provide adequate training for their guards, many security firms attempt to pass their training costs on to the guard user in the form of higher hourly rates. But although the users demand better-trained personnel to protect their property, they usually resist higher rates and often seek out the companies that charge the least.

In summary, as long as the private contract business is competitive, guards remain non-unionized, and training is not mandated by legislation, private contract and most in-house guards will remain poorly trained.

Proprietary or Contract Security Guards?

The security planner, in determining whether to use contract or proprietary (in-house) security-guard personnel, must consider several factors in regard to the general nature of the facility being protected, including its specific security needs and the overall security objectives and priorities. There are, however, certain advantages and disadvantages associated with either choice. Some of these general benefits and drawbacks are identified and discussed below.

proprietary guards

Proprietary security guards usually receive higher hourly wages than contract-guard personnel do. Therefore, they are generally higher-caliber people and provide a better service. Although it is common knowledge that a good wage will not guarantee quality work, a higher-paying position will permit the employer greater selectivity, since there are obviously more people interested in high-paying than in low-paying jobs.

Although a substantial proportion of in-house guards are untrained, members of large, well-established guard forces are often better trained than their contract counterparts. Moreover, proprietary guards, because they are usually higher-level personnel, can be trained to handle some of the more complex security duties and will be more willing to accept greater job responsibility. Also, there is less turnover among in-house guards than among contract guards, and since they tend to stay on a job longer, they are more familiar with the facilities they protect. Finally, since proprietary guards are employed directly by the user, they may tend to be more loyal to him than contract personnel would be; it follows that a loyal guard will be more concerned about his employer's well-being and will therefore provide a higher degree of protection.

There are a few drawbacks to proprietary security-guard use. Probably the most unattractive aspect of this type of service is its cost. It is estimated that in-house-guard usage costs 20 percent more than comparable (in terms of guard-hour coverage) contract-guard use. To justify this higher cost, the user should assure himself that he will receive a service of corresponding superiority and that the degree of protection provided matches his security needs. Those costs that are assumed by contract security-guard agencies, resulting in savings to the guard user, are identified in the discussion in the next section.

A common problem encountered by users of proprietary guards, particularly employers of small guard forces, is ensuring the availability of backup personnel to replace any regularly scheduled guard who, for whatever reason, cannot perform his duties as scheduled. Finally, proprietary guards may be required to join a guard union. Not only will the user have to pay a union guard force higher wages, but the effectiveness of the overall security effort may diminish owing to the familiarity and cameraderie that can develop between members of different unions.

contract guards

Contract guards are less expensive than proprietary personnel, and their use is convenient and usually constitutes less of a headache for the user.

The security-guard contractor bases his fee upon a schedule of hourly guard rates. For example, the contractor may charge his client $4.50 for every hour an unarmed uniformed security guard is on the client's premises. This guard may receive only a $2.90 hourly wage, but the user is relieved of all payroll-related responsibilities, including not only wages, but costly fringe benefits such as vacation pay and health insurance, workmen's compensation insurance, and the withholding of city, state, and federal taxes. Other personnel-related responsibilities assumed by the guard contractor are recruiting, hiring, and training expenses, as well as all the administrative headaches normally associated with any project or endeavor requiring employees.

The contractor also assumes full responsibility for the scheduling and supervising of all guard personnel. For example, it is not unusual for a security guard, after being processed, indoctrinated, fully uniformed, regularly scheduled, and broken in to his job, to walk off the job without apparent reason or notice. When this occurs, it is the contractor, not the user, who has a problem. It is the contractor's responsibility to replace the guard immediately in order to provide his client with continued coverage.

The contract-guard user also avoids the expenses of providing security uniforms, equipment, badges, report forms, and, in many cases, the watchclock. The security-guard contractor pays for these and his standard operating expenses out of the difference between what he pays his guard and what he receives from the client. It is obvious that the contractor's profit, on an hourly basis, will be a mere fraction of his hourly guard rate. As a result, if a contract-guard agency is to prosper, it must be responsible for many hours of guard coverage and must continually struggle to keep its overhead down. These two economic factors have a substantial effect upon the quality of contract security-guard protection.

There are other advantages to contract security-guard utilization that do not relate directly to matters of cost or convenience. In response to an emergency, the user of proprietary guards cannot quickly increase the number of guards on duty. Moreover, he will be unable to expand his guard coverage to include time periods previously without guard protection. For example, a user may require increased guard coverage during a labor dispute; in addition to the increased flexibility afforded the contract-guard user under these circumstances, contract guards, because of their relative objectivity, are particularly appropriate in strike situations. Guard users may also require additional and flexible guard coverage during holiday periods, special events, and periods of plant shutdowns.

Another advantage associated with contract security guards relates to the security firm's acceptance of liability in civil suits filed by third parties injured by a contract guard's negligence. In these situations, if a proprietary guard had been involved, the guard's employer would have been directly responsible. Moreover, whenever a contract guard is responsible through his negligence for a property loss or personal injury suffered by the guard user, the security firm will be responsible for the loss. Most contract security firms, because they accept this risk on behalf of their clients, purchase the appropriate insurance coverage. To be fully covered, a security agency must have personal-injury coverage (protection against false arrest, detention or imprisonment, malicious prosecution, libel, and slander), assault-and-battery coverage, property-damage coverage, errors-and-omissions coverage, and several other kinds of liability insurance protection. Because malfeasance-of-duty suits against security firms are on the increase, this type of insurance coverage has become expensive and is not easily obtained. The risk assumed by contract security-guard companies is analyzed by Bruce W. Brownyard of the W.H. Brownyard Corporation in an article in the November 1973 issue of *Security Management* magazine. Brownyard sets out several relevant case histories, including the following:

> On Christmas Eve, an altercation erupted at a department store in North Philadelphia between a [contract] security guard who was on duty in the store and a drunk and disorderly customer. The guard ordered the customer to leave the store, and the customer responded by shoving the guard to the floor. The guard got up and again ordered the disorderly customer to leave, and the customer responded by hitting the guard about the head with his fists, again knocking the guard to the floor. The guard started to get up a second time, and the customer again began to approach the guard in a menacing manner. The guard drew his gun and fired at point blank range, killing the customer instantly. A suit was filed on behalf of the widow of the deceased against the security guard firm.
>
> Over the Fourth of July weekend in 1972, the guard on the 12:00 A.M. to 8:00 A.M. shift at a Brooklyn paper factory decided to take a forklift for a joy ride around

the factory. Racing around a blind corner, he crashed into the cab of a tractor-trailer garaged in the factory. One of the forks pierced the gas tank of the cab, and the ensuing fire and explosion gutted the entire factory, causing over a million dollars worth of damage. The guard's action was found to be the proximate cause of the fire, and the guard's company was held responsible for the damage.[3]

The disadvantages of contract security-guard use have been identified and discussed in connection with the advantages of proprietary security guards.

DISCUSSION QUESTIONS

1. Why would a guard be regularly assigned tasks unrelated to his function when it is obvious that this practice minimizes his security effectiveness?
2. Why is it difficult to determine and measure, on an individual basis, the effectiveness of a security guard?
3. What, in your opinion, are some of the disadvantages of watchclock utilization?
4. What, in your opinion, are some of the security weaknesses associated with a private security patrol-car service?
5. Aside from the nature of guard work itself (low pay, few benefits, etc.), how would you explain the high guard-turnover rates that plague the contract security industry?
6. Discuss some of the reasons why security guards, especially contract personnel, are difficult to supervise.
7. Discuss some of the reasons why security guards are difficult to train.
8. What type of facility or security function would be best served by a contract rather than a proprietary security force?
9. What type of facility or security function would be best served by an in-house rather than a contract security force?

SELECTED BIBLIOGRAPHY

ASTOR, SAUL D., "Contract Guards: The Facts as I See Them," *Security World,* July/August 1975. The author strongly defends private contract-guard companies and services.

BROOK, RANDOLPH D. III, "So—What Do You Want from a Guard Company?" *Security World,* August 1977.

---

[3]"Are You Fully Protected by Your Liability Insurance?" *Security Management,* November 1973, pp. 17, 18.

DAVIS, ALBERT S. "Comparing Guards vs. Subcontracting Guards," *Industrial Security,* January 1976.

———. *Security Officer Training Book.* Knoxville, Tennessee: Training Consultants, Inc., 1975.

FEE, DWIGHT, "Training Programs, Methods, Topics and Standards for Uniformed, Nonsupervisory Security Personnel," *Security Management,* November 1976.

JONES, D.L., "Those Dangerous 'Regular Rounds,'" *Security World,* June 1977.

KAKALIK, JAMES S., and SORREL WILDHORN, *The Private Police Industry: Its Nature and Extent.* Santa Monica, Calif.: Rand Corporation, 1971.

———, *The Private Police: Security and Danger.* New York: Crane, Russak and Company, 1977.

LIPSON, MILTON, *On Guard; The Business of Private Security,* Chap. 6, "Security Personnel Practices." New York: Quadrangle New York Times Book Co., 1975.

LUKINS, RICHARD A., "Security Training for the Guard Force," *Security Management,* May 1976.

MINION, RONALD R., "Motivating Security Guards," *Security World,* June 1977.

SCHURR, ROBERT, "The Guard Force (Direct Hire or Contract)," *Security Management,* January 1976.

SILVERMAN, ALLEN B.I., "Fireams Training for Security Guards," *Security Distributing & Marketing,* December 1974.

SLUTZKY, KEN, "Upgrading Security Forces," *Security Management,* July 1977.

WANAT, JOHN A., and JOHN F., BROWN, *Hospital Security Guard Training Manual.* Springfield, Ill.: Charles C Thomas, 1977.

WHELTON, CLARK, "In Guards We Trust," *New York Times Magazine,* September 19, 1976.

WHIPPERMAN, ROBERT F., *Private Patrolman's Primer.* Los Angeles: Security World Publishing Company, 1974.

WOODRUFF, RONALD S., *Industrial Security Techniques.* Columbus, O.: Charles E. Merrill, 1974. Primarily devoted to the security-guard function in an industrial setting. Discusses use of weapons, traffic duty, report writing, patrol functions, bomb procedures, rules and regulations, and legal aspects.

Chapter 7

Intrusion Alarms

AN OVERVIEW

I. Scope of Discussion

II. Basic Alarm Systems
   A. *Central-station alarm systems*
   B. *Proprietary alarm systems*
   C. *Direct-notification systems*
   D. *Local alarm systems*

III. Principles of Operation and Applications of Intrusion-Alarm Sensors
   A. *Electromechanical alarm systems*
      1. Switches
      2. Window foil
      3. Screen alarms
      4. Pressure mats
      5. Application of electromechanical alarm systems
   B. *Photoelectric light-beam interruption systems*
      1. Application of photoelectric alarm systems
   C. *Vibration alarm systems*
      1. Vibration alarm applications
   D. *Seismic, pressure, and magnetic stress sensor alarm systems*
      1. Seismic sensors
      2. Pressure sensors

3. Magnetic alarm sensors
4. Application of seismic underground alarm systems

E. *Motion-detection systems*
1. Microwave motion-detection systems
2. Ultrasonic motion-detection systems
3. Infrared motion-detection systems

F. *Audio alarm systems*
1. Application of audio alarms

G. *Capacitance alarm systems*

H. *Thermal alarm systems*

I. *Video Alarm systems*

IV. The False-Alarm Problem

A. *False-alarm rates*

B. *Causes of false alarms*
1. Mechanical causes
2. Subscriber causes

C. *The effects of the false-alarm problem*

D. *Solutions to the false-alarm problem*

The private security industry can be divided into three basic areas: personnel services, equipment, and alarm services. Personnel services, which provide over half the industry's revenues, include security guards, investigators, and armored-car and courier services. The equipment category is made up of lighting equipment and a variety of products such as fences and electronic surveillance devices.

Alarm services bring in about 25 percent of the security industry's revenues. The products in this area are alarm and communications equipment, intrusion-detection devices, and central-station alarm operations, and the services are selling, manufacturing, installing, and responding to alarms.[1]

Scope of Discussion

In this chapter, the subject of intrusion (burglar) alarms will include a discussion of the various types of alarm sensing devices, according to their varying methods of activation, principles of operation, and security applications. The false-alarm problem will also be treated.

Merchandise alarms and their retail-security applications are discussed in

[1]The breakdown of the security industry and the estimates of revenues are from the Private Security Task Force report, *Private Security* (Cincinnati, O: Anderson, 1977), pp. 38–39.

Chapter 9; hold-up alarm devices and systems in Chapter 13; glass, window, and exit alarm devices in Chapter 4; and the subject of fire alarms in Part V.

Unlike the case with most security topics, there is a lot of literature on intrusion-alarm equipment and operating systems. Most of the trade magazines in the security field deal primarily with the types, technology, sale, installation, and service of alarms and alarm systems. The alarm facet of the overall security industry is substantial; there are hundreds of alarm manufacturing and service companies, and dozens of new alarm devices and concepts are introduced into the security market every year. For this reason, it is difficult to keep up with the continually advancing and changing alarm technology.

Basic Alarm Systems

There are four basic types of intrusion-alarm systems: central-station alarms, proprietary alarms, police-connected or direct-notification alarms, and local alarms.

central-station alarm systems

A central-station alarm system is composed of fire and/or intrusion sensing devices capable of activating an indicator panel located and monitored at a central station physically removed from the protected premises. Central-station alarm agencies employ not only sales, installation, and service personnel, but monitoring and response personnel. The monitoring function involves human observation of alarm indicators during periods when the alarm sensors are in operation. Those performing this function may also be responsible for alerting police or security personnel to respond to the scene of the activated sensor.

The largest alarm company in the United States, the American District Telegraph Company (ADT), provides alarm response personnel as a regular part of their central-station alarm service, as do many other alarm agencies. Upon the activation of an alarm sensor, the person watching the panel dispatches alarm response personnel to the scene and either calls the police immediately or waits until he receives a preliminary report from the responding security officer. If the security officer arrives at the alarmed premises and suspects that the sensor has been activated by an intruder, the police, if not already alerted, are notified.

Most alarm response personnel are instructed not to enter the premises for the purpose of searching for and apprehending the intruder, but to stand by until the police arrive. But when they have reason to believe that the alarm is false, most responding officers investigate to verify their suspicion and to determine the cause of the alarm. Because a large percentage of alarm sensor activations are unrelated to criminal intrusion, one of the most significant aspects of a central-station alarm response service is the elimination of police response to premises where, for example, alarms have been set off by employees, wind, animals, or faulty alarm equipment.

proprietary alarm systems

A proprietary alarm system is essentially the same as a central-station operation, except that in the former, the alarm panel is located on the premises containing the alarm sensors.

direct-notification systems

Another type of alarm system involves police notification through direct communication from the alarm sensors to a panel situated at the police department.

Central-station, proprietary, and direct-notification alarm systems all necessitate either line or wireless communications between the sensors and a panel that reports an activated sensor. These are commonly referred to as silent-alarm systems. Although monitoring personnel at the alarm panel are alerted when a sensor has been tripped, the intruder may not be aware that his presence is known to police or security personnel, a fact that can increase the possiblity of his being caught at the scene.

local alarm systems

A local alarm sensor is not linked to an alarm panel but notifies, by light or sound, those who are within earshot or eyesight of the protected premises. For this reason, local alarm sensors usually do not alert police or security personnel, but they do draw attention to the intruder and thus increase his chances of being detected and caught. Moreover, a ringing bell, screaming siren, or flashing light will cause many intruders to leave the scene of a burglary before completing the crime. Since local alarm systems do not require an alarm panel, they do not involve the use of monitoring or response personnel, so they are less expensive to purchase, install, and operate than are the more sophisticated, silent-alarm systems.

Principles of Operation and Applications of Intrusion-Alarm Sensors

The discussion that follows is intended to provide the student with a general idea of how the various alarm devices operate to protect a place or an object against physical intrusion. The security applications of burglar alarm systems will also be discussed in general terms. No attempt has been made to identify and discuss every type of alarm sensor currently available—just the most common and widely used.

Generally defined, an alarm sensor is a device designed to produce a signal or alarm in response to an event or stimulus within its detection area. The purpose of an intrusion-alarm sensor is to detect a physical intrusion into the protected premises or object. So many premises and objects are commonly alarmed—including entire buildings, structures, rooms, fences, vehicles, desks, file cabinets, vaults, and safes—that intrusion alarms are one of the most widely used weapons against criminal intrusion. Alarms cannot by themselves distinguish between an authorized visitor to a protected place and an intruder. For example, if the owner of a store reenters the premises at night without first deactivating the alarm, the sensing device will detect his presence and emit an alarm signal. However, an alarm that is correctly used, installed, maintained, and operated can be an effective measure against criminal intrusion.

electromechanical alarm systems

All the electromechanical alarm systems discussed in this section operate on the principle of either the breaking or the closing of an electrical circuit. That is, depending upon the system, whenever the electrical current is broken or completed, an alarm signal is emitted. For example, doors and windows in a closed-circuit system can be wired by using electrically charged strips of wire or tinfoil. When the foil or wire is cut or separated, the circuit is interrupted or broken and the alarm activated. In an open-circuit system, when the sensor is activated, a switch is closed that permits a current in the circuit, and an alarm is triggered.

Electromechanical devices are reliable and relatively service-free, although they are costly to install. Because these systems are operationally simple, they can be compromised by intruders who have limited knowledge and skill.

Switches. Doors, windows, hatches, skylights, and other hinged openings in a wall or roof are commonly alarmed through the use of electrical switches. This type of sensor is made up of two electrical contacts, one installed on the wall or ceiling (fixed surface) and the other on the door, window, or other moving surface. When the door or window is closed, the contacts are together and the electrical current is complete. When the door or window is opened, the contacts separate and the electrical current is broken, causing the alarm signal.

There are several kinds of switches of the mechanical and magnetic types. The magnetic type is made up of a magnetically activated switch and a magnet. The magnet is usually attached to a door or window, and the switch to the doorjamb or window pane. When the door or window is opened, the switch is activated by the moving magnet.

Window Foil. Window foil consists of a metallic tape that is applied to permanently closed glass openings such as display windows, permanently closed skylights, and picture windows. When the glass is broken beneath the tape, the current running through the tape is interrupted, causing the activation of the alarm.

Screen Alarms. These devices are similar in their principle of operation to window-foil alarm systems. Woven into the mesh of these screens are electrically charged wires that when cut cause an alarm situation.

Pressure Mats. These pressure-sensing devices are floor mats containing switches that are activated when stepped on or when any weight of 5 to 20 pounds per square foot is placed on their surface. This type of intrusion alarm is commonly placed either on top of or under a carpet in front of doors and stairways and beneath window openings.

Application of Electromechanical Alarm Systems. As opposed to alarms that protect spaces and areas, electromechanical alarm devices protect surfaces. As a result, they can be used only as perimeter alarms. They are used on fences, walls, and roofs, but mostly to protect doors and windows. A window can either be foiled (against breakage) or alarmed like a door (against opening). As long as the electrical contacts remain undisturbed, an electromechanical door-alarm system will not activate. Therefore, an intruder can enter the premises by cutting or chopping a hole through a door, without being detected by a mechanical or magnetic sensor switch.

photoelectric light-beam interruption systems

A photoelectric alarm system is composed of a sender device that transmits a beam of light and a receiver designed to accept the light wavelength that has been transmitted and convert light energy into electrical energy. Whenever the light beam is interrupted, a variation occurs in the amount of light received, causing an alarm signal. The beam that is sent can be either visible or infrared (invisible); the latter, of course, makes this type of alarm difficult for an intruder to detect. Infrared filters are available to place over a regular-light-beam transmitter.

Application of Photoelectric Alarm Systems. Beam intrusion-alarm systems are generally considered perimeter security devices, used both indoors and outdoors to provide an alarm barrier around a building or a fence line. The beam can be bent around an object or corner, or back and forth across a room (in which case it provides area protection) by means of mirrors. The more mirrors used, the shorter the range of the light beam. Under the most favorable conditions, light beams have been transmitted as far as 1,000 feet, but most beams are sent 300 feet or less.

Photoelectric beam alarms are not particularly adapted for outdoor use in areas where thick fog is commonplace. Moreover, before a beam can be used along a fence line, the ground under the beam path must be graded level, to avoid high spots that would interfere with the beam or low spots that would allow intruders to crawl beneath it. An ideal photoelectric alarm system produces several beams, thereby forming a "wall" of protective light. In general, beam devices constitute excellent vehicular- and employee-entrance alarms.

vibration alarm systems

Another perimeter-protecting device is the vibration alarm. These can be installed on any surface. They are commonly placed on walls, floors, ceilings, roofs, and objects such as file cabinets and safes. The sensor, a very sensitive microphone, picks up the vibrations caused when an intruder penetrates a protected area. Walls constructed of concrete block can be effectively alarmed in this manner, since concrete block is an excellent transmitter of vibration. Vibration alarms are also well adapted to metal surfaces. For example, the sound of a "silent" drill on a safe or the sounds of a lock being picked can be detected by a microphone sensor.

A device called an alarm discriminator separates most non-intrusion vibrations from sounds created by physical intrusion. Normal amounts of rain, wind, and blowing debris against a protected surface will not cause a false alarm. However, this type of alarm cannot be used in environments where there are high noise levels, such as near construction sites, low-flying aircraft, major highways, or railroad tracks.

Vibration Alarm Applications. A vibration alarm system capable of alarming an outside chain link fence has recently been developed. The system is composed of a special ⅛-inch-thick cable sensor that is attached to and strung along the fence. When the fence is climbed or otherwise disturbed, an alarm signal is emitted. The sensor can be adjusted to ignore the vibrations caused by normal rain and wind, but generally speaking, these sensors are best used in environments that are not exposed to loud noises or intense rain and high winds.

seismic, pressure, and magnetic-stress sensor alarm systems

These three sensing devices are used in a variety of underground perimeter intrusion-alarm systems. Often called "minefield-style," these alarm systems are activated when an intruder treads upon the ground above a buried sensor device.

Seismic Sensors. This type of sensor is a geophone similar to those used in geophysical exploration. The sensors are connected in a series along a line beneath a walking surface—dirt, concrete, asphalt, a wooden floor, or a roof. When someone walks nearby, each footstep causes a low-frequency disturbance that radiates in all directions from the point of contact, and the sensor closest to the footstep generates an electrical output.

Pressure Sensors. This sensor consists of two liquid-filled hoses, spaced about four feet apart. At the end of the sensor line, a special sensor device detects the change in the differential pressure under the soil as the intruder walks or crawls over the ground where the hoses are buried. When a momentary pressure change is sensed, an alarm signal is emitted. The hoses can be up to 300 feet in length and are usually buried twelve to fifteen inches under the surface.

Pressure sensors of this nature cannot be used in rocky or frozen soil, and outside vibrations in the ground caused by nearby swaying trees or vehicular traffic will cause false alarms.

Magnetic Alarm Sensors. This type of sensor (electric line) is a magnetized iron rod that senses changes in magnetic induction. It is susceptible to lightning-induced false alarms, however, and therefore not in wide use.

Application of Seismic Underground Alarm System. Seismic sensor systems are most commonly used as outdoor perimeter alarms to protect a fence line. The fact that there are no externally exposed components in these systems makes them not only hidden, but waterproof and operational in adverse weather.

motion-detection systems

Motion-detection alarms, as well as the other intrusion-alarm systems discussed in the remainder of this chapter, are generally classified as space or area alarms. Space and area alarms, unlike perimeter alarm devices, do not protect surfaces or form alarm barriers, and they are seldom used outdoors. Motion detection is one of several methods used to alarm space.

All motion-detection alarm systems use sensors that, in one way or another, respond to the motion of an intruder, but there are three categories of these alarms, based on their principles of operations.

Microwave Motion-Detection Systems. Microwave alarm systems are also called RF (radio frequency), radar, high-frequency Doppler, and radiation-resistance detector systems.

The following is a rather technical but complete description of how a microwave system works:

> A Doppler effect type of system is one which transmits electromagnetic energy at a known continuous frequency and compares the known transmitted frequency with the frequency of the energy reflected from persons or objects within

> the area being monitored. Any change in the frequency of the reflected wave with that of the transmitted wave indicates motion within the area being monitored.
>
> This change in frequency is called a Doppler shift, after Johann Doppler, who first discovered the phenomenon. The Doppler frequency shift phenomenon is also the basic principle of most ultrasonic motion detection systems.[2]

Generally speaking, a microwave system works by filling the protected space with a pattern of radio waves. When an intruder enters the alarmed area, he changes these radio-wave patterns, and the modulation of the radio waves triggers the alarm.

A microwave system includes an alarm discriminator, which filters out non-intruder-type motion, such as the movement of small animals. One of the advantages of a microwave system is the fact that it is not affected by noise or air turbulence. Microwave systems have also been designed for outdoor perimeter use.

Ultrasonic Motion-Detection Systems. Ultrasonic alarms, like microwave systems, operate on the Doppler-effect principle. With this type of alarm, an ultrasonic sensor detects the motion of an intruder as he moves through the ultrasonic (inaudible) wave patterns.

Ultrasonic devices are limited to indoor use. Although they are not affected by exterior noises in the audio range, they will detect air turbulence and set off the alarm. Even air currents created by air-conditioning units have been known to cause false ultrasonic alarms. A second drawback is that a single ultrasonic sensor will not protect as large an area as will one microwave detector.

Infrared Motion-Detection Systems. Infrared systems do not operate on the Doppler-shift principle, but respond to changes in the infrared (invisible) light that radiates from objects in a room. When an intruder enters the protected area, the intensity of the infrared light coming from his location triggers the alarm.

Unlike microwave and ultrasonic sensors, which continually transmit and receive signals, an infrared system does not transmit anything; it merely receives. For this reason, it is commonly referred to as a passive system.

Infrared sensors are not affected by moving cold-air currents, noise, or metal objects. False alarms have been caused, however, by currents of hot air, guard dogs, and radio-frequency interference. Infrared systems are used exclusively indoors.

---

[2]From Carl F. Klein, "Basic Microwave Overview," *Security Distributing & Marketing*, January 1975.

audio alarm systems

Audio alarm devices are space-protecting systems whose principle of operation is similar to that of vibration alarm systems composed of microphone sensors. An audio detection system is one in which the sensors pick up the sound vibrations caused by any forced entry into the protected area. The type of audio alarm systems discussed in this section are commonly referred to as listen-in alarms, since they consist of microphones and a control unit containing an amplifier, which is monitored.

There are two kinds of audio alarm systems: The first type uses audio equipment to hear audible sounds above a certain predetermined, preset level. When such a sound is detected, the person monitoring the alarm station is alerted and listens to determine whether it is being made by a burglar at work. This type of alarm system is necessarily sensitive and therefore active. Its sensors will respond to outside noises coming from, for example, airplanes, trains, and loud motorcycles, but these will not cause false alarms because the monitoring person will be able to identify them.

The second type of listen-in alarm operation consists of microphone sensors that are activated by other, non-audio alarm devices that have been triggered by an intrusion. For example, whenever an electromechanical alarm circuit has been interrupted (an alarmed door opened, or window broken), or when a space alarm detector is affected, the microphone sensor is activated as well. When this occurs, the person monitoring can listen in and hear what is going on inside the protected area.

The following discussion of audio alarms will primarily concern the first type of system.

Discriminators are built into audio alarm circuits so that "normal" sounds will not set off the alarm. Thus, the breaking of glass will trigger an audio alarm, but a ringing telephone will not. Sounds made by heating and cooling systems, pumps and other machinery, aircraft, and thunder are treated by the alarm as normal and will not trigger a properly adjusted audio system. Since almost all burglaries involving forced entry create noise—most often, the breaking of glass—audio systems are effective detectors of intrusion.

Because it is composed of only microphones and an audio amplifier, this is a relatively simply alarm device. Moreover, detecting an intrusion by hearing the noises made by the burglar is the original and most basic method of catching criminal intruders.

The primary problem associated with a listen-in alarm system is to adjust the sound threshold in order to filter out normal environmental noises without destroying its usefulness. For example, if the threshold is set too low, the unexpected creaking of a joist or a loud outside sound will trigger the alarm, but if it is set too high, the sounds made by a burglar will not activate it. However, in the case of an alarm caused by a "normal" sound, a person monitoring the system may be able to identify the source and nature of the noise. This aspect of audio alarms may account for their low false-alarm rate, which is particularly appreciated by police personnel. Moreover, because monitoring personnel sometimes hear the burglars speaking to each other, the police may be provided with very helpful information as they proceed to the scene of the break-in—for example, how many intruders are on the premises. There have even been a few cases in which the intruders have been overheard referring to each other by name. In these cases, even before the police arrive at the scene, the intruders are at least partially identified.

Application of Audio Alarms. Most audio systems are used in commercial or institutional settings—for example, in schools, to combat vandalism. And most of these systems are tied into central- or proprietary-station operations, although local audio alarm units are available, usually housed in stereo cabinets.

Perhaps the best application of audio detection devices is to place the microphones in vaults, where it is normally very quiet. Forcible entrance into a vault will undoubtedly make a lot of noise. Audio alarm systems, as a general rule of thumb, are least effective in poorly constructed buildings that are not insulated against outside noise. Of course, audio systems cannot be used outdoors.

capacitance alarm systems

The capacitance sensor, also referred to as a proximity alarm, is another type of space-protecting device. Capacitance is the property of two or more objects that enables them to store electrical energy in an electrical field between them. As one object is moved closer to the other, the capacitance changes.

In a capacitance alarm system, a protected object is electronically connected as a capacitance sensor to form part of a tuned circuit. The approach of an intruder changes its capacitance, which upsets the balance of the system and triggers the alarm.

The most common and best use of this type of alarm system is to protect ungrounded metal objects such as safes and file cabinets. (All metallic objects in close proximity to the protected object should be well grounded.) The alarmed object acts as one of the two plates of a capacitor in a tuned circuit, the other being the earth ground. In most instances, the intruder is detected before he touches the protected object. In this sense, then, a capacitance alarm protects the space surrounding the alarmed object.

thermal alarm systems

Thermal or heat sensors detect the temperature rise that is caused in an area by the body heat of an intruder. These sensors also respond to cutting and burning tools commonly used by safe burglars. Thermal sensors can be effectively used to alarm the interior of vaults. They have little application, however, in environments where there are rapid and extreme changes in room temperature.

video alarm systems

A typical video alarm system is composed of a closed-circuit television (CCTV) camera that sends a static picture to a comparison logic and memory evaluator. Any deviation in the picture being fed into the evaluating device—that is, any movement within the protected view of the camera—will trigger the alarm.

Existing daytime CCTV monitoring systems can be switched over at night to an automatic alarm mode, thereby converting them into video alarm systems. The use of a video tape recorder (VTR) will add another dimension to the system by allowing a replay of the activity or movement that set off the alarm and providing a permanent record of it on video tape.

The discussion of intrusion alarms in this chapter has not included every type of alarm system and alarm sensor currently on the market. For example, laser alarms, chemical sensors, and radiation detectors which have not been discussed, illustrate some of the more recent developments in intrusion-alarm technology. Also, some of the most effective intrusion-alarm systems are composed of many different types of alarm sensors and operations.

The False-Alarm Problem

Burglary alarms are considered to be indispensable weapons against criminal intrusion. The current technology permits detection of almost every kind of physical intrusion. But a few problems continue to trouble alarm users and the intrusion-alarm industry. The greatest of these is the problem of false alarms.

The most common definitions of a false alarm are (1) an alarm signal for which an investigation discloses no evidence of an alarm condition, or (2) any alarm signal not caused by the condition the alarm system was designed to detect. The following definition reflects the alarm industry's idea of how the problem should be perceived:

> False alarm means an alarm signal eliciting a response by the police when a situation requiring a response by the police does not in fact exist, but does not include an alarm signal caused by violent conditions of nature or other extraordinary circumstances not reasonably subject to control by the alarm business operator or alarm user.[3]

---

[3]From Steven B. Watts, "Multnomah County's False Alarm Research," *The Police Chief*, June 1977.

false-alarm rates

It is a universally accepted fact that nationally, 96 to 98 percent of all intrusion-alarm signals are false. That is to say, 96 to 98 percent of the alarms that have gone off have done so for reasons other than a criminal intrusion. For example, in 1973, the Los Angeles Police Department was responding to about 120,000 alarm calls a year; 97 percent of them were false.[4] Since that time, a good many steps have been taken to try and reduce the false-alarm rate in Los Angeles.

causes of false alarms

Generally speaking, the causes of false alarms are classified as either people- or equipment-connected. A third cause, which won't be discussed here, is use of the wrong type of alarm to protect a particular premises or object—such as an indoor space alarm system installed to protect an outdoor fence line.

There is considerable disagreement among police and security practitioners as to what percentage of false alarms are mechanical as opposed to subscriber-caused. (The term *subscriber* refers to alarm users rather than alarm manufacturers, service companies, or installers.) Some writers insist that people cause 75 percent of all false alarms, and others that between 60 and 70 percent of them are caused by mechanical difficulties.

Mechanical Causes. For purposes of the discussion here, the exact percentage of all false alarms caused by mechanical problems is not important. It is enough to say that malfunctioning alarm components do cause false alarms. Such a problem can originate with a sensor at the alarmed premises, an automatic dialer, telephone line or other device used to transmit the alarm signal to the monitoring station, an alarm discriminator, or a component at the receiving end of the signal.

With regard to electromechanical alarm systems, the following list names just a few of the specific equipment problems that can cause a false alarm:

1. Loose-fitting, warped, flexing doors and windows
2. Dust and dirt on an electrical contact
3. Cracked or broken glass
4. Broken wire
5. Improperly insulated wire connection
6. Shorts caused by staples in the wiring
7. Poor connections

---

[4]These figures were taken from Donald A. Shepherd, "A Systems Approach for the Reduction of False Burglary and Robbery Alarms," *The Police Chief*, June 1977.

8. Improperly adjusted contacts
9. Moving parts misaligned from dropping or a hard jolt
10. Corrosion of contacts, wires, and screws

Subscriber Causes. False alarms are frequently caused by employees and other authorized persons when they enter an alarmed building without turning off the alarm or calling the central station monitoring personnel. Such mistakes often involve personnel who have not been properly instructed as to the correct operation of the alarm system. There is often a delay between the entering of an alarmed premises and the triggering of the device. In these systems the subscriber must turn off the alarm shortly after his entry. If he forgets to do so, a false alarm results.

the effects of the false-alarm problem

False alarms are costly. In Los Angeles in 1973, each false-alarm call required about 36 minutes for a two-man radio car, with an estimated cost of $16.28. As a result, the city's estimated annual cost of responding to false alarms was $3,800,000.[5]

Besides cost, false alarms have other adverse effects. For example, after a police officer has responded to many false alarms, he is less likely to take activated-alarm situations seriously, and for an officer to react carelessly to an activated alarm without much thought or preparation is dangerous. Moreover, false alarms seriously affect police response time to alarmed premises. When the responding officer believes that the triggered alarm is not due to an actual criminal intrusion, he will avoid the risk of speeding to the scene.

Over the long range, false alarms have three general effects on the police:

1. Poor police searching of the protected premises
2. A poor attitude toward the alarm user and the alarm industry
3. A belief that intrusion alarms are more trouble than they are worth.

solutions to the false-alarm problem

One approach to the problem of false alarms is the enactment of appropriate city ordinances. For instance, ordinances have been passed in Los Angeles and Pasadena, California, requiring the owner of an alarmed premises to acquire a permit to operate the alarm system and penalizing the alarm user for false alarms. Such sanctions usually begin with warnings for initial or infrequent false alarms and end up with revocation of the user's alarm permit. At each stage of the warning system, the subscriber is urged to initiate corrective action.

[5]Shepherd, "A Systems Approach for the Reduction of False Burglary and Robbery Alarms," *The Police Chief,* June 1977.

Another anti-false-alarm measure is closer legislative control over the alarm industry, usually through licensing requirements. Such laws could set minimum standards for alarm manufacturing, installation, and service companies.

There are many steps individual alarm companies can take to reduce false alarms. The following suggestions have been made by the Western Burglar & Fire Alarm Association:

1. Sell the system right; consider the environment, habits, and routines of the subscriber. Don't over-protect.
2. Don't use space protection indiscriminately.
3. Instruct the subscriber on the proper use of his alarm.
4. Reinstruct the subscriber on the proper use of his alarm at frequent intervals.
5. Train and retrain your alarm company employees on procedures and troubleshooting techniques.
6. Maintain the system in proper working condition.

One anti-false-alarm measure that has little general support and is repellant to the members of the alarm industry is for municipalities (police departments) to charge the alarm user for each police response to a false alarm.

In summary, the extent to which false-alarm rates can be reduced depends primarily upon the individual efforts of intrusion-alarm suppliers and subscribers. Once the problem has been corrected within the security community, efforts should be made to indoctrinate public-police personnel in the immense crime-fighting potential of the use of intrusion alarms.

DISCUSSION QUESTIONS

1. Does the fact that 96 to 98 percent of all alarm signals are false alarms mean that alarms do not work properly 96 to 98 percent of the time? Explain your answer.
2. In your opinion, do intrusion alarms deter criminal intrusion?
3. In your opinion, what is the best kind of perimeter alarm?
4. Why are listen-in-type alarm signals unlikely to be false?
5. Explain the purpose of an alarm discriminator.
6. Can you suggest ways to lower false-alarm rates?
7. Is alarm technology ahead of or behind alarm application?
8. In your opinion, will alarm systems some day replace security guards as anti-intrusion measures?

9. Make an argument for and one against the notion of police departments' charging fees for each alarm response.
10. What part of a building is the least likely to be alarmed?

SELECTED BIBLIOGRAPHY

general

HOLOCOMB, RICHARD L., "Burglar and Hold-Up Alarm Systems: An Overview," *The Police Chief,* June 1977.

WEBER, THAD L., *Alarm Systems and Theft Prevention.* Los Angeles: Security World Publishing Co., 1973.

electromechanical systems

TRIMMER, WILLIAM H., "Magnetic Contacts From A to Z" (Parts I, II, III, and IV), issues of *Security Distributing & Marketing,* February, March, April, and May 1975. A thorough but technical article.

photoelectric beam interruption systems

FUSS, EUGENE, "Outdoor Perimeter Detection Systems—Part I, Photoelectric," *Security World,* June 1976.

vibration systems

"Buried Seismic System with Audio Listen-In Feature," *Security Distributing & Marketing,* April 1977.

FUSS, EUGENE, "Protection Systems—Part VII, Vibration Detection," *Security World,* May 1975.

seismic, pressure, and magnetic stress systems

FINKELSTEIN, A.B. "Watch Your Step!" *Security World,* June 1976.

motion-detection systems

FUSS, EUGENE, "Microwave Motion Detection," *Security World,* September 1975.

KLEIN, CARL F., "Basic Microwave Overview," *Security Distributing & Marketing,* January 1975.

audio systems

EVERETT, BILL, "Listening In Makes the Difference," *Security Distributing & Marketing*, April 1977.

FUGATE, LON, "The Sound Concept in Alarms," *Security Distributing & Marketing*, April 1977.

LUKS, HENRY J., "Audio Discrimination—Fact or Fiction?" *Security Distributing & Marketing*, April 1977.

MOORE, MICHAEL H., "Audio—Can You Afford to Be Without It?" *Security Distributing & Marketing*, April 1977.

capacitance systems

FUSS, EUGENE, "Capacitance Detection Systems," *Security World*, June 1975.

false alarms

GREENE, JERRY W., *A Comprehensive Review of the False Alarm Problem*, Oakdale, Calif.: Greene & Associates, 1976.

KELLEM, CARL, "Legislation vs. the False Alarm Problem," *Security Distributing & Marketing*, January 1978.

NEIL, J.P., "Paradox in the Alarm Industry," *Security Distributing & Marketing*, April 1976.

SHEPHERD, DONALD, "A Systems Approach for the Reduction of False Burglary and Robbery Alarms," *The Police Chief*, June 1977.

SMITH, JOSEPH L., "False Alarms—A Major Problem to Law Enforcement," *FBI Law Enforcement Bulletin*, May 1973.

WATTS, STEVEN B., "Multnomah County's False Alarm Research," *The Police Chief*, June 1977.

PART I SECURITY EXERCISE

You are a security consultant and have been asked to make specific recommendations regarding the security of ABC Industries, Incorporated. When making your recommendations, you may add any facts you consider appropriate or necessary. Do not hesitate to illustrate portions of your program by diagram.

ABC Industries, a manufacturer of CB radio units, is described as follows (refer to the diagram):

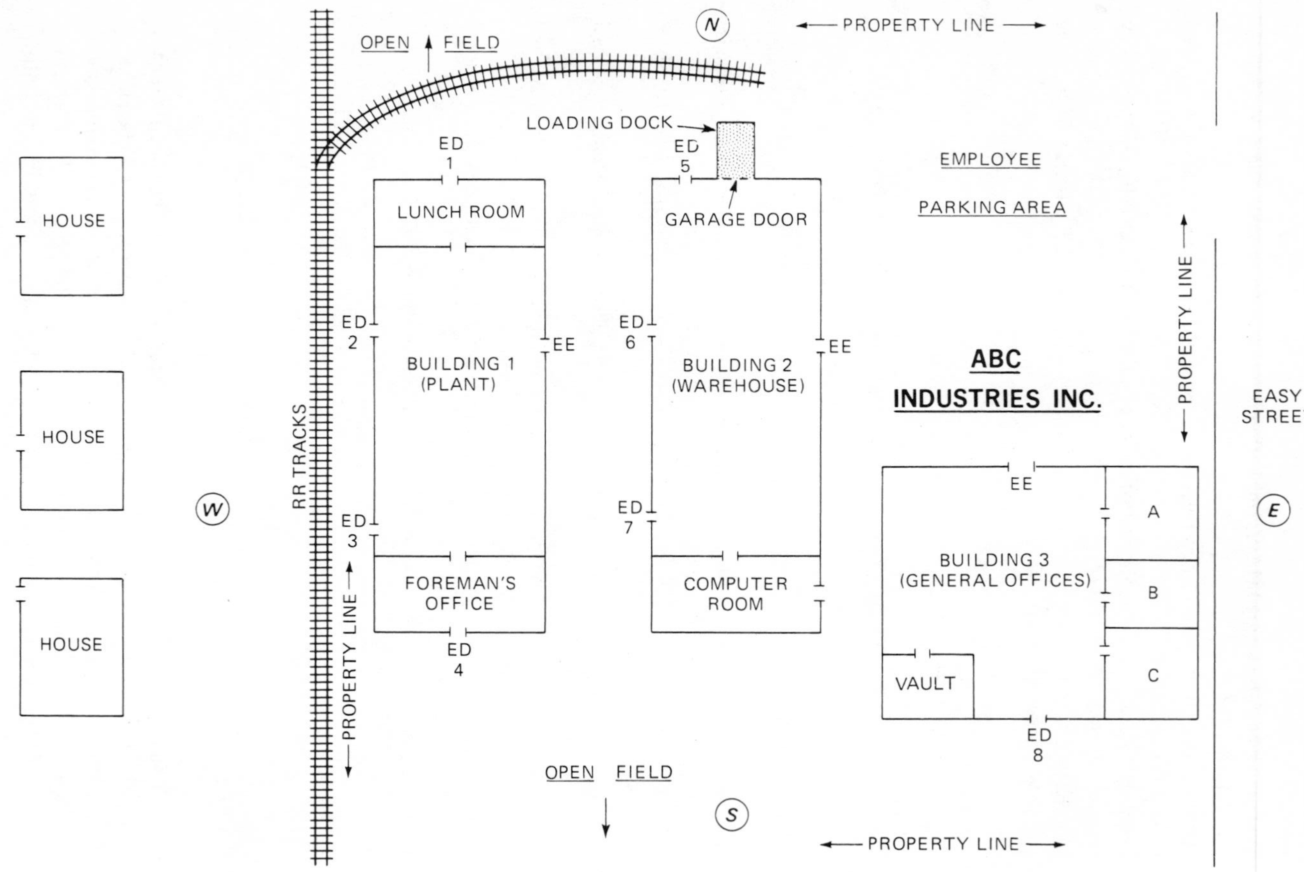
OPEN FIELD
N
PROPERTY LINE
LOADING DOCK
ED 1
ED 5
EMPLOYEE
PARKING AREA
HOUSE
LUNCH ROOM
GARAGE DOOR
ED 2
EE
BUILDING 1 (PLANT)
ED 6
EE
BUILDING 2 (WAREHOUSE)
ABC
INDUSTRIES INC.
PROPERTY LINE
EASY STREET
HOUSE
RR TRACKS
W
EE
ED 3
ED 7
A
E
BUILDING 3 (GENERAL OFFICES)
FOREMAN'S OFFICE
COMPUTER ROOM
B
HOUSE
ED 4
PROPERTY LINE
VAULT
C
ED 8
OPEN FIELD
S
PROPERTY LINE

The facility consists of Buildings 1, 2, and 3, situated on a five-acre plot in a sparsely populated and semi-isolated area on the outer limits of a small city. Building 1 is a manufacturing facility, Building 2 is a warehouse, and Building 3 is the general-office space. All the employees park in the northeast portion of ABC's property and enter the buildings through the employees' entrances marked EE on the diagram. The fire exit doors to each building are marked ED and are numbered 1–8. These exit doors, equipped with panic hardware, can be operated only from the inside. The lunchroom and foreman's office in Building 1 are equipped with lockable doors. The same applies to the two doors to the computer room in Building 2, and offices A, B, and C and the vault room in Building 3. Excluding the fire exit doors, there are eleven lockable man-doors in the facility. The large overhead door securing the loading dock can also be locked.

Easy Street runs north and south adjacent to the facility's eastern perimeter. An active railroad track runs north and south on the company's western border. Three dwellings, facing west, are situated on the western side of the property, about 150 feet from the property line. The north and south perimeters of ABC Industries face onto open fields.

ABC employs nine office people who regularly work in Building 3, Monday through Friday from 9 A.M. to 5 P.M. Five people work in Building 2 (warehouse), Monday through Saturday, 8 A.M. to 4 P.M. Fifty people work in Building 1 (plant), 25 on the first shift, 7 A.M. to 3 P.M., and 25 on the second shift, 3 P.M to 11 P.M. The facility is unoccupied during those periods when none of these shifts is in operation.

All three buildings are one story high. Building 3 has a large front window, and four standard-size windows on each of the other three sides. The only windows in Building 2 are two in the computer room. Building 1 has no windows but has skylights overhead.

In making your recommendations, take into consideration all the factors relevant to good security planning and design. For example, the cost of your program should be justifiable in terms of the degree of your protection afforded; the amount of security in any area should match the degree of criticalness or vulnerability involved; and matters such as convenience, aesthetics, and fire safety must not be sacrificed by your security program.

If there is a choice of security devices, hardware, or personnel in the solution of a particular problem, set out each alternative and note the relative strengths and weaknesses associated with each.

You have visited the facility several times. You have made the following findings of security weaknesses, and now must make corresponding security recommendations to remedy each:

1. At night, the entire five-acre ABC site is poorly lit. The only artificial light comes from a street light on Easy Street.

2. The perimeter is not protected on any side by any type of man-made barrier.
3. Neither in-house nor contract security guards are utilized at the facility.
4. None of the windows is constructed of security glazing material. They are not protected by security bars, grating, or screens. There are no window or glass alarms.
5. All the locks to the eleven man-doors are keyed alike. Every employee has a key.
6. The facility is without any type of intrusion-alarm system.
7. All nine current office employees, and five former employees, know the combination to the safe in the vault room. Three former office employees still have their company keys.
8. The owner of the company suspects that many of his blue-collar workers are leaving their work areas during their shifts with company property, which they hide in their parked cars.
9. The owner also suspects that a few of his employees are taking company property out of Buildings 1 and 2 through the exit doors and stashing it for later retrieval.
10. The warehouse foreman believes that truck drivers, while their trucks are being loaded, are stealing CB radios from Building 2.
11. The owner is worried that his employees may go on strike in three weeks. Since they all have company keys that cannot be collected once a strike is called, he wonders how he can keep them out of his buildings without changing all the locks.

PART II

RETAIL THEFT

Chapter 8

Retail Theft

AN OVERVIEW

I. The Significance of the Shoplifting Problem
   A. *The public's attitude toward shoplifting*

II. The Retail Thief—A Profile
   A. *The juvenile offender*
   B. *The housewife*
   C. *The professional shoplifter*
   D. *The kleptomaniac*
   E. *The privileged shoplifter*
   F. *The drug addict*

III. Shoplifting Laws
   A. *Elements of the offense*
      1. First fact situation
      2. Second fact situation
      3. Third fact situation
   B. *Sentencing*
   C. *Procedural aspects of the shoplifting offense*

IV. The Decision to Prosecute Shoplifters
   A. *Factors in the decision to prosecute*
      1. Age of the suspect
      2. Monetary value of the stolen merchandise

   3. A history of previous security detentions
   4. Strength of the case against the suspect
B. *Advantages and disadvantages of prosecuting shoplifters*
   1. Advantages of prosecution
   2. Disadvantages of prosecution

Retail security primarily involves the effort to prevent—or more appropriately, to reduce—the loss of merchandise through retail employee and customer theft. Part II, comprising this and the following chapter, mostly concerns customer theft; the subject of employee theft, retail or otherwise, is dealt with in Part III.

The crime of shoplifting is classified in substantive law as a larceny offense. Larceny, as distinguished from the theft-related crimes of armed robbery, bad checks, and burglary, involves stealing without the use of force, fraud, or violence and includes also such crimes as pocket-picking, purse-snatching, theft from vehicles, and theft from buildings. A shoplifter can be defined as a sneak thief who steals retail merchandise while lawfully on his victim's premises.

The Significance of the Shoplifting Problem

According to the FBI's *Uniform Crime Reports*, 6,270,800 larceny-theft offenses were reported in 1976. Of this number, 85 percent represented thefts from motor vehicles, thefts from buildings, and miscellaneous larcenies not falling within specific *UCR* offense categories. The remaining 15 percent were shoplifting, pocket-picking, thefts from coin-operated machines, and purse-snatching. According to the *UCR*, 10 percent of the larceny-theft offenses in 1976 involved shoplifting; therefore, in that year there were about 600,000 shoplifting offenses reported to the police. And according to *UCR* calculations, the average dollar value of goods stolen by shoplifters in 1976 was $39.

Using these three sets of figures, it appears that U.S. retailers suffered at least a $20 million loss that year. But studies have indicated that only one-third of all known or detected shoplifting incidents are reported to the police. Therefore, we might reasonably speculate that the monetary loss was closer to $60 million—although this figure may be somewhat high, since the unreported cases probably did not average $39 per theft.

But other calculations differ greatly. Every year, estimates of shoplifting losses are made by several organizations and agencies on behalf of the retail industry. These figures usually reflect the dollar amount of "retail shrinkage" occurring during a one-year period—inventory shortages created by dishonest customers and employees. According to a 1975 U.S. Department of Commerce publication, *Crime in Retailing*, an inventory shortage occurs when the value of the merchandise on the store's shelves is less than its book value. Unlike the *UCR* calculations, retail-industry estimations of annual shoplifting losses include those from undetected as well as known shoplifting offenses, so they are necessarily higher. For example, in 1975, the retail industry estimated that it had lost in the neighborhood of $6 billion to shoplifters. If we compare this figure to the $20 million loss attributable to detected shoplifting incidents, it appears that well over 99 percent of retail shrinkage is due to shoplifting that goes undetected at the time of its occurrence. In other words, only one out of 100 to 200 acts of shoplifting are detected when they occur.

There is no way to determine exactly what percentage of retail shrinkage is caused by customer, as opposed to employee, theft. The *UCR* provides no statistics on this, but many retail-security experts have estimated that employee theft accounts for as high as 75 percent of all shoplifting losses. And it is reasonable to assume, in the absence of data to the contrary, that both types of shoplifting occur equally undetected. For the purposes of our discussion of shoplifting, a distinction will be made between these two kinds of retail theft, and the material in this and the next chapter concerns shoplifting by retail customers.

Although customer theft accounts for only a part of all shoplifting losses, it is nevertheless a serious security problem. Because so much of it goes undetected, many aspects of this offense cannot be studied and analyzed. It is not known, for example, how many shoplifters are active at any given time, what percentage of the shopping public steals, the exact average dollar loss per theft, and which stores, by type, are the most vulnerable to the various groups and types of shoplifters. It is generally recognized, however, that the crime involves a significant portion of the public and affects every retail establishment, and a few studies have shed some light on a few aspects of the problem. The statistics and conclusions resulting from these inquiries will be referred to throughout this and the following chapter.

Most retail-security practitioners realize that generalizations regarding the frequency and volume of shoplifting offenses, as well as statistics reflecting total shoplifting monetary losses, do not necessarily have relevance to their particular function and responsibility. The extent of a particular store's vulnerability to shoplifting depends primarily upon the type of store and the nature of its clientele. In other words, national or regional shoplifting statistics will not accurately define the risk affecting any individual retail establishment.

Certain types of stores are more vulnerable to shoplifting than others. For example, a large urban supermarket may be more vulnerable than a small jewelry store in a suburban shopping center. Moreover, in discussing retail establishments, it is important to distinguish between supermarkets, variety stores (five and dimes), convenience food markets, department stores, discount stores, clothing stores, and drugstores. For example, the U.S. Department of Commerce, in its booklet *Crime in Retailing*, reports that the average annual inventory loss for a drugstore amounts to 3 percent of its yearly sales revenue. In 1974, drugstore inventory shortages totalled $500 million. This high rate of loss is due in part to the nature of drugstore merchandise such as cosmetics, costume jewelry, candy, drugs, toys, and records. In contrast, a 1976 Menswear Retailers of America survey of 9,000 participating menswear specialty stores showed a median retail shrinkage in 1975 of 1.1 percent of net sales, of which 22.1 percent occurred in the men's clothing department, 23.3 percent in sportswear areas, 26.4 percent in furnishings, and the remainder in women's, boys', teens', and shoes merchandise classifications. Other variables that may determine the risk of shoplifting include the physical design of the store and the methods by which merchandise is displayed.

Keeping these thoughts in mind, let us consider some current statistics regarding the nature and extent of the overall shoplifting problem.

In 1974, the U.S. Department of Commerce estimated that $5.8 billion worth of merchandise had been lifted from retail stores that year, an increase of more than a half-billion dollars over the preceding year. The growth of the problem is also reflected in the arrest statistics maintained by the FBI and reported in the *Uniform Crime Reports*. For example, the rate of shoplifting increased 50 percent from 1972 to 1976, with most of this increase occurring between 1972 and 1974. In all probability, this trend, in dollars lost to business as well as increased arrests, will not be reversed in the near future. Shoplifting is currently the most widespread crime affecting retail stores. Approximately 55,000 shoplifters are arrested every year in New York City alone. A survey by the Mass Retailing Institute of over 6,000 discount department stores revealed that an estimated 900,000 customers and 18,000 retail employees were apprehended for theft in 1972. This same year, the Menswear Retailers of America reported that shoplifting losses were as high as $100,000 per year in some individual stores.

A 1974 report submitted to the National Retail Merchants Association showed that out of 500 shoppers observed in a large urban department store, 42 shoplifted; that is, one out of every twelve shoppers. Other studies have corroborated these findings. Another study, also involving large urban department stores, showed one out of 20 male shoppers, and one out of 13 female, stealing from the retail establishment, with the loss per theft averaging $5.

The continued escalation of the shoplifting problem, as reflected by growing monetary losses and numbers of offenses committed each year, indicates either a security inability or an unwillingness by the retail community to prevent or detect the commission of the offense. The problem will not be solved by merely increasing the number of shoplifting arrests or the criminal prosecution of more of those caught, although these are advisable and worthwhile endeavors. It can be solved only by preventing the commission of the offense or by catching (not necessarily prosecuting) more offenders. The U.S. Department of Commerce, in *Crime in Retailing*, endorses the preventive approach to the problem by noting, "Crime prevention should be the major emphasis of a security program, since apprehension and prosecution of employees or outsiders (customer thieves) is expensive and time consuming. The costs of prosecution, as well as losses to successful thieves, can be greatly reduced through a well-designed crime-prevention program. . . ." In addition, studies have shown that the relatively mild punishment imposed upon convicted shoplifters has failed to deter the commission of the crime by people who have been convicted of it; repeat offenders are very common.

It has been estimated that at present, the cost of shoplifting accounts for an overall 15 percent increase in the price of retail goods. There is, however, a limit as to how much a retailer can pass on to his consumer. Even now, a startling number of retail establishments have gone bankrupt while struggling with the dilemma of whether to absorb shoplifting losses themselves or risk losing customers by raising prices accordingly. For example, if a store's profit margin is 2 percent of sales, the store must increase its sales by $2,500 to compensate for the theft of an article costing $50.

Shoplifting is clearly a security rather than a law-enforcement problem, and in view of its magnitude, most retailers are now looking to security for a solution.[1]

the public's attitude toward shoplifting

The attitude of the public toward shoplifting is best described as apathetic. Most consumers have little sympathy for merchants and their problems. Moreover, nonviolent crimes against property are less threatening than street crimes, so they are not uppermost in the public's mind. Shoplifting is generally thought of as a victimless type of offense that everyone, at least once in his life, has committed. As a result, the merchant should not expect customer assistance, let alone support, in his battle against retail shrinkage.

To add to his troubles, a well-meaning retailer often finds himself caught between opposing police and citizen views on shoplifting and shoplifters. To illustrate, the owner of a small convenience food market, located near a college campus, had for years suffered an extremely high percentage of inventory shrinkage as a result of student shoplifting, mostly of inexpensive items. It had been his policy, when he caught a student shoplifter, to recover the merchandise and release the offender. To combat his growing shoplifting losses, the merchant hired an off-duty police officer to patrol his store. Shortly thereafter, the officer convinced the store owner that he was not living up to his responsibilities as a citizen by releasing apprehended larcenists, so the merchant established a new policy calling for the criminal prosecution of every shoplifter caught in his store. Following this change, the owner personally caught a freshman girl leaving his store with an

---

[1]The preventive approach to shoplifting control is also costly. In 1974, a large department-store chain increased its security budget to $1.5 million and its security force to more than 150 people.

unpurchased package of lunch meat. He detained her for the police, who arrested her for shoplifting, and she was subsequently charged with this offense before a local magistrate, who set a date for her preliminary hearing. The student, under severe emotional stress, sought out the college chaplain for advice and consultation. Believing the student's story that this was her first act of dishonesty and convinced that a shoplifting conviction would ruin her life, the chaplain asked the merchant to drop the shoplifting charge. At first the store owner refused, but when the chaplain threatened to initiate a student boycott of his store, he relented and dropped the charges. The merchant tried to justify his actions to the police by explaining that 80 percent of his business came from the college, but the police were unsympathetic and warned him that crime should not go unpunished.

A few studies have been conducted to determine the reaction of an innocent shopper who witnesses an obvious shoplifting offense. These research projects usually involve sending a "shoplifter" and an observer into the store. The observer identifies those customers who have witnessed the offense and notes, among other things, whether or not the witness attempts to apprehend the thief and whether the witness reports the crime to security or store personnel. Most of these studies indicate that only a small percentage of witnesses report the crime, and that certain types of shoplifters, according to age and appearance, are more likely to be reported than others.

There are many factors that may explain why so few shoplifting incidents are reported by innocent bystanders. Some witnesses may fear being physically harmed or sued by the suspect; others would simply rather not be involved; some have an aversion to being a "snitch" or being the cause of someone else's troubles; perhaps a few applaud the retail thief, since they too are shoplifters; and finally, it is possible that because crime in general, like bad weather, has become such a regular aspect of life, it is accepted stocially by the public.

General Mills, in an effort to reverse this trend and encourage supermarket customers to report retail theft, has developed an "honesty patrol" program. Stores utilizing this service are provided with signs, brochures, press releases, and Honesty Patrol buttons. Shoppers are asked to wear these buttons and to report suspected shoplifters, and the store agrees to accept shoplifting tips anonymously, without requiring face-to-face confrontations between the reporting customers and shoplifting suspects.

The Retail Thief—A Profile

Although shoplifters' ages and backgrounds take in a wide variety of people, certain groups or types are more likely to be involved in the crime than others. In formulating profiles of typical shoplifters, retail-security practitioners have established several categories that, put together, account for almost every violator. However, one shoplifter may fall within several or none of these standard categories.

From a practical standpoint, a retail-security practitioner is interested in the profile of the shoplifter most likely to patronize the establishment under his control. By studying the categories of shoplifters and the characteristics associated with each, he can identify the groups most likely to victimize his store and initiate a security program specifically designed to protect his most vulnerable areas. Moreover, such knowledge will help him decide not only how much security to use, but what kinds of security personnel, hardware, and/or procedures are the most appropriate.

An extreme example of how shoplifter-profile awareness affects the formulation of a security procedure is a test that was conducted by two New York stores whereby they refused to admit children under the age of 15 unless they were accompanied by an adult. This procedure obviously reflected the practitioner's belief that a substantial number of his shoplifters were the very young.

the juvenile offender

Every study, survey, and set of arrest statistics indicates that shoplifting is primarily a crime of the young. It has been estimated that 78 percent of all shoplifters are under 30. According to *UCR* statistics, over 50 percent of larceny-theft offenders caught in 1976 were in their teens, 43 percent under age 18. Almost all juvenile shoplifters are amateurs who steal for kicks or status, or out of a personal need or desire for the stolen item. Various studies have shown that at least one out of every ten juvenile shoppers in a retail establishment will steal; that the most common juvenile shoplifting incident, by type of offender and item stolen, involves the teenage girl taking cosmetics; that most juvenile shoplifters prefer to steal in variety and discount stores; and that these offenders are frequently accompanied by three or four fellow shoplifters or accomplices.

It is a widely held belief that a significant percentage of juvenile offenders who have been caught stealing many times by store and security personnel continue to steal without fear of detection or police arrest. Although they normally steal items of small monetary value, the frequency with which they commit the crime, as well as the large number of offenders involved, causes juvenile shoplifting by itself to be a substantial security problem.

A private survey of shoplifting in 1973 was conducted by Commercial Service Systems, Inc., for several retail clients. The survey involved 17,876 shoplifting apprehensions made in 675 supermarkets, 75 drugstores, and 28 discount stores. Here are some of its findings relative to the ages of shoplifters: In 1973, over 40 percent of the shoplifters arrested in supermarkets and over half of those arrested in drugstores were 12 to 17 years of age. Although there were slightly more people in the United States over 60 that year than there were 12 to 17, only 7.2 percent of supermarket and 4.6 percent of drugstore arrests involved people over 60. The survey also showed that juveniles (people under 18) stole less per theft in dollar value than adults did. For example, the average value of the merchandise recovered per juvenile apprehension was $2.47 in supermarkets and $3.07 in drugstores, whereas adult averages were $5.75 and $7.90 respectively.[2]

It should be noted that this survey, and every other of its kind conducted since 1969, involves shoplifting *apprehensions*. Therefore, the statistics indicate the ages of shoplifters most frequently caught, not, say, what portion of total retail losses are caused by individual groups of offenders. And the statistics showing that juveniles as a group steal more than their share might indicate merely that young people are easier to catch than adults.

the housewife

Next to the juvenile offender, the housewife is considered to be the most frequent shoplifter. Because housewives generally do most of the family shopping, they are as a group the most frequent visitors to retail establishments, particularly supermarkets and other food stores. Like juvenile offenders, most shoplifting housewives are amateur thieves, without criminal backgrounds.

Dishonest housewives often justify their theft by citing what they consider to be unreasonably high and unfair retail prices. The theft is therefore the housewife's way of getting even with the retailer. Unemployed husbands, personal problems, and the need to make a limited budget go further are a few of the other, more common justifications.

Numerous studies have indicated that up to one out of every ten housewives steals from a retail establishment. It has also been determined that at the time of her arrest, almost every suspected housewife was in possession of enough money to pay for the merchandise she had stolen. The most common shoplifting techniques of housewives are concealment of merchandise in a purse, shopping bag, or umbrella, or under a heavy outer garment.

It is interesting to note that in France, a Paris newspaper study showed middle-aged women to be the worst shoplifting offenders and that most of them felt no guilt and did not steal out of need.

the professional shoplifter

Professional shoplifters, both male and female, are more likely to have backgrounds of arrests for other theft-related crimes. A professional shoplifter, as distinguished from most amateur offenders, steals strictly for monetary gain, so he selects more expensive items that can be easily resold or fenced. Most retail-security experts agree that as a group, professional shoplifters prefer to steal from large department and discount stores.

However, professional shoplifters are comparatively few in number, and

---

[2]Commercial Service Systems, Inc., P.O. Box 3307, Van Nuys, California 91407.

because they commit their crimes with a certain degree of skill and know-how, few are caught. For example, they can usually spot most antishoplifting measures and devices, so they avoid electronic and personal surveillance and do not attempt to steal merchandise protected by retail alarm sensors. Items such as expensive clothing, jewelry, cameras, small applicances, radios, small television sets, tape recorders, and guns should be especially protected from professional shoplifters.

the kleptomaniac

Although it is not unusual for an apprehended shoplifter to plead kleptomania, this malady is rare. Kleptomania is defined generally as a mental illness characterized by the psychological compulsion to steal. An actual case history will illustrate the nature of this illness and the effect it has on the retail community.

A 50-year-old woman was arrested following the confiscation by the police of $25,000 worth of retail merchandise from her home. She admitted stealing the merchandise, amounting to several hundred articles, from 30 area retail establishments over a period of eight years. The recovered items ranged from minicomputers to automobile wheel covers, and included expensive furs and glassware. The police determined that it had been stolen from department, book, hardware, sports, jewelry, discount, variety, and clothing stores.

Over the years, the suspect had disposed of her loot by periodic "household sales" at which the stolen merchandise was offered at half its regular price. These sales, held at the woman's residence, were advertised in the local newspaper. Shoppers who responded were usually surprised to find new merchandise being sold, some of it with price tags identifying the victim stores.

Following her arrest, the suspect admitted to the police that she had stolen, in addition to the recovered merchandise, another $15,000 worth of goods from local merchants, and that she had always suffered from the urge to steal. It was also learned that prior to her arrest, she had been caught stealing on numerous occasions by security personnel who, after recovering the property in her possession, had released her without notifying the authorities. As a result of her shoplifting activity, the woman's children refused to live with her, and they refused to shop with her after she stole repeatedly in their presence.

The police investigation further revealed that the suspect had no apparent need for the items she took. In the light of this and the other features of the case, kleptomania was considered to be the only reasonable explanation for this woman's criminal behavior. And following her arrest in this case, she continued her shoplifting activity, as evidenced by her subsequent apprehension by retail-security personnel.

The criminal prosecution of a kleptomaniac may present the district attorney with a problem when it becomes necessary to rebut the defense of insanity. Moreover, it appears that kleptomaniacs as a group are the least likely to be deterred by criminal prosecution. In view of these facts it would seem that the only security solution to the effects of kleptomania is the implementation of purely preventive measures.

the privileged shoplifter

Privileged shoplifter is a term used to describe a particular group of thieves who are neither retail employees nor customers of their victims. In this category are vendor salesmen, delivery men, visiting buyers, and former retail employees. A pilferer in one of these groups, by virtue of his ability to move in and out of the store without arousing suspicion, is privileged. More important, people in this group often have access to areas within the store that are not open to the shopping public.

Because he steals merchandise from the stockroom or from behind counters, the privileged shoplifter is not easily detected by most antishoplifting hardware and personnel. And he has the advantage of being familiar with the physical layout of the store, with the identity and work schedules of the guards and floorwalkers, and more than likely with the existence and location of electronic surveillance and alarm equipment.

Although there are no statistics as to what percentage of shoplifting losses are created by privileged shoplifters, every retail-security practitioner will agree that their contribution to retail shrinkage is substantial.

the drug addict

Shoplifters who are drug addicts can be generally characterized as numerous, desperate, and dangerous. It is not unusual for a them to steal openly, then flee the store. Their motivation is obvious: to support the cost of a drug habit. For this reason, narcotics users steal items that will bring the most cash from fences and other receivers of stolen property. These shoplifters are usually young and often have arrest records.

Shoplifting Laws

The discussion in this section involves an analysis and comparison of several state shoplifting statutes, including substantive as well as procedural aspects.

elements of the offense

Section 3929 of Title 18, Consolidated Pennsylvania Statutes, entitled *Retail theft*, reads:

a. A person is guilty of retail theft if he:
   1. takes possession of any merchandise offered for sale by any store or other retail mercantile establishment with the intention of converting it to his own use without paying to the owner the value thereof; or
   2. alters, transfers or removes any label, price tag or marking upon any merchandise offered for sale by any store or other retail mercantile establishment; or
   3. transfers any merchandise offered for sale by any store or other retail mercantile establishment from the container in or on which the same shall be displayed to any other container with intent to deprive the owner of all, or some part of the value thereof.

In Pennsylvania, as in most states, the crime of shoplifting is established whenever the offender commits an act consisting of either unlawful taking, price-tag switching, or package changing or alteration. The most common method of retail theft is the removal of the merchandise from the store by the shoplifter. If there is any difficulty in establishing the elements of the offense, it is usually in proving the suspect's *intention* to steal the item found in his possession. The central or material element in all shoplifting statutes, as well as in every other larceny-related crime, is unlawful taking, but in Pennsylvania, in order to prove this material element, the prosecution must prove that the suspect took possession of the merchandise "with the intention of converting it to his own use. . . ." And because it is obviously impossible to ascertain what is going on inside another person's head, the suspect's evil state of mind, if it is to be proven, must be inferred from his actions.

Although outward human behavior is often indicative of the actor's mental state, a person's actions can be misleading. At one time, almost every shoplifting statute required as proof of intent that the suspect leave the premises without paying for the merchandise. However, the mere fact that a customer has left the store without paying for the goods in his possession may simply indicate that he forgot to pay for it, so this statutory guideline, if applied arbitrarily in every instance without further consideration, could result in the arrest of an innocent person. Therefore, most states have incorporated a more appropriate guideline into their shoplifting statutes. The Pennsylvania statute contains the following language regarding this matter:

> (c) Presumptions.—Any person intentionally concealing unpurchased property of any store or other mercantile establishment, either on the premises or outside the premises of such store, shall be prima facie presumed to have so concealed such property with the intention of converting it to his own use without paying the purchase price thereof within the meaning of subsection (a) of this section, and the finding of such unpurchased property concealed upon the person or among the belongings of such person shall be prima facie evidence of intentional concealment, and, if such person conceals, or causes to be concealed, such unpurchased property,

upon the person or among the belongings of another, such fact shall also be prima facie evidence of intentional concealment on the part of the person so concealing such property.

The fact that the concealment of merchandise presumes theft means that the suspect, if he can convince the judge or jury that the concealment was motivated by something other than his intention to steal the merchandise, will be found not guilty of the offense. However, in most states, once the concealment element is established, the presumption places the suspect in the position of having to prove that he did not intend to steal the merchandise.

The Illinois shoplifting statute says, with regard to the presumption of theft:

Section 16A-4. P.

If any person:

(a) Conceals upon his person, or among his belongings, unpurchased merchandise displayed, held, stored or offered for sale in a retail mercantile establishment; and

(b) removes that merchandise beyond the last known station for receiving payments for that merchandise in that retail mercantile establishment, such person shall be presumed to have possessed, carried away or transferred such merchandise with the intention of retaining it or with the intention of depriving the merchant permanently of the possession, use or benefit of such merchandise without paying the full retail value of such merchandise.

Under this statute, which is more specific in this area than the Pennsylvania statute, concealment *and* removal of the merchandise past the payout area create a presumption of theft. In Illinois, as in Pennsylvania, the arrest can legally be made inside the store. In Illinois, the term *conceal* is defined under Section 16A-2.1, which states, "To conceal merchandise means that, although there may be some notice of its presence, that merchandise is not visible through ordinary observation."

The fact situations set out below show that the nature of the concealment itself usually indicates whether or not the suspect intended to steal the merchandise. Acts of concealment clearly indicating a suspect's intention to steal are statutorily defined, in many states, as the "wilful" concealment of merchandise. A retail-security practitioner, in evaluating the relative strength of a shoplifting case, or in deciding whether or not to make a shoplifting arrest, should consider the nature of the concealment itself in terms of the most reasonable inferences to be drawn from it.

First Fact Situation. Larry, aged 16, is standing near a display case that contains watches and other jewelry. The floorwalker, who has been observing Larry as he wanders aimlessly about the discount store, notices that he had spotted a watch that was left on top of the display case by a careless sales employee. Larry continues to meander, while remaining close to the display case. When the salesclerk temporarily leaves the area, Larry looks frantically about, quickly takes possession of the watch, and shoves it into his right shoe. Immediately, he walks briskly toward the main exit. He is stopped and confronted by the floorwalker before he reaches the cash-register area. When he is asked to remove his right shoe, Larry retrieves the watch and hands it over to the floorwalker. He insists that he fully intended to pay for the watch.

Second Fact Situation. Sally and her high school classmates are being watched as they browse about the main floor of a downtown department store. As Sally's two friends are being shown cosmetics by a helpful salesclerk, the floorwalker sees Sally remove a small bottle of perfume from the display area. After examining it for a few seconds, she places it in her handbag. She and her associates continue to examine cosmetic products, and Sally eventually selects an item she wishes to purchase. After the salesclerk handles this transaction, Sally and her friends start to leave the area, and Sally is confronted by the floorwalker, who removes the bottle of perfume from her purse. Sally informs the floorwalker that she forgot to include the perfume in her purchase.

Third Fact Situation. Mr. Smith is hurriedly shopping in a discount store. He is wearing a conservative suit and overcoat. After examining a pair of leather gloves, he places them in one of his overcoat pockets. The price tags, hanging from his pocket, catch the floorwalker's attention. Mr. Smith continues to shop. When he arrives at the cash-out counter, he is fumbling with an armful of items he intends to purchase. Upon completion of the sales transaction, Mr. Smith leaves the store with the unpurchased gloves still in his coat pocket. He is confronted in the parking lot by the floorwalker, who recovers the gloves. Mr. Smith asserts that he forgot to include the gloves with the other items he purchased in the store.

sentencing

The Pennsylvania retail-theft statute contains the following penalty provision:

b. Grading—
   1. Any person committing the first offense of retail theft when the value of the merchandise is less than $100 is guilty of a summary offense.
   2. Upon conviction of a second offense when the value of the merchandise is less than $100, the person shall be guilty of a misdemeanor of the second degree.
   3. Upon commission of a third or any subsequent offense, regardless of the value of the merchandise, the person shall be guilty of a misdemeanor of the first degree.

4. When the value of the merchandise shall be $100 or more, any person who shall commit the offense of retail theft, whether same shall be a first or subsequent offense, shall be guilty of a misdemeanor of the first degree.

An analysis of this provision indicates that in Pennsylvania, the severity of the punishment for violating the shoplifting law is determined by two factors: the value of the merchandise stolen, and how many times, if any, the offender has been previously convicted of this crime. A first offender, convicted of shoplifting an inexpensive item, can receive a maximum sentence of 90 days in jail and a $300 fine. A second conviction on a small theft can bring a sentence of up to two years in jail with a $5,000 fine. A third conviction carries a maximum sentence of five years in jail and a $10,000 fine. And when a Pennsylvania shoplifter is convicted of stealing an item worth $100 or more, first offense or otherwise, the maximum punishment is five years in jail and a fine of $10,000.

This statute reflects a legislative intent to discourage repeat offenders and the theft of expensive merchandise. It is interesting to note, however, that in view of the relative sentences involved, a shoplifter would be better off stealing two $75 items from two stores rather than one $150 piece of merchandise, since if he is caught on each occasion, the maximum penalty for stealing the two $75 items would be two jail sentences of two years each, whereas conviction on the single $150 theft would call for a maximum sentence of five years. Both convictions would give rise to the same fine.

In Arkansas, penalties for shoplifting are governed by the following statutory provisions:

> 41-3939. *Shoplifting—Penalty*. Any person who shall wilfully take possession of any goods, wares or merchandise offered for sale by any store or other mercantile establishment with the intention of converting the same to his own use without paying the purchase price thereof, shall be guilty of the offense of shoplifting and shall be punished by a fine of not less than twenty-five ($25.00) dollars and not more than fifty ($50.00) dollars and/or imprisonment of not less than five (5) days and not more than thirty (30) days, or both for the first offense.
>
> 41-3940. *Second offense—Penalty*. Any person found guilty of a second offense of shoplifting as defined in Section 1 (41-3939) of this Act, shall be punished by a fine of not less than fifty ($50.00) dollars and not more than one hundred ($100.00) dollars and imprisonment of not less than thirty (30) days and not more than ninety (90) days.
>
> 41-3941. *Third offense—Penalty*. Any person found guilty of a third offense of shoplifting shall be punished by imprisonment for not less than one (1) year nor more than five (5) years.

In Arkansas, the severity of the punishment does not relate to the value of the stolen merchandise but rather to the offender's history of past shoplifting offenses. First and second offenders in Arkansas receive light sentences compared to those in Pennsylvania, while third offenses in both states call for rather stiff penalties. The fines in Arkansas, for all types of offenders, are minimal.

The Florida shoplifting statute contains a penalty provision that increases the severity of a shoplifter's sentence if he "resists the reasonable effort of a peace officer, merchant or the merchant's employee to recover merchandise which the peace officer, merchant or the merchant's employee had probable cause to believe the individual had concealed or removed from its place or display or elsewhere. . . ."

In Nevada, convicted shoplifters are not only punished criminally but also subject to a civil suit by the victim retailer; the parents of a minor caught shoplifting may also be liable to the retailer for civil damages. But before a merchant in Nevada can take advantage of the right to bring such criminal and civil actions, he must post a notice to this effect in his store.

The California and Illinois shoplifting statutes also hold that parents of shoplifting minors can be held civilly liable. Under California law, however, a minor may be required by the juvenile court to perform public services, and adults who have been convicted of shoplifting may be requested to do likewise in lieu of a fine.

procedural aspects of the shoplifting offense

The Pennsylvania retail-theft provision details, among other things, the steps retail and security personnel can take pursuant to the handling of shoplifting suspects. According to the provision, Pennsylvania merchants, or those acting on their behalf, assuming that they have probable cause to act, may do the following:

1. Reasonably detain the suspect in or out of the store
2. Require the suspect to identify himself
3. Verify the suspect's identity
4. Search the suspect for unpurchased merchandise belonging to the store
5. Recover stolen merchandise found in the suspect's possession
6. Summon the police for the purpose of pressing criminal charges

This provision gives the merchant statutory protection against civil tort liability in the areas of libel, slander, false arrest, and malicious prosecution if he has acted in good faith. The fact that the merchant had reasonable grounds to believe as he did will suffice to establish good faith on his part; that is, his suspicions need not be correct, just honest and understandable. The legislative intent is to encourage the merchant to aggressively protect his assets from shoplifters.

The relevant portion of California's shoplifting law (Section 1, 490.5 [e]) states:

1. A merchant may detain a person for a reasonable time for the purpose of conducting an investigation in a reasonable manner whenever the merchant has probable cause to believe the person to be detained is attempting to unlawfully take or has unlawfully taken merchandise from the merchant's premises.
2. In making the detention a merchant may use a reasonable amount of non-deadly force necessary to protect himself and to prevent escape of the person detained or the loss of property.
3. During the period of detention any items which a merchant has reasonable cause to believe are unlawfully taken from his premises and which are in plain view may be examined by the merchant for the purpose of ascertaining the ownership thereof.
4. In any action for false arrest, false imprisonment, slander or unlawful detention brought by any person detained by a merchant, it shall be a defense to such action that the merchant detaining such person had probable cause to believe that the person had stolen or attempted to steal merchandise and that the merchant acted reasonably under all the circumstances.

In Montana, the merchant is protected by the following retail-theft provision:

> 64-213. *Right of merchant to request individuals to keep merchandise in full view—freedom from liability.* Any merchant shall have the right to request any individual on his premises to place or keep in full view any merchandise such individual may have removed, or which the merchant has reason to believe he may have removed, from its place of display or elsewhere, whether for examination, purchase, or for any other purpose. No merchant shall be criminally or civilly liable for slander, false arrest, or otherwise on account of having made such a request.

The following provision of the Wisconsin retail-theft statute defines and limits the actions a merchant or security practitioner can take to detain a suspected shoplifter:

> 939.49. *Defense of property and protection against shoplifting.* (1) A person is privileged to threaten or intentionally use force against another for the purpose of preventing or terminating what he reasonably believes to be

an unlawful interference with his property. Only such degree of force or threat thereof may intentionally be used as the actor reasonably believes is necessary to prevent or terminate the interference. It is not reasonable to intentionally use force intended or likely to cause death or great bodily harm for the sole purpose of defense of one's property.

(2) A person is privileged to defend a third person's property from real or apparent unlawful interference by another under the same conditions and by the same means as those under and by which he is privileged to defend his own property from real or apparent unlawful interference, provided that he reasonably believes that the facts are such as would give the third person the privilege to defend his own property, that his intervention is necessary for the protection of the third person's property, and that the third person whose property he is protecting is a member of his immediate family or household or a person whose property he has a legal duty to protect, or is a merchant and the actor is the merchant's employe or agent.

In summary, Pennsylvania, Illinois, Nevada, and California have the strongest antishoplifting laws.

Appendix A contains selected briefs of court decisions involving shoplifting offenses. These decisions raise and discuss issues dealing with false arrest, malicious prosecution, and slander in connection with the arrest and handling of suspected shoplifters.

The Decision to Prosecute Shoplifters

Few retail-security programs, at least in practice, reflect a rigid policy of either releasing or prosecuting every shoplifter caught. Although many of the smaller retail establishments handle their offenders on a case-by-case basis, most organized antishoplifting programs are characterized by preestablished guidelines upon which a retail-security practitioner can rely in making this decision. The material that follows consists of the identification and discussion of these criteria, and the rationale behind them.

factors in the decision to prosecute

Age of the Suspect. Studies show that apprehended juveniles are less likely to be turned over to the police than adult offenders, indicating that the age of the suspect is an important consideration in the decision of whether to prosecute.[3] Even merchants who believe in prosecuting every shoplifter may nevertheless draw the

---

[3]Commercial Service Systems, Inc., study results.

line with regard to young offenders. Those 12 years old or under are usually released by the merchant or security personnel, often after notifying the child's parents or having the child himself phone them. When speaking to the parents, retail-security practitioners usually avoid characterizing the child as a shoplifter or thief.

When a merchant calls the police or notifies a magistrate to initiate the criminal prosecution of a 12-year-old suspect, the juvenile authorities are usually bypassed through the immediate release of the child to his parents by the police or at the directive of the magistrate. As a result, nothing is gained by notifying the authorities in cases involving very young offenders, and it may also result in criticism of the merchant, which could be bad for business.

A more difficult decision concerns whether or not to notify the authorities in cases involving offenders 13 to 16 years old. Shoplifters in this age group are processed through the criminal justice system as juvenile offenders, a fact that may or may not have relevance to the merchant in his decision. A retailer may feel that juvenile offenders are not really punished by the system, and therefore, nothing is gained by his taking the time and money to prosecute. Or he may prosecute in the hope of creating a deterrent effect.

Aside from the question of retribution or general deterrence, a great number of offenders in this age group are released because the merchant or retail-security practitioner believes that the youth has been frightened by being caught, and so will not commit the offense again, or that prosecution will unnecessarily jeopardize the child's future. A street-wary juvenile offender may take advantage of a merchant's naiveté by pretending fear and concern about the adverse effect a shoplifting arrest and conviction will have on his future. But it appears that because of their increased awareness of teenage shoplifting and its contribution to retail shrinkage, merchants are becoming more willing to turn apprehended juvenile offenders over to the authorities.

Monetary Value of the Stolen Merchandise. Most, if not all, state retail-theft statutes classify shoplifting violations according to the value of the stolen merchandise, reflecting the idea that the larger the theft, the more serious the crime. This notion, under certain circumstances, may also influence a merchant's decision to prosecute. For example, a 14-year-old girl is caught stealing in a store that prosecutes most of its shoplifters. The suspect's tender years make the decision to prosecute more difficult, but the fact that she has taken a $200 camera, concealing it in her purse, may tip the scales in favor of notifying the authorities.

A History of Previous Security Detentions. Most retail-security departments and practitioners make and maintain a record of each shoplifting incident detected and handled in their store, whether reported to the police or not. These security reports, usually filed alphabetically by the suspect's name and kept according to the year of the incident, constitute the only written record of the offense in a substantial percentage of detected shoplifting incidents. The reasons behind and the uses of these reporting systems and records are numerous, but they are frequently utilized to help the security practitioner or merchant decide, in a particular case, if prosecution should be initiated. The fact that an apprehended shoplifter has been caught stealing in the store several times before, although such private records cannot be used as evidence in court, may at least indicate to the merchant that criminal prosecution, if not sought previously in connection with this person, is now warranted, and may give him the confidence and desire to pursue the matter further.

The sample retail-theft data sheet in Figure 8-1 illustrates the type of

FILE NO.__________

DATE__________

SUBJECT: ____________________________________, AKA__________
[last name, middle initial, first name]

ADDRESS:________________________________ PHONE:__________

EMPLOYED:____
[if juvenile, name of school and grade]

PARENT OR SPOUSE:__________________________________

ADDRESS:____

DESCRIPTION:

DOB__________, SEX______, EYES______, HT______, WT__________
[month, day, yr.]

HAIR________, SCARS/MARKS______________________________
[include any other characteristics]

SOCIAL SECURITY NUMBER____________________.

DATE APPREHENDED______________, PLACE APPRHENDED__________________

BY WHOM______________________________, POLICE CALLED YES_____NO_____

CONFESSION FURNISHED?_____YES_____NO.

BRIEF ACCOUNT OF ARREST AND SUSPECTED THEFT: [include description of items taken]

DISPOSITION OF CASE:

FIGURE 8-1. Sample shoplifter data sheet

information normally collected and maintained by security practitioners in shoplifting cases.

Strength of the Case against the Suspect. A retail-security practitioner should never confront and detain a shoplifting suspect unless he is absolutely certain in his own mind that the suspect has merchandise in his possession that he intends to steal. The practitioner's belief should be based upon his firsthand observation of the suspect's actions, his knowledge and ability to correctly apply the appropriate retail-theft statute to the facts at hand, and a reasonable interpretation, predicated upon his security experience, of the suspect's demeanor as reflecting his criminal intent. If a shoplifting arrest meets these criteria and there is no store policy to the contrary, criminal prosecution should be initiated even when the suspect has denied his guilt and there were no other witnesses to the crime.

Although a security practitioner may be tempted to release suspects who convincingly profess their innocence, these types of cases, more than any other, should be taken to court. When the practitioner shows weakness or doubt by releasing such a suspect, he can reasonably anticipate a false-arrest suit; and if he is named as a defendant in the action, his failure to criminally prosecute the shoplifting suspect, contrary to the merchant's policy, may be used as evidence to substantiate the false-arrest complaint. Thus, the evidentiary strength of a shoplifting case, assuming a good-faith arrest based upon the firsthand observation of every substantive element of the retail-theft statute, should not be the sole basis of a decision not to prosecute.

On occasion, a retail-security practitioner will confront a person he believes may be in possession of unpurchased merchandise even though he has not witnessed the theft. Realizing that he might be wrong in his suspicion, he may decide in advance that if his suspect is not in possession of the merchandise, or if the suspect strongly denies that it was his intention to steal the items found on his person, he will not initiate criminal prosecution; but he will press criminal charges if, in addition to catching the suspect with unpurchased goods, he elicits a confession from him. By operating in this fashion, the security practitioner may feel that he has nothing to lose, but everything to gain by recovering merchandise that would otherwise be lost to the store, and that he might also secure, in the process, the suspect's criminal conviction.

Such a practice is inadvisable for many reasons. One reason is the probability that the practitioner will eventually arrest a suspect who is not in possession of unpurchased merchandise and who, in addition to denying his guilt, may also threaten to file a civil suit against the security officer and the store. Under these circumstances, unless he is willing to commit perjury in order to establish a good-faith arrest, the security officer must release the suspect and ponder how he is going to explain to the court why he did not file criminal charges in this case. He will also be asked by the court to explain why the alleged stolen merchandise was not on the suspect's person at the time of the confrontation and detention.

advantages and disadvantages of prosecuting shoplifters

It should be kept in mind that to effectively control or solve the shoplifting problem, improvements must be made in the areas of prevention and detection rather than in the prosecution of shoplifters.

Advantages of Prosecution. The prosecution of shoplifters, to the extent that it may to some degree deter shoplifting, can be considered a preventive measure. Many shoplifters avoid stores that have reputations for prosecuting apprehended retail thieves. Before they can be prosecuted, however, they have to be sought out and caught. The effort to catch shoplifters will result in the detection of more crime and the recovery of more merchandise, an economic benefit that may well offset the cost of the security effort. And once a store has decided that the better approach to retail-theft control is to catch shoplifters rather than preventing the offense, their retail-security policy should also include prosecuting those who are caught. In addition to its deterrent effect, such a policy bolsters security morale, through both retribution and protection against civil suits.

The legislative bodies in many states have enacted shoplifting statutes calling for relatively severe penalties for repeat offenders. In the eyes of the law, however, a repeat offender is one who has been previously convicted of the offense, not merely caught committing it. So before the merchant can take advantage of these more serious shoplifting penalties, he must establish a criminal record for each offender through the prosecution of the shoplifters he catches.

Merchants in several localities, in an effort to protect themselves against habitual shoplifters, have worked with the police and other agencies to make offender information more readily available to interested parties and the courts. One method of achieving this end is by the establishment of a central clearinghouse where records of shoplifter convictions are received, maintained, and disseminated to authorized persons.

Disadvantages of Prosecution. If a store is not going to prosecute shoplifters, the only acceptable alternative is to initiate a security program geared to the prevention of the offense. There are many advantages to the preventive approach. The most persuasive argument is the fact that prevention is usually less costly for the retailer than shoplifter-apprehension programs.

The cost associated with the use of retail floorwalkers is high. Unlike many other antishoplifting measures, it is also a continuing expense; in addition to training and wage-related expenses, it involves the added cost of insurance protection to cover such activity.

The prosecution of a suspected shoplifter is a time-consuming and therefore costly procedure. Once the shoplifter is caught, time must be taken to extract a written confession from him, to notify the authorities, and to file criminal charges.

In many jurisdictions, floorwalkers have to file their own criminal complaints, a practice that requires more time and results in additional inconvenience. Whenever the suspected shoplifter pleads not guilty, the floorwalker must appear at the hearing or trial as the prosecuting witness. In many instances, salesclerks are taken from their work to testify as witnesses to the offense.[4]

The process of criminally prosecuting shoplifters also detracts, in many instances, from the effectiveness of the crime-fighting effort itself. In stores that can afford only one floorwalker on duty at a time, the premises are virtually unprotected whenever the floorwalker is in the security office interviewing a suspected thief.

In most instances, the wisdom of floorwalker use as an antishoplifting technique is questionable when compared to some of the other more effective and less costly measures. For example, the amount of territory one floorwalker can cover is limited. And floorwalkers are apt to spot, observe, and apprehend only the most obvious offenders; professional thieves often identify them and therefore avoid their surveillance. Moreover, those shoplifters whose activities have been only partially observed by the floorwalker will not, for obvious reasons, be confronted. As a result, some of the larger thefts go undetected, and others, although detected, are not handled at all.

It is not unusual for a merchant to learn that some of his most regular and substantial customers are stealing his merchandise. Under these circumstances, he may doubt the economic wisdom of criminally prosecuting these offenders; he may choose to "rehabilitate" them and so keep them as customers. It is doubtful, however, that a shoplifter will be "rehabilitated" through the merchant's failure to prosecute. Retailers who subscribe to this policy retain their customers at their own expense.

In summary, if floorwalker use is the only method for apprehending shoplifters for prosecution, then prosecution may not be the most effective or economic solution to controlling retail theft. However, since there are definite advantages to criminally prosecuting shoplifters, other methods of catching them will be considered in the following chapters, along with some preventive antishoplifting measures and devices.

DISCUSSION QUESTIONS

1. Would the criminal prosecution of every shoplifter who is caught significantly reduce retail shrinkage? Explain your answer.
2. Considering police–security relationships and functions, do retail-security practitioners augment or complement existing law-enforcement efforts?

---

[4]In an effort to speed up processing of shoplifters through the court system, the city of Chicago has established a special shoplifter's court. The "Chicago System" is discussed in full in Chapter 9.

3. Does the police function in any way complement security's antishoplifting efforts?
4. With regard to the fact situations given under "Elements of the Offense," which of these three situations, in your opinion, most clearly indicates "wilful" concealment? Justify your answer.
5. In addition to the nature of the method used by a suspected shoplifter to conceal unpurchased merchandise, what other behavioral patterns are relevant in determining whether he intended to steal the property?
6. Under the Pennsylvania retail-theft statute, would Mr. Smith (third fact situation) have a good chance of winning a civil suit brought against the store for false arrest? Explain your answer pursuant to your interpretation of the relevant statutory provision.
7. Draft a statutory provision establishing penalties for shoplifting that you consider to be the most appropriate. Be prepared to defend your law in terms of its fairness and effectiveness in dealing with the retail-theft problem.
8. What is the legislative intent behind Wisconsin's statutory provision dealing with the use of force to protect property?
9. Formulate a written security policy containing guidelines defining who shall be criminally prosecuted for shoplifting.
10. In your opinion, which of the following factors, or which combination of factors, is the most important in deciding whether or not to prosecute a juvenile offender? Justify your answer.
    a. The age of the offender
    b. The sex of the offender
    c. Whether or not the offender has an arrest record
    d. Whether or not the offender has been caught in the store before
    e. The shoplifter's attitude
    f. The monetary value of the stolen merchandise
    g. The strength of the case against the offender
11. Describe a "good-faith" shoplifting arrest.

SELECTED BIBLIOGRAPHY

BROTHERS, J., "Why Girls Steal," *Good Housekeeping*, February 1973, p. 64.

CREEDEN, JOHN J., "Shoplifting—As Seen by a Professional," *Security Management*, July 1977.

EDWARDS, LOREN E., *Shoplifting and Shrinkage Protection for Stores*. Springfield, Ill.: Charles C Thomas, 1970. This book contains an excellent discussion of kleptomania in Chapter 5.

FEIN, SHERMAN E., and ARTHUR M. MASKELL, *Selected Cases on the Law of Shoplifting*. Springfield, Ill.: Charles C Thomas, 1975.

HELLMAN, P., "One in Ten Shoppers Is a Shoplifter," *New York Times Magazine*, March 15, 1970, pp. 34–35.

RAKSTIS, T. J., "Why Our Kids Steal," *Today's Health*, December 1970.

ROGERS, KEITH M., *Coping with Shoplifters*. Los Angeles: Security World Publishing Co. (no date).

U.S. DEPARTMENT OF COMMERCE, *Crime in Retailing*, Washington, D.C., 1975. This booklet is an analysis of the available data on the various crimes committed against retailers. In addition to customer and retail-employee theft, it covers the subjects of burglary, robbery, vandalism, bad checks, credit-card fraud, and arson, and it also describes some of the techniques and programs retailers can implement to combat these crimes.

WEINSTEIN, G.W., "Truth about Teenage Shoplifting," *Parents Magazine*, April 1974.

Chapter 9

Controlling Retail Theft

AN OVERVIEW

I. Common Shoplifting Methods and Techniques
II. Utilization of Security Personnel
   A. *Security guards*
   B. *Floorwalkers*
      1. Who will make a good floorwalker
      2. Spotting shoplifters
      3. Surveillance of the shoplifter
      4. Apprehending the shoplifter
      5. Interrogating a suspected shoplifter
      6. Searching shoplifting suspects
   C. *The overall effectiveness of floorwalker utilization*
      1. Special shoplifting courts
      2. Criminal prosecution as a primary objective
III. Other Antishoplifting Measures and Devices
   A. *Measures and devices for surveillance*
      1. Closed-circuit television cameras, video tape recording equipment, and film cameras
      2. Wide-angle mirrors
      3. Sales and other nonsecurity personnel
   B. *Merchandise alarm devices and systems*
      1. Loop alarms

2. Cable alarms
3. Wafer-switch alarms
4. Ribbonswitch alarms
5. Display-case lock alarms
6. Plug-monitor alarms
7. Canvas-painting alarms
8. Tag-alarm systems

C. *Antishoplifting hangers and merchandise-locking devices*
D. *Ghosting*
E. *Merchandise presentation and display*
F. *Basic store design*

As in Chapter 8, the material in this chapter relates entirely to the customer-theft aspect of shoplifting. The stealing of merchandise by retail employees will be considered in Part III, Internal Theft.

Common Shoplifting Methods and Techniques

To be successful, the shoplifter must somehow remove from the store the merchandise he wishes to steal. The degree of difficulty associated with this task, and the corresponding risk of being detected, are determined by many factors, including the size of the item, the way it is displayed, its location in the store, and the degree and type of security protecting the merchandise. The method a thief uses often reflects his skill, determination, and imagination. Unfortunately, it cannot always be assumed that to steal valuable merchandise, the thief must use complicated and exotic shoplifting techniques; but if the proper protection is afforded such merchandise, this will usually be the case. Under these circumstances, attempts to steal the most attractive merchandise frequently involve professionals, using tools and devices especially designed or adapted for shoplifting. Retail-security practitioners who know about the methods and techniques of shoplifting are in a better position to deter, catch, or at least recognize the shoplifters they may encounter.

Active and/or professional shoplifters often wear heavy outer garments containing hidden pockets or hooks capable of holding and concealing stolen merchandise, or "booster bloomers," which are baggy pants tied below the knee. They have also been known to use a device called a "booster box"—a square or rectangular container, usually wrapped as a gift, constructed of a spring-loaded and hinged door through which the shoplifter surreptitiously shoves available items. All these shoplifting aids, if properly made and cleverly used, are extremely difficult to spot and enable the shoplifter to discreetly take and conceal large quantities of merchandise.

Smaller items can be inconspicuously carried from a store in a shoplifter's hand. A few experienced female shoplifters have learned to walk from their knees down, concealing larger items between their thighs. Wearing apparel and even small appliances have been carried out of stores in this fashion. Another method of retail theft is to take clothing into the dressing room, put it on, and wear it out of the store. Price tags have been found hidden behind dressing-room mirrors as evidence of this type of activity. During the winter months, a shoplifter may enter a store without gloves, boots, hat, or heavy coat and leave it suitably attired. Jewelry, sunglasses, and shoes are often worn openly out of a store by confident shoplifters. Items packaged in "blister packs," such as ballpoint pens, are susceptible to being torn out of their containers by shoplifters who claim ownership of them when they are confronted. Therefore, the existence of broken blister packs in a store is a sign of shoplifting activity, as is any merchandise found out of its regular display area.

Shopping bags, purses, and umbrellas are standard carriers of unpurchased merchandise from a store. Shoplifters have been known to burden their children with unpurchased merchandise that they unwittingly carry from the premises. They also steal merchandise by concealing it under their hats, up their sleeves, inside their shoes, and in their hair. Some thieves work in groups with one or two stealing while others create disturbances to divert the attention of store and security personnel.

Dishonest shoppers create bargains for themselves by removing the price tags from inexpensive items and placing them on more valuable ones, or by switching merchandise containers. Brazen shoplifters will openly grab merchandise from a shelf, off a rack, or from behind a display counter, then flee the store. Some of the more confident ones return stolen merchandise to their victims for cash refunds. Occasionally, items such as television sets and sofas are taken from layaway sections by shoplifters posing as purchasers.

Shoplifting is one of the easiest crimes to commit, so it is widely perpetrated by people of all ages, backgrounds, and degrees of intelligence. And since it also involves only a slight risk—physical or otherwise—little skill, and almost no social stigma, effective control of it is a difficult and demanding task.

Utilization of Security Personnel

Security guards and floorwalkers are the two basic kinds of security personnel utilized to combat shoplifting. Many retail-security programs are made up of a combination of security guards, floorwalkers, sales personnel, and various anti-shoplifting devices, systems, and procedures. For purposes of clarity, however, the security functions, application, and degree of effectiveness associated with each type of antishoplifting measure will be discussed separately.

security guards

Only the most careless shoplifter will steal in the presence of a security guard; so the mere presence of a guard operates to deter shoplifting within his immediate area. It follows that the use of a guard instead of a floorwalker is an effort to prevent shoplifting rather than to catch shoplifters.

Once the decision has been made to use guards, the retailer should determine how many are needed in the store and when they should be on duty. In the event the retailer does not want the expense of a guard continually on duty every hour his store is open for business, he should at least have one on the premises during the store's most commercially active periods. Although a shoplifting loss can occur whenever one shopper is in a store, the loss potential increases with the number of customers. As a result, most stores intensify their security efforts during the Christmas season, when shopping is the heaviest.

The proper size of a retail guard force will be determined primarily by the physical size of the store and the nature of its merchandise. For example, a multistoried department store having many departments that sell vulnerable merchandise may require a large complement of security guards. A force large enough to keep retail shrinkage down to a minimum, although effective, is extremely expensive, and the security administrator may have difficulty in justifying its cost to the operational executives, particularly since it is impossible to measure precisely how much shoplifting is deterred by any security measure. On the other hand, a floorwalker's effectiveness can be determined by the number of shoplifters he or she has caught within a specific time period. This statistic, however, measures the capability and talent of the floorwalker more than it does the overall security benefit resulting from floorwalker use.

In order to conduct effective retail security patrols, guards and floorwalkers should be aware of the types of shoplifters, their most common larceny techniques, and their favorite targets. They should also be capable of recognizing those shoppers whose appearance and/or demeanor makes them suspect. Proficient retail-security guards will make certain their presence is known to customers they suspect. The floorwalker, on the other hand, uses this knowledge to spot and discreetly observe those she considers most likely to steal.

If the desired result does not include the apprehension of shoplifters, just having the proper number of knowledgeable guards present in the most vulnerable areas of a store will deter a significant number of shoppers from stealing. It is the responsibility of the security administrator to determine how much guard coverage is necessary. If guards are deployed and scheduled poorly, it is possible that the same results could have been achieved with fewer personnel; if they are poorly trained, they will not produce as expected.

Some retail-security administrators believe that security-guard use is, dollar for dollar, the most effective antishoplifting measure for protecting small retail establishments. For example, one guard can adequately protect most small convenience food and drugstores. Such a preventive measure is particularly appropriate in these stores, since floorwalkers are less likely to be successful here. It is extremely difficult to watch a suspect in a small store without being identified as a security officer, and the presence of a floorwalker may make honest customers uncomfortable. Also, because convenience food and drugstores are often the victims of armed robbers, uniformed security guards on duty in these stores should be armed.

Finally, retail-security guards often perform functions that are not related to customer theft. For example, a retail guard may monitor deliveries to the store, observe employees coming to and from work, maintain order, and lock up at the close of business.

floorwalkers

A floorwalker is a retail-security officer who patrols within a store while posing as a customer. To be effective, a floorwalker must have the ability to spot customers who are likely to steal, observe them, and make the arrest if a theft does occur. Floorwalker utilization, in its methodology and primary objective, is law-enforcement-oriented, because it involves catching thieves rather than preventing theft. Its specific objectives include detecting the shoplifter in action, apprehending him, recovering the merchandise, and, if appropriate, initiating criminal prosecution. A secondary objective is deterrence, since the apprehended shoplifter, and others, may be disinclined to steal in a store using floorwalkers who criminally prosecute the shoplifters they catch.

Who Will Make a Good Floorwalker. Specific criteria regarding the kind of person best suited for this type of work are difficult, if not impossible, to formulate. Many retail-security administrators prefer to hire women between the ages of 20 and 55 as floorwalkers. Middle-class-appearing women in this age bracket usually match the profile of the largest group of shoppers and therefore fit easily into most shopping scenes, whereas a male floorwalker, regardless of his age, will sometimes look out of place in many sections of a discount or department store, making him easier to identify. As a general guideline, the security administrator should select floorwalker personnel who are the same age and sex as most of his customers and whose dress reflects their economic status.

One of the major drawbacks of using floorwalkers is the time and effort involved in finding and training them. Unlike the case with security guards, very few people are capable of becoming successful floorwalkers. Training a new floorwalker how to recognize the clues indicating that a shopper has stolen or is about to steal is not exceedingly difficult; any mature, observant person with a modicum of common sense and intelligence can learn it and, if she is quick on her feet and in good physical condition, can be taught to effectively observe shoppers while posing as a customer. However, those with floorwalker potential are separated from those without when it comes to confrontation. It takes courage and supreme confidence to accuse a person of a crime—especially a well-dressed middle-aged shopper, say, or a rough-looking 20-year-old male. Most floorwalker recruits do not go beyond this phase of the training. And even when this hurdle has been cleared, the trainee must also have the ability and know-how to conduct interviews aimed at producing admissions of guilt.

In summary, the floorwalking avocation requires physical courage, law-enforcement and security know-how, and a personality that can withstand the physical and verbal abuse that often comes from shoplifters whose hatred for law-enforcement and security personnel is not only intense but sometimes uncontrollable.

Spotting Shoplifters. Honest shoppers seldom if ever knowingly witness the commission of a shoplifting offense. There are three reasons for this: (1) They are preoccupied with their own business and are not looking for this type of activity; (2) assuming they are interested in spotting a shoplifter, they do not know what to look for; and (3) their attention spans, in this regard, are short-lived.

The efficient floorwalker, on the other hand, is constantly on watch and knows the signs of theft. The following list, although not complete, contains many of these clues:

1. Shoppers who wander aimlessly about the store, handling pieces of merchandise
2. Groups of teenagers who spend considerable amounts of time in the store without making purchases
3. Shoppers who appear nervous and glance about without moving their heads
4. Shoppers who leave the store, then immediately return
5. Shoppers who continually drop articles on the floor
6. Shoppers who place their packages, coats, and purses on top of or near merchandise
7. Shoppers who carry large purses, knitting bags, briefcases, umbrellas, and newspapers into the store
8. Shoppers who bring garments to others who are in the dressing room
9. Shoppers appearing hard to fit or difficult to please, who make repeated trips to the fitting room
10. Shoppers who distract sales personnel by engaging them in long conversations or arguments
11. Shoppers who wear coats with bulging pockets

12. Shoppers who are dressed out of season
13. Shoppers who wear loose-fitting garments
14. The female shopper who repeatedly opens her handbag for a handkerchief, handles merchandise with the same hand, then places the handkerchief back in her purse (along with the merchandise)
15. Shoppers who wear large boots that are loose-fitting or open at the top
16. Customers pushing shopping carts containing open purses
17. Shoppers pushing baby carriages and strollers

Surveillance of the Shoplifter. Floorwalking is basically a surveillance function. The floorwalker is in the store to monitor shopper activity for the purpose of detecting and handling shoplifters. She employs one of two methods of observing customer activity. The first is patrolling or moving about on the floor of the establishment; the second consists of viewing shoppers through one-way windows built into free-standing towers or walls. A floorwalker who is stationed on an observation stand or catwalk, or in a tower, watches from above. Suspicious shoppers can be observed closely from these vantage points through binoculars. Whenever a floorwalker sees, through one of these one-way windows, a customer concealing a piece of merchandise, she must either communicate this fact to another security officer on the floor or leave the observation stand to make the apprehension herself. In the latter case, this method of surveillance is risky, because the floorwalker has to interrupt her observation of the suspect taking the chance that the suspect has changed his mind or become frightened, has relinquished the merchandise, and is therefore ''clean'' at the time of his arrest. For this reason, floorwalkers who work alone usually prefer to work on the floor rather than from hidden observation points.

Apprehending the Shoplifter. A floorwalker working in a state that does not require by law that the thief leave the store before being arrested should make the arrest inside the store. A shoplifter who has been confronted after he has gone beyond the cash-out counter without paying for the concealed merchandise will find it hard to convince a judge or jury that he did not intend to steal it. In a department store, the arrest can be made anytime after the suspect has left the department he has victimized.

Probably the most important phase of the apprehension is the initial confrontation between the floorwalker and the thief. If the floorwalker's approach reflects uncertainty or fear, serious problems may result. The first thing a floorwalker should do when arresting a shoplifter is identify herself as a security officer, displaying her credentials or badge. Then she should instruct the suspect to return the item he has concealed. If the suspect hesitates or otherwise causes the floorwalker to doubt that he will give it up, she should take possession of the merchandise herself. Then the suspect should be asked to produce a sales slip showing the purchase of the item; unless the floorwalker has made a mistake, the suspect will be unable to show that he has legitimately purchased it. An experienced shoplifter may claim that he purchased the item previously, is returning it for a refund, and has lost the sales slip. The floorwalker will know the story is false because she has seen the suspect conceal the item, so she should ignore these assertions and proceed with the arrest, acting swiftly, calmly, and with authority.

The floorwalker should be as specific as possible when referring to the item that has been stolen. For example, when confronting a shoplifter who has stuffed a pair of gloves into a shopping bag and is rapidly leaving the premises, she should say something to the effect that she has seen him place in his shopping bag the black leather gloves he took from the menswear department. By immediately referring to the theft in such detail, she will usually convince the thief that he has indeed been observed and that she will not back off until the merchandise is returned. Most shoplifters, directly confronted in this fashion by a confident and quietly aggressive floorwalker, are momentarily immobilized by shock and fear, and the experienced floorwalker will take this opportunity to gain control over the suspect and the merchandise. Once this has been accomplished, it is much easier for her to maintain the upper hand.

The floorwalker should never refer to the suspect as a "thief" or "shoplifter" and should take care not to specifically or expressly accuse the suspect of theft while they are on the floor in the company of others. Once the merchandise has been recovered, the suspect should be asked to accompany the floorwalker to the security office. A salesperson should be summoned to act as a witness to the interview, since a shoplifter should never be taken to the security office and interviewed without the presence of a witness. The function of a witness is to preclude false accusations of brutality or coercion, to protect the floorwalker from being falsely accused of taking a bribe or requesting favors, and to provide an added measure of physical protection.

Interrogating a Suspected Shoplifter. The section of the Pennsylvania retail-theft law that details what a floorwalker can do in handling a shoplifting suspect was referred to in Chapter 8. That provision reads:

> (d) Detention.—A peace officer, merchant or merchant's employe or an agent under contract with a merchant, who has probable cause to believe that retail theft has occurred or is occurring in or about a store or other retail mercantile establishment and who has probable cause to believe that a specific person has committed or is committing the retail theft may detain the suspect in a reasonable manner for a reasonable time on or off the premises for all or any of the following purposes: to require the suspect to identify himself, to verify such identification, to determine whether such suspect has in his possession unpurchased merchandise taken from the mercantile establishment and, if so, to recover such merchandise, to inform a peace officer, or to institute criminal proceedings against the suspect. . . .

Thus, in Pennsylvania, as well as in most other states, security officers have statutory authority to arrest suspected shoplifters. But although the provision above outlines what a security officer can do in the detention of a suspected shoplifter, it is silent regarding the security officer's right to interrogate a person in his custody. It is common practice, however, for floorwalkers and other security practitioners to interrogate the suspects they catch; the right to do so is implied in most retail-theft statutes. The Pennsylvania provision, for example, can be reasonably interpreted to include this right, since the merchant's right to verify a suspect's identity would seem to permit relevant inquiries into the alleged offense. Even the most limited investigation would be precluded if the security officer could not question his suspect. To deny a security officer the right to solicit an admission of guilt from a shoplifter he has caught would be extremely unreasonable.

There are many specific reasons for a floorwalker to interrogate a suspect after he has been identified and the merchandise he has taken has been recovered from him. One or all of the following reasons are applicable in every case:

1. To elicit an admission of guilt
2. To elicit, in lieu of a complete admission of guilt, an incriminating declaration
3. To obtain from the suspect a signed statement that sets out in writing his full confession
4. To have the suspect sign a form releasing the security officer and others from civil liability arising from his detention and resulting interrogation
5. To acquire information regarding the existence and identity of accomplices to the offense
6. To obtain data of an intelligence nature regarding new shoplifting techniques, the existence of security vulnerabilities in the store previously unknown to the interrogator, and the identities and activities of other shoplifters

Most floorwalkers execute certain forms whenever they detain and process a suspected shoplifter. If properly filled out by the security officer and signed by the shoplifter, these usually serve two basic purposes. In addition to serving as confession forms, they also release the appropriate persons and companies from civil liability. The following clause has been taken from a standard retail-theft statement form:

> I hereby release the person or persons who detained me in connection with the aforesaid incident and his or her employees, superiors, principals and customers from any claim or demand arising out of or in connection with said incident.

An executed statement form also serves a third function, in that it constitutes a relatively complete record of the shoplifting incident. Figure 9-1 shows a retail-theft confession form fairly representative of those currently used by many stores.

[city, state] [date]

This statement is given by me, ________________ [full name]

________________ [address], ________________ [date of birth], willingly,

voluntarily, without threat, force or duress, and without any

promise of immunity. It is given in the office of ________________ [company],

and in the presence of ________________ and ________________.

I hereby release ________________ [company] and ________________ [security officer]

from any claims for damage because of this investigation.

I hereby state that on ________________ [date], I entered the premises of

________________ [company], at ________________ [address], and removed,

concealed, and took possession of the following items, knowing that

they belonged to the above company, without any intention of paying

for same:

DESCRIPTION OF ARTICLE VALUE

My accomplices were ________________.

I have read the above statement and it is a true and correct account

of the facts.

SIGNED ________________

________________ [witness]

DATE ________________

FIGURE 9-1. Retail-theft confession form

Obviously, not every person taken into custody on suspicion of shoplifting admits his guilt to the security officer. In these cases, although there may be an interrogation, there will be no executed statement form, so if criminal prosecution is anticipated, the floorwalker must rely on the available evidence—that is, her observation of the suspect's concealment and removal of the store's merchandise.

And regardless of whether or not a confession is made, the merchandise found on the suspect's person at the time of his arrest is evidence of the offense and, as such, should be appropriately handled. Although a suspect who does not admit his guilt at the time he is arrested and interrogated is less likely to plead guilty to formal charges later, the absence of a confession does not by itself rule out the possibility that the suspect will be convicted of the offense. For this reason, a security officer should never press too hard for an admission of guilt, nor should he, in cases where the suspect has orally conceded that he has been caught stealing, unduly pressure him into signing a confession form.

The U.S. Supreme Court, through its decisions, has created numerous procedural guidelines applying to state and federal police officers in connection with their investigations and handling of criminal cases and suspected criminal offenders—specifically, restrictions relating to the questioning of persons who are being arrested or who are already in police custody. Since 1936, the Court has been developing a standard of fairness against which all criminal confessions must be judged. The degree to which this judicial standard has affected the crime-solution effort reached a peak in 1966 with the now famous and controversial *Miranda* decision.[1] The following is a summary of the *Miranda* case, setting forth what is commonly referred to as the *Miranda* doctrine.

Miranda was arrested at his home on charges of kidnapping and rape. He was taken to the Phoenix, Arizona, police station, where he was interviewed by two police officers. After two hours of questioning, Miranda admitted committing the crime and signed a written statement of his full confession. He was not physically abused, threatened, or tricked, his confession was given voluntarily, and he did not request an attorney before or during the interview. However, the police officers did not specifically advise Miranda that he had a right to have an attorney present during his interview, and they also failed to specifically advise him that he didn't have to answer their questions.

At Miranda's trial, the written confession was admitted in evidence, and he was found guilty of both charges and sentenced to 20 to 30 years' imprisonment on each count.

Miranda appealed his conviction on the grounds that prior to his interrogation by the police, he was not advised of his right to an attorney and his right to remain silent. When the appeal reached the Supreme Court, the Court found for Miranda. The decision read, in part:

> Persons who are being accused of a crime through police questioning, even though they are not under arrest or in police custody at the time, have a right, pursuant to the Sixth Amendment to the Constitution, to have a lawyer present during the interview. A failure on the part of the interviewee to request an attorney does not constitute a waiver by him of this right. Moreover, a person being interviewed under these circumstances must also be advised by the police of his right against self-

[1] *Miranda* v. *Arizona*, 384 U.S. 436 (1966).

> incrimination found in the Fifth Amendment to the United States Constitution. Along with the right to remain silent, a person must be advised that any information he furnishes could be used against him in a court of law. The fact that the interviewee already knows that he has these rights will not justify a failure by the police to warn him anyway. Only through such warnings is there ascertainable assurance that the accused is aware of these constitutional safeguards.
>
> Persons interviewed following their arrest or while they are in jail must be warned of their Fifth and Sixth Amendment rights prior to any form of police questioning. The reason behind this requirement is based upon the Court's belief that the atmosphere surrounding an arrest or incarceration is, without more, coercive. The Court is of the opinion that the circumstances surrounding an in-custody interrogation of a suspect can operate to overbear his will and therefore his resistance to the interviewers. Because of this, special care must be taken whenever a suspect is arrested, to insure that he is aware that these rights are available to him.
>
> Since Miranda was not adequately warned of his constitutional rights prior to his in-custody questioning, his written confession was not admissible as evidence against him at trial.

The Court stated, as a basic rule of law, that a person in police custody, under arrest, or being accused of a crime must be advised of certain constitutional rights before police questioning, and that after he has been advised of these rights, he should not be questioned unless he has voluntarily waived them in connection with the immediate interview. Also, a waiver of one's rights, once given, can be withdrawn at any time during the interview and the interview must immediately cease.

These are the constitutional rights the person being questioned should be advised of before questioning:

1. The right to remain silent
2. The knowledge that any statement he makes could be used against him in a court of law
3. The right to an attorney, either retained or appointed
4. The right to stop answering questions at any time

The fact that the person to be interviewed already knows his constitutional rights does not remove the necessity of specifically warning him of those rights before questioning.

A confession resulting from police questioning of a person in custody, under arrest, or being accused of a crime is therefore not admissible as evidence unless the appropriate warnings and voluntary waiver preceded the interrogation.

From a practical point of view, the significance of the *Miranda* decision, as far as police officers are concerned, is the fact that if they forget to warn an interviewee of his *Miranda* rights, and if he confesses to a crime or otherwise utters an incriminatory statement in response to their questioning, this evidence has been illegally obtained and will be inadmissible in court. If the prosecution cannot prove the suspect's guilt without this evidence, he will not be convicted of the crime. The exclusion at trial of relevant, reliable, and incriminating evidence, solely because it has been acquired in a way adjudged to be in violation of a constitutional right, is called the exclusionary rule.

It is vital to note that the courts have generally limited the application of the exclusionary rule to the actions of *public* police officers. In 1921, the Supreme Court, in specifically addressing this issue, held that evidence illegally seized by a private detective was admissible against the defendant, because the defendant's right against unlawful search and seizure under the Fourth Amendment to the Constitution protects him against invasion of privacy by governmental rather than private forces. The Court has not, however, specifically determined whether a privately obtained confession in violation of the *Miranda* doctrine is subject to the exclusionary rule. Lower courts addressing this issue have yet to require security guards, private detectives, or floorwalkers to precede their interrogations with a recital of the suspect's *Miranda* rights.

However, any confession that is determined by a court to be involuntary, regardless of the fact that it was obtained by private-police personnel, will be inadmissible in court. The standard applied to security-obtained confessions is therefore one of voluntariness. Whenever a floorwalker, security guard, or private investigator obtains a confession or admission of guilt, he must be in a position to show that it was given voluntarily, without force, threat of force, or duress. Confessions that are the product of interviews using tactics aimed at psychologically coercing the interviewee, or that are obtained after prolonged questioning, will be classified as involuntary and therefore inadmissible as evidence.

For this reason, security officers frequently use confession forms containing statements that the confession was not the product of force, threat of force, or duress. Many security administrators, to be on the safe side, require their personnel to warn all suspects of their *Miranda* rights and to ask cooperating interviewees to sign standard waiver-of-rights forms.

This law of confessions applies directly to the floorwalker function. Although it is important that a floorwalker use good interviewing techniques in order to obtain as many confessions as possible, she must take care not to conduct the interrogation in such a way as to raise the issue of voluntariness. One of the best ways is to make certain that a witness is present during every interview. Moreover, interrogations should not be unnecessarily prolonged and should be conducted in a low-keyed manner. If the suspect clearly indicates an unwilligness to admit his guilt or insists that he is innocent, the interview should be terminated.

Floorwalkers who are successful interviewers are usually well-trained and experienced security officers. Although there are definite techniques that can be learned, interrogating is an art, wherein one's success or lack of it depends to a large degree upon his personality and the way he relates to people. There are many books on the subject of proper interviewing techniques, some of which are included in the bibliography following this chapter.

Searching Shoplifting Suspects. The U.S. Supreme Court based its decision in the *Miranda* case upon its interpretation of the Fifth and Sixth Amendments to the Constitution, both of which limit the ways in which state and federal governments can enforce their criminal laws. With the Fourth Amendment as its authority, the Court also restricts and supervises the methods by which police conduct their searches. The Fourth Amendment to the Constitution reads as follows:

> The right of the people to be secure in their persons, houses, papers, and effects, against unreasonable searches and seizures, shall not be violated, and no warrants shall issue, but upon probable cause, supported by oath or affirmation, and particularly describing the place to be searched, and the persons or things to be seized.

Whenever a court declares a police search to be "unreasonable," the evidence seized is not admissable at trial against the subject of the search.

Search-and-seizure law is complex, subtle, and often hard to apply to specific situations. As a result, police are never certain whether they are operating in accordance with the Supreme Court's standards. It should be noted that members of the Court themselves are not always in agreement on the reasonableness of a particular search.

Although it is impossible to formulate basic rules of law to cover every type of police-search situation, the following general outline may aid your understanding of the basic search-and-seizure principles:

1. Usually, a search of a house, office, or other fixed premises is not legal unless the person conducting the search has a valid search warrant.
2. A search warrant, to be valid, must:
   a. Describe the place to be searched.
   b. Contain probable cause that evidence of a crime is on those premises.
   c. Describe the evidence that is to be seized.
3. Legal searches can be conducted *without* a warrant:
   a. Incident to the lawful arrest of any person. (These searches are limited to the person himself and the area within his immediate physical control.)
   b. Whenever an officer has probable cause to believe that a vehicle contains evidence of a crime. (If the officer could have obtained a search warrant without risking the destruction or removal of the evidence, a warrantless search under these circumstances may be invalid.)
   c. Whenever the person having the authority to do so voluntarily consents to the search.
   d. Whenever the place to be searched is abandoned or is public in nature.

Floorwalkers and other security officers who arrest suspected shoplifters quite often conduct searches of the person. According to the case law applicable to searches of persons *lawfully* arrested by police officers, this practice is lawful and does not require a search warrant. Floorwalkers and other retail-security practitioners also have statutory authority for such searches. For instance, the relevant portion of the California shoplifting law reads, "During the period of detention any items which a merchant has reasonable cause to believe are unlawfully taken from his premises and which are in plain view may be examined by the merchant for the purposes of ascertaining the ownership thereof." Note that the term *merchant*, as defined by the California statute, includes security officers acting on a merchant's behalf. Under Pennsylvania law, the security officer, upon arresting a suspected shoplifter, may "determine whether such suspect has in his possession unpurchased merchandise taken from the mercantile establishment and, if so, to recover such merchandise. . . ." In both states, the retail-theft statutes require that the arrest and search be predicated upon probable cause to believe that the arrestee has committed a shoplifting offense.

For example, if a floorwalker, acting on vague and secondhand information to the effect that a shoplifting violation may have occurred, arrests a customer, the arrest is not predicated on probable cause and is thereby illegal under most states' shoplifting statutes. The discovery by the security officer of merchandise on the arrestee's person will not necessarily salvage the case and render it prosecutable.

The courts have continually held that the exclusionary rule does not apply to illegal searches conducted by people other than public-police personnel. However, the fact that the case above cannot be successfully prosecuted does not relate to whether or not the exclusionary rule has been applied. Because of the nature of most shoplifting offenses, the most relevant evidence is usually not the suspect's possession of the merchandise, but rather how he came by it and removed it from its original place in the store. Therefore, whether or not the exclusionary rule applies is really a moot question because, even if it does, the "evidence" excluded (possession of the merchandise), without more, would not have been enough to support a conviction.

The fact that the exclusionary rule does not apply to illegal searches by security personnel is, however, relevant in many shoplifting situations. Occasionally, a floorwalker searching for stolen merchandise will discover drugs or other contraband on the person of a shoplifting suspect. This evidence, once turned over to the police, can be used to convict him on a narcotics charge even if it was the product of an illegal search, unless the defendant can show that the floorwalker's actions were on behalf of the police.

The nonapplicability of the exclusionary rule may also have relevance in shoplifting cases where *the way the merchandise is being held* by the defendant is enough evidence, by itself, to support a shoplifting conviction. For example, if the illegal arrest and search of a shoplifting suspect results in the discovery of jewelry hidden in his shoe, a conviction is possible because this evidence will not be excluded even though the search was illegal.

The fact that the exclusionary rule does not apply to searches made by floorwalkers and other retail-security officers should not encourage them to arrest a suspect they have not witnessed committing the offense. They are still civilly liable for false arrest and other torts, particularly in cases involving illegal arrests and searches, because the statutory protection provided by many states against civil liability in shoplifting cases does not extend to instances involving bad-faith arrests.

Appendix A contains selected briefs of court decisions involving shoplifting cases. These decisions represent most of the legal points normally raised in connection with shoplifting offenses.

the overall effectiveness of floorwalker utilization

It can be reasonably assumed that merchants who employ floorwalkers consider catching shoplifters the best method of combatting retail theft, and that their primary reason for catching them is to have them criminally prosecuted. The latter assumption is reasonable because hiring floorwalkers to catch offenders merely for the purpose of recovering stolen merchandise is rather ineffective and certainly costly. The use of security personnel to monitor and control customer activity in and around the fitting room and of nonremovable-price-tag alarms, for example, are more effective and less expensive methods of catching shoplifters for the sole purpose of recovering stolen merchandise, since shoplifters caught by these measures are not as likely to be as prosecutable as those observed actually concealing the merchandise.

Therefore, merchants using floorwalkers must want more than the mere recovery of merchandise. If such a merchant puts forth an effort to catch a shoplifter and does not follow up with an attempt to secure the suspect's criminal conviction, it is evident that he is utilizing an antishoplifting measure that does not correspond to his actual security objectives.

A survey conducted by Commercial Service Systems, Inc., of 17,876 shoplifting apprehensions in supermarkets, drugstores, and discount stores in 1973 shows that in most cases, the apprehended shoplifter was not turned over to the police for prosecution or juvenile handling.[2] According to this study, the percentage of cases in which the police were called in 1973, as compared to figures dating back to 1969, shows only a slight increase. It appears therefore that the desire of merchants to prosecute did not increase during this period to any great degree. The most significant change involved adult offenders caught in supermarkets. In 1969,

---

[2]Commercial Service Systems, Inc., P.O. Box 3307, Van Nuys, Calif. 91407.

only 30.6 percent of the adults caught were turned over to the police, as compared to 42.6 percent in 1973, showing that merchants became slightly more willing to prosecute adult offenders. However, in 1973 only 38.2 percent of the adult shoplifters caught in drugstores were turned over to the authorities.

The most startling group of statistics gathered in this survey shows the infrequency of police or juvenile-authority involvement in shoplifting cases concerning juveniles. In 1973, only 18 percent of those juveniles caught shoplifting in drugstores were turned over to the authorities, as compared to 24.7 percent in 1970; and the 1973 percentage of juvenile thieves caught in supermarkets that were turned over the police, at 24.9 percent, amounted to only a 2 percent increase over the 1969 figure.

So merchants are apparently not willing to prosecute those shoplifters they catch, especially with regard to juvenile offenders. As discussed fully in Chapter 8, this unwillingness to prosecute is understandable, because of the time, inconvenience, and cost associated with pressing criminal charges. The other factors affecting the decision not to prosecute, also discussed more fully in Chapter 8, include the belief by many retailers that because convicted shoplifters are not severely punished, they are not deterred from stealing in a store that prosecutes offenders, and that a juvenile shoplifter may be the child of a regular customer whose patronage may be lost if the child is turned over to the authorities.

Although floorwalker use is one of the most effective methods of catching shoplifters, it loses much of its overall effectiveness as an antishoplifting measure when apprehended offenders are not regularly and uniformly prosecuted. Particularly since the use of floorwalkers is one of the more difficult and costly security services to implement effectively, once a merchant has decided on this technique, he must also resolve to prosecute those shoplifters he catches. However, even assuming the most efficient use of floorwalker personnel, including the prosecution of every apprehended shoplifter, a serious question still exists regarding whether or not this approach to the problem, when compared to some of the more preventive security measures, is the most effective answer.

Special Shoplifting Courts. Because criminal-court dockets are crowded with cases of serious and violent offenses, shoplifting cases seem comparatively insignificant and get little attention. A judge who regularly hears murder, assault, armed-robbery, rape, and burglary cases will seldom be in a frame of mind to carefully consider each shoplifting case sandwiched between the felony offenses, and he is not likely to impose maximum shoplifting sentences.

The Menswear Retailers of America, to encourage the criminal prosecution of shoplifters, has adopted a resolution calling for municipalities and other local jurisdictions to establish a system of lower courts to handle shoplifting cases exclusively. Proponents believe that such a system will facilitate the swift and equitable handling of apprehended shoplifters, and, because of the added convenience for the prosecuting parties, will also encourage more merchants to initiate criminal prosecution. They also believe that swift disposition of shoplifting cases will increase the deterrent effect of prosecution, and that such a court system will operate to make visible repeat offenders who are candidates for the more serious shoplifting penalties.

In 1973, Cook County, Illinois, inaugurated the nation's first shoplifting court system, via the reorganization of the existing municipal courts to allow all shoplifting cases to be exclusively heard during the afternoon, five days a week. Initially, only one court, Branch 65, was handling shoplifting cases; in 1974, 20,425 shoplifting cases were called for trial in Branch 65, an average of 85 per day.[3] Since then, three more courts have been created to handle shoplifting cases in Cook County. The location of the merchant's business determines which court will handle his case.

Despite an impressive conviction rate of about 80 percent in 1975, and an increased imposition of jail sentences and stiffer fines, there is no evidence that the shoplifting-court system has reduced the shoplifting rate in the Chicago area. A security director of a downtown Chicago department store reported that during the first quarter of 1976, shoplifting in his store increased by 25 percent over the same period the preceding year. It is true that the number of shoplifting apprehensions in Chicago's downtown stores has continued to grow under this court system. For example, during the first two months of 1976, Loop-area stores averaged from 65 to 90 shoplifting arrests per week, a 5 to 18 percent increase over the number in the first two months of 1975.[4] But officials of the Illinois Retail Merchants Association, proponents of the Chicago System, have admitted that the significant increase in criminal convictions, under a state retail-theft statute providing the nation's stiffest shoplifting penalties, has failed to stop the continued rise in Chicago's shoplifting rate. According to Judge Rosin of Branch 65, 90 percent of those shoplifters who are convicted are repeat offenders. Rosin doubts that imprisonment will necessarily deter the offenders. As quoted in *Men's Wear* magazine, he stated, "I could sentence some to 60 days or a year, and it wouldn't make a difference because as soon as they are free, they're back in my court charged with the same offense. They want to be punished!"[5]

Chicago's special shoplifting courts, however, have fulfilled their purpose of encouraging the prosecution and conviction of apprehended shoplifters; in this regard, the system has been extremely successful, and the success of a system designed to convict more criminal offenders should not be measured by whether it has succeeded in reducing the crime rate. First of all, the deterrent effect of a measure such as this cannot be determined. Second, the increase in Chicago's

---

[3]It should be noted that of these 20,425 dispositions, 11,880 (58%) were for continuances, ranging from two to three months. Defendants, by requesting jury trials and numerous other continuances, have been able to delay the disposition of their cases in Branch 65 for up to 1½ years.

[4]J.P. Donlon, "Chicago's 'Shoplifting' Courts, a Partial Solution," *Men's Wear Magazine*, June 1976.

[5]*Ibid.*, p. 54.

shoplifting rate may not necessarily reflect more shoplifting. Because merchants have been motivated to prosecute the shoplifters they catch, more crime is detected, identified, and reported, whereas undetected shoplifting losses prior to the shoplifting-court system may not have been identified as such. A more accurate indicator of the relative severity of the shoplifting problem would be actual dollar losses caused by shoplifters, but retail-shrinkage figures and percentages also include losses created by internal thieves, so a determination of this nature is not feasible.

The following excerpt from an article illustrates a typical session in Chicago's Branch 65 shoplifting court:

> The eighth floor of the central police station on South State Street becomes a traffic jam of citizens, police and court clerks shortly before 1:30 in the afternoon. An old courtroom at the extreme end of the corridor doubles as Branch 40, the prostitutes' court, in the mornings, and Branch 65, the retail theft court, in the afternoons. Associate Judge Allen F. Rosin of the Circuit Court of Cook County presides over both.
>
> Although shoplifting and prostitution are worlds apart legally, the courtroom scenarios are similar. The offenders, closely bunched and seated on the decaying wooden benches, are young, poor and overwhelmingly black. White court clerks and police matrons bark for silence but don't always get it. The more notorious violators seem to know the clerks and police, who in turn recognize them, and the judge tries not to betray an overwhelming sense of familiarity with the whole thing.
>
> The first hour of shoplifting court is the noisiest and most hectic. . . . Of the approximately 100 or more cases that come before the court each day, many are continuances that do not go to trial until some future date. Offenders are brought to the bench, the charges are read and pleas are determined all in a matter of minutes. In some cases, where the alleged violator, initially released on bond, has failed to appear in court voluntarily, warrants are issued for his arrest.
>
> Not until actual cases go to trial does one get a clear understanding of how the court operates. Although shoplifters seem to steal for a variety of reasons, the value of the merchandise stolen is inconsequential by comparison to other crimes. During the course of one recent afternoon, alleged violators were charged with taking as little as one bottle of A-1 steak sauce from an A&P or five bottles of Ultra Sheen shampoo from a Walgreen's store to bigger thefts of AM/FM radios from Goldblatt's.
>
> Often, an offender brought before the shoplifting court is found to have outstanding charges against him for other, more serious crimes. The A-1 steak sauce thief, convicted and sentenced to 90 days in jail, also had a murder indictment pending in another court. Had he not been apprehended on shoplifting charges, it is likely he would still be at large. The AM/FM radio thief had jumped bail on a charge of armed robbery. He was sentenced to a year in jail and now faces other charges.
>
> Not all violators are hardened criminals, however. Many are poor, disadvantaged women who may steal repeatedly but do so only for their immediate needs. Food thefts by women were common. When a welfare mother who had previous shoplifting convictions said in her own defense that she was "sorry," Judge Rosin's reply was: "I'm sorry to see you here too, but I didn't bring you here. You should have thought of that before you stole."

Certain cases of this type are treated with compassion. A woman first-time offender, who was brought before the court for an attempted theft of a $3.47 steak from a Jewel Co. store, immediately began apologizing for her offense before the public defender entered a plea in her behalf. Rosin quickly interrupted with, "Madam, I'm going to pretend I didn't hear that because I will be forced to admit it as evidence. We have a law in this country that states that everybody is innocent until proven guilty.

"That's a good law, don't you think? Well, I am going to remind you that anything you may say may be used against you and that you have the right to remain silent." The woman agreed to a plea of guilty but was released on her word that she wouldn't do it again.

A similar case involved the theft of a bottle of inexpensive wine by an elderly man. As the charge was being read, the judge asked the accused if the bottle of "M. & D." wine being described was, in fact, Mogen David. Later, upon releasing the thief with the admonition not to do it again, Rosin remarked ruefully, "Next time, if you're going to steal, at least wait until Passover."

"Every once in a while I go against what I know and follow my heart," Rosin added as another verbal aside shortly thereafter. A case had come forth in which three offenders released on bond had failed to appear for their trial. "I suspected this might happen, but I wanted to believe they would show up."

Once, when an offender had actually made good on his promise to appear in court for his trial, the judge was so taken aback that he spent the first three minutes of the proceedings praising the fellow for his honesty. "You mean you were out on bond and you actually showed up for your trial without forfeiting the bond. That's really good. We like to see that around here. It restores our faith in people."

Howard Treehuboff, a Glenview, Ill., attorney who works as a public defender in the shoplifting court, feels that although the Cook County courts have come to terms with the retail theft problem, there seems little they can do to discourage people from committing the crime. "Many times, I will have to defend people who I know are guilty and have a long history of similar convictions. The rate of repeaters is staggering."

Ken Malatesta, the state's prosecuting attorney, agrees. "I've only been here for a few weeks," he said. "But I can see that most of the people brought up before the court have been here before."

Malatesta's job is often complicated by the difficulty in getting store security personnel to get sufficient evidence or to bring charges with sufficient cause. In one case, a security guard who was the prosecution's only witness actually showed more hostility to the prosecutor's questions than to those of the public defender.

"Within the limits of our present judicial system," Judge Rosin later explained, "we have a good performance record. No poor person could afford the services of a lawyer, and you won't find any F. Lee Baileys defending them. Yet we have an excellent public defender who gives them every advantage under law. Because of our location, most of the people who come before me are poor and black from the South Side and West Side, but that doesn't mean that justice here is selective. The suburban courts and the theft court on Belmont and Western Streets have wealthy matrons, as well as young kids.

"The real problem is unemployment," he says. "Many people steal because they have no means to support themselves and are too uneducated to learn a trade or know how to go about finding one. Until we lick that problem we're going to be faced with these kinds of crimes indefinitely."[6]

Criminal Prosecution as a Primary Objective. Results that indicate success in terms of law enforcement goals—many arrests and a high conviction rate—do not necessarily spell success in terms of security objectives. It has not been shown that the Chicago System has produced positive security results. Merchants using or considering the use of floorwalkers to catch and prosecute shoplifters should be made aware of this fact. The floorwalking method is more a law-enforcement than a security technique; therefore, it is not surprising that when it is done well, law-enforcement goals are achieved rather than tangible security benefits. Security practitioners and merchants may have to build their programs around measures and devices that have been developed to produce security rather than law-enforcement results.

The remainder of this chapter is devoted to a discussion of those antishoplifting measures and devices that are designed to reduce shoplifting losses by detecting and/or preventing theft rather than by catching shoplifters for prosecution.

Other Antishoplifting Measures and Devices

measures and devices for surveillance

A shoplifter is less likely to steal in a store where he feels he is being observed. The following devices and measures have been designed to increase the surveillance capability of the merchant, his retail employees, and/or security personnel for the detection of those shoplifters who have not been deterred or prevented from committing the offense.

Closed-circuit Television Cameras, Video Tape Recording Equipment, and Film Cameras. One kind of closed-circuit television (CCTV) system in a large retail establishment consists of many television cameras, strategically installed throughout the store, transmitting video signals to a monitoring and control center staffed by security or store personnel. This type of system requires close communication between monitoring and security personnel. The cameras may operate from a fixed position or be remotely controlled. In the latter case, an operator

---

[6]J. P. Donlon, "Chicago's 'Shoplifting' Courts, A Partial Solution," *Men's Wear Magazine,* June 1976. Reprinted by permission of Men's Wear Magazine, June 11, 1976, copyright 1976, Fairchild Publications, Inc., a division of Capital Media, Inc.

stationed at the central control center is able to pan (move horizontally) and tilt (move vertically) each camera, and thus survey a large area of the store with great flexibility. The monitoring officer may also be able to zoom in on (magnify) specific areas—for example, the hands of a shopper who is acting suspiciously.

Television cameras that move automatically in preset patterns are another type of movable unit. These devices are capable of scanning large areas by rotating, swiveling, or moving along special tracks.

Stationary television cameras, in order to cover large areas, are equipped with many lenses pointing in various directions. These "sputnik"-like devices are in the form of half or complete globes and are usually suspended from the ceiling.

CCTV monitoring consoles, if not centrally or remotely located, may be distributed throughout the store where they can be viewed by security personnel and salespeople working on the floor. For example, the entrance to a fitting room may be conveniently observed by a person viewing a monitor in his regular working area. Monitors are also frequently placed in areas of the store where they can be viewed by customers.

When video tape recording (VTR) equipment is added to a CCTV system, the console does not have to be continuously viewed, since the video tape produced can be monitored at a later time. A VTR system has numerous other advantages when operated in conjunction with a CCTV setup. For example, when a monitoring officer sees a suspicious shopper, he may activate the VTR machine to record the shopper's actions on video tape; and VTR equipment can be programmed to periodically and automatically record the transmissions from one or several CCTV cameras.

A CCTV system can also be designed to react to unprogrammed changes in the signals being transmitted and received. The response to such a change can be in the form of a silent alarm, a local alarm, or the activation of a VTR machine to record on tape the unusual activity picked up by the television camera. This type of operation is feasible only when the CCTV camera views a static scene, such as an area in the store where most of the employees and all the customers are forbidden. In these systems, the video signals from each camera are examined electronically, and when a signal changes significantly, as in the case of an intruder coming into the camera's field of view, the change is detected and the viewing personnel notified and/or the VTR machine activated.

Another typical surveillance device is the use of film cameras that are magazine-loaded and motor-driven. One type of surveillance film camera will automatically take, for example, one photograph per second. A more economical technique is to use film cameras that are activated on command to take two photographs per second and produce up to 2,000 frames before reloading. They can be activated by a salesclerk or security officer whenever a suspicious shopper is in the camera's field of view.

Most retail users of CCTV and film surveillance equipment use it openly, in order to benefit from its deterrent effect on would-be shoplifters. Many even capitalize on this preventive aspect by specifically directing the customer's attention to the cameras, often using a decal or sign that reads, "Smile, you're on camera!" Similar results are achieved through the use of "dummy" cameras, which, although appearing authentic, are not functional devices. Displaying these inexpensive models among working cameras is another method of enhancing the deterrent effect of an electronic surveillance system.

Wide-Angle Mirrors. Wide-angle convex mirrors are an inexpensive but effective antishoplifting measure. By increasing the visibility within a store, they facilitate the detection of shoplifters. In most retail establishments, the aisles, merchandise displays, and advertising paraphernalia provide hidden areas where a thief can operate without detection. The proper installation of wide-angle reflection devices, commonly referred to as detection mirrors, will bring these obscure areas into the view of sales and security personnel. (See Figure 9-2.)

Most detection mirrors are either round, rectangular, or "roundtangular" in shape and vary in size from 10 to 36 inches in diameter. They are usually installed on ceilings, walls, and aisle pillars. For example, a mirror can be installed in such a way as to allow a cashier, from her work area, to look down an otherwise obscure aisle or see around a corner. Convex mirrors are particularly useful in smaller retail establishments such as convenience food and drugstores, in which only one or two people are working at any one time. By using detection mirrors, personnel in these smaller stores can keep an eye on customer activity while conducting regular store business.

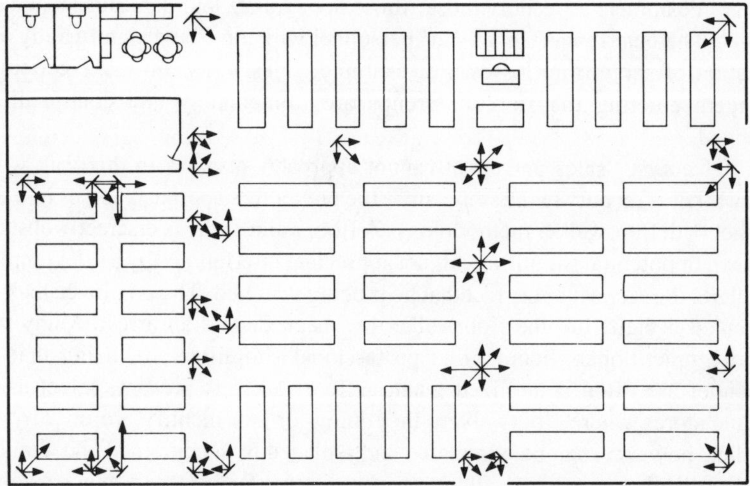

FIGURE 9-2. Typical mirror arrangement in a retail setting

An electronically driven convex mirror that continually moves back and forth provides an increased field of view. Mirrors that scan in this fashion are usually more visible than fixed mirrors, so they may produce a greater deterrent effect. However, a sufficient number of fixed mirrors will achieve the same result.

Detection mirrors are particularly valuable as fitting-room surveillance aides. For example, a well-placed mirror can expose to view an otherwise hidden aisle or hallway inside a fitting room area that may lead to an exit door. In this situation, the security officer surveying the entrance to the fitting room will also be able to monitor the exit door, thus eliminating a serious security vulnerability.

Sales and Other Nonsecurity Personnel. Retail-security practitioners are aware of the antishoplifting potential inherent in the proper use of sales and other nonsecurity employees. Alert and knowledgeable salespeople and clerks can be instrumental in preventing and detecting shoplifting, but they must first be taught how to identify those most likely to steal and be made aware of basic shoplifting techniques.

The retail-security director must not only provide this basic antishoplifting training to nonsecurity employees but also motivate them to accept this security role—and this may be his toughest assignment. Merely explaining and emphasizing the devastating effect theft has on store profits is not enough by itself to motivate most employees to contribute to a retail-security effort. However, the implementation of an employee incentive program may do it. Programs of this nature award fixed cash amounts to employees who prevent a shoplifting loss by either catching or reporting a shoplifter, or give them a percentage of the dollar value of the merchandise saved from theft.

An alert, knowledgeable, and motivated employee will pay close attention to every customer, especially those whose appearance and demeanor make them suspect. The deterrent effect of such personnel will contribute significantly to the reduction of shoplifting losses. For example, salesclerks can make certain that teenagers entering the store in groups are immediately and continually approached.

Of course, sales personnel cannot approach suspects in this way when a floorwalker is on duty in the store, since the preventive approach comes into direct conflict with floorwalker methodology. A floorwalker who is discreetly observing a known or potential shoplifter will not appreciate interference by a sales employee that alerts the suspect to the fact that he is being watched. The employee may have prevented a theft, but the floorwalker has been denied an arrest. Many retail-security practitioners believe that professional shoplifters, realizing that sales personnel are often neutralized when a floorwalker is present, select as their victims stores where floorwalkers they know or can identify are on duty. This conflict, however, can be eliminated and replaced by a combined and simultaneous floorwalker–employee attack on shoplifters. Rather than aggressively approaching suspicious customers, sales personnel can be instructed to discreetly alert a floorwalker or other security officer when they spot a suspect. This can be done through the store's intercom system by broadcasting a message in code throughout the store without drawing the suspect's attention to the fact that he has been observed.

A pocket-radio paging system may also be used as an effective communications link between sales and security personnel. When a salesclerk observes a shoplifting suspect, he can push a button under the counter to signal security-office or switchboard personnel. This signal, received in the form of a light on a panel, will indicate the identity of the sending department, and the appropriate security officer can be alerted by a beep tone followed by a voice message from the dispatcher advising him of the location of the suspect. Radio paging receivers, because they are small enough to be carried in a pocket or clipped to a belt, can be worn inconspicuously.

Sales and clerical personnel often perform retail-security functions when they monitor and control customer traffic in and out of the dressing room. This supervision is a standard antishoplifting measure. A fitting-room clerk's primary function is to make certain that whatever goes into the fitting room comes out the same way it went in, and several systems have been developed to achieve this. Issuing to each customer a plastic card carrying a number that corresponds to the number of articles the customer is taking into the fitting room is a common method.

A more fool-proof procedure involves the use of mechanical dispensers producing sequentially numbered tickets that are issued to every customer who enters. The tickets are color-coded to the number of articles taken in to the dressing room. The fitting-room clerk collects these tickets from the customers as they leave, compares the color of the ticket with the number of articles the holder carries, and makes certain that the number on the ticket falls within the appropriate range. A ticket that has been previously retained by a dishonest holder will have a number that is out of sequence. The success of a fitting-room control program depends primarily upon the performance of the retail employee charged with these responsibilities.

The problem of how to eliminate the dressing room as a security vulnerability is shared by most retail establishments. For example, in 1972, a large New York City department store began surveying customers through grilles in fitting-room ceilings and walls. The New York State attorney general's office objected to this practice, and the department store agreed to discontinue the procedure.

merchandise alarm devices and systems

The function of a merchandise alarm system is the notification, usually by sound, of store and security personnel when a protected object is removed from its display area of the store. Merchandise alarms therefore represent the preventive approach to shoplifting control, to deter as well as detect shoplifters. A variety of merchandise alarms are currently in use and are considered to be extremely effective; most users experience a significant reduction in retail shrinkage. More indirect advantages of this antishoplifting measure are less reliance upon the use of costly security personnel and the ability to display merchandise more openly without increasing the risk of theft.

Loop Alarms. A loop merchandise alarm (see Figure 9-3) is a relatively simple device consisting of one or more lengths of coaxial cable forming a closed electrical circuit. The cable begins and ends at a battery-operated alarm control unit. When the cable is cut, broken, or unplugged from the alarm box, the circuit is opened and the alarm is triggered. The use of a coaxial cable eliminates the possibility of defeating the alarm by bridging the loop (the electrical circuit). Merchandise is protected when it is placed on the loop. For example, the cable can be threaded through handles and other openings on small appliances and through the sleeves of expensive coats and jackets. A salesperson can temporarily deactivate the alarm if it becomes necessary to remove a piece of merchandise from the shelf or rack.

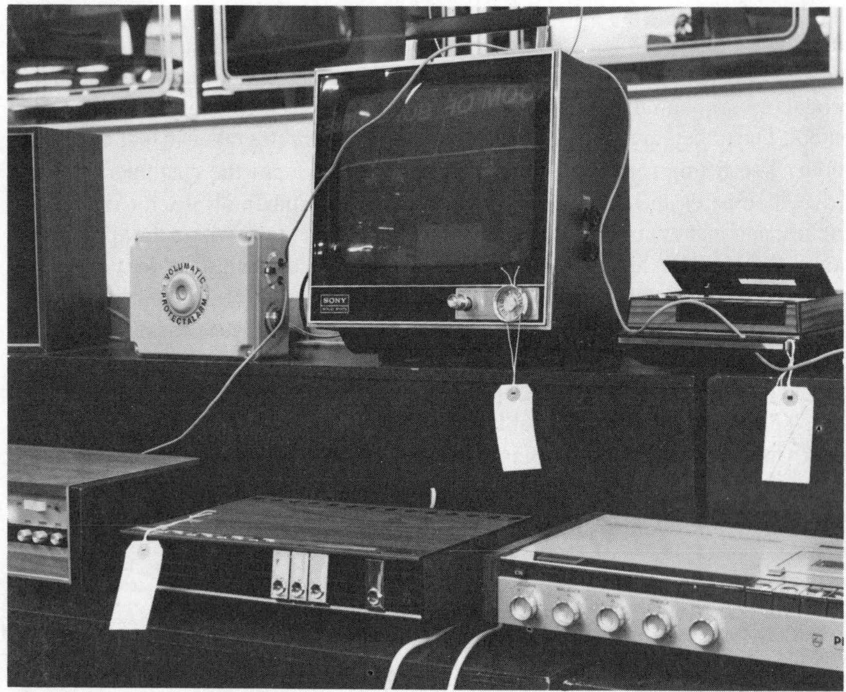

FIGURE 9-3. Loop-alarm installation

Courtesy Volumatic Limited of Coventry, England

Loop-alarm applications are somewhat limited by the fact that in order to be protected, an object must be able to accommodate the cable. Moreover, coats and jackets alarmed in this fashion cannot easily be tried on without first being taken off the loop. Articles that do not have to be removed from the shelf in order to be closely examined by a customer are the best items for loop-alarm protection.

Cable Alarms. This type of merchandise alarm consists of a coaxial cable with a small pad attached to its end. The pad adheres to the article being protected, and if it is separated from the merchandise, the alarm is sounded. The other end of the cable runs to a junction that is tied into a main alarm control unit. There must be a separate cable and junction for every piece of merchandise alarmed. Cable-alarm systems can protect a wide variety of articles. They are commonly used on calculators, typewriters, and other office machines. Unlike the loop device, they can be attached to items that do not have handles or other openings, and they make possible greater access to the merchandise, by allowing the removal of the protected article from the shelf for customer handling and inspection.

Wafer-Switch Alarms. A wafer alarm is composed of a flat, waferlike sensing device, about the size of a half dollar and very thin, over which the protected merchandise is placed. The alarm is activated when the article is taken off the sensing pad. As long as the weight of the merchandise is on the wafer, the device remains in a non-alarm status. Highly sensitive wafer-switch alarms can be set off by the removal of an item weighing as little as one ounce.

Ribbonswitch Alarms. As the name implies, a ribbonswitch alarm consists of a tape or ribbon housing a normally open electrical circuit. Although ribbonswitches have varied applications outside the retail-security field, they do have limited use as merchandise alarms. Like wafer alarms, they are pressure-activated; but whereas a wafer alarm is triggered by the removal of pressure, ribbonswitch alarms are activated when pressure is applied—even a light pressing or squeezing of the tape. Ribbonswitch tapes are often laid across pieces of antique furniture, beds, sofas, and chairs to prevent unauthorized customer use and abuse.

Display-Case Lock Alarms. Numerous devices have been designed to emit an alarm signal when a showcase lock is left open. These alarms are usually deactivated when a salesperson is present behind the display case. The weight of the salesclerk on a pressure-sensitive mat on the floor behind the showcase is one method of temporarily overriding the alarm. When the sales person walks off the mat and the display case has not been relocked, the alarm will sound.

Plug-Monitor Alarms. Electrically operated merchandise such as calculators, electric typewriters, radios, television sets, and small appliances can be protected by being plugged into an alarmed outlet. When the plug is pulled out of the socket or the article's electrical cord is cut, an alarm is triggered.

Canvas-Painting Alarms. Valuable paintings are susceptible to theft by being cut out of their frames. Alarm devices sensitive to and activated by vibration are used to protect these works of art. This type of alarm device is frequently installed on window glass as an intrustion alarm.

Tag-Alarm Systems. This type of merchandise alarm system is commonly referred to as electronic article surveillance. The system is made up of a special inventory tag that is attached to clothing and other merchandise, and an electronic sensing unit that produces sound (alarm) when one of these special tags passes it. (See Figure 9-4.) For example, a shoplifter leaving a store with merchandise containing one of these tags will be detected as he passes an electronic sensing unit installed at the exit.

The alarm tags, attached securely to the merchandise they protect, can be removed only by sales personnel with special tools. Problems occasionally arise when a sales employee forgets to remove the tag from legitimately purchased merchandise, and the customer is startled and embarrassed by setting off the alarm when he leaves the store. For this reason, sales personnel in these stores must

FIGURE 9-4. Merchandise alarm tag

Courtesy Sensormatic

continually be reminded of the importance of removing the tag from every piece of purchased merchandise.

antishoplifting hangers and merchandise-locking devices

Expensive leather and fur coats are often secured by eight-foot lengths of plastic-coated steel cable, usually of sufficient length to allow the coats to be tried on for size. Lockable lengths of case-hardened nickel-plated chain are also used to secure merchandise in this fashion.

Suit jackets and sport coats can be secured by specially designed plastic ties, threaded through the small loops sewn inside the collar of the jackets and tied to the hanger and its rack. When the customer wants to try on a jacket, the salesclerk merely clips the tie, which will be replaced if the jacket is returned to its hanger.

ghosting

Ghosting is the technique of staging or stimulating the arrest of a "shoplifter" in order to publicize the fact that shoplifters are sought out and arrested in that particular store. The ultimate goal is to frighten and deter would-be shoplifters who witness the "arrest."

merchandise presentation and display

The conflict between short-range security and retail objectives often comes into focus when the question of how merchandise should be displayed is being considered. For example, the display of merchandise in an open and appealing fashion will increase sales, and certain items displayed near exits are apt to be purchased on impulse. However, these merchandising techniques also encourage theft. In order to achieve total success in retail security, measures would have to be taken that would severely inhibit sales.

Obviously, the interests of security and merchandising have to be balanced. If, for example, too much emphasis is placed on tantalizing the customer, profits will be lost to shoplifters who have also been tempted. On the other hand, too much security will drive paying customers out of the store. Most retailers have of necessity accepted the premise that in the display of merchandise, the following security principles must be taken into consideration:

Small, valuable merchandise such as jewelry, cameras, guns, and calculators, if not alarmed, should be displayed in locked showcases. If possible, merchandise should be displayed in an orderly fashion, such as in rows or neat stacks; disorganized piles of merchandise or containers loosely filled with articles tend to encourage theft. Attractive items should not be openly displayed near exits or interior doorways. Ideally, display racks should be constructed of transparent material such as glass or abrasion-resistant acrylic materials. Security-conscious retailers often hang sport coats so that those hung next to each other are not facing in the same direction; this will prevent a desperate shoplifter from frantically pulling several coats from their hangers and fleeing the store. Finally, items particularly susceptible to theft should be displayed in areas that are highly visible to both sales and security personnel.

basic store design

Some stores, by virtue of their interior design, invite shoplifting. Every retail establishment, regardless of its type, should be well lit. The aisles should be arranged to facilitate the surveillance of customer activity by retail and security personnel. In small stores, where a single cashier is stationed behind a checkout counter, it may be advisable to place the counter near the door and to position the aisles in such a way that the cashier has a good view of the whole store. Finally, shelves, racks, merchandise displays, and advertising paraphernalia should be built as low to the floor as possible. Shoplifters frequently take advantage of the privacy created by high shelves and other impediments to effective surveillance.

DISCUSSION QUESTIONS

1. Give the reasons why a floorwalker should arrest only a shoplifting suspect she has personally witnessed taking possession of the merchandise in question.
2. Define the term *probable cause*.
3. How much force can be used to arrest a suspected shoplifter?
4. What is the difference between a full confession and an incriminating statement?
5. How important is the suspect's admission of guilt in a shoplifting case?
6. Read the *Devercelli* case in Appendix A, then tell what you, as a security officer, would have done in a similar situation.
7. What, in your opinion, would be gained by fingerprinting people charged with shoplifting?
8. What do California, Illinois, and Nevada hope to gain by statutorily holding the parents of minor shoplifters civilly liable to the victim retailer?
9. In your estimation, could there be some difficulty in prosecuting a suspect whose possession of unpurchased merchandise was not observed by a security officer but was detected by an electronic merchandise tag-alarm system?

10. In your opinion, why are merchants apparently less willing to prosecute juveniles than adults?
11. Why might a professional shoplifter select as a target a store employing floorwalkers and security guards?
12. In your opinion, what is the primary objective of retail security, criminal apprehension, or theft prevention?

SELECTED BIBLIOGRAPHY

BIERNAT, WILLIAM H., "Plug Up the Fitting Room Profit Drain!" *Security World,* April 1977.

BUNYAR, MICHAEL, "Is Shoplifting a Preventable Crime?" *Security World,* April 1977. The article deals with a shopping center's promotional campaign against retail theft.

BURKE, JOHN J., "Confessions to Private Persons," *FBI Law Enforcement Bulletin,* August 1973.

———, "Searches by Private Persons," *FBI Law Enforcement Bulletin,* October 1972.

CURTIS, BOB, "Evaluation of Store Detectives," *Security World,* April 1977.

DONLON, J. P., "Chicago's 'Shoplifting' Courts, a Partial Solution," *Men's Wear,* June 1976.

HARBIN, GEORGE, "Electronic Article Surveillance—It's Inevitable," *Security Management,* July 1977.

HARRIS, GEORGE H., "Why's and How's of Stolen Goods Recovery," Parts I and II, *Security World,* April and May 1977. A discussion of the techniques of retrieval of stolen merchandise from shoplifters, including the handling of the paperwork connected with confessions, searches, and merchandise recovery.

INDAU, FRED E., and JOHN E. REID, *Criminal Interrogation and Confession.* Baltimore: Williams and Wilkins, 1962. This is one of the most comprehensive books on the subject of interview and interrogation techniques.

PALMER, SCOTT R., "Sticky Fingers, Deep Pockets, and the Long Arm of the Law: Illegal Searches of Shoplifters by Private Merchant Security Personnel," *Oregon Law Review,* Vol. 55 (1976).

ROYAL, ROBERT F., and STEVEN R. SCHUTT, *The Gentle Art of Interviewing and Interrogation.* Englewood Cliffs, N.J.: Prentice-Hall, 1976.

Security Industry and Product News, February 1976. A special closed-circuit-television issue containing a CCTV directory and a management guide.

THORSEN, J. E., "The War on Shoplifting," *Security World,* November 1975. A comprehensive article containing a discussion of most of the mechanical and electrical devices used to deter and detect shoplifters.

PART III

INTERNAL THEFT

Chapter 10

Internal Theft

AN OVERVIEW

I. The Nature and Extent of the Internal Theft Problem
   A. *The extent of the problem*
      1. Typical motives and rationale for employee theft
   B. *The nature of the problem*
      1. Theft of cash
      2. Theft of merchandise
      3. Theft of industrial tools and supplies
      4. Theft of merchandise being shipped
      5. Theft of office supplies
      6. Theft of time
      7. Unauthorized consumption of food and beverages
      8. Theft of vital information

II. The Internal Processing of Suspected Employee Thieves
   A. *Deciding whether to accuse an employee suspect*
      1. Guidelines for determining if an accusation is reasonable
   B. *Deciding whether to terminate an employee suspect*
      1. Strength of the case against the employee
      2. Magnitude of the crime
      3. The employee's history with the company
      4. The risk of recurrence
      5. The employee's value to the company

C. *Deciding whether to initiate criminal prosecution*
  1. Advantages of criminal prosecution
  2. Disadvantages of criminal prosecution

In a business context, the term *shrinkage* refers generally to lost assets—for example, missing merchandise, cash, materials, tools, or equipment. Such losses can be explained by either vendor larceny, external theft, misplacement, inventory or bookkeeping error, or employee theft. Except for the portion that is created by external larcenists—that is, shoplifters and burglars—the major contributor to business shrinkage is the employee thief. It has been estimated that internal theft accounts for up to 70 percent of all shrinkage. Note that figures on annual dollar losses created by employee theft do not correspond to the FBI's yearly crime statistics, because a significant amount of employee theft is not detected or reported to the authorities.

An employee who has stolen his employer's property has committed a larceny-type offense—an unlawful taking committed without force or threat of force and without an illegal entry upon the premises of the victim. Such a theft also falls within a broader group of offenses commonly referred to as white-collar crime. In terms of the extent and magnitude of property loss, employee larceny constitutes the most serious form of white-collar crime.

The theft by an employee of cash that, pursuant to his job, has been placed into his care, custody, and control is a larceny offense more specifically classified as embezzlement. Embezzlement encompasses a wide range of criminal activity, including a cashier's shortchanging a cash register as well as a bookkeeper's converting large sums to his own use by altering financial records. The two elements present in every embezzlement, regardless of the method used, are larceny and trust—that is, the offender's position of trust that has enabled him to steal money lawfully in his custody.

The section of the Model Penal Code dealing with embezzlement is entitled, "Theft By Failure To Make Disposition Of Funds Received" (Section 223.8) and reads as follows:

> A person who obtains property upon agreement, or subject to a known legal obligation, to make specified payments or other disposition, whether from such property or its proceeds or from his own property to be reserved in equivalent amount, is guilty of theft if he intentionally deals with the property obtained as his own and fails to make the required payment or disposition. The foregoing applies notwithstanding that it may be impossible to identify particular property as belonging to the victim at the time of the failure of the actor to make the required payment or disposition. An officer or employee of the government or of a financial institution is presumed:

(i) to know any legal obligation relevant to his criminal liability under this Section; and

(ii) to have dealt with the property as his own if he fails to pay or account upon lawful demand, or if an audit reveals a shortage or falsification of accounts.

The internal theft of property that does not constitute embezzlement is commonly referred to as pilferage.

Part III of this text deals primarily with the overall nature and extent of the internal theft problem and how the resultant property losses can be prevented or minimized. An employee can steal from his employer in unlimited ways, using a variety of schemes both ingenious and complex; but only the most common and representative methods of employee theft will be detailed in this and the following chapter. The extent to which the topic is covered here is necessitated by the introductory nature of the text and therefore does not accurately reflect or correspond to the magnitude of its influence upon the security vocation. In reality, control of internal theft constitutes a major facet of the security effort and commands the attention of every practitioner, regardless of the nature of his particular security function.

The Nature and Extent of the Internal Theft Problem

the extent of the problem

Annual monetary losses caused by employee theft and other white-collar crime are currently estimated at $44 billion. In 1976, estimated losses amounted to $30 billion; in 1973, $10 billion; and in 1970, $5 billion—indicating that employee theft and other white-collar crime have increased at an accelerated rate.

Many security practitioners knowledgeable in this area believe that from 70 to 80 percent of all employees steal on at least an occasional basis. It is also believed that from 20 to 30 percent of them will not steal under any circumstances, whereas 30 percent will steal regardless of any security barriers placed in their path, and the remainder will steal at least occasionally if given the opportunity. It appears then that if losses created by employee larceny are to be significantly reduced, the last group must be either prevented or deterred from such behavior.

A few employee thieves, possibly one out of ten, steal sizable amounts of property on a regular, systematic basis. Quite often, this type of thief will work with accomplices and carefully plan each crime, usually stealing objects that can be quickly and profitably sold to fences and other receivers of stolen property. It is interesting to note that a six-year study of schoolboys in London, England, showed that 86 percent of those questioned had stolen something from their school by the time they were 16 years old, and that 70 percent had also stolen something from a retail establishment. In 1975, the Montgomery Ward Company disclosed that it had fired 4,000 employees in 1974—3 percent of the company's work force—for stealing $2.5 million in merchandise.[1]

It is estimated that retail prices have been inflated from 3 to 5 percent as a result of losses sustained by the business community through employee theft. The U.S. Department of Commerce has estimated that 30 percent of all business bankruptcies have been caused by internal theft. And in 1973, 1,000 retail establishments were put out of business by employee thieves.

Losses from employee larceny far exceed those created by even the most frequently committed external crimes. They are twice as high nationally as those attributable to the combined offenses of burglary, auto theft, and bank robbery. Losses caused by bad-check passers, robbers, counterfeiters, and retail customer thieves are also much smaller. Most retail-security practitioners believe that up to two-thirds of their shrinkage is caused by employee rather than customer thieves. For example, in 1975, the National Retail Merchants Association estimated that an average of $7.5 million worth of goods disappeared from stores each day and that 50 percent of these losses were due to dishonest employees.[2]

Typical Motives and Rationale for Employee Theft. An employee thief, like any other larcenist, steals for personal gain. Although there are several reasons why an employee might steal from his employer, probably the most common is the relative ease by which such an offense can be committed. Most employee thieves, like most burglars, robbers, and other perpetrators of external crimes, are opportunists. The employer is vulnerable because he must necessarily expose his property to those he employs. Even those employees who consider themselves honest will frequently pilfer small quantities of such items as pens, paper clips, and notebooks. The employee who is more committed to theft will use his position to steal in greater quantity or select objects of higher value.

A few employee thieves attempt to justify their behavior through real or imagined grievances against the employer, citing dissatisfaction with pay, fringe benefits, or working conditions, a missed promotion, or a belief that a fellow employee has been mistreated by the employer as reasons behind their pilferage.

Occasionally, an employee will find himself in what appears to be a hopeless financial predicament, often as the result of living beyond his means or of poor money management. Heavy gambling, drug use, and alcoholism are other common causes of financial difficulties. Regardless of the cause, an employee who is experiencing a serious financial problem may be more likely to resort to internal theft.

---

[1] "The Thieves Within," *Newsweek*, November 24, 1975.

[2] *Ibid.*

the nature of the problem

Theft of Cash. The theft of money from a cash register by a cashier constitutes a relatively unsophisticated form of embezzlement. Retail establishments such as supermarkets, drugstores, convenience food markets, and discount stores are common victims of this type of offender, as are restaurants and bars. This form of internal theft is commonly referred to as "knocking down."

The primary justification for the use of a cash register is to hold cash-handling employees accountable for the money they receive on behalf of their employer. Whenever a sale is rung up, the amount of the transaction is recorded onto a roll of paper tape housed inside the cash register, and at any given time, the amount of money in the cash drawer should correspond to the total amount shown on the tape. If these two figures match, the cash register is said to have balanced. But if money has been placed in the register without ringing up the corresponding sale, a cash overage will be created; that is, the amount of cash in the drawer will exceed the figure shown on the cash register tape by the amount of the unrecorded transaction. On the other hand, if cash that has been received and recorded is taken from the cash register, a discrepancy in the form of a shortage will be shown between the cash on hand and the total recorded on the tape.

So, obviously, a cash register will not operate to detect or prevent employee theft unless every cashier properly records each sales transaction, since, in order for a cashier to steal money without creating a shortage in the cash drawer, the amount stolen must not be recorded onto the cash register tape. Such an omission is usually accomplished in either of the following two ways:

1. *"No-sale transactions."* A dishonest cashier who intends to steal will, whenever possible, avoid ringing up a sales transaction. Cashiers working alone in small establishments usually have plenty of opportunities to avoid using the cash register altogether, by merely pocketing money received from customers. A cashier can usually avoid opening the cash register drawer when a customer pays the exact amount of the purchase price. But when it is necessary to make change, the cashier is usually required to open the cash drawer, and since this will be noted on the tape, the cashier is induced to ring up this type of sale. (Whether he rings up an amount equal to the sum he has received is another matter.) An employee who avoids opening a cash register drawer by making change out of his own pocket risks being reported to his employer by a customer. Probably the most common method of stealing the entire proceeds of a transaction is to handle two or more transactions without closing the cash drawer, receiving money and making change without recording these sales. By placing cash in the register without recording its receipt on the tape, the cashier creates a temporary overage in the cash drawer that can be

removed and pocketed at a more appropriate time. He will usually make certain that the amount he takes is equal to the overage he has created, so that the cash register will balance.

2. *"Underringing."* Operating on the same principle, the dishonest cashier may ring up each transaction but only a portion of the sale. For example, a cashier receives $5 in payment of a $3 purchase and rings up the sale as a $1 transaction, then gives the customer his $2 in change. Although the customer has not been cheated, the employer will lose $2 when the employee thief takes this amount from the cash register at a more convenient time.

Cashiers are not the only money-handling employees who are capable of using their positions to divert company funds. Any employee who has the job of receiving cash can merely pocket the money without executing a sales invoice or otherwise recording the transaction. Nonretail employees working with accounts receivable who handle incoming funds and credit customers' accounts may be capable of perpetrating a variety of embezzlement schemes. The following excerpt, taken from a Small Business Administration booklet, discusses a form of embezzlement called "lapping":

> . . . A somewhat more complicated type of embezzlement . . . involves the temporary withholding of receipts such as payments on accounts receivable.
>
> Lapping is a continuing scheme which usually starts with a small amount but can run into thousands of dollars before it is detected. For example, take an employee who opens mail or otherwise receives cash and checks as payment on open accounts. He holds out a $100 cash payment made by customer "A" on March 1. To avoid arousing suspicion on "A's" part, he takes $100 from a $100 payment made by customer "B" on March 5. He sends this on, together with the necessary documentation, for processing and crediting to the account of "A." He pockets the remaining $100, which increases the shortage to $200.
>
> As this "borrowing" procedure continues, the employee makes away with increasingly larger amounts of money involving more and more accounts. A fraud of this nature can run on for years. Of course, it requires detailed recordkeeping by the embezzler in order to keep track of the shortage and transfer it from one account to another to avoid suspicion. Any indication that an employee is keeping personal records of business transactions outside your regular books of account should be looked into.
>
> Sometimes an embezzler who is carrying on a lapping scheme also has access to accounts receivable records and statements. In this case, he is in a position to alter the statements mailed out to customers. Thus the fraud may continue undetected over a long period of time, until something unusual happens. A customer complaint may spotlight the situation. Or the matter may be surfaced through audit procedures such as confirmation of accounts receivable. One embezzler who also handled the customer complaints was able to avoid detection for many years. The amount of the shortage reached such proportions and covered so many accounts that he dared not take a vacation. He even ate lunch at his desk lest some other employee receive an

inquiry from a customer concerning a discrepancy in a statement. The owner-manager for whom he worked admired his diligence and loyalty. His fellow workers marveled that his apparent frugality enabled him to enjoy a rather high standard of living. But the inevitable finally happened. This employee was hospitalized with a serious ailment, and in his absence his fraudulent scheme came to light.[3]

Some of the other common methods of diverting company funds are these:

1. The padding and falsification of overtime and other payroll records
2. The creation and issuance of payroll checks to nonexistent employees
3. The creation of phony purchase orders reflecting goods and services never delivered or received
4. Inflating the cost of goods and services by, for example, purchasing personnel, who then convert these excess amounts to their own use

Theft of Merchandise. In this section, the discussion is of the theft of goods offered for sale in retail establishments, and the employees referred to are retail personnel. It is interesting to note that in a 1975 survey conducted by *Convenience Store Merchandiser*, employee theft was held responsible for 75 to 85 percent of all retail inventory shrinkage.[4]

Probably the most effective and common method used by an employee to steal his employer's merchandise is leaving the store with the property concealed on his person, just as his shoplifting counterpart does. The only difference is the considerable advantage most employees have because of their unrestricted access to the store and its merchandise. Moreover, employees who are permitted to shop in their employer's store often take advantage of this privilege by concealing stolen merchandise in packages containing items they have legitimately purchased.

Supermarkets, convenience food stores, and pharmacies, among others, experience inventory shortages caused by employees who give away or discount merchandise to friends and relatives—most commonly, food items, cigarettes, and cosmetics. It is not uncommon, however, for a clothing salesman to express his gratitude to a regular customer by throwing in a few ties with each purchase. By offering such gratuities, a salesman working on a commission can induce customers to buy from him, and the missing ties will probably be blamed on shoplifters. An employee who has been selling articles to friends or relatives at lower, unauthorized prices—a practice referred to as "sliding"—may find it difficult to discontinue, because those customers would be angered and would threaten to expose him. Employees who give away or discount large quantities of merchan-

---

[3]Christopher J. Moran, *Preventing Embezzlement* (Washington, D.C.: Small Business Administration, 1973), p. 3.

[4]*The Cost of Crimes against Business*, rev. ed. (Washington, D.C.: U.S. Department of Commerce, 1976), p. v.

dise on a regular basis usually receive substantial kickbacks from their accomplices.

There are several ways in which a dishonest retail employee can purchase his employer's merchandise at an unusually low price. For example, a salesperson working in a women's clothing department who wishes to purchase an outfit she cannot afford can place the apparel into layaway at the "request" of a fictitious customer. After it appears that the merchandise is not going to be picked up, the employee can buy it out of season at a reduced price, which is lowered even further by her special employee discount.

Another unscrupulous method of creating an employee bargain is the intentional defacing or breaking of merchandise by a manufacturing, warehousing, or retail employee. An appliance, piece of furniture, or item of clothing that is slightly but noticeably marred will usually be offered at a reduced price.

Theft of Industrial Tools and Supplies. A dishonest employee will steal any item that is useful or valuable and is within his reach; thus, industrial facilities, like retail establishments, suffer from internal theft problems. The primary difference is in the nature of the stolen property.

Like his retail counterpart, the dishonest factory worker will most likely steal his employer's property by leaving the plant with it in his possession. It is not unusual for an industrial employee to leave the plant with company tools, materials, and other items small enough to fit into a lunch pail or handbag. Dishonest employees often use their cars to steal larger objects or greater amounts of property per theft. Industrial tools and supplies are often stolen by being tossed into trash containers for later retrieval outside the plant, or by being thrown over a fence or out a window to accomplices waiting outside. Stolen property is often taken from a factory through fire exit doors that are not monitored or protected by exit alarms. An employee who leaves the premises in this fashion can often put stolen property directly into his car without being observed by management or security personnel.

Theft of Merchandise Being Shipped. It is not uncommon for stockroom and shipping and receiving employees to steal cargo directly from delivery trucks or from the dock area. Truck drivers who find excess cargo on their trucks after completing their scheduled deliveries—perhaps caused by partial deliveries inadvertently made, or by an overloading of the truck—may pilfer these items. Dishonest loading-dock personnel working in collusion with truck drivers may overload trucks intentionally for the purpose of splitting the resultant overages with the driver. On the other hand, a truck driver might intentionally deliver an amount of cargo that is less than what had been ordered so that he can steal the resultant overage; and dishonest receiving employees who are in collusion with him may knowingly accept and sign for such short deliveries, afterward sharing in the overage.

Theft of Office Supplies. Most employees, at one time or another, have taken for their personal use office supplies belonging to their employer. Individually, most of these thefts involve small quantities of items such as pens, pencils, paper clips, and paper. Because these items are inexpensive, easy to replace, and difficult to account for, most companies make little effort to prevent or deter their theft. However, pilferage of this nature is so regularly committed by so many employees that its overall cost to the business community is substantial. It is hard to determine the point at which what could be termed the unauthorized use of company property becomes theft in the employer's eyes. For example, the theft of a box of staples may be winked at by an employer who would frown upon the removal of a stapler. In this context, it is difficult to precisely define the terms *thief* and *theft*.

Theft of Time. Although the theft of time is not included in the criminal-law definition of larceny and so is not a criminal offense, it nevertheless constitutes a type of employee behavior that is costly to an employer.

Employee theft of time takes many forms. The most obvious is an employee's remaining off the job without his absence being noted. An employee who arranges for a fellow worker to punch a time clock on his behalf may get a day's pay without doing a day's work. Less flagrant are employees who punch in and out for one another to conceal late arrivals to and early departures from work. In some instances, employees have been able to report for work and then disappear until quitting time. This type of behavior is particularly feasible on large construction sites, where there are more workers than jobs. Employees who leave their place of employment without authority during working hours for personal reasons are also stealing time from an employer, as are those who take excessive lunch and coffee breaks. Some of the more subtle and less recognizable forms of time theft are daydreaming, unnecessary gossip, and the prolonged use of an employer's telephone for personal business.

Unauthorized Consumption of Food and Beverages. Another type of theft that is petty on an individual basis but costly in its entirety is the unauthorized consumption of an employer's food and drink. Typical victims of this type of internal theft are restaurants, bars, supermarkets, food-processing plants, and food-storage facilities. For example, if a few stockboys and cashiers in every supermarket in a large chain-store operation help themselves to candy bars or soft drinks every day, the annual shrinkage will be substantial.

Theft of Vital Information. The unauthorized acquisition and/or dissemination by an employee of confidential data critical to his employer can be more costly to a company than a major theft. A theft of this nature is often referred to as incustrial espionage.

Within the business community, there are corporations that will eagerly receive intelligence regarding the plans, operations, and economic status of their competitors. One of the more subtle and indirect methods of acquiring such confidential information is to recruit knowledgeable personnel employed by the competition. A more direct method is by the use of industrial spies. Information that may be useful to a competitor and therefore vulnerable to theft includes trade secrets such as marketing data, advertising concepts, rates and pricing, personnel data, and information regarding research and development.[5]

The Internal Processing of Suspected Employee Thieves

When a company is confronted with a theft or series of thefts believed to have been committed internally, the initial response is usually an attempt to identify the employee responsible for the crime. Quite often, the identity of the wrongdoer is immediately known—for instance, when the employee thief has been caught "red-handed"—thereby eliminating the need for an internal security investigation. In most cases, however, at least a preliminary inquiry is necessary to identify the thief. Such an investigation might be conducted by trained investigative personnel or by nonsecurity and noninvestigative employees. In any event, when the thief is identified, the employer has several basic alternatives in handling the situation.

The first decision is whether or not the employee is to be confronted and specifically accused of the theft. The employer may decide to avoid such a confrontation by terminating the suspect on grounds unrelated to the crime, or by waiting until such an opportunity arises. But if he decides to specifically accuse the employee of the theft, the employer must further decide what sanction, if any, he will impose. For example, a dishonest employee may be given a warning, be suspended, or be terminated. If the decision is dismissal, the victim-employer may also decide to report the theft to law-enforcement authorities for the purpose of initiating criminal prosecution.

The material that follows discusses some of the factors considered relevant by most employers in deciding what action to take against a suspected employee.

---

[5]Edward J. Anderson, in "A Study of Industrial Espionage," *Security Management*, January 1977, defines the term *trade secret* as "information which is neither patentable nor capable of being guarded under copyright laws, but which pertains to the very nature of a commercial enterprise's competitive structure. . . ."

deciding whether to accuse an employee suspect

A basic consideration regarding whether an employer should accuse an employee of a crime is the certainty and reasonableness of the employer's belief that the accused committed the offense. Assuming that it is made in good faith—that is, that the accuser's motives are not malicious—an accusation that turns out to be false could be extremely harmful to both parties; the employer will probably lose a valuable employee and/or be sued civilly for libel or slander. For this and other reasons, few employers make groundless accusations. The decision is particularly difficult when the employer does not know if there is enough evidence to legally justify the accusation. If he is in doubt over this question he will most likely play it safe and not accuse the employee.

Assuming the presence of facts that indicate an employee's involvement in an internal theft, it is usually the best policy to confront him with the evidence. If the evidence is sufficient to sustain a reasonable suspicion, the fact that the employee denies his guilt will not preclude the employer from taking further action. In any case, if an employer ignores or avoids confronting suspected employees, he may be contributing to his internal theft problem. In addition, there is the possibility that, despite evidence to the contrary, the employee is in fact innocent, and this may be determined through questioning. In a few cases, employees have confessed their crimes and have made and kept a promise to reimburse the company for its losses, meanwhile being retained on the payroll. At any rate, unless there is an accusation, there can be no sanction, restitution, rehabilitation, or criminal prosecution.

Guidelines for Determining if an Accusation Is Reasonable. Legally, the reasonableness of a criminal accusation depends upon the probability that the allegations are true. This guideline is analogous to the standard of probable cause that is a prerequisite to arrests and searches by law-enforcement officers. The probable-cause or reasonable-grounds standard is defined generally by the courts, which apply the doctrine on a case-by-case basis. With regard to a criminal accusation, probable cause exists if a reasonable man, using the same facts as are known to the accuser at the time of his accusation, would also believe that the accused committed the offense. Probable cause, however, should not be confused with a higher degree of certainty, termed proof of guilt. As a degree of certainty, probable cause is said to be less than proof of guilt but more than suspicion. The following hypothetical situation illustrates a level of certainty that does not meet the minimum standard of probable cause or reasonableness:

The manager of Company A has discovered that a small company calculator is missing from his office. Since the other eight office employees are in the habit of borrowing the calculator, the manager is not sure how long it has been gone. There has been no evidence of forced entry into the building or the office. Meeting with the office personnel, the manager determines that none of them has borrowed the machine.

At this point, the manager begins to suspect a clerical employee recently hired by Company A. He notes that prior to the clerk's employment in his office, nothing had been stolen, and he is certain that none of his other employees could have taken the calculator. When he learns that the clerk had worked late a few days earlier, alone in the office, the manager becomes even more suspicious. Then he learns from a source at the police station that the clerk had been arrested a year ago on a drug charge, so he calls the employee into his office and accuses him of the theft. The clerk denies knowledge of the crime and terminates his employment with Company A.

Although the clerk may have been a prime suspect in this case, the facts as known to the manager at the time of his accusation did not establish probable cause to believe that he had stolen the calculator. There are too many other plausible explanations for its disappearance.

As it turned out in this case, the calculator had not been stolen. Prior to going on vacation two days before the manager's discovery, the assistant manager had taken the calculator home to finish some last-minute work, and when he tried to use it, he discovered that it was broken. The next morning, as he was leaving town, the assistant manager took the calculator to a business-machine shop and left it for repairs, forgetting to notify his superior. Two days after the manager had accused the clerk of stealing the calculator, the repair shop telephoned to inform him that it had been fixed and was ready to be picked up.

deciding whether to terminate an employee suspect

After an employee who is suspected of theft has been accused of the offense, should he be terminated? The discussion below concerns some of the factors that normally influence such a decision.

Strength of the Case against the Employee. Since the suspect has already been accused, it will be assumed for purposes of this discussion that there is probable cause to believe he has committed the theft. However, because there are higher levels of certainty than probable cause, the employer may decide not to terminate a suspect whose guilt is probable but considerably less than certain. Under these circumstances, the amount, type, and quality of the evidence will be relevant in determining whether he is to be dismissed.

When discussing criminal evidence, it is helpful to define and classify it as being either direct or circumstantial. Evidence classified as direct does not require an inference. For example, an eyewitness to a crime who identifies the suspect as the offender produces direct evidence. Assuming that this witness is honest and not mistaken, the only conclusion to be drawn from this testimony is that the suspect is guilty of the crime. But witnesses are not always honest and often make mistakes, so this type of direct evidence is not necessarily strong and is often refutable. Another form of direct evidence that is much more reliable is the confession. However, even an admission of guilt will be questionable as proof if it was involuntarily given under severe duress.

On the other hand, circumstantial evidence, contrary to popular belief, can be probative, irrefutable, and very persuasive. Moreover, it is usually very reliable, especially when it is in the form of physical evidence. For example, a latent fingerprint is a common form of circumstantial evidence. The fact that a suspect's fingerprint is found at the scene of a crime constitutes direct evidence that he was there and circumstantial proof that he committed the offense. If the suspect's fingerprint is found inside a burglarized bank vault that is not legally accessible to him, his criminal involvement in the burglary is the most reasonable inference to be drawn from it. Although such evidence is circumstantial, it could, without more, establish proof of guilt.

If a suspect accused of stealing company property responds by admitting his guilt, most employers would consider the case solved and act accordingly. An employer may be somewhat less certain of an employee's guilt when the suspect denies knowledge of the theft, and the only evidence connecting him to it is the statement of an eyewitness. Still less convincing is evidence in the form of incriminatory statements allegedly made by the suspect to a third person whose reliability and motives are in question. If this is the only evidence, the employer may surely hesitate to terminate the employee.

In the absence of a single piece of direct evidence, such as testimony of an eyewitness or a confession, evidence pointing to a suspect's guilt is usually circumstantial and most likely fragmented. Therefore, an employer who as a matter of policy will not terminate an employee unless his guilt is clearly established will have to consider each case individually by evaluating the available evidence. Here are some examples of the more common forms of circumstantial evidence:

An employee may be implicated in a theft after the stolen property has been discovered in his possession. For example, if a spot search of a factory worker's lunch pail reveals a company tool, this employee will most likely be considered guilty of theft. However, he may use one of the more common defenses: that he did not know the item belonged to his employer; that it was merely being borrowed; that he had found rather than stolen it; or that he did not know it was there.

Signs of affluence on the part of an employee suspected of an internal theft may be incriminating, especially if the new, unexplained wealth coincides in time with the occurrence of the offense. For example, the purchase of an expensive car by a blue-collar employee of a warehouse immediately following the mysterious loss of several cartons of valuable merchandise may qualify this employee as a suspect.

The fact that a suspected employee is one of only a few people having access to the scene of a larceny may constitute relevant evidence indicating his guilt. And his physical proximity to the scene of the crime either before or immediately after its commission may also be relevant. Factors to be considered in evaluating the strength of this type of evidence are determinations of how many others were in the vicinity at the time and whether or not the suspect was supposed to be working near the scene of the crime.

Finally, the existence of a strong motive to steal may further implicate an employee who, for other reasons, is already suspect. Employees with serious financial troubles, or those who have voiced an intense dissatisfaction with the company, its personnel, or policies, could be considered particularly motivated to steal.

Magnitude of the Crime. In discussing this factor, it will be assumed that the question of the employee's guilt, at least in the employer's mind, his been resolved. Companies whose policy it is to automatically terminate every employee suspected of theft may do so on the premise that any larceny, regardless of its nature, constitutes a serious offense, and therefore the offender is undesirable and potentially harmful to the company. But many employers will not terminate a guilty employee without a further consideration of alternative sanctions—usually, penalties that correspond in severity to the circumstances of each case. One of the factors often considered is the magnitude of the offense, predicated upon the notion that a smaller theft is a less serious crime than a larger one, and therefore calls for a lighter penalty.

The amount of money taken, or the monetary value of the stolen property, constitutes the most obvious criterion for determining the magnitude of a theft offense, but other factors could be particularly relevant to a victim-employer. For example, a victim company may consider it absolutely necessary to recover its stolen property, particularly items that cannot be easily replaced and are critical to the well-being of the victim. Under these circumstances, the thief's willingness and ability to return the stolen property promptly may save his job. Or a company may agree not to terminate a dishonest employee in return for his promise to pay back the money he has stolen; such an agreement can also avert an embarrassing or costly scandal. By proceeding thus, the company does not necessarily minimize the offense, but rather lessens its effect.

Even when a theft does not involve a significant amount of money, the victim-employer may nevertheless perceive the offense as serious, because of the manner in which it was committed. The relationship between the perpetrator and his victim also may affect the degree of seriousness that is attached to the crime. For example, thefts that are committed on the spur of the moment by personnel low in the company hierarchy are usually not considered or treated as particularly serious offenses; but a carefully planned or vindictively motivated theft by a person employed in a position of trust will normally be considered a major offense regardless of the amount of money involved. Moreover, if it is discovered that an employee has committed a series of thefts, the entire criminal episode may be viewed in a particularly offensive light.

The Employee's History with the Company. This is another aspect of an employee's relationship with his victim-employer that may affect the decision to terminate. For example, an employee who has been mildly suspected of several other thefts, similar to the one in which he is now implicated, will most likely be treated more severely. All things being equal, the chance that a new employee will be terminated for theft is probably much greater than for a long-time employee whose work record has otherwise been satisfactory. An employee with a poor work record, and considered by his employer to be particularly disloyal, may by his theft have given the employer the long-awaited opportunity to dismiss him justifiably.

The Risk of Recurrence. If an employer believes, for whatever reason, that an employee will continue to steal, the employee will usually be terminated. For example, it is advisable to fire any employee who has been caught in a theft that by the way it was committed, clearly demonstrates his commitment to larceny as a way of life, since he will most likely steal again. An employee who justifies his theft by citing a grievance against the company may also steal again, at least until his grievance is resolved. And an employee who has admitted stealing from the company but who does not offer an excuse or show remorse for his behavior is another prime candidate for dismissal.

The Employee's Value to the Company. An employee whose termination would be immediately and severely injurious to the company, because of his knowledge, skill, or critical position, may be reluctantly retained by his victim-employer. However, many employers consider retaining such personnel even more potentially injurious. In many cases of this nature, the final decision may depend upon the magnitude of the offense, the motives of the employee, the risk of scandal, and the chance that the crime will be repeated.

deciding whether to initiate criminal prosecution

Once the decision has been made to terminate an employee suspected of theft, the victim-employer must further decide if criminal charges are to be brought against the suspect. The fact that this is not a simple or clear-cut decision is reflected by statistics indicating that only a small percentage of internal theft offenses are reported to law-enforcement agencies for further investigation and criminal prosecution. The following discussion may at least partially explain the reluctance of the business community to call upon the criminal justice system in these cases.

Advantages of Criminal Prosecution. Most of those who believe that a suspected employee thief should usually be reported to the police base this opinion on the premise that this will, at least to some degree, deter such behavior by other employees. Moreover, if all employers handle their dishonest employees in this fashion, at least the more serious offenders will eventually be convicted of larceny. And since the criminal conviction of an adult is a matter of public record in most jurisdictions, any employer who cares to inquire will learn whether an employee suspect has in fact been so convicted before.

On a more subjective level, many employers who turn larceny suspects over to the authorities do so pursuant to what they perceive as their civic responsibility to assist the police in fighting crime. Finally, retribution may be considered one of the advantages of bringing a criminal wrongdoer to justice, since the satisfaction of a victim when the person responsible for his injury is punished may be anticipated and savored by an employer-victim.

Disadvantages of Criminal Prosecution. Because the processing of a defendant through the criminal justice system is often slow, complicated, and cumbersome, most employers find that instituting criminal prosecution involves time and considerable inconvenience. From the employer's standpoint, many man-hours are lost at the police station, D.A.'s office, and courthouse. In addition, most criminal cases are characterized by a series of delays, continuances, and postponements that try the patience of victims and witnesses alike. The fact that employee thieves are often found not guilty owing to procedural errors tends to discourage most employers, and even when a defendant is convicted, it is usually the result of plea bargaining. Most of these defendants therefore receive exceedingly light sentences, usually shocking and offending their victims, who may end up seriously questioning whether coming forward was worth the effort.

Quite often, in an effort to induce an admission of guilt or a promise from the employee to make full or partial restitution, the employer will agree in advance not to initiate criminal prosecution. Such an arrangement illustrates how self-interest can destroy the long-range benefits of criminally prosecuting thieves. A terminated employee thief who has been permitted to avoid criminal prosecution by giving a confession or returning the property he has stolen will believe that he has little to lose by stealing from his next employer.

Finally, an employer may reluctantly choose not to prosecute an employee because of the effect such publicity might have on the company.

DISCUSSION QUESTIONS

1. In your opinion, at what point should the unauthorized use of an employer's office supplies be treated as theft?

2. In your opinion, should every employee caught stealing be terminated? If not, what criteria do you consider relevant in justifying a lesser sanction?
3. Discuss the proposition that an employer who fires a petty thief risks hiring a replacement who will steal more.
4. Under what circumstances would you suggest that an employee thief be criminally prosecuted?
5. Will the criminal prosecution of an employee thief necessarily result in bad publicity for the employer? Explain your answer.

SELECTED BIBLIOGRAPHY

ANDERSON, EDWARD J., "A Study of Industrial Espionage," *Security Management*, January 1977. A discussion of legal as well as illegal means of obtaining trade secrets.

GALLO, KENNETH, "All Deposits, No Returns—The Story of Suzie's Bank," *Security World*, February 1977. An article concerning the detection of underringing sales employees through surprise cash register audits.

GUGAS, CHRIS, SR., "Stealing as a Fringe Benefit," *Security World*, September 1976.

HEMPHILL, CHARLES F., JR., and THOMAS HEMPHILL, *The Secure Company*. Homewood, Ill.: Dow-Jones-Irwin, 1975. This work concerns problems related to employee dishonesty, disloyalty, and lack of interest. Numerous case histories and fact situations are drawn from labor arbitration decisions involving employee theft, alcoholism, and drug use.

HERMON, FREDERICK E., "Management Rules on White Collar Crime," *Security World*, January 1976.

MORAN, CHRISTOPHER J., *Preventing Embezzlement*. Washington, D.C.: Small Business Administration, January 1973.

ROSENBAUM, RICHARD W., "Can We Predict Employee Theft?" *Security World*, October 1975.

WEISINGER, MORT, "Employee Thievery Is Big Business," *Parade*, December 9, 1973.

Chapter 11

Common Methods of Combatting Internal Theft

AN OVERVIEW

I. Preemployment Investigations
   A. *Legal limitations on preemployment investigations*
   B. *Relevant areas of inquiry*
      1. The applicant's criminal history
      2. The applicant's financial status
      3. The applicant's past work record
      4. Interviewing the applicant's personal references
      5. Verifying the applicant's past and present residences

II. Honesty Shopping
   A. *Testing the honesty of a cash-handling employee*
      1. Reporting the employee's cash-handling methods
      2. Documenting the failure to record
   B. *Accusing a cash-handling employee of theft*
   C. *The purpose, effectiveness, and rationale of honesty shopping*

III. Basic Cash-Handling Procedures for Cashiers
   A. *Refund schemes*
   B. *Other standard cash-handling rules and procedures*

IV. Controlling and Surveying Employee Foot Traffic
   A. *Employee traffic to and from the facility*
      1. Designating employee entrance and exit doors

2. Exit door alarms
3. Monitoring employee foot traffic to and from the premises
4. Metal detectors as antitheft devices
5. Controlling employee parking
6. Time locks
7. Property-pass systems

B. *Employee traffic within the facility*
1. Employee identification cards and badges

V. Marking and Identifying Company Property

VI. The Undercover Investigation
A. *The undercover method of combatting employee theft*
B. *Administering an undercover operation*
1. The problem of in-house undercover operations
2. The operation of private undercover services
3. Placement and utilization of the undercover agent
4. Areas of investigative interest
5. Using the operative as a witness

VII. Indoctrinating Employees against Theft
A. *Methods of indoctrination*

Employee theft cannot be eliminated. It can, however, be contained and even reduced. This chapter deals with the various measures, preventive and otherwise, available to an employer in his battle against internal theft.

Preemployment Investigations

Traditionally, employers have attempted to protect themselves from incompetent, lazy, disloyal, mentally ill, dangerous, and dishonest employees by screening job applicants. In an effort to determine generally if an applicant is a poor employment risk, employers usually solicit from him personal data believed pertinent to this issue, having him record them on an application form furnished by the prospective employer. On the basis of his completed job application form, an applicant may be deemed unfit for employment on several grounds—for example, lack of formal education, vocational training, or relevant work experience.

These types of data, however, do not cover matters of a security nature. To identify the applicant who may be a poor security risk, the security practitioner should have access to personal background information specifically relevant to this determination. And he also needs to know whether the applicant has executed his job application form completely and truthfully. For him to do otherwise reflects dishonesty, a trait that may classify him as a poor security risk. Therefore, the mere verification of the information written on the application by the candidate has security relevance and purpose.

The preemployment investigation is generally regarded as one of the most effective preventive measures against internal theft. The more thorough the inquiry, the more effective.

legal limitations on preemployment investigations

Beginning in the early 1970s, an abundance of state and federal laws, collectively referred to as privacy legislation, seriously eroded the employer's ability to protect himself in this fashion from internal theft. For example, Department of Justice Order 601-75 prohibits any criminal justice agency receiving funding through the Law Enforcement Assistance Administration (LEAA) to disseminate criminal history information to non–criminal justice agencies or to confirm or deny the existence of such information for employment purposes. The Fair Credit Reporting Act, a federal statute made effective in 1971, requires that before a job applicant can be the subject of a credit bureau inquiry, his written consent be obtained. There are so many additional federal credit and privacy laws currently being considered by Congress that most employers are uncertain as to the current status of the law on this matter. For example, in 1975, there were 150 privacy bills before the legislative bodies of 49 states.[1]

Under federal and most state laws, it is currently illegal for an employer to acquire from a public law-enforcement agency any information concerning an applicant's history of criminal arrest. In a few states, even the fact that an applicant has been convicted of a criminal offense cannot be made available to an inquiring employer. In Illinois, a state law makes it illegal for a prospective employer to inquire into the existence of a criminal background on the job application unless the offense for which the candidate was convicted was job-related. One of the federal bills before Congress likewise makes it a crime to even ask an applicant if he has ever been arrested or convicted of a crime.

It is interesting to note that the increased desire for privacy, as reflected by the number of pending state and federal privacy statutes, comes at a time when the public is greatly disturbed over the rising cost of crime. The dilemma inherent in this situation affects the employer more directly by forcing him to either break the law or accept the risk of hiring employees on intuition and faith.

Notwithstanding the complex, confusing, and potentially restrictive nature of state and federal privacy legislature, the preemployment inquiry, even in its more limited form, is one of the most essential weapons an employer has against internal theft.

---

[1]Anthony N. Potter, "The Dangers of Privacy Legislation," *Security World*, November 1975.

relevant areas of inquiry

In discussing the types of data that have particular security relevance, we will consider the less obvious reasons why such information is relevant.

Unfortunately, many employers do not conduct even a cursory preemployment check. The most basic and obvious inquiries made by nonsecurity personnel can be exceedingly productive, and by merely verifying the data on each job application, an employer can effectively screen out undesirable applicants. Many employers, as a part of their preemployment testing, utilize the polygraph or the Psychological Stress Evaluator (PSE) as means of identifying high-risk applicants.[2] Another method is to have each prospective employee fill out a specially designed questionnaire that its developers claim will identify respondents who have dishonest tendencies.[3] The questionnaires usually take from 20 minutes to an hour to fill out, and applicants whose test results indicate dishonesty are often asked to take a polygraph or PSE test. This type of follow-up may be particularly applicable where the job applied for is a sensitive one.

Regardless of the method utilized, the following preemployment areas of inquiry are relevant in determining the security risk of employee applicants.

The Applicant's Criminal History. The debate over what type of background information can be kept from an employer focuses on whether or not an employer should have access to police files containing arrest data. Because most employers and security practitioners consider this type of information the most relevant in evaluating applicants as security risks, employers should be made aware of the existence or nonexistence of an applicant's criminal record. In most states, a distinction is made between the confidentiality of arrest and of conviction data. In such jurisdictions, a criminal conviction is a matter of public record, usually on file in a city or county clerk's office. Police *arrest* data, on the other hand, may not be

---

[2]Several honesty integrity matters are commonly discussed in preemployment polygraph interviews. The following subjects are identified and discussed by Kenneth Olson, in "Pre-Employment Testing," *Security Industry and Product News*, April 1977:

1. Intentional falsification or deliberate omissions on the applicant's application
2. The physical health of the applicant
3. Theft of cash and/or merchandise from former employers
4. Previous convictions
5. Degree of gambling habits
6. Use of unprescribed narcotics
7. Involvement in undetected crimes
8. Excessive indebtedness
9. Release from former employments for cause

[3]"New Pre-employment Test Can Save Business Millions," *Security Distributing & Merchandising*, May 1977, concerns the "Trustworthy Attitude Survey," an employee prescreening method developed by Dr. Alan Strand, an industrial psychologist, and Robert Cormack. The licensee for this system is the ZonLin Corporation. Another "pen and paper" lie-detector system is the "Reid Report for Job Applicants," offered by John E. Reid & Associates.

available to the employer; but in such a jurisdiction, he should at least check to see if the job applicant has been *convicted* of a crime.

If the applicant is found to have been convicted of a theft-related or other serious crime within the recent past, extreme caution is advised. However, the employer must not rely too heavily on the fact that an applicant has had no local convictions. If his application shows that he has fairly recently lived in other parts of the country, similar inquiries should be made in those jurisdictions. Keep in mind too that only a small percentage of internal theft cases are reported to the police, that only a few of these result in arrests, and that many arrests do not lead to convictions. Therefore, a clean record does not necessarily indicate that the applicant is a good security risk.

A related development in the civil law has made the employer's acquisition of an applicant's criminal history even more vital. A court in Maryland recently awarded $13 million to the husband of a woman who had been raped and murdered by one of the defendant's employees.[4] The employer, a furniture leasing company, having neglected to conduct a preemployment investigation, had hired a convicted armed robber who was at the time on parole. The rape and murder were committed by this employee in the victim's home where the employer had sent him to work.

Because of the unavailability to employers of data related to a person's criminal history, employers have been forced to rely more heavily upon other, more remote and indirect areas of inquiry.

The Applicant's Financial Status. The employer who conducts a limited preemployment investigation will normally skip any inquiry of a credit or financial nature. Some may fail to see the relevance of such data to the hiring process. Nevertheless, a correlation can exist between the degree of financial pressure on a person and his potential for theft.

In the past, investigators used credit bureaus as sources of general, nonfinancial background information. The Fair Credit Reporting Act now requires the subject's written consent for such investigation. In cases where an employee is going to be placed in a position of trust and will have access to large amounts of money, the employer would be wise to request the applicant's consent and make an appropriate financial inquiry through a credit bureau.

The Applicant's Past Work Record. The applicant's past employment record will probably constitute the most revealing part of the preemployment investigation. All former employments listed on his job application should be verified, along with the dates showing how long he worked at each. An applicant should also be asked to detail his activity during those periods not covered by his employment. It is quite possible that such time gaps will reveal previous

[4] *Blum* v *CLA*, Montgomery County, Maryland Circuit Court, 1974.

employers he has not listed. Moreover, if the employment dates listed are consistently and substantially incorrect, this fact could also indicate an attempt to hide a previous employment. Such omissions are quite relevant, since they are usually motivated by the applicant's desire to keep derogatory information from the prospective employer.

Verifications of former employments are usually made by contacting the previous employer's personnel department. Such inquiries, normally consisting of a quick review of the applicant's personnel file, will provide at least the following information:

1. The applicant's date and place of birth
2. His address at the time of this employment
3. His Social Security number
4. Dates of his employment
5. His job title and responsibility
6. The identity of his immediate supervisor

To be thorough and worthwhile, such an inquiry should also include an interview with the applicant's former supervisor. He should be asked to comment on the quality of the applicant's work, and specifically the applicant's loyalty, reliability, overall character, ability to get along with others, and attendance record. The interviewer should also determine if the applicant resigned, was laid off, or was fired, and if he resigned or was fired, what the official reason was. Former supervisors will usually answer these questions freely and with candor; however, especially when derogatory information is involved, some may avoid volunteering relevant data. For this reason, the interviewer should ask specific questions calling for answers and data relating directly to the applicant's desirability as an employee.

With regard to furnishing information of a criminal nature, most employers are uncertain as to what they can reveal about their former employee. Libel and slander law as applied to such circumstances is unclear and therefore difficult to interpret and anticipate. For this reason, one employer may not inform another of the real reason a former employee resigned or was fired, particularly when the reason is that the applicant was suspected of theft and, when given the choice, selected resignation over involuntary termination. And the former employer's reluctance will be even greater if he doubts that such allegations can be proven. As a result, prospective employers should consider it risky business to hire any applicant who is not highly recommended or endorsed by his former employer. When such an inquiry leaves the employer in doubt as to the desirability of the applicant, he might try resolving the question by interviewing past and present employees of the applicant's former employer who have worked with him.

Interviewing the Applicant's Personal References. Most employment application forms require job candidates to list three personal references. Ideally, a personal reference is a nonrelative of good standing in the community, who has known the applicant personally for several years. For this reason, references often include physicians, lawyers, ministers, teachers, and local politicians. Many employers, however, do not contact these references as a part of their standard preemployment check; it is assumed that references are chosen on the basis that they will be complimentary in assessing the applicant. Although this is often the case, interviewing personal references will nevertheless frequently reveal pertinent information about a candidate for employment. For one thing, if such a person should be derogatory in his assessment of the applicant, this information will usually weigh heavily against his being hired. Moreover, it is not unusual to find that although the applicant's list of references is quite impressive, none of those he has listed actually knows him.

Verifying the Applicant's Past and Present Residences. Preemployment investigations of a more extensive nature normally include the verification of all the applicant's places of residence during the past five years. Such verifications can often be made by reviewing telephone and city directories, and the information is also available in most employment and education records. The investigator should make certain that the applicant has listed all his past addresses. The candidate should be closely questioned regarding any periods of time that are unaccounted for on his application or as a result of the investigation. His omission of a place of residence could be relevant and must be investigated further.

If the applicant has resided in several parts of the country, the investigator should attempt to determine whether he has been convicted of a crime in any of them.

Some of the more extensive background inquiries include what are referred to as neighborhood investigations—interviews with the applicant's past and present neighbors for the purpose of determining his character, associations, and general reputation within the community.

Honesty Shopping

Honesty shopping is checking on cashiers and other money-handling employees to determine if they are pocketing their employer's cash receipts by improperly recording, or failing to record, retail sales transactions. Users of the honesty-shopping technique, commonly administered by security firms that provide what they refer to as shopping services, are supermarkets, department and discount stores, convenience food markets, and drugstores. A shopping service, whether it is a proprietary or a contract operation, uses security personnel to pose as customers and periodically visit the user's store. In honesty shopping, they purchase merchandise at the store in a manner specifically designed to give the employee an opportunity to steal the purchase money.

testing the honesty of a cash-handling employee

Of the variety of methods used to test a cash-handling employee's honesty, two of the most common and representative will be discussed here. The first, commonly referred to as the "hit and run," is usually carried out by a two-man team called a shopping crew. The first member of the team enters the store, selects an item for purchase, and then pays for it with the exact amount of change, usually placing it on the counter near the cash register. Then, as if in a hurry, he leaves the store before the employee has an opportunity to ring up the sale and give him a receipt. Because the cashier is not required to use the cash register to make change or issue a receipt, this provides him with an excellent chance to accept the money without recording the sale. Moreover, if this is done at a time when the cash drawer is open in connection with another sale, the cashier can toss the change into the open drawer, or even pocket it, if no one is nearby, without arousing much suspicion. Meanwhile, the second honesty shopper remains in the store after the first one leaves, so that he can observe and report how the tested employee handled the bait transaction.

The second shopping-service technique is referred to as the "impulse buy." It is also carried out by a two-man shopping crew consisting of a purchaser and an observer. (It should be noted that quite often, a shopping crew will include a third person, who functions as a supervisor. And on occasion, a shopping team made up of four or five people will work in a large supermarket.) The "impulse buy" is worked as follows:

The bait purchaser initiates a regular sales transaction. After the amount of his purchase has been rung up on the cash register, and just as the cashier is making change for him out of the open cash drawer, the shopper decides on impulse to buy an additional item that is displayed nearby. He pays for this item with the exact amount of change at the same time he is receiving his change from the first purchase. Given this opportunity, a dishonest employee will be tempted to place the amount received from the impulse buy into the open cash drawer without separately recording this sale. The second member of the shopping crew is positioned in line behind his partner, where he can observe and report how this transaction is handled by the employee.

Reporting the Employee's Cash-Handling Methods. Besides tempting an employee and observing his response to the temptation, a shopping crew must also furnish a report of its findings, usually on a standard form, filled out by members of the team (see Figure 11-1). In addition to stating whether or not the sale was recorded, these forms often call for evaluations of some of the less important components of a properly handled cash transaction. For example, although the employee may have properly recorded the sale, he may not have issued a receipt,

SHOPPING SERVICE REPORT

STORE NAME:____________ DATE____________

ADDRESS:____________ TIME____________

____________ DAY OF WEEK____________

EMPLOYEE:____________
(if name unknown, describe)

I. COMPLIANCE WITH CASH HANDLING PROCEDURES — CIRCLE

1. Did the cashier/sales person call back the price of each item? Y N
2. Did the cashier/sales person call back the amount tendered? Y N
3. Did the cashier/sales person count back your change? Y N
4. Did the cashier/sales person record the sale? Y N
5. Did the cashier/sales person record the sale correctly? Y N
6. Did the cashier/sales person issue a receipt? Y N
7. Did the cashier/sales person close the drawer after the sale? Y N

II. OTHER

8. At the time of the inspection business was: LIGHT NORMAL HEAVY

III. REMARKS

FIGURE 11-1. Cash-handling section of a sample shopping-service report

thereby failing to comply with one of his employer's established cash-handling procedures.

Although shopping crews are primarily engaged to catch dishonest employees, they also aid the employer by reporting on matters relating to the quality of employees' work. For example, an honest but discourteous and inefficient employee, or one who is neither neat nor clean in appearance, can be singled out by a shopping crew and replaced or corrected before too much damage is done.

Documenting the Failure to Record. In addition to the testimony of honesty shoppers, most employers require other proof of an employee's failure to record a cash transaction. Without such corroborating evidence, a dishonest employee can deny any wrongdoing or error by claiming that the honesty shopper has made a mistake.

The most common method of documenting the failure of a cashier to record a transaction is to use the cash register tape as evidence. This is done by identifying the sale immediately preceding the bait purchase and those that followed. Normally, the shopper handling the bait purchase notes and records the amount showing in the cash register window at the time he makes his purchase, thus identifying the sale immediately preceding the bait purchase; and the observing member of the shopping crew, after seeing that the employee is not going to record the money left behind by his partner, will make a purchase himself for the purpose of obtaining a cash register receipt. The number on this receipt identifies the sale immediately following the bait purchase. If the amount of the bait purchase does not appear on the cash register tape between these two transactions, the employee's failure to record the bait purchase has been documented. Under these circumstances, the best the employee can do is try to convince the employer that he honestly forgot to ring up the sale, or that he intended to do so at a later time. However, the employee's failure to record the sale at the appropriate time is a violation of a basic cash-handling procedure, particularly when the observer has provided the cashier ample time to ring up the bait purchase before he makes his own.

Many shopping-service crews use marked money that can be identified in the cash drawer or in the cashier's possession, in order to prevent the employee from denying that the bait purchase was ever made.

accusing a cash-handling employee of theft

Once a cashier's failure to record a sale has been clearly established and documented, the issue of whether such an omission constitutes theft must still be resolved. More specifically, if the employee has claimed an honest mistake, should his omission nevertheless be treated by the employer as theft?

Most security practitioners agree that one known incident of this nature does not necessarily indicate a cashier's intent to steal, but two such omissions, regardless of the circumstances, usually constitute sufficient and therefore reasonable grounds (probable cause) to make such an allegation. However, there can be other factors an employer will take into consideration when resolving the issue. For example, the fact that the cashier physically pocketed the bait-purchase money will usually be more indicative of an intent to steal than his tossing the change into the cash drawer without ringing up the sale. Then again, if the testing of a specific cashier has been predicated upon the employer's suspicion that that employee has been stealing—perhaps after several unexplained cash register shortages or overages have been discovered—the failure by the cashier to record a bait purchase will be particularly indicative of his dishonesty. Moreover, customers occasionally detect and report dishonest cash-handling employees. In any case, an employer so alerted will usually rely upon an honesty-shopping crew to confirm or deny his suspicions.

the purpose, effectiveness, and rationale of honesty shopping

Generally, honesty shopping is a method of identifying employees who are violating the employer's cash-handling procedures for any reason. More specifically, shopping services are utilized to single out and identify employees who may be stealing from their employers. An employer may also decide to use this measure as a deterrent, by internally publicizing the fact that all cash-handling employees are periodically and clandestinely shopped.

Although it is difficult to measure the effectiveness of a technique such as honesty shopping, most retail-security practitioners consider it a vital part of their overall security programs. However, to effectively control this aspect of the internal theft problem, some of the more preventive measures must also be implemented. It is also true that some of the more skilled and experienced employee thieves will be able to recognize the basic honesty-shopping methods and therefore will be able to identify members of a shopping crew, particularly in the case of a poor-quality shopper's service.

There are those who object to the honesty-shopping technique on the grounds that such a practice is unethical—that it is unfair and immoral to entice or encourage a person to steal. Their opponents argue that honest employees will not steal under any circumstances, so those who do give into this temptation should be identified and treated as security risks; that a retail employer has a right to protect his assets against dishonest cash-handling employees, and this is one of only a few measures that can effectively provide this protection; and that, in a more positive light, honest as well as dishonest employees are singled out and recognized by this technique.

Basic Cash-Handling Procedures for Cashiers

Most retail establishments' cash systems have been modified and adapted to fulfill their specific needs. As a result, there are too many rules and procedures to specifically identify and discuss. The scope of this discussion is therefore limited to the identification of a few of the universal cash-handling controls designed to prevent and deter theft of money by a casher from a cash register.

refund schemes

A cashier can cover a cash shortage in many ways. One of the more common methods is by reporting phony customer merchandise returns and cash refunds. For example, a customer has purchased a $10.50 item and has left behind the cash register receipt for the transaction. In a store without the appropriate cash register controls, a dishonest cashier could use this receipt as evidence of the return of the merchandise for a cash refund, thereby justifying a shortage in the cash drawer of $10.50, which in reality has gone into the cashier's pocket. The fact that this piece of merchandise was never returned to the store's inventory will not come to light since its physical absence can be reasonably explained as a shoplifting loss.

The opportunity for this type of employee theft can be eliminated by the establishment of merchandise return and refund procedures calling for close managerial supervision. For example, all cash register receipts reflecting the sale of items later returned for refund should be dated and initialed by the store manager or his designee. Moreover, the returned merchandise should be closely examined and personally placed back into stock by a management employee.

Fake overring slips, or cash register receipts purporting to reflect overrings, constitute a closely related method of covering a cash shortage. In this context, the term *overring* applies to any recording of an excess amount in the cash register. It is not unusual for a cashier to accidentally punch the wrong cash register key, thereby ringing up a figure that exceeds the actual amount of the sale, or to inadvertently ring up an item that should not have been included in the sales transaction. When this happens, the first cash register entry is voided, the sale is rung up again, and the incorrect receipt, as evidence of the overring, is saved to explain the imbalance or cash shortage. A dishonest employee, using a cash register receipt left behind by a customer, may claim that this receipt reflects an overring, thus covering the theft of this sum from the cash register. In order to prevent cashiers from committing this type of theft, an overring should not be considered valid unless the transaction has been supervised and approved by management personnel.

other standard cash-handling rules and procedures

The following list sets out some of the most common and universally accepted concepts and rules regarding the operation of a cash register:

1. A cash register should not be balanced by the person responsible for its operation.
2. Friends and relatives of a cashier should not be allowed to loiter about the cash-out area.
3. Each cashier should be assigned to a particular cash register. A cashier should never use someone else's cash register without prior approval.
4. Cashiers should not ring up their own purchases.
5. Every sales transaction should be rung up separately.
6. A cash register receipt should be issued whenever possible.
7. The cash register drawer should be closed after each transaction. The cashier should not handle more than one transaction out of an open cash drawer.
8. The cashier should call back the correct price of each item.
9. The cashier should call back the total amount of each sale.
10. The cashier should call back the amount tendered.
11. The cashier should count back a customer's change.

Controlling and Surveying Employee Foot Traffic

The prevention and deterrence of internal theft can be aided by controlling and monitoring employee movement to and from as well as within the place of employment.

employee traffic to and from the facility

Designating Employee Entrance and Exit Doors. When going to or leaving their place of employment, employees should be routed to specially designated doors and gates. By specifying and therefore reducing the number of doors available for this purpose, the security practitioner facilitates the observance of employees as they come and go. Where this is not done, the facility will be extremely vulnerable to losses created by dishonest employees' leaving the premises with company property. This is particularly true in connection with large retail establishments such as discount and department stores, as well as institutional and industrial facilities employing large numbers of people.

If possible, employee exit routes should be simple. If special doors are used for this purpose, each employee should be instructed to use the one nearest his work area. Employees who are discovered leaving through doors that are not proximate to their work should be watched closely and reinstructed. In designating employee exit routes and locations, the security administrator should make an effort to route employees away from high-security areas. For example, retail employees should not be allowed to leave the store through doors that are situated near valuable merchandise, but should be routed through rear or side doors that are not within the merchandising part of the store; in industrial settings or institutions, it would be unwise to route employees through the computer area.

Exit Door Alarms. Fire exit doors, because they cannot be locked from the inside, are commonly used by dishonest employees to bypass the designated and monitored employee exits. Becasue these unauthorized exit doors are often in a remote section of a facility, they are frequently used for removing stolen company property.

The most common device used to shut off employee traffic through unauthorized doors is the fire exit alarm. (See Figure 11-2.) Doors equipped with these alarms can be opened in case of a fire, bomb threat, or other emergency requiring the immediate evacuation of the premises, but when they are opened, the alarm is activated. The alarm signal can be silent—that is, appear as a light on an alarm panel elsewhere—or local. Local alarm signals are usually in the form of a loud bell, buzzer, or flashing light, or a combination of these. And some exit alarms emit a sound or light in addition to a silent signal.

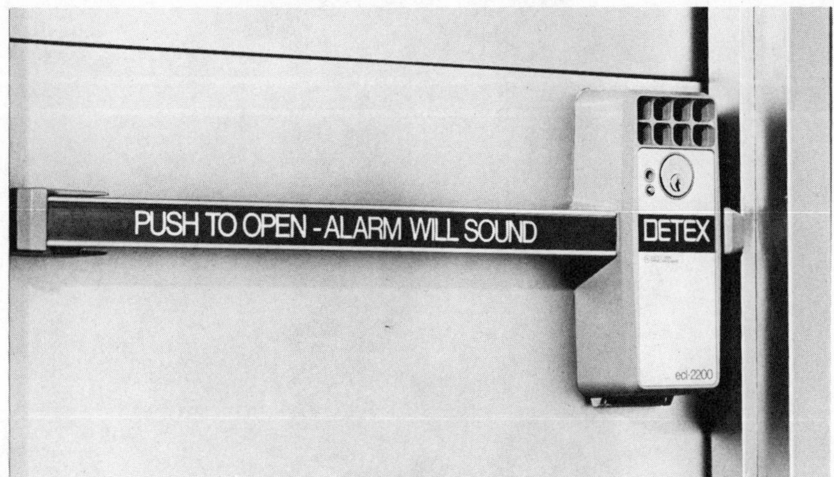

FIGURE 11-2. Fire exit alarm device

Courtesy Detex Corporation

Monitoring Employee Foot Traffic to and from the Premises. Many methods and devices are used to observe employees as they move in and out of their place of employment. The access controls and locking devices discussed in Chapters 4 and 5 as anti-intrusion measures also serve to monitor employee movement, as do security personnel stationed at employee entrances and exits.

For the purpose of preventing and deterring the flow of stolen goods from the employer's premises, the security guard may check employee identification cards, conduct spot searches, check employee packages, examine property passes that authorize the temporary removal of company property, and maintain logs and registers showing the identities and times of arriving and departing employees. A single security guard may be able to watch several employee doors and gates through the use of closed-circuit television cameras and a central monitoring station.

Metal Detectors as Antitheft Devices. Walk-through metal-detection devices like those employed at airports to detect weapons are increasingly being used as anti-internal theft devices. (See Figure 11-3.) To be effective, the metal detector

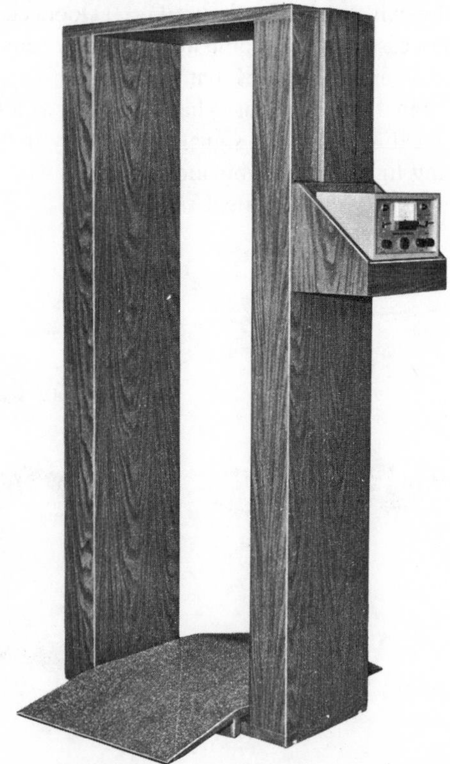

FIGURE 11-3. Walk-through metal detector

Courtesy Federal Laboratories, Inc.

employed must be one of the more advanced models, capable of detecting small metal objects while at the same time ignoring, say, paper clips. The older, less technologically advanced devices can detect only objects the size of a handgun. Besides detecting tools, parts, and merchandise from plants, warehouses, and stores, metal detectors are frequently used to protect people and courtrooms against concealed weapons and bombing devices.

In addition to revealing stolen property, the use of metal-detection devices at employee exits should also operate as an effective deterrent to employee theft. The user may exploit its deterrent value by posting appropriately worded warning signs. (See Figure 11-4.)

NOTICE: ANTI-THEFT PERSONAL SEARCH

Theft of Company property has reached alarming proportions and can no longer be tolerated or absorbed.

A few dishonest individuals make it mandatory to search all employees, plus their hand-carried possessions, with airport-type detectors at exiting. This equipment cannot harm anyone or any possessions.

We solicit your active cooperation with this security program and regret any inconvenience which may occur.

J. Jones
for Management

FIGURE 11-4. Sample warning sign

Courtesy Infinetics, Inc.; FRISKEM (TM) Division

Figure 11-5 illustrates a typical employee screening and searching station. This layout combines the use of metal detectors and a search of all exiting employees. Such a program would be particularly applicable in large facilities where small and valuable items are used as tools or material, manufactured, stored, or retailed.

Unguarded and unalarmed exit doors can be protected through the use of a metal detector and an unmanned and automatically triggered Polaroid SX70 camera. When a dishonest employee walks through the metal detector at the exit door, he is photographed by the camera, which is activated by the metal detector. (See Figure 11-6.)

The use of metal detectors as antitheft devices is a concept very similar to the utilization of article surveillance alarms in retail settings. Like metal detectors, various x-ray inspection systems and devices that detect explosives and weapons at airports are being used also to combat internal theft.

Controlling Employee Parking. Industrial facilities employing large numbers of people are particularly vulnerable to internal theft if little or no security attention is given to the matter of employee parking. Whenever employees have easy and

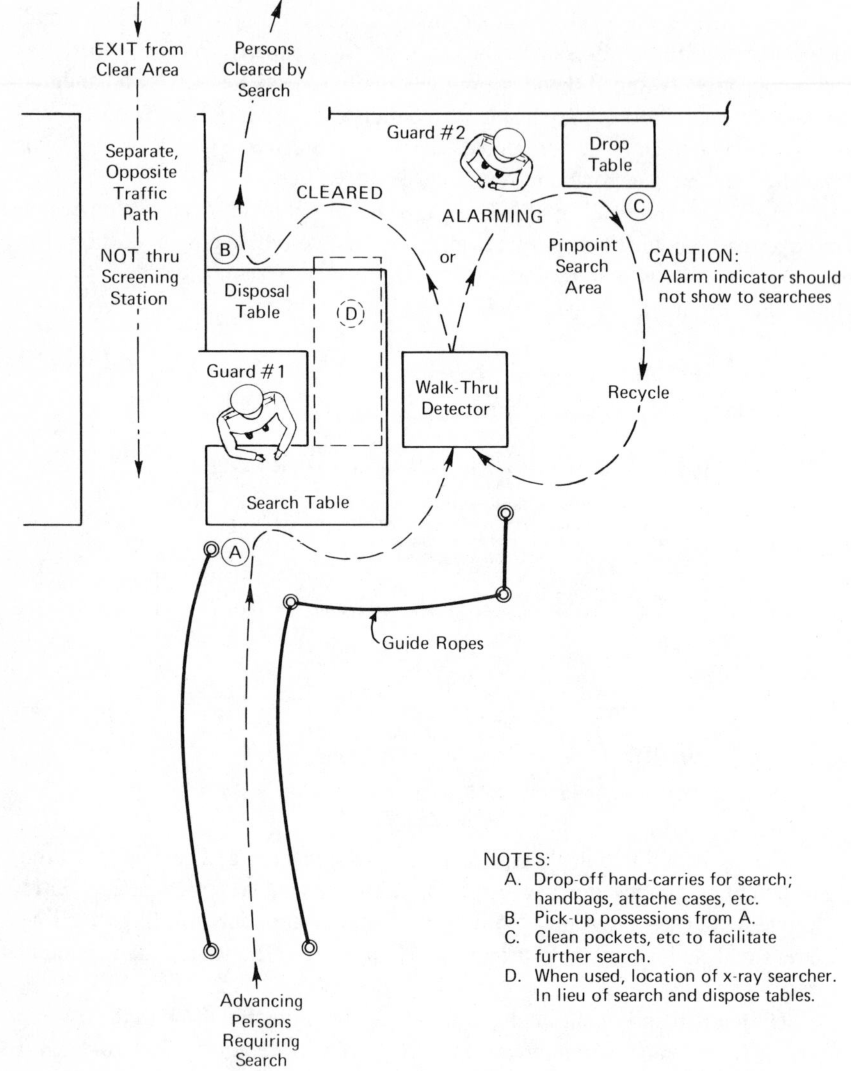

FIGURE 11-5. Screening-station layout

Courtesy Infinetics, Inc.; FRISKEM (TM) Division

unmonitored access to their cars, internal theft losses are likely to be high. For example, dishonest employees who can park their cars near loading docks or unprotected fire exit doors will find it that much easier to conceal and remove company property.

There are several procedures to help the security practitioner monitor and

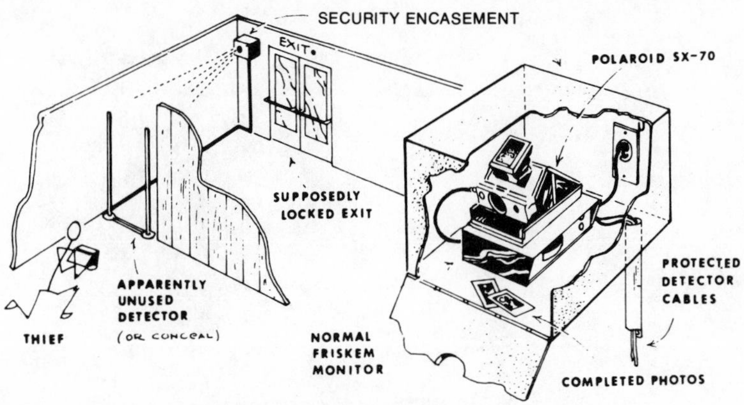

FIGURE 11-6. Unguarded surveillance station

Courtesy Infinetics, Inc.; FRISKEM (TM) Division

control an employee's movements to and from his automobile. Specific fenced-in parking areas should be designated for employee use and equipped with either automatic or manned entrance and exit vehicle gates. If possible, all man and vehicle gates should be monitored by guards stationed in the area or by closed-circuit TV cameras. The parking lot should be well lit, periodically patrolled, and situated as far from the plant as possible. As a general rule, employees should not be allowed to visit their automobiles during their work shifts. Any employee who makes an unauthorized visit to his car should be watched closely.

Time Locks. A time lock is a locking device that makes a written record of each door opening. It is composed of two basic components, the lock itself and an electronic recording unit. (See Figure 11-7.) Every locking and unlocking of such a device activates a timing mechanism within the recording unit, causing the appropriate time, date, and key number to be recorded on a pressure-sensitive tape.

Time-lock systems operate to discourage unauthorized after-hours visits to the premises by key-carrying employees. For example, the manager of a retail establishment may use his key to return to the store after it closes for the purpose of stealing merchandise, blaming the shrinkage in inventory on dishonest customers. With the installation of a time-lock system, such unauthorized reentries into the store will not go undetected.

Property-Pass Systems. Employees are often allowed to temporarily remove office equipment, tools, parts, and supplies from company premises. Within a large company, unless there is a property-pass system in effect, the guard at the door or gate will have to challenge each employee he sees coming out with company property. For example, if a guard encounters an employee leaving with

FIGURE 11-7. Time lock and recording unit

Courtesy of The Silent Watchman Corporation

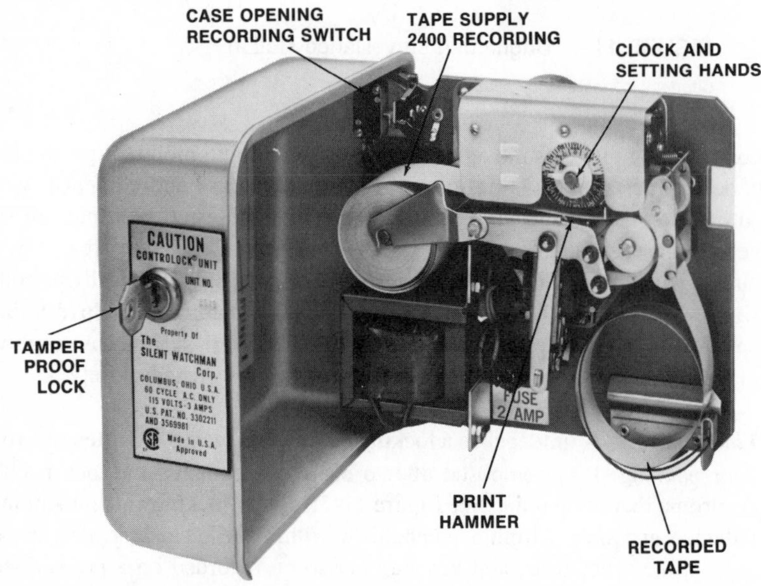

an adding machine under his arm, and the employee says the boss said it was okay, the guard would find himself in a difficult position. He would either have to take the employee's word or inconvenience him by making further inquiries to verify the authorization.

There are several types of property-pass systems, but they all operate as follows: First, the guards who monitor employee traffic at the perimeter of the facility have a set of records telling them who in the company can authorize the removal of what items, and they also have a copy of each authorizing official's signature. Second, before a piece of company property can be taken off the premises, the employee removing it must have a property pass. The typical property pass contains the name of the employee, the identity and company phone number of the authorizing official, the date, and the description and value of the item being removed. The pass may also contain a space where the reason for the property removal can be set out. Finally, after the guard collects the property pass, taking care to compare the item being removed with the description on the pass and the official's signature with the sample, he sends it back to the person who authorized the removal. The guard must also take care to make certain that the employee is who he says he is, and that the company official listed as the authorizing person does in fact have such authority.

employee traffic within the facility

Identification cards were discussed in Chapter 5 pursuant to their use as keys to various access-control systems, and in Chapter 4 as devices to distinguish employees from intruders and visitors. The discussion of identification cards and badges that follows relates to their role in combatting internal theft.

Employee Identification Cards and Badges. Employee identification, as a measure against internal theft, should involve more than simply identifying the worker as an employee; it must also identify him as an individual. For example, whenever an employee signs in or out of his work area during his work shift, the guard who maintains the ingress/egress register, by examining his identification card or badge, will be making a record of *this individual's* activities. Without such identification, there is little protection against the recording of a fictitious name.

Identification cards and badges are also utilized, by color-coding of groups of cards, as devices to detect employees who are not where they are supposed to be. For example, a blue identification card may authorize an employee to work only on the first floor, in the boiler room, in the warehouse, or within a particular building; or it may allow him to be on the premises only within a particular time period or work shift.

Employees are commonly required to wear their identification cards as badges, or to carry them and display them upon the request of the appropriate company personnel. The most effective employee identification systems involve cards containing the employee's photograph.

A guideline to the size and nature of facilities that could use such systems was outlined by Roger Kuhns, the President of Avant, Inc.:

> As a rule of thumb, any organization that has information or property worth protecting valued at roughly $100 per member and that has more than 100 members should use photo-identifications. Memory tests show that it is very difficult for authorities to remember more than 100 faces and names, especially if there is a typical annual turnover of 20 to 30%.[5]

---

[5]Roger Kuhns, "Photographic Identification," *Security Management*, March 1977, p. 89.

Identification cards are commonly used by hospitals, colleges, government installations, utilities, large retail establishments, and large factories. In facilities using them, security administrators should develop procedures to be followed when cards are lost or damaged, as well as procedures for the disposition of identification cards belonging to terminating employees and for the issuance of new cards for newly hired personnel.

The simplest and most common type of identification card is the paper-insert card, which can be produced either in-house or by a private contractor. The employee's photograph is taken with an instant camera and attached to a paper insert, which is slid into a plastic case. The case is then run through a laminating machine that forms the two pieces into a monolithic bond. This equipment—the camera and laminator—is portable and capable of producing a photo-identification card in just a few seconds. Such a card should bear, in addition to the employee's photograph, his number, a place for his signature, and the company logo.

Marking and Identifying Company Property

An employer must be able to identify a specific tool, machine, piece of office equipment, or retail item as belonging to the company, if the fact that the property has been stolen is to be established. Otherwise, the possessor of the property cannot be prosecuted and the employer cannot get it back. Items that are particularly difficult to identify include raw materials, building supplies, coins, and, since precious and semiprecious stones can be recut and reset, jewelry.

Many manufactured items are individually identified by a serial number—for example, automobiles, appliances, watches, guns, and office machines. These numbers can be used to identify an item that has been stolen and subsequently recovered, so employers should maintain files containing such data.

Many items that do not carry serial numbers can nevertheless be made identifiable by being marked in some way. It is common practice to engrave code numbers or letters on items that are not otherwise marked. Tools are often painted in such a way as to make them easily recognizable as a particular company's property. Many items belonging to a company may bear its logo. In terms of internal theft, the practice of clearly marking company property makes the monitoring of employee traffic to and from a facility much more effective. Moreover, marking and being able to identify company property operates as a deterrent to dishonest employees; they realize that the chance of being detected is easily identifiable. In theft cases, the easier it is to identify and recover the stolen property, the greater the chance of catching the thief.

the undercover method of combatting employee theft

A private undercover investigator, often referred to as an undercover operative, is a person who has ostensibly been hired as a regular employee but whose primary purpose is identifying employees who are committing theft and other crimes against their employer. As a method of combatting and controlling internal theft, the undercover technique is extremely effective. Employee thieves are often very clever and knowledgeable; they may, for example, be familiar with the employer's security program and thus be able to avoid detection easily. The placement of an equally skilled, knowledgeable, and clever undercover operative may be the only way to surprise and catch this type of thief.

Since the use of undercover security personnel is costly, it can be justified only when the employer's problem is severe and not likely to be remedied by other security techniques. Typical users of undercover operatives are large retail establishments; industrial, trucking, and warehouse facilities; and large institutions.

administering an undercover operation

The organization and operation of an effective undercover program is not an easy task. It requires planning, an administrator knowledgeable in security, and an operative with a combination of specific security and law-enforcement skills. For this reason, not all undercover programs turn out as planned; many in fact, fail miserably.

The Problem of In-House Undercover Operations. It is considered unwise for an employer to convert one of his regular employees into an undercover investigator, or to hire a new employee specifically for this purpose. The general practice is to use undercover agents who are employees of private contract security firms specializing in this service.

There are several problems inherent in using in-house operatives. In the first place, an in-house undercover investigator will not have the training required to do the job. Second, his supervisor is not likely to have had undercover experience and training. The third problem, what to do with the in-house operative at the conclusion of the investigation, is particularly difficult. Even if the operative is never identified as such, his role as an informer will eventually leak out, making him at best unpopular, and at worst, subject to reprisals that could endanger his life. The fourth problem is the selection from among one's own personnel of someone to perform in this capacity. It might well be that the employer will pick a dishonest person.

The Operation of Private Undercover Services. As stated above, most undercover operatives are supplied by private contract security firms. In companies without a security department, the service is usually contracted for by a top executive of the firm. When the company has an ongoing in-house security program, the idea usually originates with the security director. In either case, it is vital that only a few top officials know of the undercover operation.

After a representative of the security firm has met with the appropriate personnel of the client company, an operative who fills the client's employment needs is sent to the personnel office to apply for a job. The undercover operative should be hired like any other new employee; members of the personnel department should not be aware of the operation. Security firms usually provide their operatives with phony employment histories and job references to match the needs of the particular employer. Once the operative is hired, he will be on the company's payroll and compensated like other regular employees. Undercover investigators are also paid by their security employers, who bill the client for their services.

The operative is usually under strict instructions not to divulge the results of his inquiry to knowledgeable client personnel. Undercover agents usually report to their security firms daily by telephone and maintain written logs that are submitted weekly to their security employers. The security agency usually keeps the client informed daily of the operative's progress, and bases its final report to the client on the weekly logs. There should be no direct communication, however, between the operative and the client.

The length of an undercover operation will vary according to the nature of the client's problem and the success of the operative's investigation. As a general rule, most operatives are given a four- to six-week period to get acclimated to the job and their fellow employees. If an operative moves too fast and appears too eager, he might not be accepted as a regular employee and taken into the confidence of those he hopes to catch. Moreover, some operatives have to be given a significant amount of on-the-job training; under these circumstances, an operative has to concentrate, at least at first, on his nonsecurity work.

Placement and Utilization of the Undercover Agent. Undercover operatives are commonly hired as warehousemen, loading-dock employees, maintenance personnel, machine operators, mechanics, welders, stockboys, and delivery-truck drivers. If the employer-client has pinpointed the security problem to a particular employee, department, building, or operational function, the appropriate operative will be hired and specifically placed. On the other hand, if the employer is in the dark regarding the source of his problem, the operative should be placed in a position that gives him mobility and the chance to come in contact with as many employees as possible. A job on the maintenance crew, for example, may be the answer. In any case, the ideal placement of an undercover agent is in a position where the crime cannot be successfully committed without his cooperation or knowledge.

Areas of Investigative Interest. Undercover operatives are used for some or all of the following purposes:

1. To audit the employer's existing security program, to determine its effectiveness
2. To suggest how security weaknesses can be strengthened
3. To determine if there are criminal acts going on undetected
4. To identify the perpetrators of known criminal acts for termination and/or criminal prosecution
5. To evaluate and report on employee morale and related matters

Some of the more specific problems an undercover operative looks for and investigates are:

1. Theft
2. Industrial sabotage
3. Petty vandalism
4. On-the-job drug and alcohol abuse
5. Theft of time

Using the Operative as a Witness. One of the basic initial decisions to be made is whether or not to identify the operative after he has witnessed employee crimes. In many instances, the operative's observations may be the employer's only proof against an employee thief. If a contract agency is being utilized, the employer will get more for his money if he secures in advance an agreement whereby the agency promises to make the operative available as a witness in a court proceeding or arbitration hearing.

Indoctrinating Employees against Theft

It has been said that a small core of employees won't steal under any circumstances, and an equally small percentage will steal no matter what. Most employees, therefore, fall somewhere in the middle. Some security practitioners believe that the employees in this larger, middle group can be convinced not to steal.

Whether or not an employee can be indoctrinated against theft is hard, if not impossible, to determine. And where employers have set up programs to attempt it, it is equally difficult to find out how many employees have in fact responded favorably. Of course, the long-range goal of any program of this nature is the reduction of losses caused by employee dishonesty. But here are some of the more immediate objectives:

1. To clarify the notion that stealing in any form is a crime and therefore not socially acceptable behavior.
2. To instill in each employee a fear of getting caught and punished for theft. This can be done by continually reminding employees of the legal penalties for larceny and related criminal offenses.
3. To convince the employee that if he steals, the chances of his getting caught are great.
4. To suggest to the employee that once he is branded as dishonest and therefore disloyal, he will have difficulty finding another job.
5. To show the employee how theft directly hurts the company and therefore affects his own economic well-being.

methods of indoctrination

In smaller companies, employees can be indoctrinated on a personal, one-to-one basis. For the larger employer, the most common techniques include lectures, films, and posters designed to achieve some of the short-range objectives listed above.

Another technique used to indoctrinate employees is to widely publicize within the company any specific incidents of employee theft. Making examples of those who have been caught might achieve several of the objectives listed above.

There is no single internal theft measure or combination of security techniques that will guarantee positive results. Moreover, the measures identified and discussed in this chapter are not the only ways in which internal theft is battled. In order to wage an effective program against employee theft, the security practitioner must apply his security knowledge, imagination, and common sense to the specific facts and problems at hand. No two facilities or employee thieves are alike, and therefore security methods and their applications are continually changing, even within the same facility during short periods of time.

DISCUSSION QUESTIONS

1. In your opinion, what is the single most effective and economical way to combat internal theft?

2. Do you believe that higher-paid employees are less likely to steal than are lower-paid workers?
3. Identify and discuss some of the factors that make employee thieves difficult to catch.
4. Can you think of several reasons why some supervisors ignore acts of theft committed in their presence?
5. What are the advantages and disadvantages of spot searches of employees at exit doors and gates?
6. Are property-pass systems foolproof? If not, why?
7. What is the similarity between honesty shopping and an undercover operation?
8. Profile the ideal undercover investigator.
9. From a career standpoint, what are some of the drawbacks of being an undercover operative? What are some of the good points?
10. Can you think of some novel ways to indoctrinate employees against internal theft?
11. Do you believe that honesty-shopping techniques, because they tempt the retail employee, are ethically or morally wrong?
12. To what extent does shopping-service use deter employee theft?

SELECTED BIBLIOGRAPHY

preemployment

BURSTEIN, HARVEY, "Protection vs. Privacy," *Security Management*, November 1975. This excellent article proposes a preemployment screening process that would reconcile the individual's right to privacy with the businessman's right to protect his assets by trying to anticipate and prevent internal theft.

CHAMBERS, RAY W., "An Argument against Anti-Polygraph Legislation," *Security Management*, July 1977.

Compendium of State Laws Governing the Privacy and Security of Criminal Justice Information, Washington, D.C.: U.S. Department of Justice, LEAA, 1975.

GUGAS, STEPHEN E., "Making More of the New-Fashioned Application Blank," *Security World*, August 1977.

HARRIS, ERNEST, "The Struggle over Employee Backgrounding," *Security World*, October 1975.

OLSON, KENNETH, "Pre-Employment Testing," *Security Industry and Product News*, April 1977.

POTTER, ANTHONY N., "The Dangers of Privacy Legislation," *Security World*, November 1975.

URSIC, HENRY S. and LEROY E. PAGANO, *Security Management Systems*. Springfield, Ill.: Charles C Thomas, 1974.

honesty shopping

FLEISCHMAN, ALAN, "Can a Shopping Service Help Your Business?" *Security World,* April 1976.

metal detectors

WALLACH, CHARLES, and DR. ROY RICCI, "Security Metal Detection Systems," *Security Management,* July 1977.

property-pass systems

CARY, FRED W., "Property Pass Systems—A Deterrent to Internal Theft," *Security Management,* November 1975.

identification cards and badges

KUHNS, ROGER, "Photographic Identification," *Security Management,* March 1977.

MENDELSON, FRED S., "The Great (Photo-Identification) Card Game," *Security Management,* March 1977.

POWELL, GREGG E., "Identification Cards: How to Select Them," Parts I and II, *Security World,* February and April 1975.

undercover investigations

ASTOR, SAUL D., "A View from the Grass Roots," *Security World,* September 1969.

BAREFOOT, KIRK J., *Undercover Investigation.* New York: Cluett, Peabody & Company, Inc., 1975.

BRANDMAN, BARRY, "What Undercover Can Do for Business," *Security World,* June 1977.

WILLIAMS, H. E., "Undercover Investigations," *Security Management,* September 1977.

general

ASTOR, SAUL D., "Attention-Getting Program Cuts Employee Dishonesty in Supermarkets," *Security World,* April 1977.

———, "Internal Crime," Parts I and II, *Security World,* September and October 1970.

———, *Loss Prevention: Controls and Concepts.* Los Angeles: Security World Publishing Co., 1978.

CARSON, CHARLES R., *Managing Employee Honesty.* Los Angeles: Security World Publishing Co., 1977.

LEININGER, SHERYL, ed., *Internal Theft: Investigation and Control; an Anthology.* Los Angeles: Security World Publishing Co., 1975.

PART IV

OTHER CRIMES AGAINST THE BUSINESS COMMUNITY

Chapter 12

Bad Checks, Counterfeiting, and Other Crimes of Fraud

AN OVERVIEW

I. The Nature and Extent of the Bad-Check Problem
   A. *Three categories of bad checks*
      1. Forged or altered checks
      2. No-account checks
      3. Insufficient-funds checks
   B. *The extent of the bad-check problem*
      1. The most frequent commercial bad-check victims

II. Forgery and Bad-Check Laws

III. Common Methods of Passing Worthless Checks
   A. *Forged payroll checks*
   B. *Split-deposit schemes*
   C. *Personal checks*
   D. *Money orders*

IV. Procedures and Policies to Control Bad-Check Losses
   A. *High-risk checks*
      1. Two-party checks
      2. Nonlocal and certain payroll checks
      3. Counter checks
      4. Other checks that should be treated as suspicious

B. *Requiring Identification*
   1. Proper check-cashing identification
   2. Improper check-cashing identification
C. *Signature card systems*

V. Security Devices against Bad Checks
   A. *Fraudulent-check-passer identification systems*

VI. Counterfeiting
   A. *The offense*
   B. *Recognizing counterfeit money*

VII. Fraudulent Use of Credit Cards
   A. *The offense*

VIII. The Acquisition and Illegal Use of False Identification
   A. *Obtaining copies of false birth certificates*

IX. Quick-Change Artists

The Nature and Extent of the Bad-Check Problem

A check can be defined generally as a draft drawn upon funds in a bank and payable on demand to the person named on the instrument. Although there are many kinds of checks, the most common are personal checks, payroll checks, treasury checks, counter checks, money orders, and traveler's checks. The following descriptions of several types of checks are taken from a Small Business Administration booklet:

> A *personal check* (drawn on a noncommercial account) is written and signed by the individual offering it. . . .
>
> A *two-party check* is issued by one person to a second who endorses it so that it may be cashed by a third person. . . .
>
> A *payroll check* is issued to an employee for services performed. Usually the name of the employer is printed on it and it has a number and it is signed. In most instances, "payroll" is also printed on the check. The employee's name is printed by a check writing machine or typed. . . .
>
> A *government check* can be issued by the federal government, a state, a county, or a local government. Such checks cover salaries, tax refunds, pensions, welfare allotments, and veterans' benefits, to mention a few examples. . . .
>
> A *blank check* is a form not issued by a bank and not carrying its name. It may be bought at variety and stationery stores. In the proper spaces, the maker writes the name, address, account number, and branch designation of his bank.
>
> A *counter check* is one which a bank issues to depositors when they are withdrawing funds from their account. It is not good anywhere else.

> A *traveler's check* is a check sold with a preprinted amount (usually in round figures) to travelers who do not want to carry large amounts of cash. The traveler signs the check at the time of purchase.
>
> A *money order* can be passed as a check. However, a money order is usually bought and sent in the mail. [Italics added.][1]

Generally, a bad check can be defined as one that has been "submitted twice for payment unsuccessfully, or deemed uncollectible for other reasons."[2]

three categories of bad checks

Forged or Altered Checks. A check that has been changed or altered in any way by an unauthorized person is said to have been forged. The most common type is one on which the maker's signature has been forged. In such a case, the check passer falsely identifies himself as either the maker or the payee of the check. Checks are also considered to be forged when the amount payable, date, or other material portion of the document has been improperly altered.

No-Account Checks. A no-account check is one that is worthless because it is drawn on a bank account that is no longer open or in existence. The passing of a no-account check does not have to involve forgery in order to constitute a criminal offense. The fact that the check has been written on a closed bank account is in itself sufficient to make it illegal.

Insufficient-Funds Checks. A check for an amount that exceeds the sum in the bank account on which it is drawn is commonly referred to as an insufficient-funds check. In most states, in order for the negotiation of such a check to be a crime, the passer must have specific knowledge that the check was worthless. Because such knowledge is difficult to prove, and because the recipient of the check is primarily interested in payment rather than the criminal conviction of the check passer, passing this type of check does not usually become a crime until the receiver of it is certain that it is uncollectible.

the extent of the bad-check problem

Specific information regarding the extent of the bad-check problem is not readily available. For example, there is no single category covering bad-check crimes in the FBI's *Uniform Crime Reports,* where the offense falls under two broad categories of crime called "Forgery and Counterfeiting" and "Fraud."

---

[1]Leonard Kolodny, *Outwitting Bad Check Passers* (Washington, D.C.: Small Business Administration, 1973).

[2]"How Big Is the Bad Check Problem?" *Security World,* July/August 1974.

"Forgery and Counterfeiting" is defined by the FBI as "making, altering, uttering, or possessing with intent to defraud, anything false which is made to appear true." Fraud is defined in the UCR as, "fraudulent conversion in obtaining money or property by false pretenses." A majority of the arrests reflected by the statistics in these two categories involve the passing of worthless checks.

An exact evaluation of the problem's severity is also made unfeasible by the fact that banks and the Federal Reserve System do not know exactly how many worthless checks are passed. Moreover, it is estimated that only 5 to 30 percent of all bad-check violations are reported to the police. So the statistics and other data found in this section regarding the number and types of bad checks passed, the size of out-of-pocket dollar losses, the nature and types of bad-check victims, the extent of their losses, and other related facts have been taken from an article[3] based upon a study conducted by the firm of Houlahan and Balachek. The study was made pursuant to that company's intention to market a device (Veriprint) that uses thumbprints as an endorsement for checks.

It is estimated that in 1974, there was $770 million attributable to the passage of bad checks, an increase of 51 percent over the preceding year. The bad-check crime rate has been increasing over the past several years at a pace exceeding that of the overall national crime rate.

A total of 26 billion checks were written in the United States in 1973. Of these, 169 million were returned—55.8 million because of technical errors, 25.4 million because of forgery, and 87.8 million as backed by insufficient funds. Forty-three million of those returned, including 20 percent of those returned for insufficient funds, were classified as uncollectible and therefore worthless. It is estimated that nationally, 0.65 percent of all checks written are returned, and the percentage returned to commercial victims is probably much higher. By 1980, 42 billion checks will be written in the United States annually, and the dollar loss created by bad checks will be in the neighborhood of $1,168.5 billion.

Researchers Houlahan and Balachek believe (based upon 1973 statistics) that $30 is the amount of the average bad check. They give their readers an idea of the relation between the loss of this amount and the sales increases necessary to maintain the same profit margin, as follows:

> To compensate for each uncollectible check of $30, your sales must increase by:
>
> $150 if your profit margin is 20%
> $300 if your profit margin is 10%
> $600 if your profit margin is 5%
> $1,500 if your profit margin is 2%
> $3,000 if your profit margin is 1%[4]

---

[3] "How Big Is the Bad Check Problem?"

[4] *Ibid.*

The Most Frequent Commercial Bad-Check Victims. It is estimated that one-third of all bad-check losses are those by supermarkets. Department stores are a close second; they figure in 30 percent. Liquor stores and gas stations follow. Banks apparently account for only 5 to 7½ percent, but the dollar amount per bad-check incident is probably much higher for banks than for the other businesses.

Forgery and Bad-Check Laws

The offense of forgery is a felony in most states. Although they are closely related, forgery and bad-check offenses are separate violations in most jurisdictions. Forgery is the broader offense, in that it does not always involve worthless checks. The following sections of *Purdon's Pennsylvania Statutes Annotated,* Title 18, Crimes and Offenses, is representative of most state forgery and bad-check laws:

Section 4101 Forgery

(a) Offense defined.—A person is guilty of forgery if, with intent to defraud or injure anyone, or with knowledge that he is facilitating a fraud or injury to be perpetrated by anyone, the actor:
   (1) alters any writing of another without his authority;
   (2) makes, completes, executes, authenticates, issues or transfers any writing so that it purports to be the act of another who did not authorize that act, or to have been executed at a time or place or in a numbered sequence other than was in fact the case, or to be a copy of an original when no such original existed; or
   (3) utters any writing which he knows to be forged in a manner specified in paragraphs (1) or (2) of this subsection.

(b) Definition.—As used in this section the word "writing" includes printing or any other method of recording information, money, coins, tokens, stamps, seals, credit cards, badges, trademarks, and other symbols of value, right, privilege, or identification.

(c) Grading.—Forgery is a felony of the second degree if the writing is or purports to be part of an issue of money, securities, postage or revenue stamps, or other instruments issued by the government, or part of an issue of stock, bonds or other instruments representing interests in or claims against any property or enterprise. Forgery is a felony of the third degree if the writing is or purports to be a will, deed, contract, release, commercial instrument, or other document evidencing, creating, transferring, altering, terminating, or otherwise affecting legal relations. Otherwise forgery is a misdemeanor of the first degree.

Section 4105 Bad Checks

(a) Offense defined.—A person commits an offense if he issues or passes a check or similar sight order for the payment of money, knowing that it will not be honored by the drawee.

(b) Presumption.—For the purposes of this section as well as in any prosecution for theft committed by means of a bad check, an issuer is presumed to know that the check or order (other than a post-dated check or order) would not be paid; if:

  (1) the issuer had no account with the drawee at the time the check or order was issued; or

  (2) payment was refused by the drawee for lack of funds, upon presentation within 30 days after issue, and the issuer failed to make good within ten days after receiving notice of that refusal.

(c) Grading.—An offense under this section is a misdemeanor of the second degree if the amount of the check or order exceeds $200; otherwise it is a summary offense.

Under Pennsylvania law, the crime of passing bad checks is not forgery unless the check is forged. The bad-check section involves the less serious offense of passing no-account or insufficient-funds checks. Under this section, the passing of a check drawn on an account that is nonexistent when the check is negotiated creates a presumption that the check passer knew the check was worthless; thereby satisfying the element of criminal intent. The passer of an insufficient-funds check in Pennsylvania has ten days to make good on the check before criminal charges under this section can be filed.

It should be noted that the passing of a bad check may constitute a federal offense. For example, a forged or otherwise worthless check passed in a state outside the one where the drawee bank is located violates a federal statute, because the check travels interstate through normal banking channels.

Common Methods of Passing Worthless Checks

forged payroll checks

Payroll checks stolen by burglars and larcenists usually end up being cashed either by the person or persons who stole them or by other fraudulent-check passers. Once a blank payroll check is stolen, it is relatively simple to fill it out so that it looks authentic enough to cash. The bad-check offender will type in the date and forge the signature of the treasurer or other company official authorized to sign the check, and will often use a check-writing machine to insert the name of the payee and the amount payable. The payee name used is often one that corresponds to stolen identification possessed by the check passer.

Occasionally, large numbers of blank payroll checks are stolen by burglars or cargo thieves, and shortly thereafter, hundreds of merchants throughout the country are victimized by these forged documents. The larger check-passing operations or rings are loosely organized groups that act in concert to steal, execute, and pass forged payroll checks. The acquisition of false identification plays a vital role in this type of operation.

split-deposit schemes

Banks and similar financial institutions are vulnerable to fraudulent split-deposit schemes.[5] A legitimate split-deposit transaction is simply the depositing into a bank account of only part of the amount of a check made out to the account holder. After presenting the check and a deposit slip showing the sum he is placing in his account, the depositor receives from the bank in cash the amount of the difference. Because this transaction combines a deposit and a withdrawal, it is referred to as a split deposit.

A fraudulent-check passer, by making a split deposit with a stolen and forged payroll check made payable to an account holder, steals the difference between the fraudulent check and the amount on the deposit slip. If, for example, the check is in the amount of $300 and only $100 is "deposited," the check passer has fraudulently gained $200. In order to do this, the criminal must have a check that is made out in the name of a bank customer and must know his account number. Most offenders prefer using stolen blank payroll checks from nonlocal companies. The offender forges the signature of the maker and, using a check-writing machine, makes it payable to the legitimate account holder. An active check passer, armed with several stolen and forged payroll checks, can make numerous fraudulent split deposits into the same account through several or all of a victim bank's branch offices, thus fraudulently converting a substantial amount of the bank's money within a short period of time.

Many banks have been able to use their computer facilities to protect themselves against being repeatedly victimized by fraudulent split-deposit transactions. For example, when a split deposit is made, the bank teller posts (records) the transaction by computer and determines if similar deposits have been made to this account during the past 24 hours. If they have, the transaction is considered suspicious, and various steps may be taken, including the activation of a surveillance camera by the teller, and inquiries regarding the status and legitimacy of the check.

---

[5]Much of the material presented in this section was adapted from Norman L. Lawrence, "Bank Security . . . What Is Enough?" *FBI Law Enforcement Bulletin,* November 1973.

personal checks

Bad-check passers often cash personal checks that have been stolen in purse-snatchings and residential burglaries. A check passer may forge the signature of the account holder and make the check payable to himself or, more likely, a third person whose stolen identification is in his possession. If the victim account holder's identification has been stolen along with his checkbook, the check passer can make the check payable to the account holder by impersonating him. The latter technique is usually the most suitable for a check passer, since most commercial establishments are suspicious of two-party checks.

Most of the no-account and insufficient-funds checks that are passed are drawn on personal (noncommercial) accounts. For this reason, most check-cashing establishments tend to be more suspicious of personal checks.

money orders

Like payroll checks, blank money orders, stolen from their place of sale or while in transit to it, can be filled out to look authentic enough to pass. In most instances, money orders are legitimately purchased to be mailed to companies in payment of debts, but some are made payable to individuals. Upon receipt of a money order, a payee deposits it into a bank account, and the amount of the money order is credited to that account. Since a bogus check passer can forge the sender's name and the name of an individual payee, money orders made payable to individuals are usually treated as suspicious.

Also, a figure limiting the amount payable is printed on the face of most money orders, so a money order made out for an amount in excess of this limit figure should not be accepted. Quite often, the amount payable on a money order (or traveler's check) that has been legitimately purchased is altered or raised to a higher amount. For example, a money order purchased for $10 can be raised to $100 by a skillfull offender's forgery of an additional zero.

Procedures and Policies to Control Bad-Check Losses

In addition to banks and other financial institutions, almost every retail establishment must accept its customers' checks in order to function commercially. Studies involving supermarkets have shown that the average store cashes $1.50 in checks for every dollars' worth of merchandise sold. As a result most merchants are vulnerable to fraudulent-check passers. To protect themselves against bad-check losses, most retail establishments have policies regarding the types of checks they will accept, and under what circumstances. For example, it is the policy of many retail establishments not to accept checks made payable to cash. Merchants who do negotiate checks for cash usually abide by strict guidelines, such as only accepting checks from people who have applied for this privilege and have been determined to be good risks. And merchants who refuse to cash checks may still, under certain circumstances, accept them in payment for merchandise.

Some merchants are obviously more cautious than others, with the degree of caution usually corresponding to the nature of the store's vulnerability. Nevertheless, the following basic precautions are usually incorporated into even the most liberal check-cashing policies.

high-risk checks

As a general rule, certain types of checks should never be accepted unless there is a particularly good reason to do so. These types are identified and discussed below.

Two-Party Checks. Because the original maker of a two-party check can stop payment on the check at the bank, the merchant accepting the check is taking an unacceptable risk. A merchant offered this type of check would be wise to contact the maker of the check, and to obtain and record the telephone numbers and addresses of both the maker and the payee.

Nonlocal and Certain Payroll Checks. Payroll and personal checks drawn on out-of-town banks are poor risks, since bad-check passers usually pass payroll checks away from the neighborhood where they were stolen. Also, a payroll check should not be accepted until the payee's employment with the identified company is verified. Payroll checks that are handprinted, rubber-stamped, or typewritten rather than made out with a check-writing machine should be treated suspiciously as well, particularly in metropolitan areas.

Counter Checks. A few stores have counter checks for the convenience of customers. However, a counter check is not negotiable. A merchant should never accept a counter check that does not have the account holder's name, address, and account number on it.

Other Checks that Should Be Treated as Suspicious. A check that has been erased or in any other way altered should not be accepted. In the case of payroll and two-party checks, the name of the payee and the amount of the check should receive close attention. Checks that have been illegibly written or made out in pencil should not be accepted either.

Postdated checks are considered poor risks; they are frequently insufficient-funds checks. A retailer should also be wary of checks dated more than five days before the current date, and checks over six months old are usually returned to the merchant marked "stale-dated."

Caution should be exercised, especially in connection with new customers, when accepting a check for an amount more than that of the merchandise being purchased. Many retailers have set limits on these; for example, a store may accept checks up to only $10 over the purchase price of the merchandise. Moreover, most stores have preestablished limits on the size of the checks they accept either for cash or in connection with a purchase. In most stores, checks for larger amounts (if not all checks) cannot be accepted without approval by designated management personnel.

requiring identification

Even though the merchant or the bank is satisfied that the check itself is legitimate, a further determination should be made of the identity of the person presenting it—more specifically, whether he is the person who signed it or, in the case of a two-party or payroll check, the legitimate payee. Assuming that the holder is who he says he is, it is still possible that he has forged the signature of the maker of the check. Moreover, even if his identification papers match the appropriate name on the check, those papers may not correspond to his true identity. It becomes obvious that requiring identification prior to the cashing of all checks will not entirely eliminate the bad-check problem. A clever and well-prepared offender may be in possession of stolen or false identification, and only the most careful, knowledgeable, and observant bank teller or retail employee will detect such a fraud. Nevertheless, a merchant or bank, by requiring the proper identification, will significantly minimize the risk of accepting a bad check. Finally, it is important for the receiver of a check to obtain enough information about the passer so that he can be located in the event the check is returned.

Proper Check-Cashing Identification. Most stores require at least two pieces of proper identification. The following suggests what type of identification is the most useful and therefore acceptable:

1. *Current Automobile Operator's License.* If licenses in your state do not carry a photograph of the customer, you may want to ask for a second identification.
2. *Automobile Registration Card.* Be sure the name of the state agrees with the location of the bank. If it doesn't, the customer must have a plausible reason. Also make sure that the signature on the registration and check agree.
3. *Shopping Plates.* If they bear a signature or laminated photograph, shopping plates and other credit cards can be used as identification. The retail merchants' organization in some communities issues lists of stolen shopping plates to which you should always refer when identifying the check-passer.

4. *Government Passes* can also be used for identification in cashing checks. Picture passes should carry the name of the department and a serial number. Building passes should also carry a signature.
5. *Identification Cards,* such as those issued by the armed services, police departments, and companies, should carry a photo, a description, and a signature. Police cards should also carry a badge number.[6]

Employees who examine identification papers when accepting checks usually record the holder's address and driver's-license, credit-card, and telephone numbers on the reverse side of the check. After cashing the check, the employee should also initial it.

Improper Check-Cashing Identification. Many items commonly used for identification when cashing checks are easily forged and are not intended for this use. The following cards and documents have been classified by the Small Business Administration as poor check-passing identification and should be displayed only along with the holder's current driver's license:

Social Security cards
Business cards
Club or organization cards
Bankbooks
Work permits
Insurance cards
Learner's permits
Letters
Birth certificates
Library cards
Initialed jewelry
Unsigned credit cards
Voter's registration cards
Customers' duplicate cards[7]

Check-cashing employees should be trained to compare signatures of drivers' licenses and other forms of identification with the appropriate signatures on checks. They should also be instructed to compare the appearance of a check passer with any photograph on an identification card he displays. Retail employees and bank tellers should require anyone presenting a check not been made out by him (payroll and two-party checks) to endorse the check in their presence. This will provide a sample of his handwriting, which may aid investigating police officers in the case of a forgery. For example, the payee's endorsement may match the signature of the maker of the check, and both signatures may match a suspect's known handwriting.

signature card systems

Many retail establishments, especially supermarkets and discount stores, maintain files of signatures and other data on those who cash checks in their stores. These files, commonly referred to as signature card systems, are maintained

[6]Kolodny, *Outwitting Bad Check Passers.*

[7]*Ibid.*

primarily for the protection of the store and the convenience of its customers. The first time a customer cashes a check, he signs a card and also enters on it his driver's-license number, home address, telephone number, and often the name of his employer. The employee responsible for getting this information usually compares the signature on the card with the one on the customer's driver's license. The card is filed alphabetically, and every time the customer cashes a check in this store, the signature on the check is compared with the signature on his card. Depending upon the store and the degree of caution exercised, he may not be required to display identification every time he cashes a check. If a customer's check is returned, this fact is noted on his signature card for future reference in the event he attempts to cash another check in the store.

Information systems similar to this one can also be entered in a computerized system, in which data collected by many retail establishments in a chain operation can be centrally maintained and available to every contributing store. The information in such a system is easily updated and immediately available to an inquiring party.

But regardless of the kind of system used, one of the most effective measures against bad-check passers is keeping a record of every bad check passed in the store. By checking these files or lists every time a check is presented, the store will minimize the possibility of being victimized twice by the same check and/or check passer.

Security Devices against Bad Checks

Most banks and similar financial institutions, pursuant to the requirements of the Bank Protection Act of 1968,[8] use electronic surveillance systems that either deter fraudulent-check passers or aid in their identification. A bank teller who becomes suspicious of a particular check casher may choose to activate an electronic surveillance camera that either photographs, video-tapes, or takes motion pictures of the suspect. Many bank electronic surveillance systems, in fact, do not require activation, since they are in operation continuously during business hours. Although these systems are effective, their primary function is the deterrence and identification of bank robbers, so many banks, along with many retail establishments, utilize equipment designed specifically for the identification of fraudulent-check passers.

[8]The Bank Protection Act of 1968 (Title 12, U.S. Code, Sections 1881–1884) is a federal statute establishing security standards and procedures for all federally insured banks and savings and loan associations. This law was enacted to reduce the number of crimes against banking institutions.

fraudulent-check-passer identification systems

Fraudulent-check offenders, by being photographed along with the checks they pass, are more likely to be identified and prosecuted for the offense.[9] The typical check-passer identification system uses a dual-lens camera, using 16-mm film, activated by lever or foot pedal or by a remote control device. The camera produces a photograph of the offender, his check, and the identification he has displayed to cash it. The photographs themselves, constituting admissable court evidence, are widely used in the criminal prosecution of check passers and, because they depict the check passer's head, check, and identification in the same picture frame, are not susceptible to a defendant's claim that the pictures of himself and of the bogus check were mixed up by the police. Most photographs of this nature include the date of the transaction.

Check-passer identification systems are relatively simple to operate. When the check is presented to the bank teller or retail employee, he stamps it with a number that coincides with a number on the picture frame. The check and the customer's identification are then placed under the camera to be photographed along with the check passer. Most of these cameras can take up to 2,000 photographs without being reloaded. The only photographs actually developed are the ones involving bad checks; the number on the returned check identifies the picture frame that is to be developed.

Check-passer identification systems are widely used by supermarkets and discount stores. Most users of these systems believe that they effectively deter bad-check offenders, so they openly photograph their customers. Signs are usually displayed to remind the customer that the system is operated for his as well as the store's protection.

One of the problems solved by the installation and use of such an identification system is that of the child who forges and passes his parent's check. In these cases, parents are usually reluctant to believe that their children have committed forgery, and so they refuse to accept responsibility for the loss. However, once a parent is shown a photograph of the check and his child, the problem is resolved, at least for the retailer.

Counterfeiting

the offense

Generally, counterfeiting can involve the unlawful making or duplication of any object. Usually, the genuine object that is counterfeited is a thing of value, such as a statue, painting, or other work of art. In most instances, however,

[9]Much of the information in this section was taken from "Indiana Bank Reduces Fraud Losses with Cassette-Loaded Photo Units," *Security Distributing & Marketing*, October 1975.

counterfeiting is thought of in connection with the printing of false money. Only Congress has the power to print money and mint coins; therefore, under federal law, counterfeiting is classified as an offense that affects the sovereignty or the administration of government functions. Although the *making* of bogus money can be only a federal offense, a state may pass a law that makes the *passing* of counterfeit money a crime, usually classified as fraud and a crime against property.

The Secret Service, a federal investigative agency operating within the Treasury Department, has primary jurisdiction over those who print and pass counterfeit money. A person who has unknowingly passed a counterfeit bill has not committed a federal or state offense, because there was no intent on his part to defraud. But when the possessor of a bill realizes that it is counterfeit, he must turn it over to the authorities, and he will not be reimbursed for his loss; as a result, innocent receivers of counterfeit bills who do not want to be caught ''holding the bag'' often attempt to pass the money on to others. And because of this fact, when the money is finally identified as false, the person reporting the offense may not have received it directly from the counterfeiter or a member of his operation.

Commercial enterprises that accept cash as a part of their regular business are vulnerable to being victimized by counterfeiters. Restaurants and bars, because they are dimly lit, are prime counterfeiting targets. In order to avoid this type of loss, employees of banks and retail establishments are frequently taught how to recognize counterfeit money. Whenever an employee is presented with a suspicious bill, he should at least observe the passer closely, so he can give a complete description of him later if the bill is, in fact, bogus; and he might be instructed also to obtain, if feasible, the license number of the suspect's automobile. If the bogus bill is passed in a bank, the teller may have instructions to activate a surveillance camera. In most cases, employees are not required to detain, question, or otherwise confront a counterfeiting suspect, but rather to summon the manager and/or security director immediately.

recognizing counterfeit money

One of the major distinguishing features of good money is the paper on which it is printed. Genuine currency paper contains tiny blue and red fibers enmeshed in it. Counterfeiters often simulate these fibers by printing blue and red lines on their bogus bills. A close examination of the portrait and its background inside the oval will determine whether or not a bill is genuine. The background on real currency is made up of sharp and clear vertical and horizontal lines that form small, light squares. (See Figure 12-1.) On a counterfeit bill, these lines often run together, filling in the small squares. As a general guideline, it can be said that genuine money, when compared to counterfeit money, looks better. Real money is printed from steel plates that have been professionally engraved and is printed on a

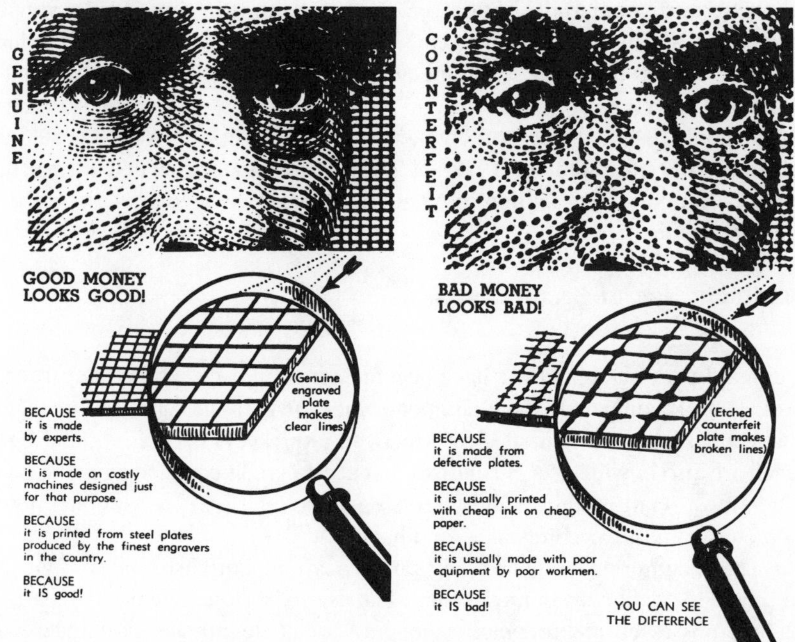

FIGURE 12-1. An illustration comparing good and bad money

Courtesy U.S. Secret Service, U.S. Treasury Department

better grade of paper. Counterfeit money is usually printed from defective plates that have been etched and therefore produce broken lines, and counterfeiters use a lower grade of ink.

Occasionally, counterfeiters take genuine $1 bills and paste counterfeited digits over the denomination numbers. For example, with the digit 20 skillfully pasted onto a $1 bill, it can be passed off as a $20 bill. This type of fraud can easily be detected by any observant employee who knows which portrait and reverse-side design correspond to each denomination. In the case above, for example, the bogus bill would carry President Washington's portrait and the U.S. Seal, rather than (if it were a genuine $20 bill) President Jackson's portrait and a picture of the White House.

Devices capable of distinguishing counterfeit from genuine bills are being used by some banks and retail establishments. For example, a counterfeit bill will produce an identifiable glow when examined under units emitting a special light. The fibers of a suspect bill can also be easily examined when the bill is exposed to a particular type of illumination.

Although counterfeiting is a crime committed by only a few, a counterfeiting operation has the potential for significant monetary losses. For example, in December 1976, police in Europe arrested four suspects in possession of over $14 million worth of counterfeit U.S. $20 bills. Around the same time, Secret Service agents seized $12 million in counterfeit $100 bills from a house near Akron, Ohio, where they also confiscated printing equipment, a camera, a platemaker, and a paper cutter.

It should be noted that most counterfeit money is seized before it is put into circulation. For example, in 1972, $22.9 million in uncirculated counterfeit currency, and only $4.8 million in circulation, was recovered.[10]

Fraudulent Use of Credit Cards

Credit-card possession and use have become commonplace. Banks, department stores, and oil companies issue and honor their own credit cards. All-purchase credit cards such as those issued by American Express, Diner's Club, and Carte Blanch are also in wide use. Businesses that accept credit cards on a regular basis include most retail establishments, service stations, airlines, restaurants, hotels and motels, rent-a-car companies, and banks.

The unauthorized use of a credit card is a criminal offense, and so is the use of a canceled credit card in most states. The user of a stolen credit card who, in addition, possesses identification belonging to the legitimate cardholder will usually encounter very little difficulty in fraudulently passing the card. Credit cards can also be acquired by offenders using fictitious identification. By the time such a card is identified, the losses attributable to its use can be substantial. Losses from the fraudulent use of credit cards cost U.S. banking institutions about $460 million in 1974.[11]

the offense

In some states, the knowing use of a stolen, forged, or fictitious credit card is prosecutable as a forgery offense. In other jurisdictions, this offense is more specifically defined. The following section of *Purdon's Pennsylvania Statutes Annotated*, Title 18, Crimes and Offenses, is representative of most credit-card laws:

Section 4106 Credit cards

(a) Offense defined.—A person commits an offense if he uses a credit card for the purpose of obtaining property or services with knowledge that:
(1) the card is stolen or forged;

---

[10] *The Cost of Crimes against Business* (Washington, D.C.: U.S. Department of Commerce, 1976), p. 9.

[11] *Ibid.*, p. 4.

(2) the card has been revoked or canceled; or

(3) for any other reason his use of the card is unauthorized by the issuer.

(b) Defenses.—It is a defense to prosecution under paragraph (a)(3) of this section, if the actor proves by a preponderance of the evidence that he had the intent and ability to meet all obligations to the issuer arising out of his use of the card.

(c) Grading.—An offense under this section is a felony of the third degree if the value of the property or services secured or sought to be secured by means of the credit card exceeds $500; otherwise it is a misdemeanor of the second degree.

(d) Definition.—As used in this section the word "credit card" means a writing or other evidence of an undertaking to pay for property or services delivered or rendered to or upon the order of a designated person or bearer.

Credit-card and major oil companies, by employing large numbers of private-investigator personnel, make a continuing effort to control and minimize this costly problem. One of the more effective security measures taken by large department and discount stores is the establishment of credit-card acceptance policies similar to those discussed in connection with the handling of checks. Employees who are knowledgeable, well trained, and motivated will also operate to significantly prevent and thereby reduce losses caused by fraudulent credit-card use.

The Acquisition and Illegal Use of False Identification

In 1976, it was estimated that people using false identification steal more than $10 billion a year. This figure includes $1 billion in check fraud, $100 million in illegally collected welfare payments, $4 billion sent out of the country by illegal aliens, and $50 million through the sale of stolen securities.[12]

obtaining copies of false birth certificates

The acquisition of a copy of a bona fide birth certificate of a deceased person is referred to as the infant-death technique. An imposter checks old newspapers or searches the records in a county clerk's office for the name of a child who died and,

---

[12]Mitchell C. Lynch, "Use of False Identity to Obtain Passports, Credit Cards Grows," *Wall Street Journal,* January 8, 1976. This article concerns the results of a Department of Justice task-force study of the use of false identification for illegal purposes.

had he lived, would have been about his own age. Then, since obtaining a copy of someone else's birth certificate is legal in most states, he gets one for that child from the county or municipal recorder's office. Since the person is deceased, there is no possibility that he will challenge the impostor's use of his identity.

The possession of such a birth certificate will enable the impostor to get, for example, a driver's license under the same name. Once he has both documents, he can apply for and receive a variety of credit cards that can be fraudulently used under the fictitious name; he can open bank accounts upon which fraudulent checks can be drawn; and he can use these documents for a variety of other illegal purposes. For example, he can rent a car displaying a fictitious credit card and a corresponding driver's license; then, since rent-a-car fees are not paid until the vehicle is returned, he can use the car until he no longer needs it, then abandon it without paying for its use. Cars rented through fictitious credit cards and supporting identification are frequently used in the commission of bank robberies and other crimes. Abandoned after the crime, such a car cannot be easily traced back to the perpetrator.

In 1974, a federal task force, made up of members of the Department of Justice, Department of State, American Banker's Association, and International Association of Chiefs of Police, was established to address the problems associated with the illegal use of false identification. Two of the major proposals drafted related to restricting the issuance of birth certificates to unauthorized persons. At present, birth records are not linked to death records; if they were, as the task force proposed, the infant-death technique would be extremely difficult. The task force also advised that, since a copy of a living person's birth certificate can be obtained by anyone telephoning the proper county or municipal office and requesting that it be mailed to him, the clerk receiving such a request should ask the party to name the parents of the subject of the birth certificate. Birth records contain this information, and such a technique would help to screen out impostors.

Quick-Change Artists

A larcenist who steals cash by short-changing a bank teller or retail employee is commonly referred to as a quick-change artist. The offense is committed by thoroughly confusing the victim. There are many techniques used; the following quick-change MOs will illustrate the nature of the offense.

The offender, dressed in conservative business attire, encounters his victims during hectic periods when they are handling many customers. Appearing somewhat confused and in a hurry, he purchases an inexpensive item with a $20 bill, getting in return one $10 bill, a $5 bill, and four $1 bills along with some change. Then he suddenly discovers that he has another $1 bill on his person. He puts it with the other four singles and asks the cashier to give him a $5 bill in return. Upon receiving the $5 bill, he puts it with the $5 bill he received before and asks for a ten.

When the $10 bill is given to him, he does not give up the two $5 bills he owes in return, but instead places the two fives with the ten he has just received and asks for a $20 bill. If the cashier is sufficiently confused, she may change the ten and two fives for a $20 bill. Since she did not receive the two $5 bills in return for the $10 bill she relinquished, she has been short-changed ten dollars.

Quick-change artists working in pairs have been known to short-change a victim in the following way: The first partner purchases an inexpensive item with a $20 bill he has previously marked. The second makes another small purchase from the same cashier with a $1 bill, and when he gets his change, insists that he gave the cashier a $20 bill. When she resists this claim, he ''proves'' his assertion by identifying the marked $20 bill planted by his partner. This bill may contain, for example, the second offender's telephone number.

Quick-change artists will not be successful in banks and retail establishments employing alert tellers and cashiers who follow established cash-handling procedures. Cash-handling personnel are usually instructed to handle only one transaction at a time. If, for example, a customer asks for change while the cashier is ringing up his purchase, the sales transaction should be completed before the change is made. When she receives a large bill, the cashier should call out the denomination, place it on the cash register ledge while making change, and put it into the cash drawer only after the customer has received his change. Finally, whenever a cash-handling employee receives a marked or torn bill, she should take special note of the customer presenting it and perhaps even call the customer's attention to it.

As a general rule, all cash-handling employees are instructed to notify management when confusion occurs at the cash register. This practice alone will deter most quick-change artists and virtually eliminate these losses.

DISCUSSION QUESTIONS

1. Under the bad-check statute quoted in this chapter, is the mere attempt to pass a bogus check a crime? In your opinion, should a check passer be prosecuted even though he has failed to defraud his intended victim and as a result has received nothing of value?
2. Why is the presentation of a no-account check more indicative of the check passer's intent than the issuance of an insufficient-funds check?
3. In addition to the check passer's handwriting on the worthless document, what other evidence might be available to connect him to the crime?
4. Do you believe that the issuance of a driver's license bearing the holder's photograph would operate to reduce bad-check and credit-card losses? Explain your answer.
5. With regard to counterfeit money, what denominations do you think are the most commonly reproduced?

SELECTED BIBLIOGRAPHY

"How Big Is the Bad Check Problem?" *Security World*, July/August 1974.

"Indiana Bank Reduces Fraud Losses with Cassette-Loaded Photo Units," *Security Distributing & Marketing*, October 1975.

KOLODNY, LEONARD, *Outwitting Bad Check Passers*. Washington, D.C.: Small Business Administration, 1973.

LAWRENCE, NORMAN L., "Bank Security . . . What Is Enough?" *FBI Law Enforcement Bulletin*, November 1973. The author discusses, in addition to the other aspects of bank security, fraudulent split-deposit schemes.

LIPSON, MILTON, *On Guard; The Business of Private Security*, Chap. 7, "Fraud Investigation." New York: Quadrangle/The New York Times Book Co., 1975. A discussion of bad-check and credit-card frauds.

LYNCH, MITCHELL C., "Use of False Identity to Obtain Passports, Credit Cards Grows," *Wall Street Journal*, January 8, 1976.

Chapter 13

Kidnapping, Robbery, and Bombings

AN OVERVIEW

I. Kidnapping
   A. *The nature and extent of the kidnapping problem*
      1. State and federal kidnapping laws
      2. The growth of the problem
      3. Well-known kidnapping cases
      4. A profile of kidnappers, their victims, and their demands
   B. *Kidnapping and the business community*
      1. Antikidnapping measures for the businessman
      2. Use of bodyguards
      3. Establishing a corporate plan of action

II. Robbery
   A. *Criminal-law definition of the offense*
   B. *The extent of the robbery problem*
   C. *The nature of robbery, robbers, and their victims*
      1. Profile of the robber
   D. *Methods, personnel, and hardware to control robbery*
      1. Robbery alarms, devices, and systems
      2. Cash-control procedures and systems
      3. Surveillance cameras
      4. Armed security guards
      5. Other protective measures
      6. Identifying the robber

III. Bombings
   A. *The nature and extent of the problem*
   B. *Common bomb targets*
   C. *Common explosives*
      1. Black powder
      2. Smokeless powder
      3. Nitroglycerin
      4. Dynamite
      5. Trinitrotoluene (TNT)
      6. Composition C
   D. *Bomb threats*
      1. Receiving and reporting bomb threats
      2. Evaluating the legitimacy of the threat
   E. *Responding to a bomb threat*
      1. The decision to evacuate
      2. Notifying the proper authorities
      3. Bomb searches

Kidnapping

Although kidnapping is committed by many types of offenders and for a wide variety of reasons, the offense is usually motivated by the desire to extort cash from individuals, families, companies, or governments that are willing to pay to ensure the victim's safe return. There are, therefore, two victims in most kidnapping cases—the abductee and the person or group subjected to extortion. A brief discussion of state and federal kidnapping laws and a review of a few well-known kidnapping cases will illustrate the general nature of the offense. Then, because our orientation here is the business community's security vulnerability, the offense will be more narrowly discussed, in relation to the abduction of business executives.

the nature and extent of the kidnapping problem

State and Federal Kidnapping Laws. The offense of kidnapping is the unlawful taking and removal of the victim. In some states, the taking and removal without the ransom element constitutes a separate and less serious offense; but in most, any unlawful abduction of another, even without a ransom demand, is kidnapping. Also, in most states, felonious restraint and false imprisonment, although they relate to kidnapping, are separate and less serious crimes. These two offenses are similar to kidnapping in that they unlawfully restrict a person's freedom to act, but they differ from it in that they do not in most instances involve the physical and forcible taking, and substantial removal, of the victim.

Pennsylvania's kidnapping law is representative of those statutes that make the unlawful taking, removal, and, under certain circumstances, confinement of another person a kidnapping offense:

Section 2901 Kidnapping

(a) Offense defined.—A person is guilty of kidnapping if he unlawfully removes another a substantial distance under the circumstances from the place where he is found, or if he unlawfully confines another for a substantial period in a place of isolation with any of the following intentions:
  (1) To hold for ransom or reward, or as a shield or hostage.
  (2) To facilitate commission of any felony or flight thereafter.
  (3) To inflict bodily injury on or to terrorize the victim or another.
  (4) To interfere with the performance by public officials of any governmental or political function.

(b) Grading.—Kidnapping is a felony of the first degree. A removal or confinement is unlawful within the meaning of this section if it is accomplished by force, threat or deception, or, in the case of a person who is under the age of 14 years or incompetent, if it is accomplished without the consent of a parent, guardian or other person responsible for general supervision of his welfare.

When the unlawful taking of a person includes his removal across a state line, federal kidnapping law has been violated. Moreover, the federal kidnapping statute creates a presumption that if the victim has not been returned within 24 hours following his abduction, he has been moved interstate. This allows the FBI to enter the case 24 hours after the crime has been committed even without specific evidence that the offenders and victim have crossed a state line. The federal statute 18USC Section 1201, reads:

> (a) Whoever knowingly transports in interstate or foreign commerce, any person who has been unlawfully seized, confined, inveigled, decoyed, kidnapped, abducted, or carried away and held for ransom or reward or otherwise, except, in the case of a minor, by a parent thereof, shall be punished (1) by death if the kidnaped person who has been unlawfully seized, confined, inveigled, decoyed, kidnapped, recommend, or (2) by imprisonment for any term of years or for life, if the death penalty is not imposed. . . .

The Growth of the Problem. Kidnapping is one of the least-committed offenses, so for most people, the risk of being kidnapped is slight. However, since the mid-1970s, kidnapping has increased at a startling rate, including the taking of innocent hostages by political terrorists. For example, from 1968 through mid-September 1975, 30 American diplomats and other U.S. officials were kidnap victims.[1] Of these, all of whom were seized on foreign soil, six were killed by the kidnappers, two were wounded, 18 were released unharmed, and four of the kidnapping attempts were unsuccessful. The United States has never paid a kidnapper's ransom. It is the government's firm policy not to pay ransom, release prisoners, or otherwise yield to terrorist blackmail.

In 1974, the FBI began compiling statistics on "hostage situations." That year, 201 offenses were committed in the United States, involving the deaths of 15 victims. During the first half of 1975, there were 124 kidnapping cases and eight victims killed. During the 1960s, however, the annual national average was only 30 to 40 kidnappings.

Well-Known Kidnapping Cases. Many kidnapping cases involve prominent or well-known victims. Because their lives and large sums of money are at stake, these cases receive considerable public attention. Probably the most celebrated kidnapping case in history was the 1932 abduction of Charles Lindbergh's infant son by Bruno Richard Hauptmann. The baby, taken from the Lindbergh home, was later discovered dead.

In 1968, Florida heiress Barbara Jane Mackle was seized by kidnappers and buried alive in a coffin-sized box in Georgia. Following the payment of a $500,000 ransom by her father, she was discovered alive by law-enforcement officers. She had managed to survive 84 hours in the underground coffin. Her kidnappers were identified and convicted.

In 1973, the grandson of billionaire J. Paul Getty was kidnapped in Rome, Italy. In order to press their ransom demands, the kidnappers cut off the victim's right ear and mailed it to a Rome newspaper. After five months of captivity and the payment of a $2.9-million ransom, 17-year-old J. Paul Getty III was released alive on a deserted Italian road. Of the nine people who were subsequently indicted for the kidnapping, only two were convicted of the crime.

In February 1974, Patricia Hearst, the 20-year-old granddaughter of publisher William Randolph Hearst, was forcibly taken from a motel room near the University of California campus. This crime cost the Hearst family a $2-million ransom in the form of food that was distributed to the poor in the San Francisco Bay area. The Hearst kidnapping, one of the most notorious crimes in history, directly and substantially affected thousands of people.

The second major kidnapping in 1974 was of Exxon Corporation executive Victor Samuelson. Samuelson, abducted in Latin America, was held in captivity for four months by Argentinian revolutionaries. Exxon arranged for the victim's safe return by paying the kidnappers $14 million, one of the largest ransoms ever paid.

---

[1]These statistics and the ones that immediately follow were taken from "Around the Globe—Outbreaks of Terror," *U.S. News & World Report,* September 29, 1975.

In 1975, Samuel Bronfman II was abducted in Westchester County, New York. His father, Edgar Bronfman, the chairman of the Seagram Company, paid the kidnappers a $2.3-million ransom. The victim was found unharmed but bound, gagged, and blindfolded, in a Brooklyn apartment, and the ransom money was recovered shortly thereafter. Bronfman's kidnappers were arrested and identified as a New York City fireman and an operator of a New York limousine service. In December 1976, the two men were tried and acquitted of kidnapping but convicted of grand larceny. One of the defendants claimed that young Bronfman had engineered the abduction for the purpose of bilking his father out of the ransom money.[2]

A Profile of Kidnappers, Their Victims, and Their Demands. Except for politically motivated kidnappers and/or terrorists, whose demands may involve the release of prisoners, changes in government policies, or the furnishing of weapons, food, or money to a revolutionary group, most kidnappers are common criminals motivated by the prospect of immediate personal gain. As a group, they are amateurs and rarely successful. In the United States, almost every kidnapping case results in the identification, arrest, and conviction of the perpetrators. The only ones who generally escape conviction are the perpetrators of mob-connected

---

[2]The following more recent kidnap-hostage incidents were reported in the March 1977 issue of *Protection of Assets Bulletin* (a monthly bulletin by the editors of *Protection of Assets Manual*, published by the Merritt Company):

In West Germany (within a ten-week period):

a. Wolfgang Gutberlet, supermarket-chain co-owner, was held hostage and released when $850,000 was paid. Four suspects were seized and the money was recovered.
b. Gernot Egolf, Hamburg brewery heir, was found frozen to death 52 days after an $850,000 demand was made.
c. Hendrik Snoek, an executive of a supermarket chain, was found chained to a shaft of an autobahn bridge after his father paid a $2.1-million ransom.
d. Richard Oetker, son of one of the richest men in Germany, was released after $8.3 million was paid. This was the largest ransom ever paid in Germany.
e. Six-year-old Eustachius Hell was found dead two days after $85,000 was demanded.

In the United States (in early February 1977):

a. February 8: An Indianapolis, Indiana, mortgage-company executive was held for 63 hours by a man with a shotgun. The hostage was released after authorities said they would not prosecute the attacker.
b. February 9: A Silver Springs, Maryland, bank's employees were held hostage for several hours by a young man who eventually surrendered.
c. February 11: Eight hostages were held at gunpoint in a home for unwed mothers in Cincinnati, Ohio, by a couple who was looking for a son they had put up for adoption a number of years ago.
d. February 12: A man held his six-year-old son hostage for five hours in Wheaton, Maryland, while he sporadically fired a rifle at police.
e. February 14: A man with a rifle killed five men and wounded five others where he worked in New Rochelle, New York, before killing himself.

In Spain, in a little more than a year, 53 business executives and government officials were kidnapped and held hostage. A number of deaths resulted.

abductions. These kidnappings are seldom reported to the police, and it is assumed that when the kidnappers are identified and caught by the victims or their colleagues, they are punished.

Besides the fact that they are amateurs, most common kidnappers are caught because of the difficulty of successfully committing the offense. For example, the capture and holding of a hostage involves planning, timing, and skill, and the victim must be housed and fed inconspiciously during his incarceration. Moreover, arrangements must be made by the kidnappers to communicate with those who will pay for the victim's safety, and once the victim's family or employer has agreed to pay the ransom, the kidnappers must figure out how to pick up the money without being observed, identified, or apprehended. This phase of the crime is usually the most difficult for both the offender and the victim. Even if the kidnapper takes possession of the ransom money without being caught or identified, he must be careful in spending it, since it will have been either marked or recorded as such. Finally, offenders who commit this violent and desperate crime are not only detested by the public, but are the subjects of the most intense and professional crime-fighting effort law-enforcement personnel can muster. For these reasons, kidnapping is not usually committed by professional criminals.

kidnapping and the business community

As reflected by the discussion above of some of the more notorious kidnapping cases, kidnap victims can be government officials, infants, children of the rich, or business executives. Businessmen have become increasingly aware that they are prime kidnapping targets, not because they personally have money, but because their employers are wealthy. One form of kidnapping that threatens a particular group of businessmen is the seizure by bank robbers of bank officials or members of their family as hostages, in order to ensure full cooperation from the officers and employees of the victim bank.[3]

For the victim and the offender alike, kidnapping is a dangerous and costly crime. Since members of the business community have become potential victims of this offense, their protection has become a major security concern. The following discussion is of some of the corporate and individual security policies and measures that can be implemented to reduce a businessman's risk of being kidnapped.

Antikidnapping Measures for the Businessman. One of the most basic antikidnapping measures businessmen can take is to vary their daily routines, thereby eliminating patterns that might be helpful to would-be abductors. For example, a businessman should not frequent the same restaurant the same night of each week, or even patronize the same restaurant more than twice a month. He should take

[3]In 1975, 128 bank employees and patrons were taken hostage by bank robbers.

different routes when traveling between his home, office, club, restaurant, and associates' residences. By not regularly using the same taxi stand, for example, he eliminates the possibility of being picked up by a phony cab.

The protection of top executives may warrant more severe measures. To make the executive less visible to the public, his name should be taken out of the telephone directory and off his mailbox, and he should not have his initials on his car or license plates. The executive should also make certain that his vacation plans stay out of the newspaper's social pages. Because expensive cars are a giveaway, more and more business executives are driving medium-priced cars, which have been specially equipped with bulletproof glazing materials.

The executive must also be secure in his home. The installation of a residential intrusion-alarm system, quality locks on solid wooden doors, proper window security, and adequate lighting usually provides sufficient residential protection. Having peepholes in all exterior doors and buying a watchdog will also help.

As other steps a businessman can take to reduce his chance of being kidnapped, he should:

1. Not give out personal information about himself or his family to unknown information collectors.
2. Be suspicious of persons who don't seem to belong around his home or place of business.
3. Never meet with strangers in out-of-the-way places.
4. Keep his car doors locked and his windows rolled up when driving.
5. Let people know of his destination and time of arrival when traveling or just commuting between home and office.

Use of Bodyguards. Since the mid-1970s, security firms providing bodyguards have had an increased demand for this service. Although their clients have traditionally included entertainers, sports figures, and other celebrities, a significant and growing portion of their business now consists of providing for the personal safety of the corporate executive.

The increase in the use of executive bodyguards, an extreme and costly measure involving only a small percentage of the country's top executives, has paralleled the rise in the nation's kidnapping rate. The following excerpt reflects the nature of the bodyguard function:

> How do bodyguards protect the VIP's in their custody from assassins, kidnappers, extortionists, terrorists, kooks and crowds? Understandably, the security agents are reluctant to discuss the secrets of their trade, but here are some details they were willing to reveal:
>
> If a client is one who travels around making speeches, a study is made of photographs of crowds taken at his previous public appearances. If the same face is

spotted more than once, blowups are made, and turned over to the FBI for possible identification. . . .

When a client attends a banquet and, during the invocation ceremony, all heads are bowed in silent prayer, the bodyguard is the one man whose head remains erect. Similarly, he will not stand frozen when the national anthem is played. For these are the perilous moments when a candidate for assassination is most vulnerable. During these intervals a bodyguard must be more alert than ever, scanning the entire audience for a danger signal, checking all the doorways.

When [the client] checks into a hotel, the bodyguard will have seen to it that the right and left rooms adjacent to his suite have been rented, so that no one can occupy them. The rooms directly above and below will also have been preempted. Vents and pipes are carefully examined. These precautions make it impossible for anyone to drill through walls, floor and ceiling in order to introduce some sophisticated gas or explosive.

In addition, all locks on these rooms will be changed. Maids, waiters and other hotel personnel who have access to the suite will be double-checked. The security net will even cover the occupants of all the other rooms on the same floor. If their credentials can't establish them as solid citizens, they will be discreetly reassigned rooms on other floors far away from this "off-limit" area.

"You can't hit 'em if you can't find 'em," says Wackenhut's Don Richards. "Whenever we take on a client we examine his work habits, family patterns, the routes he takes to the office and the normal activities of daily living. Then we recycle his entire life style so that most of his movements are unpredictable. The harder we make it for a criminal to pinpoint his whereabouts, the easier our job. . . ."[4]

The piece above graphically illustrates the intensity and professionalism associated with providing a bodyguard service. In terms of their training, experience, and ability, bodyguards are an elite group of highly paid security practitioners. Because of the cost and inconvenience to the bodyguard user, this measure should be considered only in connection with situations where the risk of kidnapping is perceived as great.

Establishing a Corporate Plan of Action. Although it is difficult to completely prepare for kidnapping—which, by its nature, involves an unlimited number of unforeseen contingencies—many important decisions can be made in advance. If a kidnapping does occur, there will be no time to carefully consider the ramifications of each decision, so a corporate kidnapping victim caught without a preestablished plan may react indecisively or make his decisions too hastily.

A complete kidnapping plan should include not only what will be done by the company but also how its policy will be implemented. These procedural matters might include, for example, the assignment of specific duties to key company personnel, the establishment of lines of communication, and the creation of a definite chain of command.

---

[4]Mort Weisinger, "The Bodyguard Business Is Booming," *Parade,* April 28, 1974.

The corporation should formulate in advance a policy regarding how it will respond to a kidnapper's demands. The basic issue here is whether or not the company will, as a matter of policy, pay a ransom in exchange for the return of the abducted employee. Corporate personnel who might be affected by this decision should be made aware of policies concerning it. Other matters that must be considered are decisions regarding police notification and the handling of the media. It should be noted that the role of the media in kidnapping cases is a complex and delicate issue, since the right of the public to know often comes into direct conflict with the well-being of the kidnap victim.

Corporate policy makers, while in the process of developing a kidnapping plan, should consult with the security director regarding matters relating specifically to the offense. For example, company officials confronted with a possible kidnapping situation should take steps to ensure that the alleged victim has actually been abducted. This precaution will protect the company from paying a ransom to a swindler impersonating a kidnapper when his "abductee" has voluntarily disappeared for his own reasons. Then, once the abduction has been verified and contact has been made with the kidnappers, the company should insist upon some proof that the victim is alive and in the abductors' custody. This can be in the form of a letter in the abductee's handwriting, which responds to questions that only the victim can answer correctly.

If corporate leaders consider the matters above and a general kidnapping plan is outlined, the firm will be in a better position to handle this type of emergency.

Robbery

criminal-law definition of the offense

Robbery is generally defined as the unlawful taking of property by force or the threat of force. Because of its assault facet, robbery is normally thought of as a crime against the person. Some states, however, classify robbery as a theft-related crime against property, and others place the offense in a separate category. Regardless of how it is classified, robbery is made up of two basic elements, the use of force and an unlawful taking. The use or threat of force against a human victim distinguishes this crime from burglary and larceny, crimes committed without the intention to physically harm or threaten the victims. Note that an offense is not robbery unless the force that is used or threatened is *physical,* thus distinguishing robbery from offenses such as blackmail, where the offender makes a nonphysical threat in order to obtain money.

Under many state statutes, there must be an actual theft before the offender is considered to have committed a robbery. In these states, for example, a holdup man who enters a supermarket with a gun, then flees the scene empty-handed after his threat has been ignored, has committed not robbery but attempted robbery. Pursuant to the Model Penal Code version of robbery, however, any attempted theft by force or threat of force would constitute robbery, regardless of whether the offender was successful. The Model Penal Code definition is:

Section 222.1 Robbery

(1) Robbery Defined. A person is guilty of robbery if, in the course of committing a theft, he:
   (a) inflicts serious bodily injury upon another; or
   (b) threatens another with or purposely puts him in fear of immediate serious bodily injury; or
   (c) commits or threatens immediately to commit any felony of the first or second degree.

   An act shall be deemed "in the course of committing a theft" if it occurs in an attempt to commit theft or in flight after the attempt or commission.

(2) Grading. Robbery is a felony of the second degree, except that it is a felony of the first degree if in the course of committing the theft the actor attempts to kill anyone, or purposely inflicts or attempts to inflict serious bodily injury.

It should be noted that under the Code, an offender has committed robbery if he has stolen pursuant to a threat to immediately commit a felony upon the victim or a third person—for example, if he has forced a woman to give him money under the threat of rape.

Robbery, like the offenses of murder and aggravated assault, is a crime of violence committed against the person and, as such, it is treated as a serious offense. It is classified as a felony in every state and gives rise to penalties ranging up to 20 years in prison. Under certain circumstances, robbery is also a federal crime—for example, the robbery of a federally insured bank or savings and loan association—and is investigated by the FBI.

Since robberies involving armed offenders can result in the killing of robbery victims, witnesses, and responding law-enforcement personnel, a brief discussion of the felony-murder rule is appropriate. This is the concept that whenever a killing takes place during the commission of a felony, every person involved in the felony can be held criminally responsible for the death, regardless of whether the killing was specifically intended or whether the offender was himself involved in the homicide. For example, the driver of a getaway car, waiting outside a bank where a security guard is accidentally killed by a bank employee who is shooting at one of the robbers, can be prosecuted for homicide under the felony-murder rule. If one of the robbers is killed by one of the victim's employees, a guard or a policeman, the accomplices, under this rule, can be held legally responsible for his death.

the extent of the robbery problem

Robbery, unlike shoplifting and many other offenses, is always detected. Moreover, since almost all robberies are reported to the police, offense data in the *Uniform Crime Reports* pertaining to robbery quite accurately reflect the overall extent of this problem. Statistics from the 1976 *UCR* will be cited here to illustrate the magnitude of the problem.

Robbery is defined by the *UCR* as "stealing or taking anything of value from the care, custody, or control of a person by force or by violence or by putting in fear, such as strong-armed robbery, stick-ups, armed robbery, assault to rob, and attempt to rob."

According to the *Uniform Crime Reports*, 420,210 robberies were committed in 1976, making up 4 percent of the FBI's total crime index and 43 percent of all crimes of violence. The rate of robbery in 1976 reflects a 10 percent decrease over the previous year. Between 1972 and 1976, the rate of robbery in the United States increased by 12 percent, with much of the increase attributable to the victimization of chain stores and banks. For example, between 1972 and 1976, chain-store robberies increased 50 percent, and bank robberies 74 percent. With regard to the nature of robbery victims, in 1975 over 50 percent of these crimes took place in the street. It is interesting to note that street robbery, commonly referred to as mugging, decreased from 1975 to 1976, by about 5 percent, as compared to bank robbery, which jumped about 3 percent during this period. In 1976, 43 percent of all robberies were committed through the use of firearms, 13 percent were by the use of knives or cutting instruments, and 8 percent by the use of other weapons. The remainder of the reported robberies were strong-arm where no weapons were used.

Total robbery losses in 1976 amounted to approximately $140 million, whereas ten years earlier, they were estimated at $50 million. These losses are small when compared to the annual cost of such crimes as larceny, burglary, and bad checks, and losses from unreported employee pilferage far exceed robbery losses. However, the robbery statistics do not reflect the personal loss and suffering experienced by those who are injured every year in robberies.

In 1976, law-enforcement personnel solved 27 percent of their robbery cases, but only 72 percent of the adults arrested for robbery were prosecuted. Of those prosecuted, only 56 percent were convicted of robbery. About one-third of those arrested for robbery in 1976 were juveniles who were turned over to the juvenile court system for processing.

The average monetary loss in 1976 robberies was $338, but, as in other years, there were several individual cases involving far more substantial losses. For example, in November of the previous year, four armed robbers reportedly stole $135,000 from an Illinois bank. In December of that year, two robbers shot and killed the vice-president of a Georgia bank while he was at home for lunch, then attempted to extort $60,000 from his bank, stating that the victim would be killed if their demands were not met. They were arrested as they left the victim bank with the $60,000. And banks are not the only facilities vulnerable to large robbery losses. For example, armored cars, large supermarkets, race tracks, and liquor stores often relinquish large sums to robbers.

The violence and danger always associated with robbery are reflected in the following two cases, which occurred during the latter part of 1976:

Two female employees of Chicago's South Side currency exchange were taken hostage by robbers who were trapped inside the facility by responding police. After an exchange of gunfire resulting in injuries to both armed robbers and a policeman, the offenders took their hostages to a nearby apartment and held them captive, along with an occupant of the apartment, for four hours. They finally released the hostages unharmed and surrendered to the police. While the Chicago robbery was taking place, four bandits in Brussels, Belgium, held up a labor-union headquarters. Armed with tommy guns and pistols, they opened fire inside the headquarters, then fled the scene, spraying bullets throughout a busy shopping area. After wounding six people, including a security guard, the robbers escaped arrest by losing the police in heavy downtown traffic.

the nature of robbery, robbers, and their victims

The following statement aptly describes the nature of the robbery offense: "Robbery, by definition, combines violence and theft, is almost always committed by the predatory stranger and is thus distinguishable from such other crimes of violence as homicide, rape, and assault where the victims and the perpetrators in most cases are known to one another."[5] Whereas the business community is vulnerable to bank, supermarket, service-station, liquor-store, drugstore, and convenience-store robbery, individuals become vulnerable to mugging the moment they leave the relative security of their homes. And because robbery involves unprovoked assault upon innocent persons by strangers, the public reaction to robbery is particularly strong.

Robbery is generally a nighttime offense.[6] With the exception of bank robberies (since banks are closed at night), five times as many robberies are committed during the night as during daylight hours. As a general rule, commercial robbery victims are carefully selected by offenders, and so only the most vulnerable banks and stores are robbed. For example, when studying robbery rates in connection with a group of convenience stores, the researchers found that 13

---

[5]John E. Conklin, *Robbery and the Criminal Justice System* (Philadelphia: Lippincott, 1972), p. viii.

[6]In this section, much of the material regarding the nature of robbery and robbery victims is based upon the findings of an eight-month study (January 1 to August 31, 1975) involving 120 7-Eleven stores in the Los Angeles area. The study was conducted by the Western Behavioral Sciences Institute, a private, nonprofit research institute, and funded by the National Institute of Law Enforcement and Criminal Justice (NILECJ) and the Southland Corporation, operators and franchisers of 5,400 convenience food stores. The results of the study are discussed in "Convenience Stores Find an Answer," *Security World,* April 1976.

percent of the stores accounted for 72 percent of the robberies, and that certain stores were never robbed, whereas others were continually being victimized. The researchers found similarities in those stores that were constant victims, primarily involving physical characteristics that tended to draw robbers. The socioeconomic character of the neighborhood appeared to have no relationship to a store's individual robbery rate.

More robberies are committed during November and December than during any other two-month period. Also, they occur not just on weekends but somewhat evenly throughout the week. Most robbers wait until the customers have left before entering a store, and they usually pose as customers before announcing the robbery. Most robberies last only a few seconds, seldom involving lengthy instructions or conversation between the offender and the victim.

Almost every robber uses a gun or a knife to perpetrate the offense:

> . . . The first function served by a weapon is that it creates a *buffer zone* between the offender and the victim. The firearm is most effective, for it instills the greatest amount of fear in the victim. Many interviewed robbers stated that "no one would try to take a gun away from you" and that "it's easier to control people with a gun." Some felt that a knife did not serve this function as well as a pistol, since a victim might try to take a knife from the robber. A firearm is more dangerous and covers a greater area, since harm can be inflicted from a distance. . . .
>
> The second function of the weapon, *intimidation* of the victim, is related to the creation of a buffer zone, in that if the offender can frighten the victim sufficiently, the latter will be less apt to resist and more willing to give up his money, minimizing the chance of struggle and injury. Quite a few inmates said that they used weapons, especially firearms, to avoid the need for violence. A few offenders expressed fear of the "hero"—the victim who resists even in the face of a loaded weapon, and is seen as highly irrational and unpredictable. . . .
>
> If the presence of a weapon does not intimidate the victim enough to induce cooperation, the offender may try to increase the level of intimidation. One offender cocked the pistol he carried to frighten the victim, and another robber sometimes held the pistol to the victim's head. Both tactics proved successful in eliciting victim cooperation. If the victim continues to resist, the offender may use his weapon for a third purpose, to *make good the threat* which the presence of the weapon implies. A few offenders will stab or shoot a victim to complete a robbery, but a more common response is to use the weapon, particularly a loaded firearm, as a blunt instrument. The offender will strike the victim on the side of the head or in the stomach to show him that he "means business." The weapon is thus used in a nonlethal manner to indicate to the victim that the offender is willing to use force to complete the theft. . . .
>
> A fourth function of the weapon is to *insure escape* from the scene of the robbery. Robbers know that if they can get away from the scene rapidly, their chances of being arrested for the offense are significantly reduced. A weapon can be used to keep victims, witnesses and even police officers from blocking their escape. The type of weapon employed is important, a knife being of little value in facilitating an escape, since it can be used effectively only in a physical struggle. Robbery offenders are more apt to fire a gun to insure escape than they are to overcome victim

> resistance, since they face incarceration if apprehended for their crimes but can find other victims to rob if they encounter an uncooperative one. More is at stake in escaping from the scene than in completing the robbery or a particular victim. . . .[7]

In the case of store and bank employees who have been held up, the fact that they have not suffered a personal monetary loss or been injured or roughly handled by the robber does not necessarily mean that they won't experience some after-effects of the crime. Only a small percentage of robbery victims are injured or killed by robbers, but many state that since being robbed, they trust people less; and quite a few quit their jobs after a robbery.

With regard to the actual use of physical force by a robber against the victim, Conklin found that if the robber is in possession of a weapon, he is less likely to use physical violence against the victim than if he is unarmed. Conklin's findings showed that in three-fourths of the unarmed robberies, some type of force was used:

> . . . Often the force was in the form of holding or restraining the victim so that he would not try to escape or call for help. Having no weapon with which to convince the victim that a threat exists, the offender will grab or push the victim to show that he "means business." In this way, the physical behavior of the offender functions as a weapon, in that it serves to intimidate the victim and permits him to make good his threat if he feels it is necessary to do so in order to complete the robbery. If the offender is carrying a knife, he uses physical force about two times in five; and if he has a firearm, he uses physical violence about one time in five. There is thus a clear tendency for the offender to use less force as the weapon he carries becomes more threatening to the victim. The relationship between type of weapon and use of violence is close, but there is no relationship between type of weapon and victim resistance, even though one might expect that armed offenders would resort to force less often than unarmed robbers *because* their weapons reduce the probability of victim resistance. . . . If the offender has a knife, he is almost twice as likely to use force if the victim resists as if he does not resist. If the offender has a firearm, he is three times as likely to use force if the victim resists. This indicates that if the robber is unarmed, he must often use some type of force to intimidate and restrain the victim to complete the robbery. If he has a weapon, he is more apt to use force only when the weapon does not sufficiently intimidate the victim and he feels he must resort to violence to complete the theft. . . .[8]

Every robber, regardless of whether he is armed or not, is potentially dangerous and should be treated as such. Employees of stores where the risk of robbery is perceived as substantial usually receive instructions on how to act when confronted by a robber, in order to reduce their chances of death or injury. If the five procedures listed below are followed by a robbery victim, the risk of violence will be minimized:

1. Cooperate with the robber. Do what he says. If he wants you to lie down, do so. Otherwise, he might knock you down or tie you up.

---

[7]Conklin, *Robbery and the Criminal Justice System*, pp. 110–12.

[8]*Ibid*, pp. 116–17.

2. Do not engage in unncessary conversation with the robber. The longer he is on the premises the more chance there is for violence.
3. Never argue with a robber. Robbers are usually nervous and if angered, often become violent.
4. Never attempt to disarm or attack a robber.
5. Never chase or follow a robber. Robbers often shoot at their pursuers. There is also the chance that the police will think that you are a robber.

Profile of the Robber. According to the 1976 *Uniform Crime Reports,* robbers, like most other offenders, are usually young. In 1976, there was a significant decrease in the percentage of young people among those arrested for robbery. The total number of robbery arrests decreased by 16 percent from 1975 with the number of young offenders arrested decreasing by 19 percent. More than one-third of these were 17 years old or younger, 56 percent were under 21, and 76 percent were under 25. In addition, 59 percent were black, and 7 percent of the total arrested for robbery in 1976 were female—a 10 percent increase over 1974. These statistics indicate that a robber (at least, one who is arrested) is most likely to be a young, black male.

John E. Conklin established four distinct categories of robbers, distinguishing them by their movitation for theft, methods of operation, and degree of commitment to crime as a way of life. What proportion of all robbers fall into each category is not known, but here are the four basic types:

1. *The professional robber.* Robbery, unlike some other offenses, requires little skill or special ability, so the term *professional* in this context is used in the broadest sense. The professional robber does, however, utilize some skill and planning in committing the offense. Conklin defines professional robbers as "those who manifest a long-term commitment to crime as a source of livelihood, who plan and organize their crimes prior to committing them, and who seek money to support a particular lifestyle that may be called hedonistic."[9]

Few professional robbers have regular, full-time jobs. An offender might commit several robberies a year, depending upon how long his supply of money holds out between crimes. A professional robber will usually commit the offense with a firearm and accomplices. His plans usually entail the careful selection of a vulnerable and lucrative victim, the assignment of duties to each accomplice, and the establishment of an escape route. Getaway cars are often stolen or rented. To further protect their identity, robbers often wear disguises when confronting their victims, and after committing the crime, they usually leave the area for a period of time.

Professional robbers can be divided further into two subgroups, one of offenders who commit robberies exclusively, and the other of professional criminals who specialize in other crimes, such as burglary and check passing, but

[9]Conklin, *Robbery and the Criminal Justice System,* p. 64.

occasionally commit a robbery. Members of the latter group, although they do not consider robbery their primary offense, nevertheless commit it with a degree of skill and planning.

2. *The opportunist robber.* Offenders in this group usually commit other offenses, such as shoplifting, and rob only when the opportunity arises. Thus they seldom plan their robberies in advance. This is probably the largest group of robbery offenders.

This type of robber victimizes only the most vulnerable targets, so his robberies usually involve only small amounts. Common targets for opportunists are people caught alone on the street late at night, those working alone in all-night convenience and drugstores, drunks, elderly people, and cab drivers.

Opportunists rob, not for a living like professionals, but rather for extra pocket money, and they tend to be younger than their professional counterparts. Conklin says, "Professional robbers tend to be white, in their mid-twenties, and from middle- or working-class backgrounds; opportunists are usually black, in their teens or early twenties, and from lower-class families."[10]

3. *The addict robber.* Conklin divides addict robbers into two subgroups—users of opiates such as heroin, and users of pills such as amphetamines and LSD. Heroin addicts steal for a fix rather than for a living, he says, whereas robberies by pill users are not always motivated by the need for drugs—they are frequently the result of the effects of these mind-altering agents.

Members of both groups, although they are usually active thieves, are not highly committed to robbery; it is a dangerous method of stealing, so they generally rob only as a last resort. Conklin suggests that when, for example, shoplifting is made risky by the increased use of retail-security measures, addicts are encouraged to rob rather than shoplift. But it has been presumed that if security-related reductions in shoplifting give rise to corresponding increases in robbery, the robbery victims will not be the users of these security measures—so Conklin's notion raises an interesting question: Do effective security measures cause an increase in the incidence of street crime?

Because the addict robber is more desperate and therefore careless in the commission of the offense, he is more apt to be caught than is the professional robber. It is interesting to note that in 1975, the head of the District of Columbia police department's bank-robbery squad estimated that 70 percent of the bank robberies in Washington were dope-related.[11]

4. *The alcoholic robber.* This type of robber is drunk when he commits the offense. Alcoholic robbers are not committed to robbery as a way of life and do not, as a rule, commit other crimes. Their robberies are unplanned and usually

---

[10]*Ibid.*, p. 69.

[11]This statement, reportedly made by Sgt. Jim King, appeared in "An Unhealthy Place for Bank Robbers," *Parade*, February 15, 1976.

committed on the spur of the moment. The motives behind them tend to be varied and somewhat vague. It should be noted here that alcohol and drug use are not legally recognized defenses to crime.

methods, personnel, and hardware to control robbery

Robbery Alarms, Devices, and Systems. Most holdup alarm systems are nonproprietary and of the silent type. Also, unlike burglar alarms, which are activated by the offender, robbery alarms are usually activated by the victim, who operates a signaling device concealed behind sales, cash-out, or bank counter. Holdup alarms are commonly triggered by depressing what is referred to as a "panic button." (See Figure 13-1.) The alarm signals are received at panels situated on alarm-company premises, in police stations, and/or at FBI offices.

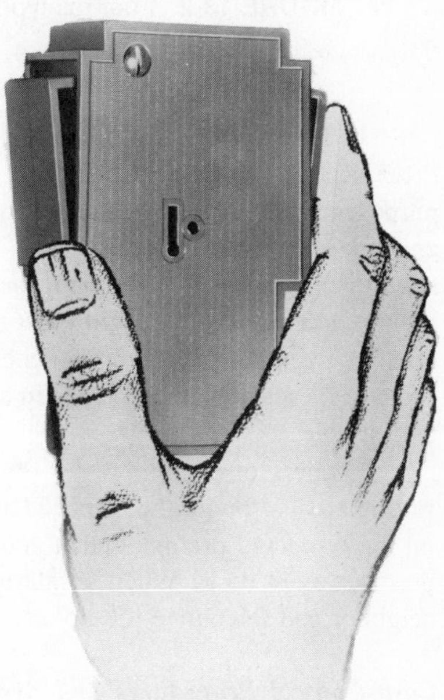

FIGURE 13-1. Holdup switch. The two side levers must be depressed simultaneously before an alarm is triggered.
Courtesy Ademco, Syosset, N.Y.

For obvious reasons, signaling devices are installed in places on the protected premises where they can be inconspicuously activated. A robber who observes a victim tripping an alarm may panic or become angry, and resort to violence. A money-clip or bill-trap signaling device constitutes an easy and safe method of activating a holdup alarm. These devices are designed for installation in cash registers and cash boxes and at bank teller's windows. Two bills are placed into the clip, which is hidden beneath a stack of money in the drawer or cash register. When the bills on top are removed from the drawer, the alarm is not activated, but when the two bottom bills are pulled out of the drawer and the money clip, it is.

Holdup alarm signaling devices can also be foot-operated. (See Figure 13-2.) For example, the upward movement of the victim's toe from beneath the foot rail may activate the alarm.

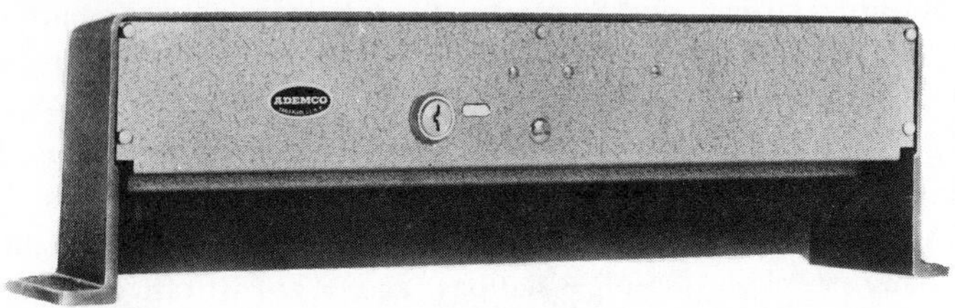

FIGURE 13-2. Foot-rail-type holdup alarm signaling device

Courtesy Ademco, Syosset, N.Y.

In New York City outdoor signs that flash the words "ROBBERY IN PROGRESS" have been installed on several Chemical Bank buildings. The purpose of this innovative but controversial holdup alarm system is to alert police and citizens who are in the vicinity, and also perhaps the deterrent effect it might have upon robbers. At any rate, the question that has not been resolved is how witnesses and the police will react to an activated sign. It is quite possible that armed citizens might try to apprehend or kill the robbers, and such a response, because it escalates the violence in an already violent and dangerous situation, is undesirable.[12]

Owners of smaller stores often install inexpensive holdup alarm devices referred to as "buddy-buzzers." This type of system consists of a switch, hidden on the protected premises, that activates a buzzer, bell, or flashing light at the premises next door. When an alarm is tripped by a robbery victim, his alerted neighbor can telephone the police.

Cash-Control Procedures and Systems. Robbery losses can be minimized, especially in retail establishments, by controlling the amount of cash on hand. In most instances, a cashier or bank teller can operate with a relatively small amount of money. When the cash level exceeds the amount necessary to operate the cash

---

[12]In November 1976, a manager of a service station, who had staked the place out to catch would-be robbers, shot and killed one of three robbers who tried to hold up the station. The oil company that owned the service station responded by firing the manager for violating a company policy prohibiting the possession of firearms on or about the premises. A spokesman said it was the company's policy to prohibit such private crime-fighting effort by employees.

register, cash box, or teller's window, the excess money should be deposited in a vault, safe, or minisafe. Also, retail customers should be encouraged to make their purchases with bills of smaller denominations. Such cash-reduction procedures will not only reduce the size of the loss when a robbery does occur, but make the store a less lucrative target if the store publicizes the fact that it keeps only small amounts of cash on hand.

The installation of a minisafe equipped with an electronic time lock is a convenient and effective method of controlling the amount of cash available to a robber. An employee cannot remove the cash from this type of safe without first having access to a remotely located control unit. When the proper key has been inserted into the keyway on the control unit, the minisafe can be opened after a preset time lapse of four to twelve minutes.

The maintenance of only small amounts of cash is an extremely effective antirobbery procedure. However, in order to ensure its proper and regular implementation, every cash-handling employee should be repeatedly indoctrinated regarding its importance, and cash registers and drawers should be checked regularly by management and security personnel to make certain that the procedure is being followed.

Surveillance Cameras. Banking institutions are probably the most common users of antirobbery film and closed-circuit-television surveillance systems. The purchase and use of motion-picture, closed-circuit-television, and video tape recording equipment is an expensive security measure. For this reason, smaller retail establishments, such as drugstores and convenience food markets, use smaller and more economical cameras that take still photographs. Upon activation by a victim employee, these "Super 8" cameras can be set to take from one frame every second to one every 90 seconds.

Regardless of the type of camera or suveillance system, cartridge- or magazine-loaded cameras should be used, because they are easily loaded and unloaded by nonspecialized store or bank employees. The most common photographic surveillance cameras are 8-, 16-, 35-, 70-, and 105mm devices. Because its primary purpose is to identify the robber, the camera should produce a photographic negative that can be enlarged to an identifiable one-inch face image of the subject.

Armed Security Guards. Unless they are armed, uniformed security guards should not be used to protect facilities vulnerable to robbery. For one thing, a robber who unexpectedly encounters a uniformed but unarmed security guard will probably react as if the guard were armed. Moreover, only an armed, desperate, and therefore dangerous robber will knowingly rob a facility that openly employs a uniformed security guard, so it is obvious that a uniformed but unarmed guard working in a store or financial institution is in a perilous position.

Although the practice is not required by the Bank Protection Act of 1968, banking institutions commonly use armed and uniformed security guards. Other robbery-prone guard users are late-night convenience food markets, liquor stores, supermarkets, and drug stores. These types of establishments are the prime targets of opportunist, addict, and alcoholic robbers, who seldom victimize facilities protected by uniformed security personnel, as armed security guards function here to prevent robberies rather than to catch or identify robbers.

Armed guards can be extremely effective, but, because they are higher paid than unarmed guards, they are costly to use. Most banks employ in-house security-guard personnel, but many small retail establishments hire off-duty policemen to protect their stores. Private security firms also supply armed security guards. To be completely effective, at least one armed guard should be on duty whenever the facility is open for business. If such complete coverage is not feasible, a guard should be on duty during after-dark business hours.

Another consideration in the use of armed security guards is that of safety. With regard to safety, the ideal situation would be the presence of a capable, appropriately trained, emotionally stable, and fully equipped guard on premises that are not likely to be robbed. On the other hand, the worst possible safety risk is the use of an untrained, inadequately equipped, immature, and emotionally unstable armed guard on duty in a busy, crowded, and vulnerable facility. Many states are attempting to minimize the dangers in the use of inadequate guard personnel by enacting laws requiring the certification and training of armed guards. Even in the states where such security standards are strictly imposed and uniformly enforced, armed-guard situations are seldom ideal in terms of safety. The users of armed guards for antirobbery purposes should be made aware of the safety risks normally associated with this security measure.

Other Preventive Measures. The following robbery-prevention techniques are particularly applicable to convenience food markets, liquor stores, pharmacies, and other small retail establishments doing business after dark.

The study involving the 120 7-Eleven stores in the Los Angeles area, referred to earlier, supports the notion of a relationship between store's physical characteristics, including its design, and the chance that it will be robbed. For example, the cash register should be placed where it can be seen from outside the store. Robbers do not like taking the chance that they will be spotted by police officers passing by in their car. For this reason, brightly lit premises will also tend to discourage robbers, and signs and merchandise displays should not block an outsider's view of the store interior.

A store staffed by active employees is less likely to be robbed. For example, when there are no customers in the store, a clerk who is working alone should be out from behind the counter, stocking shelves; the average robber is on his victim's premises for only 60 to 90 seconds, and he will not want to spend time ushering a clerk back to the cash register. A retail clerk who closely observes and verbally greets every person who enters the store will also discourage a few would-be robbers. His close attention to his customers makes it more difficult for a robber to loiter in the store waiting for the most opportune moment to surprise his victim. Moreover, a robber who feels that he has been closely observed prior to the robbery may fear later identification and therefore decide against committing the offense. Clerks should also be alert to people loitering outside the store, since they may be planning to rob it later. The police should be called whenever a clerk observes a suspicious person or vehicle in the vicinity. An employee who goes one step further by writing down the description of a suspicious person, and descriptions and license numbers of suspicious vehicles, is especially appreciated by the police, who consider these types of data vital to the crime-solution process.

Identifying the Robber. Most bank and retail security administrators, realizing that the risk of robbery cannot be totally eliminated, have established educational programs to prepare potential robbery victims for the crime, by training them how to act when they are robbed so as to minimize the chance of violence. Employees are also told what they can do to aid the police in identifying the robber.

Robbers, unlike burglars, seldom leave physical evidence behind that can be used to link them to the crime. For example, burglars often leave tool marks, latent fingerprints, shoe impressions, or burglary tools at the scene of a breakin. But at a robbery scene, in establishments without surveillance cameras, the only evidence left may be the impression the robber leaves with the victim witnesses. Even in cases where a robbery note has been left behind, a surveillance camera has been activated, or the robber's latent fingerprints have been taken from the victimized premises, the key to a rapid identification of the robber lies in how well the victim witnesses can describe the offender. Moreover, once a robbery suspect has been identified, apprehended, and charged, his robbery conviction will not be possible without at least one eye-witness to positively identify him as the robber. The procedures set out below for victim employees are not preventive security measures, but rather investigative and prosecutive aids.

A victim employee should observe the robber and his accomplices as closely as possible, so that he can provide the responding police with a complete general physical description of each offender. A witness should be able to mentally note and remember at least the following physical characteristics of a robber: his sex; his race; his age; his approximate height and build; and his general appearance. A mark placed six feet high on a doorframe may be used to help a witness judge a robber's height as he leaves the premises. A relatively calm and observant witness may be able to furnish the police with a more detailed description of the robber's clothing and facial characteristics. With regard to describing a robber's face, some of the more detailed points of observation are illustrated in Figure 13-3.

Immediately following the robbery and before the arrival of the police, each witness should make separate notes on the physical description of each robber. Witnesses should not discuss or argue over their respective perceptions of the offenders; the police will not be interested in composite descriptions. This type of

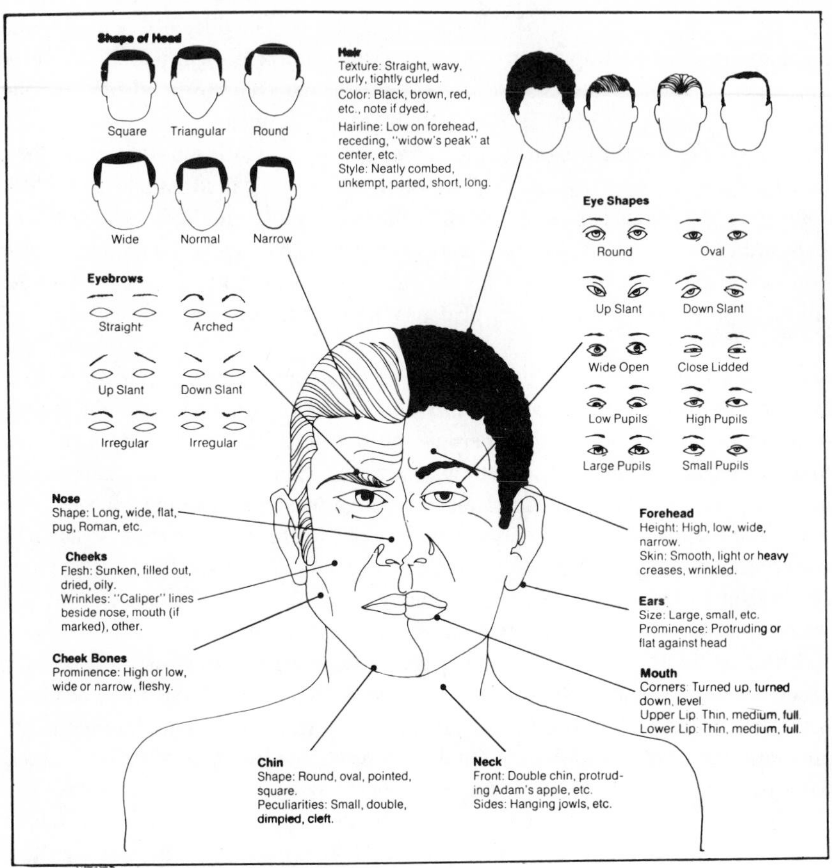

FIGURE 13-3. Facial description guide

From Crime in Retailing (*Washington, D.C.: U.S. Department of Commerce, 1975*).

descriptive data, because they consist of a series of compromises, are worthless and usually misleading.

As the robbers leave the premises, witnesses should attempt to determine the appearance and license number of the getaway vehicle and its direction of travel. Also, if a robber has been observed touching something on the premises, this area should be protected and pointed out to the police immediately upon their arrival. Finally, it may be appropriate for an employee to secure the names and addresses of nonemployee witnesses who, for one reason or another, may not be present when the police arrive.

Employees of facilities victimized by robbers should not divulge to television and newspaper reporters the amount of money stolen, but should refer such inquiries to their supervisors or to the head of security. This is because the victim will become even more vulnerable if the successful robbery of his facility is publicized.

The use of bait money is another—commonly used by banks—to aid in the investigation and prosecution of robbers. The serial numbers of a few designated bills are recorded, and victim bank employees are instructed to make certain they give the robber this bait money, which may later help identify the offender or connect him to the crime.

Bombings

For purposes of this discussion, a bombing offense is the criminal manufacture, possession, delivery, and/or placement of an explosive or incendiary device. Political terrorists, vandals, arsonists, extortionists, and hijackers are common perpetrators of bombing offenses. Bombs and incendiary devices have also been used specifically as murder weapons, particularly in contract killings and executions related to underworld activities, where a bomb is usually placed in a victim's car.[13] Explosive devices are occasionally used also by burglars to open safes and vaults.

False bomb threats, even though they do not involve actual bombing incidents, are also classified and treated as bombing offenses. Such criminal hoaxes, perpetrated upon both private and government facilities, have become commonplace. Because they are costly, disruptive, disquieting, and sometimes dangerous, such threats are a major security concern.

the nature and extent of the problem

In terms of the annual number of bombing incidents in the United States, the worst may be behind us.[14] The three-year period from 1973 through 1975 was a high point in the number and severity of these offenses. In 1973, there were 1,955 bombing incidents in the United States and Puerto Rico; 22 people were killed and 187 injured in them. In 1974, there were 2,041 bombings, involving 24 deaths, 206 injuries, and property damage amounting to $10 million. In 1975, although the number of bombings remained about the same, more than twice as many people were killed in them, and property damage also doubled.[15] During the first

[13]In June 1976, reporter Don Bolles of the *Arizona Republic* was killed by a bomb that had been placed in his automobile. At the time of his death, Bolles had been investigating suspected land frauds in Arizona.

[14]The bombing statistics cited in this section have been taken from several issues of the *FBI Law Enforcement Bulletin*. They can also be found in the FBI's *National Bomb Data Center Reports*.

[15]One bombing incident accounted for a $14 million loss in 1975.

ten months of 1976, 42 people were killed and 186 injured in 1,330 bombing incidents in the United States and Puerto Rico—figures that represent a slight decline in the number of incidents, deaths, and injuries over the same period the preceding year.

Basically, there are two kinds of bombing devices. The first is made up of an explosive substance, and the second is the incendiary device, commonly referred to as a fire bomb, of which the most familiar type is the "Molotov cocktail." Slightly over half the bombing incidents in 1974 were caused by explsoive devices; the remainder involved incendiary bombs. With explosive devices, detonation occurred 79 percent of the time; for incendiary devices, 83 percent.

During 1973 and 1974, 73 percent of all bombing incidents in the United States and Puerto Rico occurred between 6:01 P.M. and 6:00 A.M. In 1973, the most incidents occurred on a Tuesday and the least on a Sunday; in 1974, the highest-frequency day was Monday and the lowest Saturday.

common bomb targets

The leading targets of bombing incidents for the years 1974 and 1975, in the order of their victimization, were as follows:

1. Residences
2. Commercial operations and office buildings
3. Vehicles
4. Schools
5. Law-enforcement personnel, buildings, and equipment
6. Utilities

Geographically, in 1974 and 1975, the Western states reported the highest number of bombing attacks, followed by the Southern states. The North Central region was third, and the Northeast reported the fewest, only half as many as the West.

In 1973, about 40 percent of all bombing incidents occurred in cities of over 250,000 in population, and California led the nation in the number of bombings.

Based upon the data above, the profile of a vulnerable bombing target might be that of a commercial operation or office building situated in a large Western city. Since most bombings occur after 6 P.M., such a facility will be particularly vulnerable if it is not adequately protected against nighttime intrusion. Moreover, because many bombs are equipped with timing devices, facilities without effective daytime access-control measures may also be especially vulnerable.

common explosives

Black Powder. Black powder can be in the form of small grains or larger pellets of irregular shapes.[16] The grains or pellets are covered with a black, shiny coat of graphite. This substance is easily ignited by friction or spark and therefore must be handled very carefully. Once ignited, black powder gives off a dense white smoke that produces a "rotten egg" odor. Unlike most explosive substances, black powder can be destroyed by immersion in water.

Smokeless Powder. This substance is not really smokeless. Moreover, it is not a powder, but rather is in the form of flakes, strips, pellets, sheets, or cylindrical grains. It is usually coated with graphite and when ignited produces a light-colored smoke. Smokeless powder can be ignited by sparks or flames. It will not burn when wet.

Nitroglycerin. Nitroglycerin is a thick, oily liquid that is colorless in its pure state but when prepared has a pale yellowish color. This explosive is very sensitive to shock and should therefore not be moved in its liquid state. A small drop of nitroglycerin on the skin will cause a violent headache, accompanied by nausea. Nitroglycerin is not usually moved until it has been absorbed in sawdust or otherwise neutralized.

Dynamite. Dynamite consists of porous or absorbent material such as wood-pulp, sawdust, or a similar substance that has been saturated with nitroglycerin. It is formed into cylindrical sticks and wrapped in heavy waxed paper. The sticks range from six to twelve inches in length and are from 1¼ to 1¾ inches in diameter. Dynamite that is in good condition can be handled with relative safety, but it is unsafe when wet or when the nitroglycerin has seeped through the wrapper. It is detonated through the activation of either an electric or a nonelectric blasting cap.

Trinitrotoluene (TNT). This explosive substance is composed of flakes pressed into blocks of a light straw color, then coated with a fibrous material to keep the blocks intact and waterproof. TNT will not detonate from friction or shock and will not usually explode from the impact of a rifle bullet, so it is capable of being handled safely. Like dynamite, it is detonated by blasting cap.

---

[16]The material in this entire section has been drawn from the Department of the Army's Field Manual FM 19-30, *Physical Security,* Appendix IV, "Identification and Disposal of Common Explosives."

Composition C. This is a plastic explosive material that is yellow or white in color. It is usually pressed into blocks two inches square by eleven inches long and encased in glazed paper or a plastic wrapper. Like TNT, it is insensitive to shock, but it is more powerful than TNT and can be destroyed only by detonation.

bomb threats

Common victims of bomb threats are schools, hospitals, airlines, banks, office buildings, government facilities, retail establishments, industrial complexes, and law-enforcement agencies. Most bomb threats are made by telephone, and most of these are hoaxes. Moreover, only a few bombing incidents are preceded by warnings or telephoned threats.

Receiving and Reporting Bomb Threats. In a nonresidential setting, the receiver of a bomb threat is usually an employee who has telephone-answering responsibilities. Because security-guard personnel often answer telephones after regular business hours, they usually receive training on how to handle bomb-threat calls. But every potential receiver of such a threat should be specifically instructed on how to respond to the caller.

Frequently, the employee is trained to activate a tape recorder upon receipt of such a call. In many facilities, telephone switchboards are equipped with devices, called "traps," that increase the possibility of tracing a call back to the caller's telephone. They do this by keeping the line open until the receiver of the call, not the caller, terminates it. In a normal situation, the calling party eliminates further tracing of the call when he hangs up the telephone; by installing a trap, the receiving party can keep the line open by not hanging up, and can notify the police or telephone company via another telephone. (It should be noted, however, that long-distance calls, despite the presence of a trap, cannot be traced.)

Most facilities do not have traps built permanently into the telephone service, but they can request that the telephone company install one temporarily if they receive this type of threat. Many law-enforcement-agency switchboards, however, are permanently equipped with these devices.

The federal government has formulated the following series of questions that should be asked of a bomb-threat caller:

1. When will the bomb explode?
2. Where is the bomb now?
3. What kind of bomb is it?
4. What does it look like?
5. Why did you place it?

Security guards and other potential receivers of telephoned bomb threats are often provided with report forms to fill out upon receipt of such a call. These forms call for information to aid in identifying the caller and in determining if the threat is real. For example, every bomb-threat report should require the receiver to determine, if possible, if the caller is a man, woman, or child; if the voice has any recognizable accent, pattern of speech, or speech impediment; and whether the caller sounds as if he might be under the influence of drugs or alcohol. Most of these report forms also solicit data that might provide a clue regarding the origin of the call—for instance, background noise such as music, typing, traffic, machines, airplanes, or children.

Evaluating the Legitimacy of the Threat. The nature and severity of a victim's reaction to a bomb threat will reflect the degree of credibility he places on the threat itself, as well as the amount of harm that would be caused by an explosion on the premises. It is therefore obvious that every reaction to a bomb threat, whether preplanned or not, is preceded by an evaluation of the caller's credibility.

There are numerous factors and circumstances that would make a victim believe strongly that a bomb-threat call is a hoax—for example, a call made obviously by a child whose friends can be heard giggling in the background. This is particularly true in those situations where the call follows others of a similar nature. Under these circumstances, the victim's only response may be to record the call and report the incident to the appropriate authorities for the purpose of identifying the caller. If, however, there is any doubt regarding the legitimacy of such a call, a search of the premises may be in order, but these situations do not usually call for an evacuation of the premises.

On the other hand, the substance and form of a bomb threat call may engender a real concern regarding its legitimacy. For example, a serious and articulate adult caller who describes in detail the bomb and its location will usually cause a severe reaction on the part of the victim, regardless of the probability that the call is a hoax. Another factor to be considered is whether the threatening party could have had physical access to the alleged bomb site. For example, if the caller claims to have planted the bomb in an area of the facility where only a few people have access, the threat is more likely to be a hoax; but before a final evaluation of the threat, the alleged bomb site should be checked to determine if it has been the scene of a forced intrusion. Moreover, every person who has access to this area should be accounted for and, if possible, questioned. If there is no time to complete this type of inquiry, the bomb threat should be treated as if it were real.

responding to a bomb threat

Because most bombing incidents occur without warning, victims seldom have the opportunity to react to or prepare for the explosion. For this reason, the most important aspect of a bomb-oriented security program should be prevention—a facet of the problem that unfortunately is not often emphasized. The most effective method of minimizing the chance that a bomb will be planted within a facility is to implement an effective access-control system. Any kind of access-control system—the use of guards, electronic surveillance devices, employee I.D. cards, visitor registration procedures, protective fencing, lock hardware, or a combination of these—if it at least operates to deny the bomber easy access to the more vulnerable areas of the facility, will constitute an effective antibombing measure.

If, despite these preventive measures, a bomb threat is made that is perceived to be real, certain steps can be taken.

The Decision to Evacuate.[17] Evacuating every occupant in a threatened facility is one of the more drastic responses to a bomb threat, particularly in connection with big and complex premises occupied by large numbers of people. Even the partial evacuation of a plant, office complex, or institution is costly and highly disruptive, and in addition, it may expose the evacuees to even greater danger. For these reasons, evacuation should be relied upon only after alternative safety measures have been considered and rejected.

When it is known that a bomb may have been planted in a building, its doors and windows should be opened to vent the explosion. If the exact location of the bomb is known, the evacuees should be routed so that no one comes within 300 feet of the device.

Even though a bomb-threat situation may call for the evacuation of a building, numerous arguments against total evacuation have been advanced by people who are knowledgeable in the field. Probably the most persuasive argument concerns the risk of exposing a greater number of people to the blast, particularly when the location of the bomb is not known. It is believed that whenever evacuees are moved about in large groups, the potential for personal harm is increased. Moreover, the total evacuation of a densely populated facility may create panic among the evacuees. Widespread panic often leads to stampeding, which itself creates a very hazardous situation.

The possibility exists also that the bomber's placement of his device has been specifically predicated upon a knowledge of the victim facility's evacuation patterns and procedures, and that a large number of evacuees will thereby be exposed to the bomb. And finally, the dramatic effect of a mass evacuation may encourage or excite potential callers of false bomb threats, enhancing the possibility of repeated hoaxes.

Whenever total evacuation is deemed unwise for any of these reasons, a partial evacuation may be the most appropriate alternative. Moreover, in a situation where the threatening caller has indicated that the explosion is imminent, there may not be enough time to effect a total evacuation. A partial evacuation involves

---

[17] Much of the material in this section was drawn from Edward L. Lee II, "Physical Security and the Police Facility: A Total Program," *FBI Law Enforcement Bulletin*, November 1976.

moving only those occupying areas of the facility most likely to be destroyed by the explosion. In most cases, damage from an explosive device is confined to a specific area; very few bombs have the capacity to destroy an entire building. Partial evacuation is therefore particularly appropriate when the exact location of the bomb has been determined. For example, if a bomb has been planted on the third floor of a ten-story structure, a partial evacuation may include only the occupants of the third floor and those on the floors directly above and below.

In designing a bomb-threat evacuation program, a security planner should devise a method by which those affected by the threat are notified of the situation. Such notification can be made through a preexisting public address system, through the use of security guards or other messengers, or by activating a local alarm.

Notifying the Proper Authorities. Following any explosion that has occurred without warning, the fire department should be immediately notified. If injuries have been sustained as a result of the blast, medical assistance must be summoned as well. And because a bombing incident is both a state and a federal crime, the local police and the FBI will be called upon to investigate the matter.

When a bomb threat is received by telephone, the receiving party has usually been instructed to immediately notify a supervisor or a member of the security department. In either case, the person ultimately in charge of handling such a threat will have the further responsibility of notifying appropriate outside fire, medical, and police (bomb squad) agencies. If the threat is perceived as real, the notifications will follow the same lines as discussed in connection with an actual explosion. If it is an obvious hoax, the call should nevertheless be immediately reported to the local police for investigation, since a false bomb threat constitutes a criminal offense in every state. Under these circumstances, the telephone company should also be notified by the police or directly by the victim.

Bomb Searches.[18] When the maker of a bomb threat omits details regarding the specific location of the device, the task of verifying the bomb's existence as well as its location is made all the more difficult, particularly in facilities that are not protected by effective access-control measures. In such facilities, no areas can be safely eliminated as potential bomb sites, so every inch of the premises must be searched. In most facilities, however, most employees, vendors, or visitors, or people impersonating them, are capable of carrying a bomb onto the premises without being discovered. Bombs can also reach their target by car, truck, or railway car, or can be delivered to the victim through the U.S. mail, parcel post, United Parcel Service, air freight, or any commercial courier or delivery service.

---

[18]Some of the material in this section originated in an article entitled "Bombs and Bomb Threats," which was published by Oak Security Inc. in 1972. It was one of a series of security briefs that is no longer in publication. Copies of this and other security-related articles can be obtained from Nickerson & Collins Co., Publishers, 2720 Des Plaines Ave., Des Plaines, Illinois 60018.

It is not uncommon for a bomber to place an explosive device in an area of a facility that, in terms of access, offers the least resistance. Areas that are normally unlocked and unwatched are likely bomb sites. Examples of such vulnerable spots are washrooms and lavatories, janitor's closets, lobbies, telephone switchboards, hallways, elevators and stairways, scrap piles, locker rooms, and lunchrooms.

Participants in a bomb search should be instructed not to touch or move any suspicious object they encounter. Many kinds of explosive devices are sensitive to shock, and the methods by which a bomb can be detonated are varied and often ingenious. For example, a bomb might be triggered by a photoelectric cell that causes it to explode when exposed to light; another type of bomb, equipped with a mercury switch, will detonate if it is tilted. For these reasons, the removal, deactivation, or destruction of an explosive device should be handled by professional bomb-disposal personnel.

There are, however, a few basic procedures to be followed in most bomb-search situations. In addition to the general rule that a suspicious object should never be touched or moved by a layman, the following guidelines will most likely be applicable:

1. Security guards should be positioned about the perimeter of an endangered area to keep people and vehicles away.
2. Personnel who are searching for a bomb in a darkened area should not turn on the lights, because the light switch might be the triggering mechanism.
3. Walkie-talkies should not be used within an endangered area. They could detonate an electric blasting cap.
4. The search itself should be well planned and coordinated, to avoid wasted effort and time caused by searching the same area more than once.
5. The search should be conducted by personnel who are familiar with the physical layout of the facility—security guards, janitorial personnel, department heads, foremen, and plant engineers.

Those who have been selected to conduct the bomb search should be cautioned that explosive devices are of many shapes and sizes and often do not look the part, so they should not only look for the bomb itself but seek out any physical deviation in the facility. For example, if a searcher encounters a briefcase resting on a washroom sink, it should be treated as a potential bomb until its presence is fully explained. And a bomb search can be supplemented by the use of a specifically trained dog capable of detecting explosive substances, or by a bomb detection device manufactured and designed to perform this function.

Whenever a bomb or a suspicious object is located, these procedures should be followed:

1. Doors and windows in the vicinity of the bomb should be opened to reduce shock waves in the event of an explosion.

2. All available fire extinguishers should be readied and in position to combat any fires caused by the explosion.
3. If time allows, highly flammable objects and liquids should be removed from areas immediately surrounding, or otherwise endangered by, the bomb.
4. The bomb should be surrounded with sandbags or similar shock-absorbing objects, such as specially constructed bomb blankets. One of these blankets can cover an area of up to 16 square feet.
5. Valuable and irreplaceable documents, files, and other papers should be taken from the endangered area.

Most security administrators, regardless of their specific function or job responsibility, are necessarily aware of basic bomb-prevention and bomb-threat measures and procedures. Many who are employed by facilities commonly victimized by bombings and false bomb threats are quite knowledgeable in this field. Bomb-disposal specialists are usually military or law-enforcement personnel; however, the matter of bombs and bomb threats is basically a security concern.

DISCUSSION QUESTIONS

1. Discuss the arguments for and against complying with a kidnapper's demands.
2. The bank-robbery rate increased 20% between 1974 and 1975, while street robbery (mugging) rose only 5%. How would you explain this variance in crime-rate increases?
3. Discuss the possibility that effective security measures, because they discourage the robbery of stores and other commercial facilities, cause an increase in the incidence of street robbery.
4. In addition to the points discussed in this chapter, can you think of any other disadvantages inherent in the use of robbery alarm systems that alert people by exterior signs that a robbery is in progress?
5. In your opinion, should the employees of service stations, pharmacies, liquor stores, and convenience food markets be prohibited by company policy from keeping guns on the premises?

SELECTED BIBLIOGRAPHY

kidnapping

"Around the Globe—Outbreaks of Terror," *U.S. News & World Report*, September 29, 1975.

AXTHELM, PETE, "A Crime That Doesn't Pay," *Newsweek,* August 25, 1975.

DARLING, DON D., "Action Security for 'That Crisis Situation,'" *Security World,* November 1974.

GOLDMAN, PETER, "The Bronfman Drama," *Newsweek,* August 25, 1975.

JOSEPH, RAYMOND A., "Bodyguard Business Booms as Kidnappings and Crime Rate Rise," *Wall Street Journal,* November 20, 1975.

MATHEWS, TOM, "The Story of Patty," *Newsweek,* September 29, 1975.

"Patty's Twisted Journey," *Time,* September 29, 1975.

SHAW, PAUL and JAN REBER, *Executive Protection Manual.* Scheller Park, Ill.: Motorola Teleprograms, Inc., 1977.

"Terrorism: Growing and Increasingly Dangerous," *U.S. News & World Report,* September 29, 1975. An interview with Robert A. Fearey, Special Assistant to the Secretary of State and Coordinator for Combatting Terrorism.

WEISINGER, MORT, "The Bodyguard Business Is Booming," *Parade,* April 28, 1974.

robbery

BLUMENTHAL, FRED, "An Unhealthy Place for Bank Robbers," *Parade,* February 15, 1976. This article concerns the success the police in Washington, D.C., have had in identifying and arresting bank robbers.

CONKLIN, JOHN E., *Robbery and the Criminal Justice System.* Philadelphia: Lippincott, 1972.

"Convenience Stores Find an Answer," *Security World,* April 1976.

MCCLINTOCK, F. H., and EVELYN GIBSON, *Robbery in London.* London: Macmillan, 1961. One of the most complete studies of robbery and robbers.

MACDONALD, JOHN M., *Armed Robbery: Offenders and Their Victims.* Springfield, Ill.: Charles C Thomas, 1975.

MILLIGAN, WILLIAM F., "The Savings Bank Security Officer and the Bank Protection Act of 1968," *Security Management,* January 1976.

MYLER, JOHN A., "Bank Security Regulations—Should They Be Revised?" *Security Management,* May 1976.

RISSLER, LARRY E., "Displaying Robbery Surveillance Photographs," *FBI Law Enforcement Bulletin,* December 1975.

SHERER, R. E., "A Candid Overview of Photographic Surveillance Cameras," *Security Distributing & Marketing,* December 1975.

"The 'Small Security' Solution," *Security World,* April 1976.

bombings

COX, DONALD L., and JOHN M. DE MARCO, "Bomb Threat Response: The Facility Self-Protection Plan," *Security Management,* January 1977.

KNOWLES, GRAHAM, *Bomb Security Guide.* Los Angeles: Security World Books, 1976.

LEE, EDWARD L. II, "Physical Security and the Police Facility: A Total Program," *FBI Law Enforcement Bulletin,* November 1976.

PIKE, EARL A., *Protection against Bombs and Incendiaries: For Business, Industrial and Educational Institutions.* Springfield, Ill.: Charles C Thomas, 1973.

STOFFEL, JOSEPH, *Explosives and Homemade Bombs*,.2nd ed. Springfield, Ill.: Charles C Thomas, 1977.

WALSH, TIMOTHY J., and RICHARD J. HEALY, *Protection of Assets Manual.* Santa Monica, Calif.: The Merritt Company, 1975. See Chapter 26, "Bombs and Bomb Threats."

PART V

FIRE SCIENCE

Chapter 14

Fire Prevention and Safety

AN OVERVIEW

I. Fire, A Major Security Problem
  A. *Relevant fire statistics*
  B. *The major causes of fire*
    1. Causes of residential fires
    2. Causes of industrial fires

II. The Nature of Fire
  A. *The four stages of fire*
  B. *Killing agents of fire*
  C. *NFPA classification of fires*

III. Fire-Prevention Devices, Systems, and Programs
  A. *Fire-alarm sensing devices*
    1. Ionization detectors
    2. Photoelectric detectors
    3. Infrared detectors
    4. Thermal detectors
  B. *Fire-alarm reporting systems*
  C. *Sprinkler systems*
    1. Wet-pipe sprinkler systems
    2. Dry-pipe sprinkler systems
  D. *Standpipe systems*
  E. *Portable fire extinguishers*
    1. Soda acid extinguishers

2. Foam extinguishers
3. Dry chemical extinguishers
4. Carbon dioxide extinguishers
5. Carbon tetrachloride extinguishers
6. Water extinguishers

F. *Fire doors*
G. *Fire emergency programs and procedures*
H. *Fire-prevention and safety surveys*

IV. OSHA
A. *Scope of OSHA*
B. *Purpose of the OSHA Act*
C. *Enforcement of the OSHA Act*
D. *OSHA and the security function*

V. Arson
A. *Definitions*
1. Criminal-law definition
2. The Model Penal Code version

B. *The nature and extent of the arson problem*
C. *Motives for arson*
D. *Arson prosecutions*

Most security practitioners, whether in-house or contract, white collar or blue, and working in retail, institutional, or industrial settings, are professionally involved in varying ways and degrees with fire prevention and safety. The security function involves private fire fighting and prevention as well as private crime fighting and prevention, so a knowledge of fire science, like police science, is necessary. Security practitioners supplement and augment the public fire-fighting effort carried out by hundreds of municipal and volunteer fire departments.

Chapter 14 is intended as a general, nontechnical overview of the major topics in fire prevention and safety.

Fire, A Major Security Problem

relevant fire statistics

In 1976, there were more than 900,000 building fires in the United States. (Nonbuilding fires include aircraft, ship, motor vehicle, and forest fires.) The total monetary loss from these business and residential fires that year was over $2 billion.[1]

[1]Unless there is an indication to the contrary, the statistics cited in this section have been compiled and published by the National Fire Protection Association (NFPA), 470 Atlantic Ave., Boston, Mass. 02210.

In 1976, 70 percent of all fire deaths resulted from residential fires. During that year, 8,800 people died in fires, and 108,000 were injured in them. About one-third of the residential-fire victims were under the age of 16. The primary cause of death of fire victims over 16 and under 60 is heavy ingestion of alcohol, which seriously impedes the ability to respond properly to an emergency.

The majority of fatal residential fires occur between 9 P.M. and 6 A.M., and take place in the winter months.

Of the nonresidential building fires in 1976, 43 percent of the firms either failed to reopen or went out of business within six months after the fire.

the major causes of fire

Causes of Residential Fires. A study of the causes of *fatal residential* fires by the National Fire Protection Association produced the following findings:

Cause	*Percentage*
Smoking	56.0
Faulty heating equipment	13.8
Faulty electrical wiring	7.5
Cooking stove	7.0
Arson	4.3
Other	11.4

Causes of Industrial Fires. In 1976, a study was conducted by Factory Mutual to determine the causes of industrial fires.[2] The results of this study are set out below:

Cause	*Percentage*
Electrical	26.3
Hot surfaces	11.0
Friction	9.0
Overheating	8.7
Cutting/Welding	7.5
Smoking	7.3
Incendiarism	6.4
Chemical action	6.3
Open flames	5.8
Miscellaneous sparks	5.4
Molten materials	4.1
Exposure fires	2.2

[2]Factory Mutual (FM) is an association of fire insurance companies that insure only manufacturing plants of superior construction and maintenance. It has made numerous contributions to fire science, particularly in the field of loss-prevention research. FM's research facility is located in West Gloucester, Rhode Island.

It is estimated by Factory Mutual that 75 percent of all industrial fires are caused by human error and carelessness, and that during the past ten years, deficiency in housekeeping practices contributed greatly to the large monetary losses suffered in nineteen major industrial fires.

The Nature of Fire

the four stages of fire

"Fire is primarily defined as rapid oxidation, accompanied by heat and light. In general, oxidation is the chemical union of any substance with oxygen. . . . Fire can usually take place only when three things are present: *Oxygen* in some form, *fuel* (material) to combine with the oxygen, and *heat* sufficient to maintain combustion. Removal of any one of these three factors will result in the extinguishment of fire."[3] *Combustion* is the act or process of burning; combustible material (fuel) can be in the form of solids, liquids, or gases.

> Fire starts in one of two basic ways: a source of heat—a match, burning fuel, faulty electrical equipment, for example—is permitted to come in contact with a combustible material; or the material is permitted to enter a state in which it creates enough heat itself to trigger combustion. This is known as spontaneous ignition and most commonly occurs in piles of discarded rags or trash which have been impregnated with oils, cleaning fluids or other volatile fuels.[4]

As a fire starts and develops, it goes through four distinct stages, and in progressing from one stage to the next, it becomes increasingly more hazardous. A fire-alarm sensing device (discussed later in the chapter), depending upon its type and principle of operation, will be activated when a fire reaches one of the following four states:

1. Incipient stage—Invisible products of combustion are given off. At this point the fire is not visible. Smoke and flame cannot be seen. There is no appreciable heat at this stage of a fire.
2. Smoldering stage—Combustion products are now visible in the form of smoke. There is no flame or appreciable heat at this point.
3. Flame stage—An actual fire now exists. Flame and smoke are visible. There is still no appreciable heat. Heat will follow, however, almost instantaneously.
4. Heat stage—At this final stage there is uncontrollable heat and rapidly expanding air.[5]

---

[3]Loren S. Bush and James McLaughlin, *Introduction to Fire Science* (Beverly Hills, Calif.: Glencoe Press, 1970), p. 34.

[4]From "Detection Devices for Early Warning and Control of Fire in Buildings," a pamphlet published by LCN Closures, Princeton, Illinois.

[5]Lasier, "Detection Devices," p. 27.

killing agents of fire

Contrary to popular belief, most fire fatalities are caused not by burns (flame), but rather by the toxic gases produced by the combustion process (smoke). These gases, which can be odorless, often penetrate a victim's circulatory system, causing physical impairment that makes his escape considerably more difficult. Some of the toxic gases that can be produced by combustion are carbon monoxide, hydrogen fluoride, nitrogen dioxide, styrene monomer, and hydrogen chloride. Most fire deaths from gases are probably caused by carbon monoxide, but this is not necessarily the most deadly product of combustion.

Exposure to smoke can cause serious lung damage. Wood smoke, for example, kills the cells lining the throat and respiratory tract, causing fluid in the lungs to hemorrhage. If the victim survives the fire, he still runs the risk of pneumonia. And besides producing toxic gases, smoke also creates panic, which is considered another killing agent of fire.

The following are the lethal factors in a building fire:

1. Presence of noxious or toxic gases
2. Presence of smoke
3. Development of extremely high temperatures
4. Reduction of oxygen concentration, accompanied by an increase in the concentration of carbon monoxide
5. Development of fear
6. Direct consumption by fire[6]

NFPA classification of fires

The National Fire Protection Association has established the following four types or classifications of fires according to the nature of the material (fuel) being burned:

1. *Class A Fires* are fires in ordinary combustible materials, such as wood, cloth, paper, and rubber.
2. *Class B Fires* are fires in flammable liquids, gases, and greases.
3. *Class C Fires* are fires that involve energized electrical equipment where the electrical nonconductivity of the extinguishing media is of importance.
4. *Class D Fires* are fires in combustible metals, such as magnesium, titanium, zirconium, sodium, and potassium.

---

[6]Carl F. Klein, "The Nature and Detection of Fires in Buildings," *Security Distributing & Marketing*, June 1977, pp. 30–34, 58, and 59.

These fire classifications will become relevant in our later classification of fire extinguishers according to the types of fire they can put out.

Fire-Prevention Devices, Systems, and Programs

fire-alarm sensing devices

A fire-alarm sensor, like an intrusion-alarm sensor, is designed to react to a particular situation. Fire sensors, components of automatic fire-alarm systems, are triggered by either heat, combustion, or flame. The four basic kinds of fire-alarm sensor are:

1. Ionization detectors (detect invisible particles of combustion)
2. Photoelectric detectors (detect smoke)
3. Infrared detectors (detect flame)
4. Thermal detectors (detect heat)

These four types of sensors correspond to the four stages of a fire. An ionization detector provides the earliest warning of fire, since it is activated at the first (incipient) stage of a fire; photoelectric sensors are activated when the fire reaches the smoldering stage, when smoke is visible; infrared detectors react when flame is present; and thermal sensors respond when the fire reaches its fourth and final (heat) stage.

Ionization Detectors. Ionization sensors are the only types capable of detecting a fire at the incipient stage; therefore they are considered overall the most effective fire-detection device. They react to the invisible combustion particles emitted during this initial stage of a fire.

Photoelectric Detectors. Photoelectric sensors, commonly referred to as smoke detectors, are considered early warning devices because they are activated prior to the flame and heat stages of a fire. There are two types of photoelectric devices. The first operates on the principle of photoelectric-beam interruption. When the smoke interrupts or disturbs the beam, an alarm is triggered. In the second type, which is more common, the presence of smoke in the sensor reflects the photoelectric beam and directs it into a photocell device, activating the photocell sensor. Some manufacturers produce photoelectric sensors equipped with a backup heat-detection capability.

Infrared Detectors. Since these sensors respond to the infrared radiation emitted from a flickering flame, they are commonly referred to as flame detectors. They are not triggered until the fire has reached its third or flame stage, so they are not classified as early fire-warning alarms.

If a flame detector is inappropriately placed, it can cause a false alarm. For example, a flame detector can be activated by reflected sunlight from windows, passing cars, bodies of water, and flickering neon signs, or by the opening of venetian blinds. An infrared sensor, therefore, is more appropriately used in places where a fire, once started, will develop very quickly through (or without) the incipient and smoldering stages—for instance, where ignition can be instantaneous, such as places where combustible gases and flammable liquids are stored.

Thermal Detectors. Thermal detectors, commonly referred to as heat detectors, are triggered when the temperature in the protected area reaches a predetermined level (fixed-temperature devices) or when the rate of temperature rise exceeds a predetermined norm. Fixed-temperature detectors will usually initiate an alarm when the temperature in the protected area reaches 135° F., but higher-temperature sensing devices can be utilized in abnormally hot environments. A thermal detector, because it is not activated until the heat stage, is not an early warning device. Thermal devices are used, however, in boiler rooms, kitchens, garages, and manufacturing areas where invisible combustible products, smoke, and flame are normally present and capable of activating ionization, photoelectric, and flame sensors.

fire-alarm reporting systems

The two basic elements of a fire-alarm system are the ability to detect a fire and a device that reports this finding. Regardless of whether the fire is detected by one of the sensing devices discussed above or by a human being, or both, the system is not complete without some type of alarm signaling capability. An alarm report must accomplish two purposes: to notify the occupants of the fire-endangered premises and to alert the fire department.

The local reporting device usually consists of a horn, gong, and/or light, which alerts the occupants so that they can leave the premises. This type of device should be distinctive, so that it is recognized as a fire-warning signal. In noisy locations, or in places where deaf people work, the signal should be visible. In these situations, a flashing light would be appropriate. Local alarm mechanisms should be installed so as to provide complete premises coverage; they should be periodically tested; and they should be designed and installed in a way that makes accidental or malicious activation difficult.

The second reporting function of an alarm system, the notification of the fire department, can be accomplished in many ways. One of the simplest and most common fire signaling devices is the pull box. Fire-alarm pull boxes are used to alert the fire department once the fire has been detected. Fully automatic systems are capable of mechanically detecting the fire, reporting it locally, and then notifying the fire department directly over a municipal fire-alarm circuit or over telephone lines. Automatic telephone dialers and recorded-message devices are frequently used to alert the fire department or call the person monitoring a central or proprietary alarm station. In a less automatic system, an automatic dialer may alert one or more employees of the endangered facility over their office telephone or at home. In these systems, the alerted employee is responsible for calling the fire department. Also, it is not unusual for fire department personnel and other designated persons to be thus notified simultaneously.

When the fire-alarm signal is transmitted by telephone (or otherwise) to a central or proprietary alarm station, the person monitoring the alarm panel (fire and intrusion) has the responsibility of notifying the fire department. Sophisticated fire-alarm systems also have automatic announciator devices, which advise the alarm-signal receiver of the specific location of the fire within a facility. For example, when a fire truck is dispatched to a college campus, the responding firemen should at least know which building is supposedly on fire. In the less-automatic systems, the firemen, once they reach the endangered building, can be informed by a security officer of the exact location of the fire.

Regardless of the method by which a fire is detected or how the alarm signal is transmitted and to whom, the ultimate objective of all alarm systems is the same: to save life and property. This is done by alerting those endangered by the fire and those who will put it out.

sprinkler systems

A fire-protection sprinkler system can be defined generally as a network of underground and overhead pipes designed to carry and automatically disperse water inside a building in the event of a fire. A sprinkler system consists of a suitable water supply, a fire-activated sprinkler devices (heads), water control valves, and a water flow mechanism that releases an audible alarm signal whenever a sprinkler head is activated and in operation. Sprinkler heads are usually heat-activated, spraying water when the temperature in the room reaches a predetermined level. Most sprinklers will operate at temperatures between 130° and 165° F.

There are a variety of water-supply arrangements, including, among others, gravity tanks, pressure tanks, and direct connections to a city water main.

Wet-Pipe Sprinkler Systems. A wet-pipe system is composed of sprinkler devices attached to pipes that are water-filled. When the sprinklers are activated (opened) by the appropriate temperature in the room, the water in the pipes and in the main water supply is released through the sprinklers. Wet-pipe systems cannot be used in unheated buildings located in areas where the temperatures drop below freezing, because the water in the pipes will freeze, rendering the system inoperative and subjecting it to serious damage.

Dry-Pipe Sprinkler Systems. In dry-pipe systems, the pipes leading to the sprinklers contain air under pressure. When a sprinkler is activated, air is released through it, opening a valve that allows a flow of water into the pipes and out of the sprinkler. Since dry-pipe systems are not susceptible to freezing, they are utilized in unheated buildings located in cold climates.

Security guards and maintenance personnel who are charged with the daily maintenance of a sprinkler system check the system's gauges frequently to make certain that the proper amount of air pressure is being maintained in the pipes. And regardless of the type of sprinkler system, security personnel are usually made aware of the location of the large "riser" pipes through which the water supply to the entire system is delivered. "Risers," often located in buildings' exit stairways, have valves that can be turned to shut off the water supply to an entire system. In the case of a broken sprinkler, it becomes necessary to turn off the main water supply in order to avert serious water damage.

standpipe systems

A standpipe system is similar to, and often an extension of, a sprinkler system. Standpipe systems are categorized according to their water supply and release operations. Generally defined, a standpipe system is a fire-fighting device in which water is brought to the fire by a hose; therefore, its main components are a riser, a water shutoff valve, and a fire hose.

portable fire extinguishers

A fire extinguisher is a pressurized cylinder containing a dry chemical or some other agent that, when discharged on the appropriate type of fire, will put it out. The type of fire extinguisher used should correspond with the classification of fire being put out. For example, a fire extinguisher that discharges water will not put out a Class C fire, which is an electrical fire. Since water conducts electricity, the use of water on a Class C fire not only will be ineffective, it could be very dangerous. (At this point, it might be helpful for the reader to review the section in this chapter that discusses the four NFPA classifications of fire.)

Fire extinguishers can be classified according to their fire-fighting agents and the kinds of fire they are capable of extinguishing.

Soda Acid Extinguishers. Soda acid extinguishers are filled with water, bicarbonate of soda, and acid. To operate this type of fire extinguisher, one must turn the cylinder upside down. This mixes the contents, thereby producing carbon dioxide gas, and the gas forces the water out of the extinguisher. Soda acid fire extinguishers are effective against Class A (wood, paper) fires.

Foam Extinguishers. A foam extinguisher disperses a foamlike substance that in essence smothers the fire, since combustion cannot be sustained without oxygen. Foam extinguishers put out Class A fires and are effective against Class B (flammable-liquid) fires. They should not be used on Class C or Class D fires.

Dry Chemical Extinguishers. Dry chemical fire-fighting agents have the same effect on a fire as foam substances. There are several types of dry chemical extinguishers, according to the nature of the chemical used. Each type is labeled to show what classification of fire it has been designed to put out. Generally speaking, this type of extinguisher is most effective against Class B (flammable-liquid) and Class C (electrical) fires.

Carbon Dioxide Extinguishers. Fire extinguishers that disperse carbon dioxide put out a fire by cooling and smothering the burning material. Carbon dioxide is heavier than air, fireproof, and cold. Because carbon dioxide does not conduct electricity, these extinguishers are effective against electrical fires. They are also used to extinguish flammable-liquid fires.

Carbon Tetrachloride Extinguishers. This type discharges a lethal gas that cools and smothers a fire. Because of the deadly nature of carbon tetrachloride, this type of extinguisher should be used only outdoors. It works well on electrical fires but it must not be used in a closed room, regardless of the classification of the fire.

Water Extinguishers. Water is probably the original fire-fighting agent. Whether it is discharged from an extinguisher or from a hose or bucket, it operates to cool the burning material. Water is effective against Class A but not Class C fires, and on a flammable-liquid fire it may also be inappropriate, since the water flow could operate to spread the liquid and the fire.

It is usually advisable to place an adequate number of standard ABC-type extinguishers throughout the protected premises. An ABC extinguisher is one that has been designed to effectively extinguish most fires. To augment standard fire-extinguisher placement, specialized devices can be placed in areas that are susceptible to specific types of fire. For example, a foam extinguisher could be installed in any room where flammable liquids are stored. Also, extinguishers of the appropriate size must be used, and installed extinguishers should be regularly checked to see that they are in working order.

fire doors

A fire door is a device used to impede the spread of flame and smoke. It also provides a barrier that separates people from the toxic by-products of fire. Automatic fire doors are held open until there is combustion. When a fire starts, these doors are shut, or shut automatically. Less sophisticated fire doors are rigged with ropes and pulleys; modern ones contain door-closing mechanisms housing built-in fire sensors. For example, some automatic door closers have built-in ionization sensors that, when activated at the incipient stage of a fire, cause the door to close. (See Figure 14-1.)

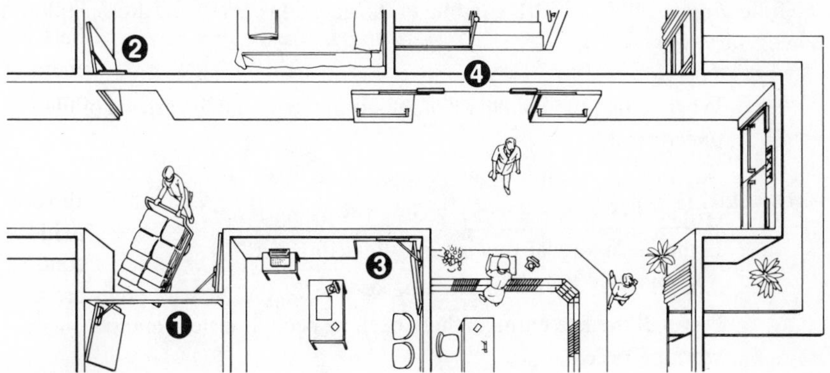

FIGURE 14-1. Floor plan of a health-care facility with automatic fire doors
Courtesy LCN Closers

fire emergency programs and procedures

One of the most important aspects of a fire emergency plan is getting all the people safely out of the endangered facility. Frequent fire drills using predetermined escape routes will facilitate premises evacuation in a real emergency. In some of the larger facilities that have highly developed emergency programs, a fire warden is appointed and trained. Many of these facilities also have fire brigades, consisting of qualified people assigned to either the security or the maintenance department. Members of a fire brigade are usually under the direction of a specially appointed fire warden, fire safety engineer, or, in their absence, a security administrator with a knowledge of fire prevention and safety. In the event of a fire, the fire brigade responds by bringing fire-fighting equipment to the site of the blaze and containing the fire until the arrival of the professional fire-fighting agency. It is also responsible for grounding all elevators and rescuing employees and visitors who may be in immediate danger. When the fire department arrives on the scene, its commanding officer takes full charge of the fire-fighting and evacuation functions.

An effective fire emergency plan will also include the development and maintenance of a fire alert system, an emergency communications plan, and the appointment and supervision of personnel to staff an emergency first-aid station.

fire-prevention and safety surveys

Surveys should be conducted periodically to determine the existence, readiness, and effectivenss of fire-prevention equipment, procedures, and personnel. The following checklist illustrates some of the questions asked and areas explored in such surveys:

1. What is the time lag between the notification and the arrival of the fire department?
2. Are fire evacuation plans posted throughout the facility?
3. Are all the fire-sensing devices in working order?
4. Is the alarm-signal reporting system in order?
5. Are all local alarms in working order?
6. Have all the fire extinguishers been inspected, tested, and put in good working order?
7. Is there a first-aid capability available?
8. Have all the employees received instructions on how to use the fire extinguishers?
9. Do the employees know which type of extinguisher to use on each type of fire?
10. Are fire drills being conducted regularly?
11. Has the sprinkler system been inspected, tested, and put in good working order?
12. Are all fire hydrants accessible and in working order?
13. Are all smoking regulations being strictly enforced?
14. Are highly combustible materials properly stored and appropriately safeguarded?
15. Are the fire escapes in good condition?
16. Have fire doors been installed where they are needed?
17. Are standpipe hoses in good repair and appropriately located?

This checklist, although not complete, serves to illustrate the broad and diverse nature of the fire-prevention and safety function.

OSHA

scope of OSHA

OSHA stands for Occupational Safety and Health Administration, a federal agency within the Department of Labor and the Department of Health, Education and Welfare. It was established to administer the William-Steiger Occupational Safety and Health Act, which was signed into law in December 1970, to become effective in April 1971.

The act has broad application. It covers every employer "affecting commerce." This means that virtually every employer (with one or more employees) is subject to OSHA's safety standards.

purpose of the OSHA act

The act states, ". . . the Congress declares to be its purpose and policy . . . to assure so far as possible every working man and woman in the nation safe and healthful working conditions. . . ." In its "General Duty" clause, it states that every employer must furnish to each employee a place of employment free from recognized hazards that are causing or are likely to cause death or serious physical harm. The employer is also required to comply with all the occupational safety and health standards and regulations promulgated by the act.

In addition to these general statutory requirements, OSHA has already codified a large number of specific safety standards.

enforcement of the OSHA act

The U.S. Department of Labor is responsible for enforcing OSHA standards and proposing penalties for violators. It should be noted that penalties apply only to employers. Although the act requires employee compliance with all safety and health standards, rules, regulations, and orders, it is the employer's responsibility to see that his employees comply.

Under the act, all employees must have access to OSHA regulations and standards. An employee may request an OSHA inspection of his place of work, and he has the right to ask for medical or health tests to determine if he is being exposed to unhealthy conditions.

Up until recently, OSHA representatives and inspectors could enter an employer's premises without prior notice at any time, provided that the inspection was otherwise reasonable. These surprise OSHA visits were unpopular with most employers, and a small businessman in the Midwest contested the practice by not allowing an OSHA inspector on his property without a search warrant. In May

1978, the U.S. Supreme Court, in a 5–3 decision, ruled that government agents checking for safety and health hazards may not make spot checks of a business without a warrant. The Court held that such inspections amounted to an invasion of the Fourth Amendment's ban on unreasonable searches and seizures. The warrant however, does not have to be based upon the probability that safety or health hazards are present on the premises to be inspected. Prior to this ruling, and certainly after, representatives of management, employees, or both had the right to accompany an OSHA inspector as he checked the premises.

The act requires employers to keep certain safety and health records for five years. These files are subject to OSHA review. Examples of the type of data that must be maintained by the employer are:

1. Logs of occupational injuries and illnesses
2. Supplementary records of occupational injuries and illnesses
3. Summary of occupational injuries and illnesses

OSHA and the security function

Loss prevention, as a security concept, was traditionally thought of as preventing and minimizing losses from internal and external crime, fire, and disaster. But because of the criminal justice nature of OSHA—specifically, its regulations, enforcement policies, penalties, and review hearings—it was felt that security practitioners were the ones best suited to administer safety programs. As a result, the security function is gradually being expanded to include safety responsibilities as well. Security practitioners who are involved in safety matters are often given titles such as Director of Loss Prevention, which reflects the dual security and safety functions.

A loss-prevention administrator responsible for corporate safety, for example, might be responsible for conducting safety audits and surveys, indoctrinating management and labor personnel, supervising the maintenance of OSHA-required records, keeping informed of and enforcing specific OSHA regulations, seeing that OSHA violations are corrected, and dealing with OSHA representatives.

A few of the specific concerns of a loss-prevention officer might be:

1. Falls
   a. Slippery floors
   b. Pavement in disrepair
   c. Articles left in corridors
   d. Spilled substances
2. Collisions and falling objects
   a. Improperly stacked material
   b. Improperly stored ladders

   c. Reckless driving
   d. Stationary equipment extending into aisles
3. Cuts
   a. Proper storage of pointed and sharp-edged implements
   b. Use of gloves by certain employees
4. Fire
   a. Proper storage of flammable liquids
   b. Keeping sprinkler systems unobstructed
   c. Keeping fire exits clear
   d. Enforcement of no-smoking regulations
   e. Elimination of overcrowding
   f. Training of guard force in matters of fire fighting, fire prevention, safety, and rescue

Arson

definitions

Criminal-Law Definition. The common-law offense of arson generally consisted of the willful and malicious burning of a dwelling (house) of another. Under common law, therefore, the burning of a barn, field, or one's own home was not arson. A common-law arson was thus limited to a very specific fact situation:

1. A willful and malicious (set intentionally by one with an evil motive)
2. burning (not scorching or charring)
3. of a dwelling (does not include unfinished homes)
4. of another.

Modern-day statutory arson is much broader in scope. It reflects the modern problems of fire insurance fraud (involving homes, business premises, and motor vehicles), malicious bombings, and the use of fire to cover other crimes. Contemporary statutory arson applies not only to the traditional common-law notion of the offense but to numerous arson-related situations.

The Model Penal Code Version. The Model Penal Code definition of arson is representative of most contemporary arson law:

Section 220.1 Arson and Related Offenses

(1) Arson. A person is guilty of arson, a felony of the second degree, if he starts a fire or causes an explosion with the purpose of:
   (a) destroying a building or occupied structure of another; or

(b) destroying or damaging any property, whether his own or another's, to collect insurance for such loss.

(2) Reckless Burning or Exploding. A person commits a felony of the third degree if he purposely starts a fire or causes an explosion, whether on his own property or another's, and thereby recklessly:
(a) places another person in danger of death or bodily injury; or
(b) places a building or occupied structure of another in danger of damage or destruction.

(3) Failure to Control or Report Dangerous Fire. A person who knows that a fire is endangering life or a substantial amount of property of another and fails to take reasonable measures to put out or control the fire, when he can do so without substantial risk to himself, or to give a prompt fire alarm, commits a misdemeanor if:
(a) he knows that he is under an official, contractual, or other legal duty to prevent or combat fire; or
(b) the fire was started, albeit lawfully, by him or with his assent, or on property in his custody or control.

(4) Definitions. "Occupied structure" means any structure, vehicle, or place adapted for overnight accommodation of persons or for carrying on business therein, whether or not a person is actually present. Property is that of another, for the purposes of this section, if anyone other than the actor has a possessory or proprietary interest therein. If a building or structure is divided into separately occupied units, any unit not occupied by the actor is an occupied structure of another.

the nature and extent of the arson problem

Arson is regarded as one of the country's fastest-growing crimes.[7] According to the Insurance Information Institute, the direct dollar loss from arson in 1976 amounted to $2 billion, an increase of nearly 70 percent over the 1975 figure of $1.2 billion. The National Fire Protection Association reported that the number of arson cases has tripled since 1963. It appears that the rate of arson is increasing by from 20 to 25 percent each year. In New York City alone, about 36,000 housing units are burned (and not replaced) every year. It is universally believed that in the United States, 11 percent of all building fires are arson-related. The average dollar loss per arson incident is $4,399, as compared, for example, to $1,457 for motor vehicle theft. Finally, in 1975, more than 1,000 people were killed by arson-caused fires.

---

[7]Most of the statistics used in this section are found in Seattle Police Chief Robert Lee Hanson's article, "A Fire in Your Pocketbook," *The Police Chief,* June 1977, pp. 20, 21.

motives for arson

Arson is unique in that, unlike other crimes, its commission is the result of a variety of motives. For example, the motive for robbery is usually a monetary gain, but an arsonist may set a fire for any of the following reasons:

1. *Insurance fraud.* Many residential and commercial fires on insured premises are set by desperate homeowners and businessmen to collect the insurance benefits. The incidence of this type of insurance fraud seems to increase whenever the general economy worsens. Some insurance executives familiar with this problem believe that the high increase of business-related fire losses in December and January can be explained in part by the fact that business is usually off in January, and that the usual April increase in fire losses may be due to the April 15th deadline for income taxes.
2. *Vandalism.* Many fires are set by juveniles, who use fire as another way to senselessly destroy property. Vandal-set fires in public school buildings have become a serious problem.
3. *Revenge.* This is probably one of the more traditional motives for arson. The revenge may be personal, business-related, or political in nature.
4. *Fires to cover crimes.* Crimes such as murder, rape, burglary, and embezzlement are often followed by a burning of the crime scene. Such a fire may be set to disguise the real cause of death or to destroy evidence. In one 1974 arson case, a burglar set fire to a bowling alley in an effort to cover his crime, and an adjacent nightclub caught on fire, killing 24 patrons.
5. *Extortion.* Arson, or the threat or arson, is often used by extortionists as a method of coercing reluctant businessmen into making their "protection" payments. By burning down the property of an uncooperative victim, the extortionist sets an example to intimidate other victims.
6. *Pyromania.* A small percentage of arson cases involve pyromaniacs. Pyromania can be defined generally as a mental affliction characterized by an uncontrollable impulse to set fires. Pyromaniacs receive sexual gratification through setting and/or watching a fire. One type of pyromaniac is commonly referred to as the "hero" type; after setting the fire, he remains at the scene to help battle the blaze. The prosecution of a pyromaniac is made difficult by the fact that the pyromania provides him with a built-in insanity defense.

arson prosecutions

Arson is considered one of the most difficult crimes to solve. One reason is that the fire itself often aids the arsonist by destroying any evidence he may have left at the scene of the crime. Another is the lack of trained arson investigators. An arson investigation is a highly technical and specialized endeavor, and there are not enough people trained and experienced in handling the rapidly increasing incidents of arson-related fires.

Nationally, there are arrests in only 26 percent of all arson cases, and fewer than three arsonists in 100 go to jail. In the suburbs, arrests are made in only 7 percent of the cases. These depressing statistics provide perhaps the strongest argument of all on behalf of the necessity for security personnel to maintain the highest possible level of fire prevention and, indeed, protection against all the hazards of intrusion.

DISCUSSION QUESTIONS

1. In your opinion, what type of fire-alarm sensor is the best for residential use? Explain your answer.
2. In your opinion, what type of fire-alarm sensor would be best for each of the following? Explain your answers.
   a. Boiler-room use
   b. Computer-room use
   c. Office use
   d. Garage use
3. Why should a night watchman be familar with the operation of the building's sprinkler system?
4. Cite at least one additional question to be added to the fire safety checklist in this chapter.
5. In your opinion, what type of arsonist (according to motive) is the most dangerous? Explain your answer.

SELECTED BIBLIOGRAPHY

AMOROSO, LOUIS J., "Where Do We Stand with OSHA?" *Security World,* July 1977.

BRYAN, JOHN L., *Fire Suppression and Detection Systems.* Beverly Hills, Calif. Glencoe Press, 1974.

BUSH, LOREN S., and JAMES MCLAUGHLIN, *Introduction to Fire Science.* Beverly Hills, Calif.: Glencoe Press, 1970.

Guard Service in Fire Loss Prevention (NFPA No. 601). Boston: National Fire Protection Association, 1968.

HANSON, ROBERT L., "A Fire in Your Pocketbook," *The Police Chief,* June 1977.

KLEIN, CARL F., "The Nature and Detection of Fires in Buildings," *Security Distributing & Marketing,* June 1977.

LASIER, THOMAS R., "Detection Devices for Early Warning," *Security Distributing & Marketing*, June 1976.

MACDONALD, JOHN M., *Bombers and Firesetters*. Springfield, Ill.: Charles C Thomas, 1977.

SCHENKELBACH, LEON, *The Safety Management Primer*. Homewood, Ill.: Dow Jones–Irwin, 1975. Contains an appendix that lists several reference publications regarding OSHA.

Standard for Guard Operation 1975 (NFPA No. 601a). Boston: National Fire Protection Association, 1968.

THORSEN, J.E., "Security and the OSHAct Puzzle," *Security World*, July 1977.

APPENDIXES

Appendix A

Briefs of Selected Court Decisions Involving Shoplifting Cases

Martinez v. *E. J. Korvette, Inc.*, 477 F.2d 1014 (1973)

Facts:

The plaintiff, Mrs. Ruth Martinez, accompanied by her husband and brother-in-law, went to one of the defendant's stores in the suburban Philadelphia area, planning to buy a new coat. Before trying on any of the new coats, she took off her old trench coat and laid it on top of the display rack. After looking at new coats for a period of time and deciding to make a purchase, the plaintiff could not find the coat she had worn into the store. At this time, she went to another part of the store to look at other merchandise. While she was at the check-out counter in this part of the store, she advised the sales clerk that since her old coat had disappeared, she would wear the new coat home. The plaintiff, at this time, paid the clerk for the coat with a credit card and was given a sales slip and a cash register receipt which reflected the purchase. After the plaintiff walked out of the store she was confronted by a floorwalker, who questioned her about the coat. The plaintiff accompanied the female security officer back into the store, where the plaintiff displayed her sales slip. At this time, the plaintiff and the floorwalker were unable to locate the sales clerk who had handled the sale. The plaintiff was taken to the security office where the floorwalker had the plaintiff's old coat, which had been found on a hanger on the rack by security personnel. The plaintiff refused to sign a release form and was immediately taken before a justice of the peace. The floorwalker and the plaintiff testified before the magistrate at this time. The justice of the peace found the plaintiff guilty of shoplifting and sentenced her with a fine.

The plaintiff appealed her shoplifting conviction before a court of Common Pleas which reversed the conviction. She then brought a malicious prosecution suit against the defendant in a U.S. District Court. When the lower federal court held in favor of the defendant by dismissing the plaintiff's case, she appealed to the U.S. Court of Appeals, Third Circuit.

Court: For the defendant.

Decision:

Before a plaintiff can recover in a malicious prosecution suit, he must carry the burden of proving that the defendant, in making the arrest, lacked probable cause. Probable cause does not depend upon the guilt or innocence of the accused but rather upon the honest and reasonable belief of the person making the arrest. The facts in this case clearly indicate that the floorwalker had probable cause to arrest Mrs. Martinez for shoplifting. The fact that she was later found innocent of the shoplifting offense does not make a *prima facie* malicious prosecution case.

Dissenting opinion:

The fact that the justice of the peace had found sufficient evidence to convict the plaintiff of shoplifting in the first instance does not, by itself, support a finding here that the floorwalker acted on probable cause. Prior to the decision to charge Mrs. Martinez, the security officer was aware that she had a register receipt which she claimed was for the coat, that the receipt was in fact for the coat, that she had taken the coat and the receipt and had verified that in fact that the receipt was genuine, that she had thereupon attempted to coerce Mrs. Martinez into executing a paper releasing Korvette's from any charge of harassment, and that only when she refused to sign the release did she decide to charge her despite her knowledge that the receipt was genuine.

Grennett v. *U.S.*, 318 A. 2d. 589 (1974)

Facts:

Grennett entered a Washington, D.C., store and proceeded to the stationery counter, where he took possession of two notebooks. Placing the two notebooks into the inside breast pocket of his coat, he left the stationery department and walked past three cashiers without tendering payment for this merchandise. He then shopped in several other sections of the store and did not, during this period, offer to buy the notebooks from any of the numerous cashiers located within the areas of the store he visited.

Grennett was arrested in the store by a security officer. A scuffle ensued and it became necessary for the security officer to restrain Grennett. Grennett was taken to the security office at which time the notebooks were recovered from his inner breast pocket.

Grennett was charged and convicted of shoplifting. He appealed his conviction on the grounds that his actions, and the recovery of the notebooks, did not constitute sufficient evidence of his guilt.

Court: For prosecution.

Decision:

The behavior represented by the facts in this case comprises sufficient evidence to support a shoplifting conviction. [There were no dissenting opinions in this case.]

State v. *Fitzmaurice*, 314 A. 2d 606 (1974)

Facts:

When Fitzmaurice was approached by the manager of a food store, he fled to the rear of the store. The manager, at this time, saw Fitzmaurice dispose of three packages of meat (lamb) into the turkey case. Fitzmaurice was taken to the front of the store where he was arrested by a police officer. When Fitzmaurice was searched he was found to be wearing a T-shirt which had been stained by the meat and three belts or straps used to hide articles.

Fitzmaurice was convicted of shoplifting. He appealed his decision on the following grounds.

1. The evidence in this case does not support the finding of his guilt.
2. The New Jersey shoplifting statute, under which Fitzmaurice was convicted, because a presumption of theft is created whenever merchandise is concealed, violates principles of due process since it eliminates criminal intent as an element of the shoplifting offense.
3. The shoplifting statute, because of the above inference, violates the defendant's presumption of innocence by forcing him to prove that he is not guilty.
4. The shoplifting conviction is invalid because the defendant was arrested before he left the interior of the store.

Court: For prosecution.

Decision:

The defendant's stained T-shirt, the belts, his flight and his disposal of the meat constitute ample evidence to support a finding of guilt.

The use of a statutory presumption in a criminal law case is proper so long as there is a rational connection between the fact proved and the crime which is presumed from this fact. There is a rational connection between the concealment of merchandise and the *prima facie* inference that the reason merchandise is concealed involves an intention, on the part of the person so concealing, to steal it.

The New Jersey shoplifting statute, by creating this presumption, does not force defendants charged under the statute to prove their innocence. The state, under this statute, must still carry its burden of proof. The statutory inference simply creates *prima facie* evidence of guilt. The statute permits, but does not compel, a finding of guilt upon proof of certain basic facts.

The language of the New Jersey statute clearly indicates that in light of the presumption created by the concealment of merchandise, it is not necessary for the defendant to leave the store before a shoplifting conviction is possible.

May Department Stores Company v. *Devercelli,* 314 A. 2d 767 (1973)

Facts:

Devercelli and his wife went to the defendant's store in Arlington, Virginia, for a "Private After Hours Sale." Devercelli had difficulty walking due to numerous physical disabilities, including partial paralysis resulting from his former dependence upon an artificial kidney and then later from a transplanted kidney. When he entered the store Devercelli was handed a shopping bag by one of two of the defendant's employees who were greeting customers at the door. It was Devercelli's understanding that the bag was given to him for shopping purposes. Devercelli's eyes were bloodshot; his arms were black and blue and showed needle marks; he walked with a faltering gait; he appeared nervous and he moved in erratic patterns. All of these characteristics were directly or indirectly a result of his kidney problem. Because of the defendant's appearance, he was noted and surveyed by store security personnel soon after he entered the establishment.

Devercelli proceeded to the men's department where he stopped at a table containing bargain ties. He placed four ties over his shoulder then walked to the far end of the table where shirts were on display. At this time a floorwalker approached him and stared at his arms. Devercelli responded by explaining to the security officer that his reliance upon a kidney machine caused the marks on his arms. It should be noted that the floorwalker denied having this conversation with Devercelli. According to Devercelli, the floorwalker, upon hearing about his medical condition, moved away from him but contined to keep him under surveillance. At this time Devercelli collected four shirts, placed them under his arm and walked to the end of the table where cuff links were on display. As he was examining the cuff links, Devercelli knocked several to the floor. After picking up the cuff links and placing them into his shopping bag, he selected additional cuff links by comparing those on the counter with those in the bag and keeping the ones he liked the best. After spending ten minutes selecting cuff links, Devercelli started towards the belt counter. According to Devercelli's testimony, he was, at this time, apprehended by two male store detectives. According to the testimony of one of the arresting store detectives, Devercelli, after selecting shirts, ties and cuff links, went to the sporting goods department where he placed these items into his shopping bag before returning to the men's department. The security officer's testimony also differed from Devercelli's in that, according to the security officer, Devercelli was apprehended in front of the escalator after he had left the cuff link table.

Upon arresting Devercelli, the two security officers took him to the detention room located on the lower level of the store. There was conflicting testimony as to the extent of force used by the officers in escorting him to the security office. Devercelli testified that he was forced to walk at a pace too fast for his physical condition and as a result he was almost carried along by the officers, who ignored his pleas to slow down. On the other hand, the store detective testified that Devercelli was merely escorted, without incident, to the detention room.

A search of Devercelli in the detention room determined that he was in possession of $3.00 in cash and a valid May Department Store charge card. Devercelli was advised of his rights, and the crime of "willful concealment" was explained to him. The pertinent section of the Virginia shoplifting statute reads:

Va. Code 1950, Section 18.1-126

> *Concealment of merchandise on premises of store a misdemeanor.* Whoever, without authority, willfully conceals goods and merchandise of any store, while still upon the premises of such store, shall be deemed guilty of a misdemeanor and upon conviction thereof shall be punished as provided by law.

After being taken to the detention room, Devercelli was interrogated at length by the security officer. A security officer read him his rights from a preprinted card. One of these rights involved the right to make a telephone call. Nevertheless, Devercelli's request to call his employer and/or his wife was denied. Before the questioning began, one of the security officers paced the floor slapping his gun. After it became apparent that Devercelli was not going to confess to a shoplifting offense and the interrogation was about to end, the security officers asked Devercelli to sign a civil release form, telling him several times that he could not leave the store until he signed. Devercelli was also advised that if he refused to sign the form he would go to jail. After being in custody an hour and a half, Devercelli reluctantly signed the release and was allowed to go free. Upon his release he was cautioned not to mention his arrest to anyone. Devercelli, at this time, asked for an apology. None was forthcoming.

The portion of the Virginia shoplifting statute dealing with the exemption of civil liability states:

Va. Code 1950, Section 18.1-127

> *Exemption from civil liability in connection with arrest of suspected person.* A merchant, agents or employees of the merchant, who causes the arrest of any person pursuant to the provisions of Section 18.1-126 (concealment of merchandise), shall not be held civilly liable for unlawful detention, slander, malicious prosecution, false imprisonment, false arrest, or assault and battery of the person so arrested, whether such arrest takes place on the premises of the merchant, or after close pursuit by such merchant, his agent, or employee, provided that, in causing the arrest of such person, the merchant, agent, or employee of the merchant, had at the time of such arrest probable cause to believe that the person committed willful concealment of goods or merchandise.

Devercelli, as a result of the above incident, filed a civil complaint against the May Department Store Company charging false imprisonment, assault and battery and slander. The trial court jury, believing Devercelli's account of what transpired, found that the security officers arrested Devercelli without probable cause to believe that he had willfully concealed the merchandise. The lower court held that because the arrest was without probable cause, the detention was illegal. It was also held by the lower court that the statutory exemption from civil liability did not apply to the fact of this case because the security officers' arrest was not based upon probable cause. Moreover, the lower court found that the security officers' questions regarding Devercelli's use of alcohol and drugs were accusatory and slanderous.

As a result of the above findings of facts and law by the trial court, Devercelli was awarded $165,000 in damages.

The May Department Store Company appealed the lower court decision to the District of Columbia Court of Appeals, basing their appeal on the following grounds:

1. Appellant argued that the question of whether or not an arrest is based upon probable cause is a matter of law, not fact, and as such should not be decided by a jury.
2. As a matter of law, Devercelli's actions comprised probable cause to believe that he had committed a shoplifting offense. His arrest and interrogation were therefore legal, and the exemption from civil liability clause in the Virginia retail theft statute precluded recovery by Devercelli in this case.
3. Assuming Devercelli's arrest was illegal, his signing of a civil release form relieved the appellant of any civil liability.

4. The security officers' inquiries as to Devercelli's use of alcohol and drugs, under the circumstances of this case, were allowable and therefore did not constitute slander.
5. The size of the monetary damages, because they were the result of passion and prejudice on the part of the jury, are excessive.

Court: For Devercelli in connection with the May Company's liability for his false imprisonment and assault and battery.

For May Department Store on the issue of slander. [The court held that the security officers' question of Devercelli regarding the use of drugs and alcohol was not malicious and therefore not slanderous.]

The appellate court also noted that the appellant's (May Company) assertion that the size of the damages was the result of passion and prejudice had been overlooked by the lower court. As a result, the lower court was directed to resolve this issue which was raised by appellant's post-trial motion.

Decision:

Under Virginia law, issues regarding probable cause can be decided by a jury. The Virginia courts have defined probable cause as follows: "Probable cause is knowledge of such state of facts and circumstances as excite the belief in a reasonable mind, acting on such facts and circumstances, that the [suspect] is guilty of the crime of which he is suspected."

The facts of this case clearly sustain the jury's finding that the arrest was made without probable cause. The placing of merchandise into a shopping bag, without more, will not, as a matter of law, give rise to a finding of probable cause. In this case the jury decided to believe Devercelli's account of what transpired, and according to his statement of the facts, the security officers acted unreasonably and without restraint. Had the officers made a preliminary and low-keyed inquiry into Devercelli's activities without taking him to the detention room, the matter could have been resolved without the lengthy interrogation and all that followed.

Because the jury found that Devercelli had signed the civil release form under duress, it cannot operate to preclude recovery against the party responsible for the involuntary nature of the release. The jury's finding of duress was amply supported by the evidence.

Dissenting opinion:

The issue of probable cause in a criminal case is a question of law for the court to determine when there are no material issues of fact. In this case there is no question that the security officers acted on probable cause. The unfortunate condition of Mr. Devercelli colored the jury's finding of fact with regard to the probable cause issue and influenced its award of excessive damages. The following excerpt, comprising an excellent discussion of the various probable cause and requirements under differing retail theft statutes, has been taken from the body of Associate Judge Nebeker's dissenting opinion:

> . . . a determination of probable cause cannot be colored by facts not known or reasonably apparent to the officer making the apprehension. The court must view the situation through the eyes of the officer. In doing so, these are the facts. Mr. Devercelli gave all the appearance of a most desperate shoplifter. The majority concedes this. His explanation to the female security officer of the reason for his appearance does not dispel the high degree of suspicion already apparent, for such "explanations" are easily fabricated. But in any event, this attempt to divert the suspicion, which even Mr. Devercelli recognized by explaining his condition to the female security officer, cannot, on this record, be imputed to the arrest officer. In selecting ties and then shirts, Mr. Devercelli next proceeded in a manner quite consistent with an effort by a thief to conceal the items. He dropped or caused to fall to the floor other small items (cuff links, located a short distance away from the shirts). In recovering these items, and while in a stooped or crouched position, he placed other items in the bag. It is important to note that he could have overtly placed the items in the bag as he selected them. Instead, knowing he was behaving suspiciously, he undertook what reasonably appeared to be a familiar effort to conceal his actions. He "dropped" items to the floor and then, while seemingly retrieving them, dropped other items and, in the ensuing confusion, placed small and large items in the bag. Little wonder the arresting officer acted at that point. It must be remembered we are here dealing with an offense called wilful concealment, not larceny. It is thus irrelevant whether Devercelli attempted to leave the store or the specific area without paying for the items concealed in the bag. Neither is it relevant that the bag was given Devercelli by a store employee, nor what he considered the purpose for the bag. Shopping bags are usually available within department stores for use by customers, and unfortunately they are also available to a thief.
>
> I respectfully submit that the evidence in testimony regarding Mr. Devercelli's movement in the store is immaterial. The majority's concession that it "is not surprising that the suspicions of the appellant's detectives were aroused" and that they could have "displayed more restraint and attempted to acquire more information" is astounding in view of their holding. I assume the majority is importing into the area of law a concept of a limited "seizure" of the person as in *Terry* v. *Ohio*. They would seemingly permit the suspect to be stopped and questioned in full view and hearing of other customers. I can think of no faster way to produce embarrassment and a damage suit or slander suit and false arrest.
>
> As to the majority's view that the cases cited by appellant contained additional circumstances to support probable cause, I believe a careful reading of those cases will show they support appellant's assertion that probable cause did exist. *Delp* v. *Zapp's Drug and Variety Stores*, 238 Or. 538, 395P.2d 137 (Or. 1964), pertains to a statute which required, unlike the Virginia statute here in question, the additional element of taking "with the intent to convert to his own use without paying the price." Clearly, then, in order to establish probable cause it was necessary under the Oregon statute to wait until the suspect had proceeded past the check-out counter. This additional element, however, would not be required under the Virginia statute to establish probable cause and is not constitutionally required, for probable cause always requires less than proof beyond a reasonable doubt. *Cooke* v. *Newberry & Company*, 96 A.J. Super. 9,232 A.2d 425 (1967), pertains to a New Jersey statute

that indeed contained a presumption that concealment of the merchandise in the store was *prima facie* evidence of intent to convert to the use of the taker without paying the purchase price. A careful reading of *Cooke* will show that the court did not question the probable cause for the arrest, nor did it purport to establish a minimum level for probable cause as the majority implies. The New Jersey statute clearly states that the mere concealment of the merchandise would created probable cause. Finally, *Bettollo* v. *Safeway Stores, Inc.*, 11 Cal. App. 2d 430, 54 P. 2d 24 (1936), expressly supports the view by holding: "The undisputed evidence shows reasonable and probable cause for the detention. Johnson [the security officer in this case] had seen the respondent [the suspect in this case] pick up the candy and conceal it in his pocket. . . . (Id. at 431, 54P. 2d at 25)." In spite of the majority's statement to the contrary, the court did not hold that the additional circumstances of proceeding through the check-out counter without paying was necessary to constitute probable cause.

Appendix B

ASIS Security Survey—Questionnaire and Results

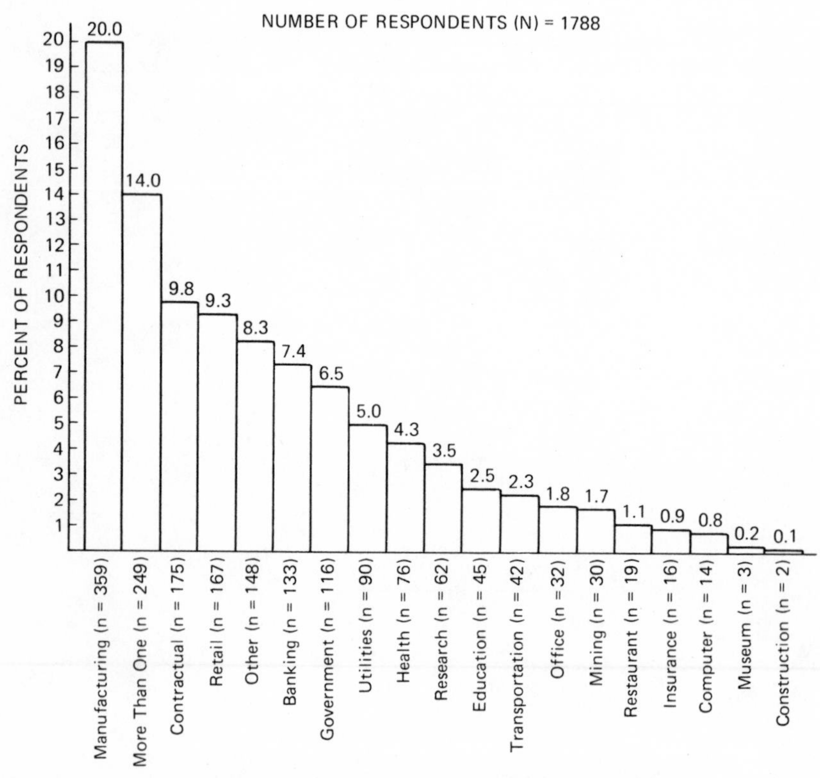

By permission of the American Society for Industrial Security. Published in the January 1976 issue of *Security Management*.

SUMMARY OF RESPONSES TO ASIS SURVEY, 1975

Question 2a:
Does your security responsibility include safeguarding U.S. classified materials?

Yes	37%
No	62%
No response	1%

Question 2b:
Is your security force unionized?

Yes	18%
No	79%
No response	3%

Question 3:
The activities of your firm are basically in:

Government	10%
Proprietary	55%
Combination	34%
No response	1%

Question 4:
The security force in this firm is:

Contractual	26%
Proprietary (In-house)	50%
Both	24%

Question 5a:
Among your security personnel, how many are uniformed? 79%

Question 5b:
Of the uniformed personnel, how many carry a firearm? 45%

Question 5c:
Among your security personnel, how many are not *uniformed?* 30%

Question 5d:
Of the not uniformed personnel, how many carry a firearm? 30%

Question 6:
With what frequency do security personnel in your firm have contact with public police personnel?

Daily	47%
Weekly	24%
About twice a month	10%

Monthly	11%
Don't know	7%
No response	1%

Question 7:
Would you classify your firm's relationship with the public police as:

Excellent	57%
Good	30%
Adequate	10%
Poor	2%
Unknown	1%

Question 8:
Have public-police attitudes toward support of your private security efforts been:

Positive	66%
Neutral	24%
Negative	3%
Unknown	5%
No response	2%

Question 9:
Which of the following items could foster improved communication between public police and private security?

Hold periodic meetings with supervisor/manager	14%
Hold informal meetings between police officers and security personnel	25%
Have formal training sessions on each other's roles	7%
Have formal written policy regarding operating procedures of security personnel	7%
Other	5%
Multiple response	38%
No response	1%

Question 10:
In general, should private security personnel have the same legal authority as public police?

Yes	16%
No	74%
Undecided	9%
No response	1%

Question 11:
Under ordinary circumstances, how frequently are your security personnel mistakenly identified as "public" police by private citizens?

	1	2	3	4	5	
Often	3%	4%	9%	33%	47%	Never

Question 12:
To differentiate private-security personnel and public-police personnel, which of the following do you prefer?

Style of uniforms	19%
Color of uniforms	23%
Cloth badges	5%
Distinctive color of hat	1%
Other	10%
Multiple responses	37%
No response	5%

Question 13:
Are credentials carried by your security personnel:

Similar to public police	17%
Different from public police	56%
None issued	22%
Don't know	3%
No response	2%

Question 14:
Does your organization carry personal liability insurance which will protect the "individual security worker" from:

False arrest action	
Yes	37%
No	19%
No response	44%
Liability as a result of negligent action	
Yes	45%
No	12%
No response	43%
None	
Yes	6%
No	15%
No response	79%
Both	
Yes	31%
No	6%
No response	63%

Question 15:
What type of legal assistance is available for your security personnel?

None	8%
Formalized legal training courses	3%
Legal counsel of corporation or company	61%
Training obtained prior to employment	4%
Other	3%
Multiple response	17%
No response	4%

Question 16:
What is the approximate monthly wage for the following security personnel within your enterprise?

	None Employed		*Under $500*		*$501-$750*		*$751-$1000*		*$1001-$1250*		*Over $1250*		*No Response*	
	Prop.	*Cont.*	*Prop.*	*Cont.*	*Prop.*	*Cont.*	*Prop.*	*Cont.*	*Prop.*	*Cont.*	*Prop.*	*Cont.*	*Prop.*	*Cont.*
Unarmed uniform guards	16%	9%	7%	39%	24%	29%	18%	4%	5%	1%	1%	1%	29%	17%
Armed uniform guards	18%	15%	3%	19%	17%	30%	15%	6%	6%	1%	1%	1%	40%	28%
Investigators/detectives	14%	16%	1%	0%	9%	18%	12%	18%	14%	6%	12%	3%	38%	39%
Middle mgmt./supervisors	3%	5%	0%	0%	4%	7%	14%	25%	27%	26%	36%	18%	16%	19%
Owner/general manager	7%	7%	0%	0%	0%	1%	2%	3%	6%	9%	49%	46%	36%	34%

Question 17:
Are written job descriptions available in your firm?

Yes—for *all* security job functions	66%
Yes—for most security job functions	18%
Yes—for a few security job functions	6%
No job descriptions available for security job functions	9%
No response	1%

Question 18:
Do you have different hiring qualifications (other than age) for an individual performing the following functions?

Carrying a firearm	
Yes	35%
No	37%
No response	28%
Requiring primary contact with general public and employees	
Yes	37%
No	51%
No response	12%
Infrequent contact with public or employees (monitor controls, patrol during nonworking hours, etc.)	
Yes	25%
No	55%
No response	20%

Question 19:
Indicate the percentage of your present security personnel with previous police, military security, and/or intelligence experience prior to joining your organization.

No response	4%
No such experience	5%
1–25%	36%
26–50%	20%
51–75%	15%
76–99%	12%
100%	8%

Question 20:
Do you provide a formal in-house training program for newly hired security personnel?

Yes	68%
No	28%
No response	4%

(Number of hours ranged from 4 hours to 2 weeks.)

Question 21:
Do you require formal training on an annual basis for all security personnel?

Yes	48%
No	46%
No response	6%

a: *In-house training*

Yes	43%
No	2%
No response	55%

(Number of hours ranged from 2 to 80.)

b: *Externally conducted training*

Yes	21%
No	10%
No response	69%

(Number of hours ranged from 2 to 80.)

Question 22:
With what frequency do you utilize criminal justice record systems? (i.e., license check, arrest records, etc.)

Never	16%
Daily	27%
Weekly	30%
Monthly	18%
Yearly	4%
No response	5%

Question 23:
Indicate your accessibility to public criminal justice records for private security business.

No response 7%

	1	2	3	4	5	
Not accessible	19%	18%	26%	14%	16%	Very accessible

Question 24:
Indicate the types of information you need to know from the criminal justice system.

	Yes	*No*	*No response*
a: Arrest verification	75%	11%	15%
b: Conviction verification	84%	4%	12%
c: Alleged misconduct	49%	20%	31%
d: Driver license check	57%	18%	25%
e: Vehicle check	65%	13%	22%
f: Other	10%	0%	90%

Question 25:
Which information agencies do you utilize for the given types of investigations?

Investigations		*Federal*	*State*	*Local*	*Private (i.e. credit)*
Personnel Selection					
	Yes	24%	39%	64%	55%
	No	33%	25%	13%	17%
	No response	43%	36%	23%	28%
Background					
	Yes	27%	36%	62%	56%
	No	28%	25%	13%	16%
	No response	45%	39%	25%	28%
General					
	Yes	20%	31%	57%	48%
	No	32%	27%	14%	20%
	No response	48%	42%	29%	32%
Credit					
	Yes	5%	9%	27%	56%
	No	41%	39%	32%	17%
	No response	54%	52%	41%	27%

Question 26:
Do you feel the private security industry needs "a set of standards"?

Yes	87%
No	6%
No response	7%

If yes, indicate the relative importance of having "a set of standards" developed in each of the following areas.

	Very Important	*Somewhat Important*	*Not Important*	*No Opinion*	*No Response*
Personnel Selection	78%	12%	1%	1%	8%
Training and Education	76%	15%	1%	0%	8%
Performance standards for security personnel	69%	21%	2%	0%	8%
Performance standards for security equipment	51%	34%	4%	2%	9%
Licensing and regulation	51%	28%	9%	3%	9%
Regulations by insurance companies	19%	31%	27%	12%	11%
Industry wide voluntary Code of Ethics	53%	27%	8%	3%	9%
Formalization of private/ public police relationships	57%	26%	5%	3%	9%

Question 27:
In what state is your business located?

Responses were received from ASIS members in every state, and 258 (14%) indicated they do business in more than one state.

Index